JEWISH SPACE LASERS

MIKE ROTHSCHILD

JEWISH SPACE LASERS

THE ROTHSCHILDS AND 200 YEARS OF CONSPIRACY THEORIES

MELVILLE HOUSE
BROOKLYN • LONDON

JEWISH SPACE LASERS:
THE ROTHSCHILDS AND 200 YEARS
OF CONSPIRACY THEORIES

First published in 2023 by Melville House
Copyright © 2023 by Mike Rothschild
All rights reserved
First Melville House Printing: July 2023

Melville House Publishing
46 John Street
Brooklyn, NY 11201
and
Melville House UK
Suite 2000
16/18 Woodford Road
London E7 0HA

mhpbooks.com
@melvillehouse

ISBN: 978-1-68589-064-3
ISBN: 978-1-68589-065-0 (eBook)

Library of Congress Control Number: 2023939600

Designed by Beste M. Doğan

Printed in the United States of America
1 3 5 7 9 10 8 6 4 2

A catalog record for this book is available from the Library of Congress

This book is dedicated to
the Rothschilds of Vernon Hills,
and to Michael J. Reagan.

"People call you this or they call you that. But I can't respond to that, because then it seems like I'm defensive, and, you know, what does it matter, really?"
—BOB DYLAN, *ROLLING STONE,* JUNE 1984

"A Rothschild stopped off at an inn in a small Russian *shtetl* where he was served two eggs for breakfast. At the meal's end, he was handed a bill for twenty-five rubles, an enormous sum."

"'This is absurd,' Rothschild thundered angrily. 'Are eggs so rare here??'"

"'No,' said the innkeeper. 'But Rothschilds are!'"

—TRADITIONAL JEWISH STORY, AUTHOR UNKNOWN

CONTENTS

"DISTANT JOURNEYS AND PRODIGIOUS CHALLENGES"

The heiress was fake, but the name was real. Sort of.

Anna de Rothschild seemed like a natural among the usual ornate displays of wealth and power that make up the poolside and golf course scenes at former President Trump's Mar-a-Lago club in South Florida. She wore a fancy watch and drove a $170,000 black Mercedes, which she stood next to in the pictures she took with rappers and finance bigwigs. She spoke the language of the land, effortlessly telling stories of luxury real estate developments in Monaco and the Bahamas, sprawling vineyards, her $13 million Miami Beach mansion, and the vast country estates where she grew up. She had founded charities devoted to children, took selfies on private planes, made smooth golf shots, and had face-to-face meetings with some of the most powerful people in the Republican Party.[1]

And why shouldn't she? Anna de Rothschild wasn't some billionaire tech kid in a hoodie or obnoxious political operative looking for face time with The Donald. Striking, confident, and dark-haired, she was a descendant of the Russian branch of the Rothschild family. Yes, *those* Rothschilds—the legendary European banking dynasty that rose up from the Frankfurt ghetto to become the kings of continental finance, lending, mining, and railroads. Their largesse, their wealth, their old money class, their ability to make or break nations with a loan of mere peanuts (to them), and their sheer *everything* are famous around the world. And their heirs are still out there, still working in banking, finance, art, literature, and philanthropy.

So maybe it was the name, or her affect, or the loosey-goosey, endless party vibe at Mar-a-Lago. But nobody questioned Anna de Rothschild. Allegedly, nobody bothered to background check her or vet her ancestral claims during any of the four visits she made to the club. Because she carried herself like she'd never been among anyone other than rich and powerful people. She was so convincing that after posing on the Mar-a-Lago golf course with Trump and South Carolina senator Lindsey Graham, the guest who took the photos joked about charging her for the pictures, saying, "Anna, you're a Rothschild—you can afford one million dollars for a picture with you and Trump."[2]

She couldn't. Because she wasn't.

Instead, Anna de Rothschild, according to FBI officials, was actually 33-year-old Ukrainian immigrant Inna Yashchyshyn. She wasn't a member of the Rothschild family; "Anna de Rothschild" doesn't exist in any family lineage, nor was there ever a Russian Rothschild branch. Instead, she's alleged to have built a fake identity to help run charity scams, fraudulent business ventures, and a variety of grifts where she inserted herself into wealthy circles based on the power of her name. For her part, Yashchyshyn denies ever having taken on the persona of a wealthy European heiress and instead claims she's the victim of an abusive former partner, a Florida-based Russian businessperson who she said forced her into these schemes. And the story gets even more sordid—said former partner was soon shot dead in a small Quebec resort town by a purported member of the Canadian Hells Angels, while Yashchyshyn herself seems to have fallen afoul of Russian organized crime, allegedly owing $150,000 to a tattooed member of a Russian criminal syndicate who, in turn, threatened to kill Yashchyshyn.[3]

One might be tempted to focus on how a person with such dangerous and criminal associations could get into the orbit of the former president and current members of the US Congress. But the answer might lie in how her chosen *nom de grift* opened the door in the first place. "De Rothschild" almost certainly wasn't picked at random, but chosen precisely because of its connotations. And it was a wise choice. Another Mar-a-Lago member remarked in the *Pittsburgh Post-Gazette* piece that broke this story that guests "fawned all over her and because of the Rothschild mystique, they never probed and instead tiptoed around her with kid gloves."[4]

"The Rothschild mystique" was all it took to get an accused grifter and associate of the Russian mob past the Secret Service and next to Donald Trump. Such is the power of the history and legend of the Rothschild name. People heard the name and were able to be convinced that the person who held it had access to vast familial wealth passed down through generations. And sure enough, if she had been a Rothschild, that would have been true.

But that mystique has a longstanding dark side that goes much deeper, and is much more profound, than one alleged con artist.

There's an alternate history of the Rothschild banking family that portrays them not as a family of accomplished businesspeople but as puppet masters who control all but a few central banks, have funded both sides of every war since the American Revolution, hold as much as 80 percent of the world's wealth in their coffers, and are part of a sick occult web of rituals that involve murder and human sacrifice. The Rothschild mystique walks alongside a Rothschild conspiracy theory industry that is, unfortunately, tied to some of the most violent spasms of antisemitism of the last two centuries.

It started with inflammatory pamphlets on the streets of Paris, continued through pro-Union US newspapers of the 1860s, morphed into whispers of Jewish control of the Federal Reserve and the rise of fascism, then wormed its way into the deepest recesses of Cold War paranoia, Clinton-era anti–New World Order hysteria, and the internet hate culture of this very moment. And in the twenty-first century, the industry dedicated to smearing the Rothschilds turned against a more recent public figure of

Jewish wealth, the Hungarian billionaire George Soros, while continuing to attack the Rothschilds for things they haven't done and a scale of wealth that nobody possesses.

Almost all conspiracy theories are rooted in antisemitism, and almost all antisemitism is rooted in conspiracy theories. Jewish people will always be scapegoats for some people, and the Rothschilds are some of the best-known Jews in modern history. In many ways, the story of Rothschild conspiracy theories *is* the story of modern antisemitism. That is how inseparable they are.

Antisemitism is an ideology that's easy to exploit and lucrative to monetize any time there's a major political upheaval, health crisis, economic disaster, military setback, or degradation of "traditional" social mores—which is to say, all the time. Some of this stereotyping is benign enough: jokes about how cheap Jews are, books extolling "Jewish business wisdom," and the like. But Rothschild conspiracy theories have been used as fodder for pogroms, riots, blood libel panics, terrorist attacks, and mass shootings. And they played a critical role in ginning up the necessary level of hate and bloodlust to make the Holocaust possible.

And it's still happening. The antisemitism powered by Rothschild conspiracy theories has seen a considerable upswing during and after the Trump years, with neo-Nazis and antisemites emboldened enough to pass out antisemitic fliers at Broadway shows, harass people on the street, hang anti-Jewish signs on overpasses, vandalize Jewish property, and, in some cases, commit overt acts of violence.[5] Celebrities and conservative influencers now openly speak to huge online audiences of how much they love Hitler, and of Jews being a lesser, disloyal race, while controlling banking and entertainment—all accusations consistently leveled at the Rothschild family, but often couched in the past in equivocations like "we don't hate all Jews, just *these* Jews."

The echoes of the hoaxes and myths written about the Rothschilds in generations past ring out clearly in the attacks on Soros and other prominent Jews today. The new attacks are, with the exception of a few names changed and a few dollar amounts inflated, the same attacks as before. The impact of these theories on the Rothschilds themselves is hard to quantify, but for the Jewish people, the harm is obvious. Modern Jews are still battling the myths that started in a game of telephone almost two hundred years ago.

To understand Kanye West ranting on Alex Jones's show about how great Hitler was requires understanding the influence that John Birch Society speechwriter Gary Allen's 1971 book, *None Dare Call It Conspiracy*, had on Jones, an effect which he has spoken of many times. Allen's book, which sold millions of copies by attacking Jewish "insiders" like the Rothschilds, was inspired in part by *Secrets of the Federal Reserve*, a bestselling conspiracy book funded by the antisemitic and openly pro-fascist poet Ezra Pound. And Pound was inspired by that deathless work of anti-Jewish paranoia, *The Protocols of the Elders of Zion*, which emerged from the antisemitism of Tsarist Russia at the start of the twentieth century.

These tropes, in turn, were based on those that came out of France in the 1890s, which were inspired by the same tropes coming from the United States's gold-versus-silver debate at the same time. And all of it can be traced back to the anti-wealth fervor of the European Revolutions of 1848 and the fallout of an obscure train crash outside Paris—on tracks owned by one of the sons of Rothschild dynasty founder, Mayer Amschel Rothschild, whose other son had gained a reputation among cranks for having manipulated the outcome of the Battle of Waterloo to do nothing less than take control of global finance.

All these conspiracies and events, and so many more, led us to the place where we are now. This book is a study of that dark and winding path. It is not a biography of the Rothschilds, nor is it a deep archival study of their various business ventures and loans. It's also not an examination of the political and societal forces at play in the Rothschilds funding England's purchase of part of the Suez Canal, or their misadventures with Cecil Rhodes in South Africa, or the family's internal conflicts over Zionism. And it's not a glossy look at the opulence bought with their wealth. Many of those books already exist—and most don't touch on the lurid and bizarre whispers about them.

Instead, this is the biography of an idea, and it's a simple enough one:

that Jews control everything, and that the Rothschilds are the "Kings of the Jews." Behind this notion lies a tangled web of absurdities that are equal parts bizarre and deeply sad. And it's not all conspiracy theories, either. When popular culture has needed a rich family, particularly a Jewish one, to satirize or caricature, writers and artists pick the Rothschilds as a stand-in simply because they're the best known of the bunch. Some of these portrayals are positive and others deeply weird, but most are negative—or at least based in negative stereotypes. And while the left/right divide in the United States has calcified into constant partisan argument, a 2022 study of whether American conservatives are more likely to believe conspiracy theories found that of the most popular fringe ideas of the last decade, belief that the Rothschilds are secret global controllers was split directly down the middle between conservatives and liberals.[6]

It is a sprawling story, told over centuries and continents. There are fake Russian counts, Parisian pamphlet wars, lizard people, internet memes and extremist newsletters, masked balls full of servants in cat costumes pawing each other, arcane feuds, luxury saunas in Siberia, Broadway songs about interest rates, a poem called "Lord Rothschild's Soliloquy" that doesn't rhyme, and a pro-silver tract called *The Secret of the Rothschilds* that doesn't actually mention the Rothschilds. There are crank political parties, assassination attempts, war and disaster, revolutions, economic calamity, Crosses of Gold and fascist Silver Shirts, heroism and aspiration and frenzied escapes from evil. There are appearances by T. S. Eliot and Boris Karloff and Ed Sullivan and Thelonious Monk and Stanley Kubrick. There are Anne Frank sanitary napkins. There is that very famous, yet misunderstood, "Jewish Space Laser" that lends this book its title even though the person alleged to have said it never actually did. There are even *more* fake Rothschilds.

But there are no real Rothschilds telling their story, at least not in this book. While there are hundreds of living descendants of the sons and daughters of Mayer Amschel Rothschild, the family rarely consents to interviews and is even more reluctant to discuss the conspiracy theories that have dragged behind the name for two centuries. As such, no Rothschild heirs agreed to my requests for interviews, nor did the family have any say in the book's contents. So it falls to me, a Rothschild not related to *these* Rothschilds, to make an attempt. With many of the most virulent antisemites featured in this story long dead, instead I relied on primary sources—the books they wrote, the speeches they gave, the cartoons they drew, and the rumors they spread.

Sadly, I found them everywhere: in newspaper archives, the Congressional record, heretofore forgotten books and pamphlets in the public domain, archives of long-dead web pages, TV broadcasts watched by millions, extremist newsletters, and commercially available films and songs. And I find them constantly in the responses to my work, where conspiratorial accusations of "of course a Rothschild would say that" or of covering up for "my family" are a daily occurrence. There were so many Rothschild conspiracy theories to sort through and so many mentions of the family in extremist and crank literature that inevitably I had to omit some, truncate others, and leave many inviting rabbit holes undisturbed. A note on these sources: While the temptation is to think one must read them to understand them, many are extremely vile and full of propaganda while also being incomprehensible. My intention in exposing them is not to platform them for future readers but to explain how they fit into the greater antisemitic conspiracy sphere. Most should remain obscure and hard to find.

And while I wanted to give the Rothschilds the opportunity to tell their side of the story, there's a very good reason they didn't. As their London-based archivist told me over email, to address the rumors would force family members to do something that essentially can't be done, which is prove a negative. They would have to prove they *don't* have $500 trillion, that they *didn't* conspire to use the Civil War to divide the United States between Britain and France, or that they *didn't* sell their Austrian hunting lodge in a rush because QAnon found out that they hunted humans for sport there. Such negative proofs are impossible, because the burden of proof lies with the accusers. And the accusers wouldn't believe them anyway.

Not that everyone thinks this way, of course. For many Jews, the Rothschilds have been a beacon of hope in dark times, a reminder that anything is possible with unity and a steadfast devotion to family and tradition. They have inspired beautiful writing and timeless music, and they have made their mark on Jewish life and culture in innumerable ways. And their business savvy has reshaped the world, brought nations closer together, and helped transform industry and finance as we know it. That Rothschild mystique, it turns out, is well-earned.

As the Nobel Peace Prize–winning author of *Night*, Elie Wiesel, wrote when extolling a revival of the 1970 Broadway musical *The Rothschilds*, even just a mention of the family during his childhood in the isolated mountains of Romania had magical connotations:

[The name Rothschild] summoned up distant journeys and prodigious challenges, luxurious chateaux and magnificent banquets, and all that we were deprived of: stability, security, liberty and power. Envied by the high society that accepted them reluctantly, the Rothschilds were our princes and protectors, recalling the glory and pride of ancient days. Innumerable stories about them circulated, and still do, each more picturesque and improbable than the others. On the highest rung of the social ladder, they could seek anything, win anything, permit themselves anything. Aware of their power, they spoke to earthly potentates as equals. A word from them, a gesture, sufficed to free prisoners, victims unjustly condemned, from their gloomy dungeons.[7]

They were, and in some parts of the world still remain, Jewish royalty. And as some of modern history's most visible Jews, they've absorbed more than their fair share of blows, accusations, and myth. Both positively and negatively, the Rothschilds and Judaism are one in the same. To answer the question of "Why is it always *these* Jews," then, we first have to start with a simpler question: "Why is it always *the* Jews?" And the answer, like almost everything in Judaism, goes back to the very beginning.

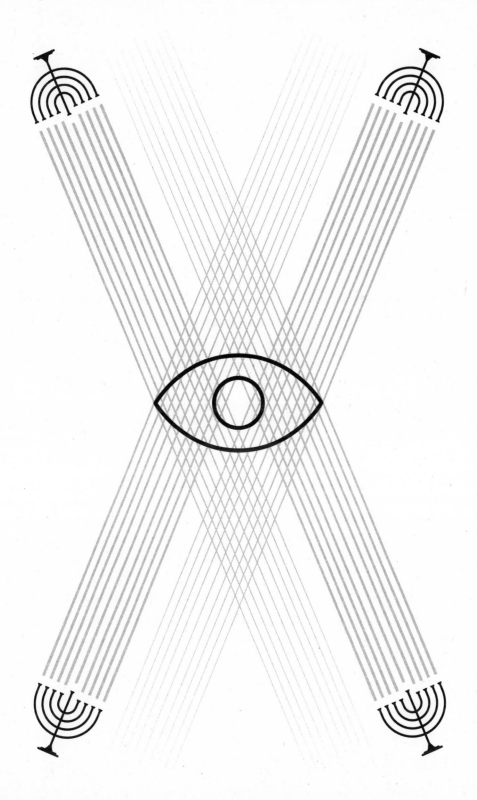

GREEDY, CHEAP, AND BLESSED: THE HISTORY OF JEWISH MONEY TROPES

A powerful leader gathers a massive army to resist the machinations of a cabal behind every major world calamity in history. This vile cult is a cadre of greedy and conniving schemers, with their own language, their own customs, and a devotion to keeping outsiders out. They have a total stranglehold over the financial system, load crushing debt on any nation that won't bow to their whims, and dispose of any leader who gets in their way.

Their ultimate goal?

The establishment of a world government exerting total domination over media, finance, entertainment, and commerce, creating a slave race of disposable workers devoid of freedom or human dignity.

But one leader finally stood up and said no.

This courageous truth teller confronted the cabal, expelling them and their crooked banks out of his nation. Their "one world government" would never come to pass as long as this leader stood in the gap, declaring total war on the enemies of freedom and their lackeys. Nothing less than the fate of the free world was at stake. Battle was joined, and the streets ran red with the blood of believers and nonbelievers alike. But through it all, despite the cabal's limitless resources, their control over the media and the courts and the banks, the leader held firm. And the cabal finally did one thing that they had never done before, in all their eons of control over the masses: they got nervous.

It won't shock anyone that the "powerful cabal" in this scenario is the Jewish people at large, and the wealthy, powerful Rothschild banking family in particular. But who is the courageous leader supposedly fighting them to the death?

It could be Napoleon Bonaparte, a figure deeply wrapped up with Rothschild mythology who is said to have remarked while in exile on St. Helena in 1817 that "the Jews are a nasty people, cowardly and cruel," as well as "[the] most contemptible of people."[1] Or it could be the Roman emperor Hadrian, who crushed the Jewish revolt of 132–136 C.E. to the point where as many as 588,000 Jews were killed, and of which the historian Dio wrote, "thus nearly the whole of Judea had been made desolate."[2]

Was it King Edward I of England, whose Edict of Expulsion of 1290 removing Jews from the United Kingdom would stand for over 350 years? Was it Joseph Stalin, a vicious antisemite who conspired against the Jewish medical intelligentsia of Moscow up until the moment of his death? Adolf Hitler? Someone else?

In this case, the historical leader "standing firm" against the "evil cabal" isn't a historical figure, but Vladimir Putin. The Russian president's evangelists in Europe and the United States embraced Russia's invasion of Ukraine in February 2022, an act that Putin claimed was a mission to "de-Nazify" the country. Presumably, this included arresting its openly Jewish and democratically elected president, Vladimir Zelynskyy. As part of the drive to convince the West that Putin was invading Ukraine for its own good, conservative pundits and social media influencers regurgitated a slew of decades-old myths about Putin taking on the deep state, pushing back against the New World Order, and, in this case, "kicking out" the Rothschilds and nationalizing Russia's central bank.

One high-profile believer in this was Fox News contributor and former *60 Minutes* correspondent Lara Logan. As part of her overall embrace of fringe theories about supposed Jewish desire for global domination, Logan reposted an incomprehensible 2011 post from a blog called "Political Vel Craft" alleging that Putin had ended "Russia's financial dependence on the Teutonic Zionist financiers" who had engineered "THE ASSASSINATION OF PRESIDENT ABRAHAM LINCOLN BY OBAMA PUPPET MASTERS [sic] ~ THE ROTHSCHILDS."[3] After praising Putin as "the man to stand up to the New World Order," Logan would go on the conspiracy theory podcast *And We Know* to falsely claim that the Rothschild family "employed [Charles] Darwin" to come up with the theory of evolution as part of their drive to promote a godless one world government.[4]

But what sounds like a bizarre, deranged conspiracy theory that was invented on the spot is just the latest iteration of a myth that's been around for thousands of years. It has demonstrated remarkable durability and resistance to facts. And it's driven both titanic world events and the careers of some of the most prolific cranks and conspiracy spreaders of the last two centuries. The myth is that the Jews dominate global finance, and the Rothschilds are their kings, handing down funding and orders for their peons in the wider Jewish community to carry out.

The conspiracy theories and stereotypes about Jews and money—from the miserly Jew who haggles over the slightest bargain to the more anodyne "good with money" East Coast Jew trying to infiltrate the gentile country club to the Jewish financial advisor plugged into "ancient wisdom"—are everywhere in Western culture.

Any minority with its own language, customs, clothing, and culture is bound to be resented by the majority. But historically, only Jews have found outsized professional success through that majority—loaning it money, managing its finances, settling its legal disputes, entertaining it, and the like. And they've suffered outsized resentment because of that success. Antisemitism and Jewish wealth are bound up in each other, and Jewish success is at the core of the conspiracy theories about them.

Of course, Jews are demographically overrepresented in banking, finance, the legal profession, the sciences, and the entertainment industry. The reasons why have nothing to do with a cabal of puppet masters, but instead stem both from the historical Jewish emphasis on literacy and from the opposite—highly placed Jews deemphasizing their Judaism in favor of success in the secular world.[5]

And while many of these references are outwardly antisemitic, some are complimentary or even aspirational: there is a genuine belief that Jews are born with intuition for making money, as seen in countless books with titles like *Ancient Jewish Wisdom for the Wise Investor*[6] or "15 Reasons Why JEWISH People Are RICHER"—a YouTube video with over 1.6 million views from people presumably looking for Hebraic insight into easy wealth.[7] There's even a legend about this intuition that's become attached to Nathan Rothschild, once the richest man in the world and a critical figure in Rothschild family conspiracy theories, stating that he possessed a physical "Hebrew Talisman" bringing him great wealth through divine luck.

But that's not the image that antisemites have in mind when extolling Putin or Hitler or Hadrian for their harsh treatment of greedy Jews. The image of the hunched-over, hook-nosed Jew obsessed with accumulating wealth at the expense of Gentiles is so deeply embedded in our culture that we fall back on it without even realizing what we're saying—or where it came from.

It is impossible to understand why conspiracy theories about the Rothschilds endure without understanding the endurance of tropes about Jews and money—that they are innately good with it, are too cheap to part with it, and use it to infiltrate Gentile social circles.

THE GREEDY JEW

The trope of Jews being greedy, untrustworthy, and conniving has existed since the earliest days of Christianity. There are a number of references in the New Testament that were later interpreted to be about Jewish greed—particularly Jesus referring to the Temple as a "den of thieves" in Matthew, Mark, and Luke. But Jesus and his earliest disciples were all Jews and would never have struck out against other Jews performing financial business. The money changers who Jesus ejected from the Temple in Jerusalem could easily have been Roman or some other nationality, and were tossed out because Jesus believed they were overcharging for their services, not because they might have been Jews.[8]

So if the trope of Jews cheating, overcharging, and hoarding didn't originate with anything Jesus actually said, where does it come from? Like all durable conspiracy theories, there's a grain of truth to at least some of the history behind the stereotype, in that Jews did play outsized roles in the finances of Christian life. Pushed out of professions that revolved around physical labor, particularly agriculture, Jews *were* often the only ones in a community who would lend money or exchange the currency of one kingdom for another. And they *did* charge for their services—often in violation of Christian prohibitions.

Ultimately, Jewish "greed" is just one part of the stereotype about Jews and money—but it's the part that's most often weaponized against them.

The traditional explanation that's usually given for why Jews and money are so intertwined is that in the Middle Ages, Christians were forbidden from working in professions where interest was paid out. Usury was strictly forbidden by both the Old Testament, in Exodus, Leviticus, Deuteronomy, and Proverbs, and the New Testament, in Mark. The practice was formally banned by the Catholic Church at the Council of Nicaea of 325 C.E. Some early Christian thinkers even went all the way back to Aristotle for inspiration and made the argument that since "metal can't beget metal" (i.e., inorganic material can't make more of itself), interest runs counter to the laws of nature.[9]

But by the Middle Ages, European Jews were also forbidden from working in the majority of other professions—particularly agriculture, which was the most prevalent "career" of the time. This led Jews to embrace lending money at interest and changing currency for a fee, primarily as a means of economic survival. So the prohibitions on lending at interest in the Torah were essentially suspended by rabbis of the time out of necessity. Without concepts of natural law or mortal sin, and with rabbis of the time being an eminently practical sort who wished to see their people prosper in the few arenas in which they were allowed to prosper, these considerations simply didn't apply.[10]

Jews also emphasized literacy and education to a much higher degree than non-Jews. Starting with the destruction of the Second Temple in 70 C.E., every Jewish man had to be able to read the Torah, and Jewish families traditionally sent their children to school earlier and at a much higher rate.[11] This emphasis on reading and arithmetic meant that they were often literally the only ones in a community who had the ability to track who was lent money and how much. During the tenth through thirteenth centuries, Jews of the Middle East fled the Mongol invasions of Persia and Iraq, with many settling in Western Europe, England, and North Africa. Because of their emphasis on education and financial acumen, the Jews of the diaspora were in a strong position to integrate into their new communities as merchants, craftsmen, and bankers. And while usury was still forbidden, Christian officials of the time up to the twelfth century C.E. either turned a blind eye or actively encouraged Jews to lend money at interest for a simple reason: someone had to do it. Jews would come to have a near-monopoly on moneylending as a result, with many Jewish bankers and their descendants becoming extremely wealthy.[12]

Hence, Jews of the Middle Ages gained a reputation of being not only "good with money" but the ones you had to go to if you needed it—at a price.

But this uneasy balance wouldn't last, and by the middle of the twelfth century, the Church essentially declared war on lending at interest—a war that was almost entirely directed at getting Jews out of moneylending. The Council of Vienne declared usury as heretical in 1311, putting it on par with murder and incest. Royal permission would begin to be required of Jewish bankers to lend money at all, and Jewish estates were made property of the king if the banker died without an heir. It became harder and more expensive for Jewish lenders to operate, meaning they had to charge even higher fees— while dealing with more competition from the growing number of Gentile bankers. The cycle often ended in violence or outright expulsion for Jews.[13]

With the German Reformation of 1517, canon law and finances officially became less enmeshed. Thinkers of the emerging Protestant movement began to see the charging of interest as much less of a mortal sin and more of a necessity. It could even be seen as a positive, fueling the growth of cities and the building of churches, efforts that demanded more financial resources than virtually anyone, including royalty, had at their disposal. And while nobles traditionally went to the Jewish community for loans, now they had other options as more Christians became involved in banking and Jews were pushed out.[14]

Over the next few centuries, the Christian view of lending at interest evolved to the point where in *The Wealth of Nations*, published in 1776, Adam Smith extolled the risk the moneylender takes, which "affords him the opportunity of making this profit"—though Smith still cautioned against "the extortion of usury."[15]

Essentially, Christianity at the time when the Rothschilds began to establish themselves condoned some charging of interest on loans while continuing to castigate "usury"—a vague and undefined term that was almost always linked to work deemed "unproductive" or impactful only to the Jewish community, a stereotype that's still prevalent in the form of the Jew who "can't make anything" other than money off Christians. The result was a constant cycle of repression, violence, and removal based on the self-perpetuating notion that Jews were greedy, lazy, and sinful.[16]

The "greedy Jew" stereotype is, therefore, intrinsically linked with the supposed sin of usury. Everyone from virulently antisemitic (and specifically anti-Rothschild) poet Ezra Pound to Osama bin Laden would conflate lending at interest, which is the backbone of modern banking, with the biblical concept of usury and point their finger at the Jews. Bin Laden, for example, would castigate the United States for "permitting usury, which has been forbidden by all the religions" as proof that "the Jews have taken control of your economy" in his "Letter to America" in 2002.[17] And the word is often used in mainstream media publications to denote exorbitant rates on loans given by unscrupulous banks or loan sharks.

Terms like "usurer" or "loan shark" are often interchanged with another word that's become a shorthand for a greedy Jew: shylock. Maybe the most well-known fictional Jew, Shylock of *The Merchant of Venice* demands payment for a loan in the form of the flesh of his borrower and is relentless in getting what he believes is coming to him. Most historical portrayals of Shylock presented him as either a cruel and repulsive clown or as a stock Jewish character whose greed gets him what he deserves—forced conversion and poverty. It's only been in more modern scholarship that Shylock has been seen as a reflection of the antisemitism of Elizabethan England, with recent staging of the play presenting a more sympathetic approach to his conduct. His very name, despite not being Jewish in origin, has been adapted as a verb often used in context of Jews—to *shylock* someone is to cheat or overcharge someone, and it's not a compliment.

Jewish moneylenders were routinely blamed for outbreaks of bubonic plague and lawlessness, while tens of thousands of Spanish Jews were killed in the late 1300s because of their economic success, with those unwilling to convert to Christianity singled out. Ultimately, usury would be one of the justifications given for Spain's edict of 1492 demanding either the baptism or expulsion of the kingdom's three-hundred-thousand-strong Jewish population—a justification repeated with the expulsion of Spain's Moorish population in 1609.[18]

And the old canard of deicide—the Jews killing Jesus Christ—has been dredged up again and again to justify organized violence against Jews, often linked to the supposed greed of the biblical Judas and his acceptance of thirty pieces of silver to identify the Messiah—never mind that both Judas *and* Jesus were Jews. The trope is so durable that it resurfaces in 2004's film *The Passion of the Christ*, where director Mel Gibson (no friend of the Jewish people) depicts Pontius Pilate as essentially blackmailed into executing Christ by Jewish authorities after Judas betrays him.[19]

The greedy Jew trope was born from the success of Jews. And this success has a cost: the innumerable cultural depictions about how "they own" some industry or other. Witness Irish rock legend Van Morrison, never known for antisemitism, who was pilloried by music writers and the Jewish press alike for including a vitriolic track called "They Own the Media" on his 2021 album *Latest Record Project Volume 1.* The song never mentioned who "they" are, but they're bad and they run your life—"they control everything you do" and "keep on telling you lies" and "control the media."[20] For his part, the singer tweeted shortly after the album's release that "they" referred to the government of then–UK prime minister Boris Johnson. Regardless of his target, Morrison was nodding to classic tropes of Jewish control of the press, even if that wasn't his intention.[21]

But even if the cranks and antisemites of the Middle Ages found pay dirt in exploiting Christian fears of Jewish success, there was one group of highly placed gentiles that began to rely more and more on Jewish financial acumen—nobility. And it's in the intertwining of Jewish monetary success and European royalty that we can find the seeds of both Mayer Amschel Rothschild's success and the industry of conspiracy theories about his family.

THE JEW AS FINANCIAL SOOTHSAYER

As the most visible wealthy Jewish family in the world, the Rothschilds are unfairly linked to some of the worst stereotypes imaginable, particularly when it comes to usury. They're often seen as profiting off loans to both sides in wars—when, in reality, they often found themselves helplessly watching two nations or empires they had business in go to war with each other.

"They are rumored to control the world through debt and usury and as of today, while withdrawing somewhat from banking, they seem to have put much of their wealth into natural resources and food," is how a 2019 blog post under the banner of the nominally independent research think tank *Institut Européen des Relations Internationales* with the subtle title "Banksters and Warmongers" put it. And this kind of outlandish paranoia is found throughout both antisemitic literature in general and anti-Rothschild writing specifically.[22]

Of course, the family did make a fortune, starting with their dealings in textiles, rare coins, and medals—niches that many other Jews were also able to take advantage of for cultural reasons. Thanks to their success as money-lenders and bankers, Jews began to be saddled with a reputation of not just being "good with money" but having a kind of ancient wisdom, something secret and strange that others didn't possess.

An entire occupation grew out of this belief that Jews were tapped into the secrets of money in ways Christians weren't: the arcane position of "court Jew." It was when he became a court Jew in 1769 that Mayer Amschel Rothschild first began to make his fortune, picking up a thread from a long line of Jewish financiers and bankers who didn't merely have more money, they *just knew* what to do with it. As Dutch Rabbi Menasseh ben Israel wrote in a 1655 petition to Oliver Cromwell to restore citizenship to British-descended Jews, "it is a thing confirmed, then, that merchandizing is, as it were, the proper profession of the Nation of the Jews."[23]

Court Jews (also known as court factors, court bankers, court agents, or *Hoffaktor* in German) occupied an extraordinarily precarious and con-tradictory position in both royal and Jewish life. They were essentially the private bankers of European royal courts, hired because of their financial acumen and ability to loan their own money and borrow from other Jews without religious restrictions. Mayer Amschel Rothschild was one of the last major court Jews in Europe, but wealthy Jewish lenders with no formal position in a court date back to England in the 1100s. In the decades af-ter the Norman Conquest, British Jews like Josce of Gloucester and Aaron of Lincoln—likely the wealthiest man in Britain at the time of his death—funded the expeditions of their kings with their own money. By the 1500s, royals in the Holy Roman Empire, Spain, Portugal, Russia, Sweden, the Ottoman Empire, and England all made use of the services of court Jews as military suppliers, merchants, financial gurus, obtainers of rare items, and funders of wars of conquest.

They had no political power and posed no threat to the ruler. There was great money to be made in the position of court Jew, and just as much peril of the money running out, or losing the favor of the court that gave it to you. Those holding these positions were devoid of rights and often had little other option than to do business with their rulers—becoming wealthy with money that could be stripped from them at any time. In recompence, they gave lavish gifts to their employers in thanks for their protection, but often inscribed those gifts with Jewish iconography. And their personal collections of fine art and objects rivaled those of their employers—German court factor Alexander David left so much ornate Judaica behind when he died in 1765 that it formed the core of what was essentially the world's first Jewish museum.[24]

Jewish families would loan and engage in commerce with other Jews in the employ of European noble houses and the Catholic Church, with their royal patrons buying everything from precious metals and consumer goods to rifles and ammunition with which to wage war. In return, court Jews were allowed a portion of the profits, special privileges in where they lived and what they wore, and access to European nobility for their own dealings. Some were even granted noble titles themselves—a far cry from the ghetto squalor that many of their fellow Jews occupied.[25]

But like everything else involving Jews of the Middle Ages and beyond, this position was fraught with violence and persecution. Criticism from both within and without the Jewish community was inevitable—and sometimes deadly.

Other Jews often criticized court bankers for the outsized role they played in ghetto life. Many court Jews took on the role of *shtadtlan*, an unelected diplomatic envoy from the royal court to the ghetto—and they were resented for it. These envoys presented petitions from the Jewish community to the ruler and, through this role, laid down guidelines for education and discipline, had the right to collect taxes from other Jews, and ensured that other Jews didn't run afoul of restrictive anti-Jewish prohibitions, which often didn't apply to court Jews themselves.[26] The *shtadtlan* was not selected by the community and answered to his Christian patron, not his Jewish brethren. While sometimes these envoys played a critical role in opening up European cities to Jewish settlement, they also perpetuated the ghettoizing and othering of Jews, well into Mayer's time.

There were darker implications to this type of dual role, as well. Court Jews often worked for nobility who either actively oppressed Jewish communities or had ministers and military officers who did. It was a contradiction that political theorist and philosopher Hannah Arendt pointed out in her 1952 review of Selma Stern's *The Court Jew*, the first book to chronicle the ascent and peril of the position of court factor in the Holy Roman Empire. Arendt criticized Stern for not delving into this apparent paradox, situations where "the Jews were protected by one man only and opposed by everybody else." For Europe's Jews of the time, the protection of one patron, even a powerful one, had limits.[27]

Despite their lavish lifestyles, many court Jews died with little to their name. They could be saddled with crushing debt if a ruler was unable (or simply decided not) to pay back his Jewish lender, or the lender's Jewish associates. There was no way for a Jew to collect the debt of a Christian ruler, and constant anti-Jewish sentiment ensured that there would be no repercussions for the ruler who refused to honor those debts. Beyond that, when a court factor's royal patron died, the successor often had no use for them— leading to their bankruptcy, exile, or even execution. Court Jews may have been courtly, but they were still Jews.

One particularly gruesome example of a court Jew's wealth leading to misery for other Jews was after the death of Aaron of Lincoln in 1186. As was the usual custom, King Henry II seized Aaron's massive fortune after he died, but Aaron had so many debtors that it took over a decade to untangle the estate. One debtor, Richard de Malbis, attempted to destroy the records of his debt and believed that a former agent of Aaron, located in York, had the paperwork. Richard formed a local mob and began attacking the Jewish community, whose members gathered in York Castle for protection. After a siege, the entire group were either burned to death or took their own lives. The 150 Jews, mostly women and children, killed in the York Massacre were victims of one of the worst pogroms of Norman English history.[28] A century later, Jews were expelled outright from England.

Another act of violence against a court Jew would have reverberations for Jews for centuries afterward—the sham trial and execution of Joseph

Süss Oppenheimer, known later in history simply as "Jew Süss." In 1733, Oppenheimer was court Jew of Carl Alexander, the duke of Württemberg, one of the most highly populated states of the Holy Roman Empire. Oppenheimer had a brilliant financial mind and was trusted with printing and moving vast sums of money. But he was personally indiscreet—which included having sexual affairs with Christian women. Years after coming to power, Carl Alexander died of a sudden stroke, leaving his nine-year-old son as the leader-in-waiting. Resentful local authorities saw an opportunity to get rid of Oppenheimer, and he was arrested the same day that Carl Alexander died.

Charged with a bizarre array of financial and vice crimes, he was subjected to months of brutal interrogation and a long trial, which at least one source claims was intentionally dragged out to force Oppenheimer's estate to cover the costs. The charges against him were never made clear, and no evidence was presented, but the verdict and punishment were inevitable: guilty, and death.[29] Oppenheimer refused a final offer of converting to Christianity to spare his life and was executed in a gruesome and public spectacle—taken to the top of a forty-foot ladder and strangled in front of as many as twenty thousand people. To add extra indignity, his body was placed in a custom-made iron gibbet and exhibited until the duke's son finally had it removed and buried as an example to other Jews.[30]

The execution of Joseph Süss Oppenheimer was plainly an act of antisemitic political violence, spurred by his wealth and dalliances with Gentile women. With Oppenheimer tarred as a servant of Satan and an example of Jewish greed bringing misery on good Christians, German authors and artists would spend centuries exploring what drove the frenzy that led to his execution. The best-known work was likely Jewish German author Lion Feuchtwanger's 1925 novel *Jud Süß* (*Jew Süss*), adapted into film in 1934 in England, with Oppenheimer played by actor Conrad Veidt—later famous for his role as Major Strasser in *Casablanca*.

But another film adaptation, also called *Jud Süß* and released in 1940, would immortalize Oppenheimer in what many scholars have called the most antisemitic film of all time. This *Jud Süß* portrayed the court Jew not just as a schemer but as a violent rapist who profited off the starvation of the people and imposed punishing taxes on them, before his arrest and execution for trying to overthrow the government. A major financial and cultural success in Nazi Germany, the film became a pillar of Joseph Goebbels's propaganda machine's effort to dehumanize and scapegoat the Jews of Germany in preparation for the next phase of anti-Jewish repression across the Reich, along with two other Nazi propaganda films of the time that specifically targeted the Rothschilds.

The trial, execution, and posthumous smearing of Oppenheimer had a profound effect on how Europe, and in particular Germans, would see Jews and money going forward. Every court Jew—or Jewish merchant of any renown—could be a Süss in disguise, scheming to take control from the pathetic Christians they lorded over while defiling their women and keeping all the riches for themselves.

THE CHEAP JEW

Did you hear about the Jewish car? It not only stops on a dime, but it picks the dime up.

Do you know why Jews have such big noses? Because air is free.

How was copper wire invented? Two Jews fought over a penny.

The Rothschilds can't be considered stingy, given both the lavish sums they've spent on their own lifestyles and the enormous amounts they've given away. But no discussion of Jewish money tropes can ignore the one about the Jew who was *so cheap*—particularly given the reputation of wealthy Jews as keeping their money either for themselves or in their clannish communities.

You'll hear jokes like the ones above freely told both about and by other Jews, often ones who have become wealthy themselves in entertainment. Jerry Seinfeld, Larry David, and Jon Stewart have all made careers at least in part off their riffing on Jews refusing to pay retail, negotiating past the point of all reason, cheaping out on tips, and being stingy with gift giving. And they're hardly alone.

Born Benjamin Kubelsky, the Jewish comic who went by Jack Benny had a stage persona who was so cheap, his most famous bit involves him "thinking it over" when a gun-toting thug demands "your money or your life." When staying at a hotel, Ross Gellar on *Friends* stuffs his suitcase full of complimentary soaps, grooming goodies, notepads, and instant coffee. When TV mob boss Tony Soprano owes a vast sum of gambling losses to Jewish loan shark Hesh Rabkin, he complains over and over to his therapist not about his own bad choices, but about Hesh fitting the stereotype of the miserly Jew.

Most of these portrayals are Jewish performers exploiting an extant stereotype for their own benefit. And there are exceptions to the entertainment trope of the cheap Jew. Jerry Seinfeld's version of himself on *Seinfeld* is extremely free with money (his parents, not so much), as is the Jewish character Schmidt on the sitcom *New Girl*, to the point of being willing to bankrupt himself to spend on a lavish wedding.

But when easy laughs are needed about a Jewish character, it seems fairly harmless to insinuate that they'd do anything to save a buck. Even works with complimentary depictions of Jewish characters often throw in references to them being bad tippers or being a bit too bargain hungry. And why not? Does anyone of any religion want to pay more for anything than they have to? We all clip coupons, look for deals, and maybe tip a little less than we should. Isn't this a backhanded compliment? *Jews! They're just like us!*

The problem with these depictions isn't that cheapness is only a Jewish attribute—every culture has some other culture they think of as more miserly than they are. For some, it's East Asians, for others, Scots or Germans or Norwegians. Even different parts of the United States stereotype other Americans as unreasonably cheap—particularly New Englanders. But issues start to arise for Jews because this perceived extreme frugality is wrapped up with extreme greed. Nobody likes to spend money they don't have to, but Jews don't just hoard money, they'll cross lines other groups won't to get their hands on it—from Judas to Jew Süss.

And as European Jews poured into the United States in the 1800s, the

twin stereotypes of greedy and cheap came with them. Broadsheets, satirical magazines, and plays of the nineteenth century played up the stereotype
relentlessly, particularly in New York, where hundreds of thousands of Jews
settled, usually in squalor. In the mostly forgotten 1885 hit play *A Ready-
Made Suit*, two Jews give testimony against a woman accused of marrying
nine men in quick succession with the excuse (delivered in a typical German
Jewish accent) that they married her together because "one wife between
us . . . will be less expensive."[31]

As Jews began to find success in their new homes, the responses of non-
Jews were often shot through with resentment—not just at the Jew getting
money, but at what the Jew did with his money. They kept it. Or they gave
it to other Jews through Jewish philanthropic organizations. Ill feelings
over Jewish business acumen and generosity were becoming so linked in the
United States that in reaction to the mid-nineteenth century benevolent organization Society for the Amelioration of the Condition of the Jews, meant
to help ease the financial burden of immigration, the upper-crust New York
weekly *The Spirit of the Times* rhetorically asked its readers, "Why don't we
have a Society for Ameliorating the Condition of the Jewed?"[32]

Maybe more than any other manifestation of the cheap Jew stereotype,
the notion of being "Jewed down" permeates the way we talk about Jews
and their relationship to money. It is the essence of Jewish money stereotyping. And despite it being transparently antisemitic, it's somehow become
the phrase of choice for how to talk about taking the worse end of a bargain,
from people who claim not to know what it really means and "would never
say anything antisemitic."[33]

And a lot of people claim to not know what it means. During a
2022 Kentucky state senate hearing regarding the state leasing two
storm-damaged buildings for a dollar so they could be repaired,
Republican Rick Girdler asked if there were any questions, to which fellow Republican Walker Thomas laughingly asked if the state could "Jew
them down on the price."

"We got a representative up here who [wants to] see if you can Jew 'em
down a little bit on the price," Girdler responded, quickly catching him-

self. "That ain't the right word to use. Drop 'em down, I guess."[34] Both reps quickly apologized, claiming the phrase was just something people used when talking about getting a good deal.

An Ohio State professor got in trouble for declaring to her class that "Jewing people down is the way" for tourists to get better deals on trinkets in Mexico, managing to insult two different ethnic groups at once.[35] An Oklahoma state senator used the phrase "try to Jew me down" in a 2013 debate, then when he was called out on it, offered a smiling apology "to the Jews," who are "good small businessmen as well."[36] And a county commissioner in Washington state was caught using the phrase twice trying to negotiate a deal at an antique show, then apologized with the claim that he had "the utmost respect for the Jewish faith."[37]

Sometimes they don't even bother with the apology, like the New Jersey council member who asked that a Jewish attorney dealing with settling a lawsuit against the county "wait her out and Jew her down" and was defended by colleagues for using "Jew down" as a verb meaning negotiate, not a hateful slur.[38]

With the cultural depiction of Jews so dominated by the tropes of the greedy, inscrutable, cheap Jew, it's no wonder that antisemitic thinking about the Rothschilds is so intertwined with conspiracy theories. The demonstrably false idea that one clan of powerful, wealthy Jews dominates all other powerful, wealthy Jews is the core of how the family is portrayed in the media, literature, and politics. Even flattering depictions of the family can't help but imbue them with a supernatural ability to make money. And the unflattering depictions cast them as almost fanatically devoted to keeping their riches in their own family—and doing anything to expand that wealth.

Of course, all of the myths of Jewish wealth and power are just that—myths. Even with Jewish "overrepresentation" in business and other professional fields, Jews around the world are born into poverty as much as anyone, are as middle class as anyone, and have the same debts and business failures as anyone. The majority of leaders in business and politics are still Christian—and many of the firms they started refused to hire Jews until well into the twentieth century.[39]

Even after religious restrictions on usury began to fall away in the late 1700s, the ancient prejudices didn't. So the Jews of Europe would have to start their own private banks in their own communities, beholden to the whims and rules of the majority—a majority that still came to them for loans. The most impactful of these Jewish private banks would be the one that arose out of the segregation and squalor of the Frankfurt Jewish ghetto of the 1700s. It was the brainchild of Mayer Amschel Rothschild, a coin dealer and friend of royalty who, along with his sons, would transform the way we coexist with wealth and power as we know them today.

A BRIEF
HISTORY OF THE
ROTHSCHILDS,
PART I:
1565–1868

Frankfurt in the era of the Holy Roman Empire was a bustling center of commerce and culture. But its Jewish people were essentially detainees, penned into the forced squalor of the *Judengasse*—"The Jews' Lane." Its three thousand residents lived almost on top of one another in a narrow corridor packed with buildings and houses. Its high walls were accessible only through three heavy gates, which were guarded by armed soldiers and locked at night and on Sundays. It was about a quarter of a mile long and much narrower—less than twelve feet in some places. Only a small piece of one of those walls remains in the ghetto's old location east of the center of the city, as what wasn't torn down or incinerated by one of the ghetto's routine fires was almost totally destroyed by Allied air raids in March of 1944.[1]

The Jews kept inside were restricted in travel, free association, and employment. Like all Jews in the Holy Roman Empire, they were second-class citizens who ostensibly lived under a decree of protection of the emperor, first issued in 1090. But they were also subject to varying degrees of *actual* protection depending on the whims of whoever held the crown. And as always, they were beholden to their local monarch's need for money. Sometimes it was lent freely, other times it was extorted. Organized pogroms, individual acts of anti-Jewish violence, forced conversions, and even expulsion were a constant threat, as the Jews of Frankfurt were kicked out in 1349, only to be allowed back eleven years later.[2]

The community at the time of Mayer Amschel Rothschild's birth was limited to just twelve weddings per year to keep the Jewish cohort from getting too big for their walled lane to keep in. If a Christian demanded "Jew, *pay your dues*," they had to step aside, hat in hand, and bow. They couldn't linger in public spaces outside the walls and couldn't sell their goods to or buy from Christians except on special occasions. Until 1726, Jewish men of the ghetto had to wear a special insignia—two interlocking yellow circles. Buildings routinely collapsed, and every doorway and alley seemed to be crowded with humans. Even the cemetery was neglected, never being expanded after its initial opening in 1241.[3]

But the *Judengasse* was not without the things that made life bearable. There were synagogues and public spaces and houses with colorful names. Forbidden from owning even the land their modest houses stood on, Frankfurt's Jews sold textiles or silk, exchanged currencies, and dealt in secondhand goods. Because of its central location and status as a free city directly subordinate to the Holy Roman Emperor, Frankfurt was (and continues to be) one of Europe's most important hubs of trade, transportation, and commerce. Its merchants and nobles, including the emperor himself, had outsized financial needs, and the city's Jews were happy to oblige through loans.

The seeds of conspiracy theories and distortions about the Rothschilds and their financial empire would be planted long before Mayer Amschel Rothschild's birth into that squalor. Mayer's story, and that of his entire family, isn't atypical of other Jews in that sphere—modestly prosperous, hemmed in by culture and tradition, and trying to keep their own company as pressure increased for them to convert.

FROM ISAK TO MAYER, FROM ELCHANAN TO ROTHSCHILD

Mayer's earliest known ancestor, related through an unknown line, was Isak (or Isaac, or Isaak), son of Elchanan—also written out simply as Isak Elchanan, reflecting the Jewish tradition of men taking their father's name as their surname. The vast majority of Isak's life is lost to history, even his birthday, but tax records in the Rothschild archives reveal that he was a fairly prosperous merchant, dealing mostly in textiles.

Around 1565, Isak was able to build a house, christened *zum roten Schild* after a standard of a red shield hung on the outside.[4] Isak died in 1585, and his grandson Naftali eventually moved out of the *roten Schild* house into the rear portion of a different house, christened *Hinterpfann*,—"warming pan" or "saucepan." The Jews of Frankfurt weren't allowed to take last names at the time, so Isak's successors went by a variety of surnames, usually the first name of their father. One of those eventually discarded surnames, Bauer, was sometimes used by Mayer's grandfather Moses Kalman Rothschild and surfaces in conspiracy theory lore as "proof" that the Rothschilds changed their names for some unknown but definitely villainous reason.[5]

Like Isak, little is definitively known about the early adopters of the Rothschild name, other than they built on Isak's slow upward mobility while continuing to cram into the tight quarters of the house "in the back of a saucepan"—a house which burned down at least twice during that time.[6] Mayer's great-grandfather Kalman (sometimes anglicized as "Carl"), grandfather Moses, and father Amschel Moses continued building the family textile business while expanding into money changing—the swapping of one state's currency for another, an endless need demanded by the Holy Roman Empire, which comprised nearly three hundred separate states, duchies, and free cities—each with its own currency. They also began acquiring rare military medals and coins to sell during the special times they were allowed outside the walls of the ghetto.[7]

Amschel soon worked his way into becoming the court Jew to Crown Prince William (also called Wilhelm), son of the Landgrave of Hesse-Kassel, one of the wealthiest states in the empire, making its fortune largely off renting out professional soldiers, dubbed "Hessians," to various European powers needing foreign mercenaries. As the Landgrave's personal supplier of collectable coins, Amschel rapidly ascended, giving him access and privilege—and a connection that would prove critical to the financial empire his son would build.[8]

It was into this contradiction, a well-heeled family lending money to one of the wealthiest states in the Holy Roman Empire while simultaneously living in squalor as near prisoners, that Mayer Amschel Rothschild was born in 1744, the fourth of five children who survived. Like his ancestors, young Mayer's life was mostly unrecorded, and after a brief time at rabbinical school, he entered the family business after losing both parents due to smallpox outbreaks in the ghetto. At age twelve, Mayer was an orphan with four other siblings to help take care of, and little money to do it with. He had to go to work.

After studying business in Hanover, young Mayer made a fortunate connection in becoming the apprentice to another prominent Jewish banker, Jacob Wolf Oppenheimer. Jacob's grandfather Samuel had been the court Jew for the Austrian emperor, and his family's bank routinely did business with wealthy clients from a variety of nationalities. Living for nearly a decade in the much less outwardly anti-Jewish Hanover, Mayer's link with Oppenheimer meant he was quickly introduced to the rarified air of the bankers and financiers working around European nobles.[9]

Mayer finally returned to Frankfurt in 1763, where his connections gave him the opportunity to work for Crown Prince William as his personal dealer in rare coins and military medals. Most of Mayer's transactions were minor, but they were profitable enough that in 1769 he was given the title his father once had, *Hoffaktor*, to the future ruler. He married seventeen-year-old *Judengasse* resistant Gutle Schnapper the next year, and they would eventually have ten children who survived childhood—five sons and five daughters.

William's patronage and his own business ventures selling textiles, coins, art objects, and rare items to minor nobles provided Mayer a good enough living. The crown prince was moving up in the world, as well. William fattened his bank accounts selling professional soldiers to his cousin—King George III of England. These were, of course, the same detested Hessian mercenaries (many of whom weren't actually from Hesse and weren't mercenaries but conscripts) whose presence in the Thirteen Colonies would eventually be one of the twenty-seven grievances included in the Declaration of Independence.[10]

While his court Jew position wasn't especially lucrative, it afforded the ambitious and clever Mayer the opportunity to travel the Holy Roman Empire and make contacts that would be vital to future business ventures. He expanded into selling textiles and food goods, and even started making small bank loans. The year 1785 brought the death of William's father, Fredrick II, and Mayer's benefactor ascended to the throne as William IX, Landgrave of Hesse-Kassel, a title that later became William I, Elector of Hesse in 1803 after he became one of the college of rulers who chose the Holy Roman Emperor. He'd rule the state for the next forty years.

As revolution in France turned into war in Europe, Frankfurt became a target. Mayer signed contracts to supply Austrian soldiers billeting in Frankfurt with food and supplies. Soon enough, France invaded Hesse, and the conflict quite literally destroyed the *Judengasse* when a French artillery barrage fired during the siege of the city missed its target and hit the ghetto, with the cramped wooden houses, including the old *Hinterpfann* house, going up in flames. By a stroke of what many would later see as divine intervention, when much of the ghetto was destroyed, Mayer survived and was able to use the opportunity to rent office space in the city center of Frankfurt. Mayer and Gutle, along with oldest son Amschel, would still live in the *Judengasse*, but the days of the walls holding in the Jews of Frankfurt were ending.[11]

As the French Revolutionary Wars raged, William needed money, and Mayer had ready access to the Landgrave's massive treasury, making loans and deals as he saw fit. He was now likely one of the richest Jews in Frankfurt, with Rothschild business quickly becoming a European affair. Mayer was now working with Amschel making loans to both other principalities in the empire and other nations. And they were earning high interest rates—necessitated by the constant needs of funding war. Mayer needed people he could trust supervising the work, and he found them within the family—his sons.[12]

One common misconception blatantly fueled by later antisemitic propaganda was that Mayer "sent" his sons out into the world at the same time to simultaneously conquer the financial capitals of Europe. Such an act is depicted in numerous biographies of the family, including the 1934 Hollywood film about Mayer, *The House of Rothschild*. But they all moved out gradually over years, for different reasons, and with different levels of ambition and acumen. Some Rothschild houses were established years after Mayer's death, and no such "order" to disperse was ever given.

For the time being, Amschel stayed in Frankfurt to help his father, working alongside several of the Rothschild daughters in supervising their growing portfolio. In 1800, Mayer and Amschel were appointed Crown Agents of Holy Roman Emperor Franz II—a prestigious honor, even with the empire just a few years away from total collapse and the reorganization of its member states.[13] Third son Nathan had already settled in Manchester, England, in 1798 to expand on the family's growing textile business. Jakob, the youngest and maybe the most ambitious son (who later Anglicized his name as James), settled in Paris in 1811 at the age of nineteen to help safeguard Rothschild business against plunder by the forces of Napoleon. And second son Salomon and fourth son Calmann (Carl) eventually opened banking houses in Vienna and Naples in the 1820s, as the Frankfurt, London, and Paris houses had grown into juggernauts that needed more international capital.

By that time, much of the family fortune had been made—and much of its lore already cemented.

THE BIRTH OF THE ROTHSCHILD MYTH

The emergence of Mayer's children as business leaders in their own right, particularly Nathan in England and James in France, would be the key to elevating the Rothschilds to an international dynasty, putting them in a position to lend money to nations in desperate need. The Napoleonic Wars offered almost unlimited opportunities for the Rothschilds to profit, as members of the coalition against France needed a constant flow of cash and gold to equip their massive armies. In due course, the Rothschilds lent to almost every state in opposition to France, earning interest on the loans the whole time.

Over twelve years between 1803 and 1815, on and off, Napoleon's France sent more than two million men at arms into battle, with as many as three million men arrayed against them, led by England and Prussia. Those millions of men needed equipment, food, uniforms, horses, artillery, and provisions for long campaigns—the British alone spent 13.7 million pounds equipping their army just in 1813, a huge amount at the time.[14]

After his victory at the Battle of Jena in 1806, Napoleon's army marched on Hesse. And even though the Elector had promised to remain neutral, he had also leased Hessian mercenaries to Prussia to fight against France. So orders were given to arrest the Elector and confiscate his vast estate, meaning William and his family needed a quick escape—or as quick as one can make when packing up a massive treasure of gold, jewels, and priceless business papers. They put on civilian clothes and disappeared into exile—leaving it to Mayer and Amschel to get the money where it was needed.

French forces immediately began looking for the loot, and the Elector tasked his court factor Mayer with hiding at least some part of it—the birth of another legend that would outlast the family patriarch, that of the Rothschilds stealing the vast "Elector's treasure" and profiting from it while funding all of the nations at war and making money off the misery.

The money that the Rothschilds made off investing the Elector's estate was hugely important to the spectacular growth of the House of Rothschild, to the point where Carl wrote in an 1814 letter that "the Old Man made our fortune," with the Old Man being William.[15] Through a complex system of purchases, distributions, cooked books, and loans made through outside parties, the Rothschilds managed the Elector's investments and funneled much of the fortune away from Napoleon and toward the armies fighting him. In doing so, they were increasingly taking the risk of running afoul of the substantial police and military forces France had committed to stopping money from flowing to their enemies.

Mayer and several of his sons were arrested by French authorities, though later released without charge, at least once. Letters of the time record Mayer and his sons corresponding with the exiled Elector using fake names and codes in letters delivered in secret compartments and written in archaic Hebrew script.[16] Nathan and James concocted a risky plan to smuggle gold back and forth across the Channel so it could be used as collateral in loans that would then go to fund Wellington's troops. The family made a huge amount of profit off both interest on the loans and fluctuations in the exchange rate of gold. As with most of the legends about the Rothschilds, the exact amount of gold Nathan bought, who he bought it from, how he and James moved it, and how exactly James staved off arrest all tend to vary depending on who is telling the story. But England desperately needed currency to pay and equip their army, and the Rothschilds were the only European banking house that could consistently provide it.[17]

With such huge amounts of money being transacted, and with the failing health of both patriarchs and Napoleonic police still searching for William's money, the family firm officially reorganized as "Mayer Amschel Rothschild and Sons." This partnership saw the family wealth equally divided between the five male heirs, and lasted for nearly a century.[18] The timing couldn't have been better—the already ailing Mayer was increasingly bedridden and died in September 1812, leaving a warning to his sons not to squander what he'd left them through wasteful spending, and to stay united no matter what the financial world threw at them. Gutle would remain living in the *Judengasse* until her death over three decades later.

There was little time to mourn. War was raging, and the Rothschild sons were in the thick of it. With France blockaded, London-based Nathan became the "commanding general" of the family and the principal financier of the British effort against Napoleon, with James his right-hand man in Paris. European forces relied heavily on mercenaries, who needed to be paid in the coin of their own realm or else they wouldn't fight. The Rothschild brothers were the main vessel through which money was smuggled in and out of the continent, and they made a fortune on both the commissions they took and interest on the loans they made— one estimate claims the family's wealth increased tenfold during the first half of the 1810s.[19]

In April 1814, Coalition armies took Paris, and Napoleon was exiled to the island of Elba in the Mediterranean, expected never to leave. Less than a year later, he escaped, headed back to France, and reclaimed his title of emperor. A final battle beckoned, and in June 1815, massive British and Prussian armies—financed in large part by the Rothschilds— defeated Napoleon's rebuilt army in battle at Waterloo in Belgium. The tyrant was exiled again, this time to tiny St. Helena in the South Atlantic, and never left.

The legend of how the Rothschilds learned of the victory at Waterloo, and what they did with that news, is so baked into the fabric of Rothschild family conspiracy theories that it deserves its own chapter. But the upshot is that while Nathan received the news quickly, there was no massive windfall. In fact, the Rothschilds likely saw Napoleon's quick defeat as a potential catastrophe. Anticipating a prolonged conflict after Napoleon's escape from Elba, the brothers duly bought up more gold to pour into Wellington's forces—only for the renewed conflict to be over in just a few months. Faced with the depreciation of their gold, Nathan frantically bought up British stocks that had collapsed with the country in financial trouble due to its massive war debt. When stocks rose over the next months, the family saw immense profit. British papers ran stories about Nathan's good fortune buying up these depleted stocks, and the first stirrings of a legend were created. And to reflect Nathan's new role as leader of the family, Rothschild business was now done through Nathan's company, N. M. Rothschild, founded in 1811 and headquartered in London.[20]

By the 1820s, the Rothschilds dominated European finance, almost singlehandedly developing what would become the international bond market. They were counselors and lenders to European royalty, the Vatican, prime ministers, and King George IV himself. And they were now bankers to the Holy Alliance—the treaty group of Russia, Prussia, and Austria that emerged to combat future French militarism. Rothschilds and their agents worked over the next few years to defuse a number of tense situations that easily could have exploded into war, by using letters as unofficial diplomatic channels, and by loaning money to cash-strapped kingdoms in return for promises of peace.[21]

One financial adventure around this time, Nathan Rothschild's saving the Bank of England from collapse in 1825, would provide yet another durable canard and conspiracy theory for cranks to distribute. But as with Waterloo, the truth is much less operatic than the conspiracy theories: When a gold price collapse put the Bank of England at risk of failing, N. M. Rothschild stepped in with a large loan. The Bank of England paid the loan back with interest, and the deal was just one more step on the road to N. M. Rothschild becoming the biggest bank in the world, likely ten times the size of its competitors.[22]

Conspiracy theory fodder about the family wouldn't be limited to their financial acumen, though. After 1824, Rothschild sons began to marry their children off to children from other branches. While intermarriage sounds like a shocking, incestuous practice confined to the Middle Ages or hemophilia-stricken Hapsburgs, marriages of convenience of this type were common in wealthy dynasties, to the point where high-born English Jews were referred to as "The Cousinhood."[23] For the Rothschilds, intermarriage was a way to keep the five houses from drifting away from each other and to keep their fortune from being taken by outsiders; also, by this point the family was so rich that nobody else was in their social strata. Yet cousin marriages were prohibited in many branches of Christianity and in the US, and Rothschild familial marriages were used as an excuse to oppose Jewish emancipation.

Fortunately, great care was taken in selecting mates for family members, and the Rothschilds avoided the recessive genes that plagued European royalty. Some Rothschild cousin marriages were loveless shams, while others, like the match between Nathan Rothschild's son Lionel and Charlotte, the daughter of oldest son Amschel, was a social triumph—making them the wealthiest couple in England.[24]

To house their expanding families, Rothschild sons began buying up country estates and palaces and climbing the social ladders in Paris and London. They started taking the prefixes of European nobles, such as "von" for Austrians and "de" for French and English members. Journals and newspapers praised the family's generosity, the extravagance of the décor of their homes, the size of their gardens, the jewels and precious metals they displayed, and their affinity for fine art, food, and architecture. Papers of the time (and writers to come) drooled over these luxurious furnishings and tapestries and gold-tinged lighting fixtures the way modern audiences marvel over megamansions and million-dollar cars.

The family gave a seemingly endless series of lavish balls and parties, where guests and the press alike marveled at the grandiosity of their homes and hospitality. As the family expanded into more palaces and estates, it took up the stereotypical pastimes of the idle rich—hunting, horse racing, art collecting.[25] The Rothschilds displayed a certain ambivalence toward all this social climbing, with many claiming they did it only to raise the social profile of Jews in Europe in general. But Rothschild largesse and refined taste would become a defining feature for how wealth and privilege were depicted after the Napoleonic Wars—a distinction that even got its own name: *Le Style Rothschild*.

A GERMAN IN NEW YORK

Financially, the family was diversifying from selling bonds to governments into selling commercial bills to private businesses. The family made great fortunes in precious metals, grain, sugar, copper, and mercury—mined in Spain and vital to refining silver and gold. By necessity, Rothschild business expanded into new cities, with agents taking the place of actual family members as the conduits for their dealings in newly wealthy enclaves like Madrid, St. Petersburg, Havana, and American cities like New Orleans and New York.

The biggest hindrance to the Rothschilds turning the United States into another jewel in their crown was that third generation Rothschilds didn't want to go there. It was too rural, too agricultural, and too cut off from the continent. It was a grave mistake that would have far-reaching consequences for both the family and American banking.

With family members not wanting to leave their lives of luxury for the hinterlands, the family's reliance on outside agents had to be stepped up. Often starting as clerks in family employ, agents handled correspondence, accounting, personnel matters, and, increasingly, running offices without actual family members there. Many were highly skilled businesspeople and provided critical intelligence to the family on the goings-on in far-flung nations. It wasn't unusual for Rothschild agents or their children to marry other agents, start their own firms, or profit off their association with the family. Agents were a hugely important part of how the family was able to keep so many business interests going without modern communication tools, but the agent system had its limits—and those limits were going to be severely tested by events both worldwide and familial.[26]

Even though the family leaned on agents, major decisions were made by the brothers, and only the brothers. Soon, there was one fewer brother. When Mayer Amschel died in 1812, the Rothschilds were still a small but growing financial powerhouse with branches in a few of Europe's biggest capitols. When his son Nathan died twenty-four years later, they were gods of money—and the world was much more complex.

Nathan's death was about as inglorious as it gets, with the scion plagued by a recurring anal abscess, or "a disagreeable boil in a most inconvenient place," as his wife put it in a letter.[27] After an extremely painful surgery to drain it, a second wound became infected. More abscesses appeared, with Nathan lapsing into fever, likely from sepsis. By the end of July, he was clearly on his deathbed, and after echoing the last days of his father in hastily rewriting his will to ensure the family partnership would survive, he died. A carrier pigeon of the Rothschild communication network conveyed the message to London with three simple words—*il est mort*.[28]

The shock to the financial market was considerable—Nathan was the head of the most powerful financial empire in Europe and the richest man in England, and therefore almost certainly the wealthiest man in the world at the time. Estimates have Nathan's personal fortune at around 3.5 million pounds, with the entire family having personal capital of around 6 million pounds—about $676 million in current value.[29]

With Nathan gone, James became de facto head of the family, and he put his time and effort chiefly into funding France's burgeoning railway system. But he struggled to keep the houses from feuding with each other, as the Paris, London, and Frankfurt branches were now almost equally wealthy. With their expansion into Spanish mercury bringing opportunities in the Americas, the next logical step for the Rothschilds would be to conquer the financial markets of the United States as well. But the family's forays into US banking and commodities were beset with failure—and their actual footprint in American finance is dwarfed by the legends and hoaxes about it.

With no family member willing to move to New York, the family appointed an agent to head business in the US, a Jewish employee named August Schoenberg. Sent to Havana to check on Rothschild interests in Cuba, he stopped in New York in 1837, and because the Rothschild agents at the time had gone under in the Panic of 1837, he never left. He changed his name to Belmont, converted, and announced he was acting as an agent of the Rothschilds, but he was mostly working for his own benefit. He soon got involved in Democratic Party politics, diplomacy, and horse breeding. His son, August Jr., financed the construction of the original New York Subway system and lent his name to both the Belmont Stakes horse race and the Belmont Park racetrack. The relationship between Belmont and the Rothschilds was complex, as while the financier helped buoy the Rothschilds' holdings in the US, he also did an enormous amount of business for himself. As such, the Rothschilds were kept out of the rapidly expanding Wall Street banking community, and their exclusion would be a critical event in family history.[30]

Confounded by the litany of state and federal laws they had to deal with, the family began making loans to the governments of individual states, only to see most of them flounder. Back in London, relations with the Bank of England were beginning to sour, too, and other countries began to chafe under the influence that the Rothschilds had over international banking. But for as much as the family tried to stay out of European political intrigue, they were pulled into what became known as the Damascus Affair, the disappearance of a Capuchin monk and his Muslim servant in that city— blamed on a group of influential local Jews accused of murdering him and using his blood to make matzo.[31]

Several of the accused Jews were tortured to death or forced to convert, and both police working for the deeply antisemitic French consul and local mobs committed numerous acts of violence against the Jewish community, including seizing dozens of Jewish children to attempt to extract the loca- tion where "blood rituals" were being held. The revival of the blood libel galvanized European Jews in their quest for emancipation. It also codified a growing antisemitism in Europe, particularly France, because Syria at the time was under French control. James and Solomon Rothschild made pleas to French and Austrian officials to put an end to the pogrom, and the hos- tages were released. But the storm of accusations and libel against the Jewish community were devastating, both for attempts to hasten Jewish emancipa- tion in much of Europe and for the public image of Europe's Jews.

Much of this ire was directed toward the Rothschilds. They were visible targets because of their wealth, their public role in advocating for Jews in the aftermath of the Damascus Affair, their refusal to convert to Christianity as so many of their competitors had done, and, in particular, what was seen as the family's outsized ownership of European railways. Combined with rev- olutionary fervor in 1840s France and the rise of socialism in response to European industrialization, numerous legends about the family would take root around then, spurred by the revolutionary upheavals of 1848.

THE 1848 REVOLUTIONS

Starting in January 1848, Europe went through tremendous political and social tumult. Spurred by advances in industrialization, frustration with the control of absolute monarchies, demands for political reform and press freedom, and growing anti-rich sentiment, workers across Europe began to rise. The French monarchy was overthrown again and replaced with a presidency held by Napoleon's nephew, Louis-Napoleon (also known as Napoleon III), while many of the German and Italian states had to liberalize their laws, and open warfare broke out in city streets across Europe.

One of the driving factors in the revolutions of 1848 was the liberation of the growing European middle class, and Jewish emancipation was a major part of that. Jews and non-Jews alike fought for the ending of special laws and taxes on Jews. And Jews even won political offices in nations that had been deeply hostile to them. But the revolutionary fervor put the Rothschilds in a difficult spot—they were ardent in their support of emancipation, but also seen as a huge part of the capitalist rot that had to be thrown off.[32]

As the revolutions went on, the growing populist backlash put Jewish wealth at the center of the storm, with the Rothschilds tarred as the figurehead of Jewish control of capitalism. Even their one-time ally, British prime minister Benjamin Disraeli, spoke openly of the need for the Rothschilds to "lose everything everywhere except [London]."[33]

Beyond the danger posed by the financial upheaval of 1848, the Rothschilds faced physical danger. Family properties were ransacked, their possessions were stolen, Rothschild heirs were sent fleeing, and the press turned against them with increasingly Jew-hating fervor. James de Rothschild, a focal point for attacks because of his ownership of French railroads (his railway stations and bridges were hit with arson attacks), sent his family away from Paris, while Solomon barricaded himself in his Palais in Vienna, with his son Anselm fleeing the city for a month when armed revolutionaries set up camp on his office's roof.[34] Amschel Rothschild's windows were smashed three different times by protestors in Frankfurt, to the point where he too fled, and the attacks were satirized in cartoons of the day.[35]

If ever there was a moment when an "old money" house of wealth would be toppled, it was 1848. Rumors swirled that the storm of attacks James was facing would force him to flee France for good, while the Vienna house teetered on the brink of collapse, threatening the Frankfurt house, which held a great deal of Vienna's debt—the legendary Rothschild interconnect-edness finally becoming a danger. The London house had to bail out the others, which it could do only thanks to August Belmont, who (attempting to stave off being fired) kept it floating with a large shipment of silver sent from New York.[36]

Thanks to James's tenacity, the unity of the houses, and the natural burnout of the 1848 revolutions, the family survived. But public sentiment had turned on them, especially in France. In some ways, it would never en-tirely turn back. The days when, as a quote attributed to multiple sources put it, "There is but one power in Europe and that is Rothschild" were waning.[37] The decades between Waterloo and 1848 had been peaceful and prosperous for the family, but the next three, until the Franco-Prussian War began in 1870, were tumultuous and violent. One house wouldn't survive, and others nearly collapsed.

The family's political influence was left diminished by 1848, and many of the monarchs they'd been counselors and bankers to were gone. Beyond that, the world that the Rothschilds had mastered was changing. The Rothschilds' complex system of using private couriers carrying dip-lomatic bags to ferry information at top speed was revolutionary when they started it in 1814, but every other bank was now doing it as well. New technology made the need for private couriers obsolete, but the Rothschilds resisted such modern communication, and the family had a peculiar disdain for the telegraph, with James grousing in a letter to Nathan that the device was making people "too well informed, and there is little opportunity to do anything."[38]

Private banking, the lending of money directly to nations by individu-als, was also being replaced by joint stock banking, or banks that issue stock and are owned by private shareholders. And nation-states began selling bonds of their own directly to their citizens, rather than to wealthy banks like the Rothschilds.

After the revolutions of 1848, Rothschild money and influence in-creasingly couldn't prevent wars, and the family's accumulation of wealth wasn't admired as much as it was scorned by new socialist thinkers who demanded equality for all, no matter the cost. Around the same time, the family suffered a slew of deaths, including matriarch Gutle, who died in 1849 at the age of ninety-six, while brothers Carl, Solomon, and Amschel all died in 1855.

The family was still struggling to break into the United States, as the problems with Belmont in New York were compounded by those with their West Coast man, British banker Benjamin Davidson, whose father happened to be Nathan's brother-in-law. After gold was found in California, the Rothschilds sent Davidson from Mexico to San Francisco, where he sent massive gold shipments back to the family but also made lavish real estate purchases against the family's orders. But like with Belmont, it wasn't bad enough to send a family member there to take charge.[39]

Europe's upheaval was bad for the family at home, as well. The Vienna house's near-collapse saddled the family with a massive amount of debt, while the new Prussian delegate to the German Confederation was less than impressed with the decaying remnants of the first generation of Mayer's children.[40] A descendant of wealthy landowners, the ultra-nationalistic Otto von Bismarck disdained the older generation of Rothschilds and believed they were more interested in parsing out inheritances than doing business. There were political considerations as well—growing tension between Prussia and Austria put multiple Rothschild houses at risk, leading Bismarck to borrow through his personal banker, the Berlin-based Rothschild agent Gerson von Bleichröder, not the family itself.

Although its influence on European leaders was on the decline, the family began to get into politics more directly. Lionel de Rothschild, son of Nathan, became the first British Jew ever to take a seat in the House of Commons, other than Disraeli, who was born Jewish but converted to Anglicanism at twelve. Jews had been elected to the House of Commons before but had always been prevented from sitting due to the explicitly Christian language of the Oath of Abjuration. It was abolishing these oaths that became the focus of the Rothschilds' political activism, and even though a bill passed by the House of Commons did away with the oath, Lionel was still made to be sworn in on a Christian bible—which he refused after his election in 1847. It would take until 1858, after he'd been elected again, for Lionel to finally be allowed to take his seat.[41]

But business would continually be threatened by the outbreaks of wars between and inside nations that the Rothschilds had either made loans to or had major holdings in—specifically Germany, Austria, and Italy, as well as the United States during the American Civil War.

INTERESTS ON BOTH SIDES

Often, the Rothschilds would have financial involvement in both sides of a conflict—truthful echoes of future conspiracy theories that the family "funds both sides of every war." But this was not because they would make money no matter who won, as so many cranks would later allege. It's because the family had expanded so much that little of Europe didn't have at least some link to them. It's why they worked so hard for peace, and often refused to make loans or buy bonds from nations threatening war in the decades after Napoleon—no matter who would win, the Rothschilds would lose.

When war broke out in the Crimea in 1853 between Russia and an alliance of England, France, and the Ottoman Empire, leaders of Europe again turned to the Rothschild family. Nathan's son Lionel, the heir of the London branch, lent over sixteen million pounds to support the war against Russia just in 1854. And James floated a nine-figure loan in francs to support France.[42] All that money was lent to fight a nation that the Rothschilds had also once lent to, including a six-million-pound loan made by Nathan in 1822.[43]

That war did much to shore up the Rothschilds prestige as bankers to the world, but it was becoming inevitable that with the Rothschilds loaning so much money, eventually some of their clients would go to war with each other. When Austria and Prussia fought in the summer of 1866 over the administration of the northernmost German state Schleswig-Holstein, it was a brief and bloody conflict called the "Seven Weeks' War." The Rothschilds would seem to be on the side of Prussia and Bismarck, with Mayer Carl (son of Vienna head Carl) having become banker to the Court of Prussia and the Rothschilds making a large loan to Bismarck's government through Bleichröder, both for war and for railroad expansion.[44] But the Austrian Empire was home to massive Rothschild holdings in mining and the railroad industry. It seemed that no matter who won, the family stood to lose. Bismarck would quickly lead the Prussian Empire to victory and the creation of the North German Confederation—expelling Austria in the process, which went on to merge with Hungary to form the Austro-Hungarian Empire. These machinations would have dire consequences for the future of Europe.

In the same weeks in June 1866, the Austrian Empire also went to war with the Kingdom of Italy in the Third Italian War of Independence. Again, two foundational Rothschild houses, Vienna and Naples, were pitted against each other. The Austrian Empire buckled under the strain of two wars, and while the Naples house had closed in 1863 following Italian Unification three years earlier, the family still had deep financial ties to the Vatican, along with considerable holdings in the Kingdom of Italy.[45] Italy would win against Austria and annex precious territory on its way to completing unification in 1871, when the Kingdom of Italy took over Rome and the Vatican states. Germany, too, would unite in the same year, with Bismarck as the first chancellor of the German Empire.

Across the ocean, unification was the last thing on anyone's mind, including the Rothschilds'.

The misconceptions about the Rothschilds' role in the American Civil War will be fully explored in subsequent chapters. But the family's involvement in the war between the Union and Confederacy was typical of their misadventures in nineteenth century America: limited, confused, and seemingly at odds with itself. It was also at least somewhat ambivalent toward the South, with some sources incorrectly claiming the Confederacy had sold vast quantities of bonds to the Rothschilds.

There were other harbingers of bad times to come. By 1868, James de Rothschild was the last son of Mayer Amschel. While his brothers spent much of their final years ailing, the founder of the powerful French house of the family remained healthy and vigorous up until the end, and his death was a cultural touchstone, with tens of thousands of Parisians, Rothschilds from across Europe, and royalty all turning out to pay their respects. He had made the Paris house into a financial juggernaut, its portfolio growing hundreds of times over from his initial investment in 1815. And in his will, he attempted to keep his father's ethos of family unity, admonishing his heirs to "never forget the mutual confidence and fraternal accord" the brothers enjoyed.[46]

It didn't last. The remaining houses feuded over how to react to Prussia's growing power and the potential of Germany uniting under Bismarck, the plight of Eastern European Jews, how to handle Napoleon III in France, whether to expand more into the Americas, the increasing opposition and antisemitic rhetoric the family faced, and their overall waning influence in Europe's capitols as a new generation of leaders swept away old alliances.

There would be great successes to come, in Europe and around the world. But the last of the founders of the great houses passing, combined with the looming threat of war between France and Prussia, signaled the end of the family's dominance as bankers, peacemakers, and soothsayers. On the other hand, the first century of Rothschild growth, financial dominance, Jewish advocacy, and largesse had provided an almost inexhaustible well for conspiracy theorists, antisemites, and crank thinkers to draw from. And there was one legendary incident that would be the foundation for so many myths and canards: Nathan Rothschild and his reaction upon finding out the outcome of the Battle of Waterloo. While the battle was fought in 1815, the myth would emerge decades later—and has been continuously embraced by some of the worst people imaginable.

THE WATERLOO CANARD: THE ROTHSCHILD MYTH TO END ALL MYTHS

By the time of James's death in 1868, there had already been decades of cultural depictions of the Rothschilds. At least some were flattering, or at least not overtly antisemitic. The 1817 cartoon "A View from the Royal Exchange" shows Nathan in what would become a much-referenced depiction—plump, red-faced, top-hatted, and holding a piece of paper while executing one of the many bold moves that made him the richest man in the world. In short, he looks like any other wealthy British stockbroker, just more so.[1]

Other cartoon depictions of the Rothschilds followed the same gently satirical tone. The British Museum has an entire collection of Nathan cartoons, showing the tycoon hobnobbing with royalty or bestowing favors on his friends while inside a giant top "spinning a loan." In one example that will become crucial to future myths, a popular cartoon depicting Nathan at the London Stock Exchange standing next to what was said to be his favorite column is literally called "A Pillar of the Exchange."[2]

Literature of the early 1800s extolled the Rothschilds as new royalty, equal parts canny and clairvoyant, bankers to the world, and wealthier than anyone could imagine. Much of this work, though fawning, was also shot through with dark jabs. An early poem by *Vanity Fair* author William Makepeace Thackeray, appropriately titled "N.M. Rothschild, Esq" extolled "pillar of the [Exchange]" Nathan as "First Baron Juif" and "not the 'King of the Jews' but the 'Jew of the Kings'" who "plays with new kings" like a child playing with dolls.[3] The twelfth canto of Lord Byron's legendary poem *Don Juan* provides the answer "Jew Rothschild" to the question "Who hold the balance of the world? Who reign / O'er congress, whether royalist or liberal?" And future British prime minister Benjamin Disraeli's 1840s trilogy of novels *Coningsby*, *Sybil or the Two Nations*, and *Tancred* contain characters based on both Nathan and his eldest son Lionel de Rothschild, depicted with fabulous wealth and diligent observation of Jewish ritual.

It's not clear what the Rothschilds thought of the growing media fervor around them. Some accounts claim Nathan was amused by the cartoons about him, pinning a few to the wall of his office and laughing at his portrayal.[4] But the tide of public sentiment was beginning to turn against the Rothschilds, particularly outside England, as socialism rose in response to growing wealth inequality and small nation-states began to coalesce into the major nations we know today. One cartoon would be the harbinger of future Rothschild depictions and conspiracy theories to come—a grotesque German drawing anonymously published in 1845 and known as *Die Generalpumpe*—"The General Pump"—dehumanizing Mayer Amschel Rothschild as a giant spigot, pumping gold into the clutches of bankers and tycoons while common people suffer.[5]

Other such depictions of the Rothschilds as pigs sustaining the banks and royals of the world, gluttonous kings devouring the world, and other antisemitic imagery would soon follow. Even fictional works by authors who were financially assisted by the Rothschilds seemed awestruck by the sheer amount of wealth they'd acquired in such a short time. German poet Heinrich Heine, a close friend of the family, believed the Rothschilds were revolutionaries creating a new aristocracy that they would lead as the very richest of the new money to emerge in the nineteenth century. And his 1841 declaration in a letter to a German newspaper that "money is the god of our times, and Rothschild is his prophet," made after he visited James's office in Paris, would be reproduced in countless antisemitic internet memes 150 years later.[6]

Despite being a close friend and financial beneficiary of James de Rothschild, French author Honore de Balzac bitingly satirized his patron in the 1837 short story *La Maison Nucingen*. The greedy French Jewish banker of the title, Baron de Nucingen, who appears in numerous Balzac stories, serves as an outrageous fictionalized caricature of James, and might have planted the first seeds of the most enduring and iconic conspiracy theory about the Rothschilds ever—that Nathan made a fortune by buying depressed stocks before news of the French defeat at Waterloo was known by the public. But it would be another document, written by an obscure pamphleteer under the pseudonym "Satan," that would insert the story into the popular consciousness, launching a thousand conspiracy theories in the process.[7]

THE MANY MYTHS OF NATHAN ROTHSCHILD

The story of Nathan Rothschild and his great windfall after Waterloo has been told so many times with so many conflicting details that even tracking the most consistent version is difficult. Adding to the complexity is that the first popular versions of the tale originated decades after the battle, and weren't in English. This allowed fragments to be warped and twisted by both pro- and anti-Rothschild writers alike—with a thousand different versions of the same story.

If there's one thing about the Battle of Waterloo that's filtered into popular culture, save the ABBA song "Waterloo," it's probably that the Rothschilds made some uncountable fortune off getting the news of the battle's outcome first and exploiting it to the fullest possible extent. This belief can be found in print material of all kinds, in magazine articles, films, plays, and novels from every generation since the tale first emerged. It's in history books, investment books, guides to business management and finance, self-help and technology manuals, documentaries on money printing and war, histories of London, of Jews, of the Rothschilds, of France, and of Germany, and even encyclopedias. It's in broadsheets of the early nineteenth century, conspiracy tomes of the twentieth, and viral videos of the twenty-first.

The myth that Nathan Rothschild manipulated Waterloo for his own ends is so adaptable that the 1940 Nazi propaganda film *The Rothschilds' Shares in Waterloo* bastardized what was itself an ahistorical take on the Waterloo story, the 1934 Hollywood film *The House of Rothschild*. Even the Duke of Wellington himself, the great architect of the victory, told a story a decade after the battle positing that a Rothschild agent witnessed a messenger deliver the news of the triumph to exiled French king Louis XVIII—and made haste to bring the news back to his boss Nathan first.[8]

More than any other member of the original generation of Rothschilds, even more than his father Mayer, myth and mystique surrounds Nathan Rothschild. And where myth and mystique meet outsized wealth and great historical events, conspiracy theories are sure to follow. When historical cranks and modern antisemites have needed someone to spew venom at, it's been Nathan—the man who "made millions" off Waterloo by "getting the news first," who "saved the Bank of England" and afterward set himself up as the "unelected ruler of Europe," and who some quotes say dared make the claim that he "controlled the British money supply."

Nathan was uniquely positioned to become the focal point of the Rothschild myth because he was the head of the family after Mayer's death. He was the wealthiest of the sons, an extremely gifted businessperson who saw the Rothschilds grow from a well-off banking family to an international dynasty. And he didn't suffer fools or get sucked in by dreams of outsized gains—one letter in the Rothschild Archives demonstrates how a Scottish adventurer named Gregor MacGregor attempted to swindle Nathan with the prospect of investing in a Jewish colony in a fictional Central American territory called Poyais—a scam that defrauded hundreds of others in the fifteen years that MacGregor ran it—only for Nathan to ignore it.[9]

Because of his wealth and location, Nathan has the most English-language material written about him, but paradoxically, we know the least about his inner life. While thousands of letters written to and from the other Rothschild sons lie in the family archives, only a few of Nathan's letters have survived.[10] His first recorded correspondence from England is from 1800, and the next year, his older brother Salomon was sent over to help manage his growing textile business in Manchester. But even though the surviving records show that Nathan was still subordinate to Mayer in his dealings, little remains of the intricacy of how he made his millions.

We do know that he did well enough to buy a house on "the most elegant street in Manchester," and was successful enough during boom times that he could ride out the busts germane to the textile business.[11] What hampered the growth of his empire more than anything was war.

Napoleonic France may have been a nominally equal and friendly place for Jews, with the 40,000-strong population of French Jews granted equal rights under Napoleon. But France had occupied Hesse-Kassel in 1806, exiling the Elector, William I (patron of Mayer), for his support of Prussia. This was still the cradle of the family, still the home of Mayer and Gutle, and much of the *Judengasse* had been destroyed by French guns. If Napoleon's forces won, the debts owed to the family by Britain, Russia, Prussia, and the other nations allied against France would likely never be made whole, and the family might have to live under occupation.

Because England imposed a blockade against France in May 1806, and Napoleon retaliated with an embargo against all outside trade into France six months later, Nathan had to fund the war from afar. He had already cornered the market on British gold with the collapse of his biggest competitor in 1810, and oversaw its smuggling over the English Channel, making loans to the nations in the coalitions against France. With that money, and heavy borrowing from William I's fortune—the "Elector's Treasure," often spoken of by Rothschild opponents as ill-gotten gains—N. M. Rothschild went about bankrolling the fight against Napoleon.[12]

The system by which money and information were moved back and forth between England and the Continent was complex, but the young, dynamic Nathan excelled at it. In the process, the family did well, earning interest on British government debt (sold in the form of bonds called "consols" that were only finally paid off in full in 2015) and the other loans it was making to the nations at war with Napoleon. Mayer also hid away part of William's fortune for himself, while selling off much of his collection of coins and medals to ensure more of it could be laundered to Wellington.

William's money was just one part of the vast sum of treasure that bounced back and forth across the English Channel. But the mythos of the "Elector's Treasure" began to take on a life of its own in 1826, spurred by the growth of socialist anti-Rothschild sentiment in France and the massive reparations the losers had to pay to the victors, with the Rothschilds administering French repayment to England. Stories began circulating in the socialist press that their gains during the Napoleonic Wars had mostly been made through war profiteering—especially the selling of "Hessian" mercenaries—and was being used by the conniving Rothschilds to bloat their own fortune at the expense of the young men who died in battle.[13]

Such overblown myths about Mayer and Nathan's exploitation of "blood money" would surface again and again in future writing about the family. The Elector's Treasure is an obscure bit of history, couched in hopelessly complex financial arcana and unfolding through archived letters. As Rothschild conspiracy theories go, it's fallen by the wayside. But the Waterloo myth lingers to this very day, demonstrating an almost supernatural ability by Nathan to divine the future, a ruthless ambition to exploit it, and a deep hate of Gentile working men in doing so.

"IMPETUOUS DARING"

While the details (and the intent) vary, every version of what supposedly happened during those days in June 1815 has a few events in common. They all revolve around Nathan taking advantage of the Rothschilds' extant system of foreign agents by either transmitting the news through messengers, or of Nathan personally using that system to get himself to London before anyone else. As the outcome became clear, Rothschild messengers (or

Nathan himself) rushed from the battlefield or from Brussels to a ship waiting at the port of Ostend, crossed the Channel at great peril, and got back to the London Stock Exchange with the news printed in a hot-off-the-presses paper, which the British government did not believe but Nathan did. And in sharing the news that France had won, he either triggered a sell-off by panicked British brokers who misinterpreted his slumped-over affect or simply lied about the outcome of the battle.

With the "panicked sell-off" in full swing, Nathan then used his network of agents to secretly buy up depressed consols just before the rest of the world found out what really happened. When news broke of Wellington's victory and stocks went back up in value, Nathan made a fortune. According to the legends, nobody knows how much Nathan made that day, but it was enough to ensure that the Rothschilds controlled England and ruled the financial world after that.

Like much of the scholarship and fiction regarding the family, a good number of these stories seem to admire Nathan for his cunning and bravery in taking control of the world's finances in one swift stroke. Post-Waterloo authors would write that his actions were taken with the best information at hand, not out of malice but merely with a willingness to risk buying when everyone else was selling.

One typical complementary American version came in a 1903 article in *The Windsor Magazine* called "The Money Kings of the Modern World," and was one of the many profiles of the family that saw them as a kind of new royalty. After leaning hard on the legends of the Elector's Treasure and of the family's various name changes before Mayer's birth, the article claims that Waterloo "marked decisively the establishment of the new dynasty" that Mayer and sons were building. Messengers of the legendary Rothschild courier system first brought Nathan local papers with the news of Prussian military collapse, which sent stocks spiraling enough for Nathan to buy, then sent the subsequent news of ultimate victory over Napoleon—boosting those stocks up higher than ever. Nathan's triumph was total, sending "every government in Europe, cap in hand [asking Nathan] to accept the position of their financial agent." Which, of course, he did.[14]

Other complementary retellings are even more action-packed, such as the 1905 version of the tale in *The American Monthly Review of Reviews*, itself remarking on a March 1905 article in *Cosmopolitan*, "The Empire of Rothschild." The *Review* author applauds Nathan for his "coolness, judgement, and impetuous daring" and claims Nathan was "a spectator on the battlefield" where he saw French troops besting the "exhausted" armies of Wellington and his Prussian counterpart, Blucher. Nathan then rode on horseback to the port of Ostend, paying a handsome sum to a boatman to brave a terrible Channel storm and get him back to London, where his slouching and defeated expression while leaning against his favorite column at the Stock Exchange was enough to cause a sell-off. And of course, "Nathan's agents [. . .] bought, bought, bought" the whole time.[15]

More versions of the story would come in the generations to follow. They would be pumped full of lurid, irrelevant, unconfirmable details. The amount of money Nathan made veered wildly between a few million pounds and well over 125 million. There were fine horses carrying couriers on midnight rides, perilous storms nearly sending the news carriers to their death, Rothschild-trained carrier pigeons valiantly taking the news across the water, and Nathan standing so close to the battlefield that he could smell cannon smoke and see the faces of men blown to bits. Or he was given the news in a secret paper from Amsterdam delivered to him by a hardy sea captain named Cullen, or by a fast cutter contracted by the Rothschilds and waiting at the port of Dunkirk, and there was even a once-hidden letter from an American diplomatic envoy named James Gallatin in London confirming that "they say Monsieur Rothschild dispatched couriers from Brussels to Ostend" with a ship standing by to bring the news.[16]

In his hugely popular 1928 biography of the family, *The Rise of the House of Rothschild*, Austrian author Egon Caesar Corti doesn't put Nathan at Waterloo himself, but instead lauds the Rothschild courier system for making sure he had the news early, singling out one Europe-based agent "whose name was Rothworth" for "obtaining the first newspaper account of the successful issue of the battle" and speeding it across the Channel to Nathan, who "applied it to his own profit in his business dealings." But Corti also applies certain skepticism to the legend, allowing that the public made much of it up as they looked for an explanation as to how intertwined Nathan had become with British finance.[17]

In his 1963 memoir *The Craft of Intelligence*, CIA head Allen Dulles (who had previously helped German Jews escape Berlin) praised the Rothschild courier system that allowed Nathan to get the news of British victory first in London. Decades later, in part one of his epochal two-volume history *The House of Rothschild* (a frequent source for this book), Niall Ferguson would apply more skepticism to some of these myths, writing that Nathan was likely expecting the War of the Seventh Coalition to drag on far longer and was finding the buying of British consols to fund the war to be increasingly less viable. And while Nathan likely had at least some early knowledge of the outcome, and that "no doubt it was gratifying" to get the news fairly soon after Wellington's victory, restrictions on the amount of consols one could buy at one time meant his profit on Waterloo "could not have been very great."[18]

"ROTHSCHILD KNOWS"

While the details vary, none of these stories seem particularly anti-Jewish. Some lean harder on tropes than others, but they all cast Nathan as a crafty businessperson who saw an opportunity for profit and took it at great risk. But there are versions of the story that are much more conspiratorial, casting Nathan as manipulating both the battle and the transmission of the news for his own ends, or deliberately announcing that Wellington had lost while funding both sides of the conflict, and even ensuring Napoleon's defeat through a bribe to a French marshal.

The 1887 John Reeves book *The Rothschilds: Financial Rulers of Nations* might be the earliest popular English-language dissemination of the "Nathan was at the battle" legend. The book isn't quite as antisemitic as its title, as Reeves goes on at length about the persecution and scientific accomplishment of Jews who merely "like to make the best bargains they can" and "maintain a proud reserve and never solicit aid from any but co-religionists."[19]

But about the Rothschilds themselves, Reeves is unsparing—he writes that they "belong to no one nationality, they are cosmopolitan"—a chilling early version of the "rootless cosmopolitan" canard that would power Soviet persecution of leftist Jews in the 1920s and '30s.[20] But more than that, Reeves claims that not only did the family fund Napoleon's enemies, they also funded Napoleon as well: "they were ready to grow rich at the expense of friends and foes alike."[21]

Through Nathan taking a front-row seat at the battle, Reeves explains, he learned of Napoleon's defeat "long before" anyone else and acted quickly to take advantage of the news. As a wealthy baron, Nathan, naturally, was so disdainful of the fate of the Gentile boatmen carrying him from Belgium to England that he simply offered more and more money until one hardy sailor, taking up the challenge for 2,000 francs, demanded the money be sent to his wife because he didn't believe he would survive. Like in every other tale, the John Reeves version of Nathan made it back and took it upon himself to announce the grim news of French victory—while his agents secretly bought depressed stocks "on a gigantic scale." Then he announced the "real" outcome, with the windfall of Waterloo making him "nearly a million sterling" and the Rothschilds now so powerful that no nation would ever dare make a financial move without the brothers' approval.[22]

Other stories taking the improbable idea that Nathan Rothschild had personally witnessed the Battle of Waterloo as gospel have a similar tinge of anti-Jewish sentiment. One such version was enshrined in a speech on the floor of the House of Representatives in 1900, with Nathan Rothschild's scheme seen as a warning of the "dangers of causing a panic [...] when it can be turned to profit"—a clear sign of the "greed and avarice enforced by someone in power to compel submission."[23]

Playing off Reeves's canard that "Napoleon's fall was Rothschild's rise" (itself a false trope repeated over and over by different chronicles), then–Stanford University president and ardent eugenicist David Starr Jordan wrote a scabrous contribution to the Maryland Peace Society Journal in 1910 claiming the "gifted son Nathan Rothschild caused the fall of the house of Bonaparte to ensure the rise of the house of Rothschild," lording over every financial transaction by every nation on the Continent as "the actual ruler of Europe." If war was coming to Europe, Jordan reasoned, then it would be the money of the Jew—and the machinations of the Rothschilds—that would load the first cannon.[24]

Writing in the 1913 biography *The Romance of the Rothschilds*, Ignatius Balla puts Nathan as a spectator at Waterloo, his soul hardened by the sight of "the dead and the wounded," and upon seeing Napoleon's defeat, he rushed back to London through Ostend, ferried by the omnipresent terrified sailor who accepted Nathan's lavish payment of 2,000 francs. Exhausted and broken by his perilous journey, Nathan leaned against his favorite column in the London Stock Exchange, where the uncertainty about the battle and Nathan's appearance fueled a sell-off based on rumors of French victory—while Nathan's agents bought up everything they could for a profit of "nearly a million sterling in a single day."[25]

The accusation found even more new eyes when it was included in the *Dearborn Independent* articles that made up Henry Ford's 1920 screed *The International Jew*, which served as the first time the text of the infamous Russian forgery known as *The Protocols of the Elders of Zion* was widely circulated in English.[26]

And while the *Protocols* would be enormously influential in how antisemites around the world saw Jewish wealth in the next century, the more immediate impact of Ford's Jew-baiting was on how they saw the Rothschilds. Ford's hugely popular series of articles includes a direct reference to the "Nathan lied to the Stock Exchange" legend in the first volume, *The World's Foremost Problem*, as an illustration of how Jews value control of the media. Why else would Nathan, a "coward" who was "always afraid of danger," take the risk of going to the battlefield himself? He needed the news first—and with the outcome known only to him, he braved the Channel storm, glumly leaned against his favorite column at the Stock Exchange, pretended France had won, and had his minions buy up the depressed consols, making "$10,000,000 [sic]—all as an affair of news!"[27]

Even the authors of books that seem to admire the family weren't immune to conspiracy theory and the echoing of antisemitic canards. Biographer Frederic Morton's dishy 1963 *The Rothschilds: A Family Portrait* was a National Book Award finalist that attempted to put a pop spin on the rise of the dynasty. In discussing Waterloo, Morton both gushed at Nathan's "very hard work and very cold cunning" in pulling off a "multi-million-dollar [sic] scoop" and, unfortunately, echoed the claim that he'd engineered it on purpose. As Morton tells the tale, the trusty agent Rothworth (who, since his debut in Corti's book, had appeared in both the 1934 and 1940 film versions of the story) "jumped into a boat in Ostend" clutching a freshly printed Dutch paper telling of French victory. Nathan was informed in due course and went right to the Stock Exchange. Arriving disheveled and seemingly upset, he duly leaned against his favorite pillar and "dumped consols." As Nathan's "pudgy fingers . . . depressed the market with each sell signal," breathless whispers of "Rothschild knows" and "Waterloo is lost" rippled through the building. Nathan bought a huge number of consols "for a song," then made millions when he suddenly announced the news of Coalition victory.

"We cannot guess the number of hopes and savings wiped out in this engineered panic," Morton gravely wrote of the "scoop" that gave the Rothschilds the fortune to buy uncountable paintings, race horses, and palaces.[28]

The Waterloo myth carries enormous power and weight to this day. It was recycled in a 2022 email by a cryptocurrency company advising investors that "the best time to buy bitcoin is whenever blood is on the street, everyone is panicking and no one's talking about it," an adaptation of an apocryphal Nathan Rothschild quote regarding the battle.[29] Nathan receiving the news early "thanks to his extensive network of carrier pigeons" was included in an otherwise anodyne article about Rothschild investing practices in *Forbes* in 2014, despite there being no such pigeon post at the time.[30] And in his 2007 film *Endgame*, conspiracy maven Alex Jones tells yet another version of the story in a grave tone while stock footage and public domain images keep viewers on the hook for his theories:

"On the eighteenth of June, 1815, agents of the British arm of the Rothschild family looked on as Emperor Napoleon Bonaparte fought desperately to save his army from the jaws of a British-Prussian pincer attack," Jones announces. "A Rothschild agent was able to get the news of Napoleon's defeat at the hands of Lord Wellington to Nathan Rothschild a full twenty hours before the news reached London. Nathan, the head of the British arm of the Rothschild family, put out the rumor to the London Stock Exchange that Napoleon had *won* the war! Stocks plunged by 98 percent. Rothschild was then able to buy up the entire British economy for pennies on the pound. When the news of Napoleon's defeat finally arrived, stocks soared. Britain was now the undisputed ruler of Europe. And Rothschild ruled England."[31]

THE REAL NEWS FROM WATERLOO

With a story repackaged and rewritten as often as the Rothschild/Waterloo legend, where does one even start to find the truth? Did Nathan actually get the news first and make a killing off it? If he didn't, then who did? It's a question that at least some chroniclers of both the Rothschilds and Waterloo have attempted to explore beyond the ludicrous stories of Nathan's supposed adventures related to horses, storms, ships, or pigeons.

Author and war correspondent Virginia Cowles's 1973 biography *A Family of Fortune* makes some effort to shoot down some of the contradictory and fanciful stories. Allowing that there are "a dozen different accounts" of what exactly happened during those days in 1815, Cowles dispenses with the notions of carrier pigeons ferrying the news, Nathan personally watching the cannonballs fly, and Nathan making a fortune off the delayed news of the outcome. Instead, she writes that Nathan was simply one of the first people to get the news from a middle-of-the-night edition of a Belgian paper that had been brought across the Channel on a normal, though hurried, journey by a family courier.[32]

Ferguson's biography, maybe the most clear-eyed attempt to separate the Rothschild myth from reality, doesn't get into the details of how Nathan heard the news at all, given that the more fantastical elements "have long ago been debunked."[33] Like Cowles, he downplays the windfall from

Waterloo, pointing out instead that the family's sloppy accounting and the unexpected end of the war left them in at least some peril in the immediate aftermath of Napoleon's defeat because they held too much gold, bought in anticipation of a long conflict, that was no longer needed.[34]

And while numerous sources prove that the family made an enormous amount of money off the final few years of struggle against Napoleon, that aforementioned poor accounting means that nobody really knows exactly how much. It's clear that the Rothschilds profited immensely off the interest they made from buying consols and lending gold—enough to establish the family as the preeminent heads of European banking. But the exact figures are unknown.

About the Waterloo windfall, Ferguson uses letters from the brothers and exchange rates at the time to determine that Nathan made a profit of just over 7,000 pounds—about $615,000 at late 2022 exchange rates.[35] Hardly the stuff of "ruling nations." Cowles also makes no effort to speculate, saying only that Nathan neither depressed the consols market nor made a fortune off its rise, because he "already had his fortune."[36] The Rothschild Archive also doesn't guess at an exact number, allowing only that it was "very considerably less than a million pounds."[37] Certainly, it was nowhere near the 10 million pounds or 125 million pounds or "the entire British economy," as some less reputable sources claim. Records from the time show the family *might* have made a million pounds for the entire year of the Battle of Waterloo—but certainly not from the battle itself.[38]

But what of the other details—Nathan leaning against the column, the terrified sailor's 2,000 franc payoff, the trusty courier "Rothworth" and his freshly printed paper, the Dunkirk fast cutter, the panicked sell-off crashing 98 percent of British stock, the letter from American envoy Gallatin, the story of Nathan personally seeing the battle? Were they all made up by journalists and gossips?

In his 2015 book *The News from Waterloo*, British journalist Brian Cathcart attempted to get past the legends using newspaper accounts and letters written at the time to find who, exactly, was the first person who knew of Wellington's victory. If it wasn't Nathan—and few reputable historians believed it was by then—who was it? For one thing, as Cathcart writes, Nathan isn't the only person pointed at by history as the first to know the triumphant news; there were various unconfirmable stories floating around of an aide to Lord Wellington dispatched via horseback to Ostend and braving a Channel storm, a sailor on a yacht in the Channel somehow learning of it, a fog-obscured semaphore signal that managed to only convey the first two words of the message "Wellington defeated Napoleon at Waterloo," and various colorful figures washing up on various shores declaring the news of Wellington's win to baffled locals.[39]

The reality is that there were likely two different ways the information was delivered—one involving the first person in London to know, and the other being the first person to inform Nathan Rothschild. Of the first, Cathcart uses newspaper archives to track a story from the Edinburgh newspaper *Caledonian Mercury* that an English gentleman known as "Mr. C from Dover" learned the news in Ghent, Belgium, by observing messages of the victory being given to exiled French king Louis XVIII. After finding out Wellington had won, "Mr. C" rushed back to London and met with ministers in London three days after the battle. There is no record of who "Mr. C" was, but he almost certainly was the first person to bring the news of the victory to London, almost a day before the arrival of Wellington's actual messenger—a soldier who actually *had* crossed the Channel in a boat from Ostend.

As for Nathan, he certainly learned of it early, likely from a letter sent to him by a family agent in Ghent who would have learned of the victory around the same time as "Mr. C."[40] A different story from the *Caledonian Mercury* makes mention of a letter from Ghent "received by Rosschild [sic], the great stockbroker." Nathan is said to have reported the contents of the letter to the Foreign Office, then set about his usual business—making a small profit in the immediate days after Waterloo that was never big enough to mention in his recorded letters. Other traders almost certainly did much better off the news from Waterloo.[41]

As for the rest, it's all a post-hoc invention. There was no panicked sell-off spurred by a broken and exhausted Nathan leaning against a pillar, since Nathan knew nothing that would panic anyone. And historical attempts to retrofit "Mr. C" as a Rothschild agent who crossed the Channel on behalf of Nathan or claiming that he was the "Captain Cullen" of various stories related to the news aren't based in fact, either. There's no evidence the two had any connection, or that Nathan did anything of note with the information from the letter. That letter, taken from Ghent, would have reached Nathan after the London Stock Exchange closed on the Wednesday after the battle, and the news was already breaking in London by the next morning, when government bonds began to rise.[42] The Gallatin letter was revealed as a fake written around the end of the nineteenth century, the 2,000 franc payoff to the terrified sailor never took place, there was no storm of note in the Channel that day, and the "Dunkirk fast cutter" story was invented nearly a century after the battle by a journalist belatedly tasked by the Rothschilds with debunking the Waterloo story.

The legend of Nathan's "windfall" likely came from several different primary sources in the aftermath of the victory. One was immediate post-Waterloo reporting about various bankers profiting off Waterloo, including a report in the newspaper the *St. James's Chronicle* of a "stockholder (Mr. R) who availed himself of his priority of intelligence respecting the victory at Waterloo" and made a large profit off the gains of consols after the battle.[43]

The other is a letter sent by a Rothschild employee in Paris to Nathan a month after the battle, declaring, "I am informed [. . .] you have done well by the early information which you had of the victory gained at Waterloo." The writer of that letter was Rothschild agent John *Roworth*— almost certainly the "Rothworth" written about by Corti, Morton, and other biographers as the actual messenger from Ostend, although he definitely wasn't in Belgium at the time of the battle.[44] And the "done well" is almost certainly a reference to getting the letter from Ghent, not a financial gain, because there wasn't one of any significance. Likewise, Nathan's oft-quoted remark that Waterloo was "the best business I ever did" is related much more to the impact of his smuggling of gold to Wellington during the entirety of the Napoleonic Wars, and not some kind of double-cross pulled off in the aftermath of Waterloo.[45]

The Nathan Rothschild/Waterloo legend is just that. It's a fanciful story spun out of a mundane one: part truth, part misinterpretation, part fake. It was a way for onlookers to explain how Nathan had gotten so rich off the war—there had to be deception and conspiracy, because nobody just makes that much money that quickly. And with the Waterloo story examined, we can see every later Rothschild conspiracy theory told through its distorted lens. The later canard that Nathan "saved" the Bank of England from a catastrophic run in 1825 is almost beside the point when compared to the chicanery of 1815. If, as Alex Jones put it, British finance controlled the world and Nathan Rothschild controlled British finance, what did it matter what he did with his billions? Him bailing out the Bank of England was just an example of the control he gained through Waterloo. What good is being a "financial ruler of nations" if you can't save them on a whim to protect yourself?

Who, then, was the first to connect Nathan Rothschild to the news of victory at Waterloo, and then to a massive financial gain? The Duke of Wellington's oft-told story from the decade after the battle is the logical conclusion at first glance. After all, Wellington told a number of highly placed people that the news of Waterloo was brought to Nathan Rothschild by a Jewish Rothschild agent who, in turn, learned of it at Ghent from a message to Louis XVIII, and then duly rushed across the Channel from Ostend to inform his employer.

But that story was told privately, and Wellington's tale wasn't popularly printed until the end of the nineteenth century. And while it does have elements of truth (the letter from Ghent, Wellington's messenger crossing the Channel at Ostend), one major falsifying factor is that it's mostly hearsay. Wellington was also a bit busy actually fighting the battle to have firsthand knowledge of how the news of its outcome made it to London. His story says nothing about Nathan being at the battle, or about him exploiting the early news for a world-controlling profit, and Wellington would have known such things were fanciful inventions.[46]

Nathan Rothschild isn't even the only Jewish banker rumored to have made a vast profit off the Battle of Waterloo. A parallel legend claims that the "Mr. R" quoted in the *St. James's Chronicle* was actually the British economist David Ricardo, believed to have profited handsomely off his advanced knowledge of the battle—as much as a million pounds, according to disreputable sources who often conflated him with Nathan. Like the Rothschilds, Ricardo's actual gains off the news of Waterloo were far less interesting than papers of the time claimed.[47]

With so many stories drawing on other stories, it's here that we circle back to the "Satan" pamphlet—an obscure document written decades after the battle in which the Waterloo canard was only one attack in a vicious broadside against the Rothschilds. And that was far from the only accusation made by the ersatz Dark Lord against the world's wealthiest family.

THE SATAN PAMPHLET: ROTHSCHILD CONSPIRACY THEORIES EMERGE AFTER WATERLOO

The rapid growth of railroads across Europe gave people a faster and more efficient way to travel than anyone had ever seen. It also offered a more gruesome way to die than many people were comfortable with. As train travel became more common both inside and between cities, newspaper and magazine accounts eagerly described the many stomach-churning things that could happen to the human body when railroad travel went wrong. And, of course, it did go wrong.

Papers around the continent reveled in graphic depictions of railroad trauma and death, putting readers there on the scene as mangled bodies and severed limbs were pulled out of wrecked cars in England, the German states, France, and elsewhere deep into the nineteenth century.[1] The Rothschilds had funded or outright owned many of these lines, including the Kaiser Ferdinands-Nordbahn railway in Austria, the first major steam railway on the continent and a vital link between Vienna and Krakow, as well as the Tannus Railway going in and out of Frankfurt, and other lines going well into Eastern Europe. James was the fulcrum for Rothschild railway expansion and would eventually connect ten nations to each other, with the centerpiece being his *Chemin de Fer du Nord*—also called the Nord Line.[2]

The derailment of a Nord Line train near Fampoux in northern France on July 8, 1846, would seem to be just another consequence of rapidly evolving technology struggling to meet increasing demand—something for the papers to write gruesome testimonials about, then move on. It wasn't the first train accident in French history, nor was it the worst. The best estimate is that seventeen people died in the Fampoux derailment, though there are accounts of the event that claim a significantly higher death toll. Contrast that with the fifty-seven known to have died, and hundreds of others burned or otherwise injured, on May 8, 1842, when a train traveling on the Versailles Railway south of Paris broke an axle, sending passenger cars piling into each other and causing a catastrophic fire. It was the worst railroad accident in the world at the time.[3]

Other than a few lurid newspaper articles and satirical pieces written in the weeks after the disaster, the Fampoux derailment would mostly be forgotten. Scholars might know it best from a metaphorical mention in Hugo's *Les Misérables*, written sixteen years after the event, where an "off the track" Inspector Javert is written as having a passing "Fampoux of a rectilinear conscience, the derailment of a soul."[4] The event is so obscure it doesn't even have an English-language Wikipedia entry. But Fampoux lingers not because of what happened, but because of who was involved: the Rothschilds. It was James de Rothschild who owned and had funded the recently inaugurated Nord Line off whose tracks the train derailed. And it happened at the same time as antisemitic attacks on Jewish wealth were cycling back up in certain corners of the French press. So while the Rothschild competitors who owned the Versailles Line got a pass from a shocked French public for the horrible accident in 1842, James and his family weren't so lucky with Fampoux just four years later.

We've seen that the Rothschilds, and Nathan in particular, played a critical role in funding the effort against Napoleon. And James was so pivotal to linking France together through his funding of railroad expansion that one of the Rothschilds' French competitors wrote in the years before Fampoux that "the involvement of the Rothschild bank in the railway from Paris to Saint-Germain is not only of great importance for this particular venture, it will also necessarily have a determining influence on the later realization of all the great industrial undertakings."[5] The Rothschilds were inextricable from French industrial progress, and when one went wrong, it was assumed to be the fault of the other.

UTOPIAN HATE: THE RISE OF FRENCH ANTISEMITISM

Conspiracy theories often find their roots in the linking of events that have little to do with each other—"they" don't want you to know that these two things are actually the same thing. With a family as sprawling and influential as the Rothschilds, it's not surprising when the undertaking of one branch of the family is linked to that of a different branch and put together as "proof" of Rothschild overreach or control. And so it was with Fampoux, which was combined with the already extant rumors about the Rothschilds and Waterloo by a hack pamphleteer who went by "Satan" and had a deeply personal axe to grind.

Nathan had been dead for a decade when the Fampoux derailment took place. But just the linkage of Nathan and James as brothers was enough for "Satan" to combine Waterloo and Fampoux in an unhinged pamphlet that tarred the Rothschilds as a demonic force of greed and evil, controlling everything and elevating themselves to the status not just of kings but of kings of kings. And the climate was ripe for such a screed to take hold in popular consciousness; much of the French public was becoming deeply disenchanted with the social and economic order and looking for someone to blame for it.

The restoration of the Bourbon monarchy following the fall of Napoleon saw the continuation of the emancipation of French Jews that quietly had started in the late eighteenth century with the French Revolution, when Jews were granted civic and legal equality. A difficult period of adjustment followed as Jewish communities confronted a new political order. But as time passed, French Jews began to express a more nationalistic sentiment as they integrated more into French politics and society. France as a whole recommitted to its revolutionary spirit, and this extended to the country's Jewish population. The Bourbon Restoration of 1815 and the years that followed it saw the establishment of French-language Jewish newspapers and schools and the emergence of a distinct Franco-Jewish identity.[6]

That renewed spirit once again sent French revolutionaries into the streets in late July of 1830, overthrowing King Charles X and elevating his cousin, Louis-Phillipe, to the throne in the revolution that would inspire *Les Misérables* and send socialist shockwaves through Europe. The so-called July Monarchy that followed would attempt to fully emancipate French Jews and put them on a level with Catholic and Protestant French citizens. It was a unity that, while never fully achieved, was unthinkable for French Jews who less than half a century earlier had still been subject to poll taxes and severe restrictions on where they could settle.[7]

As the rights of Jews in Europe increased, so too did the wealth of its growing middle class. But such societal transformation inevitably leaves some people behind and embitters others. By the mid-1840s, a distinct nationalist and anti-capitalist populism was taking hold in France, and socialist yearning for true financial equality was gaining steam. Not all of it was anti-Jewish, and anti-rich sentiments were high on both the French far right and far left. But there was a growing perception among French socialists that wealthy Jews were puppet masters and arbiters of who gets money and how much they get. And these socialists weren't alone. This was the era when cartoons like *Die Generalpumpe*, depicting Mayer Amschel Rothschild as a grotesque spigot of cash, took off in popular European culture.

And there was one more element to add to this already toxic stew: growing backlash against the Damascus Affair, when local Jews were accused of the ritual murder and consumption of a Capuchin friar and his assistant in 1840. Fueled by the revival of the blood libel canard and stereotyping of Jews from that part of the world as sexually aggressive and libertine, French Jews (including James and Solomon Rothschild) who supported their "Oriental" coreligionists had their loyalty doubted and their motives questioned again and again.[8] A new generation of outwardly antisemitic, far-left writers like Alphonse Toussenel, Pierre-Joseph Proudhon, Charles Fourier, and Pierre Leroux struck gold tarring the Jews as kings of finance, otherworldly beings too enmeshed in their own community to ever truly be French, and the Rothschilds as royalty above even all other Jews. The works they produced and their posthumously published private writings were hyperbolic in their antisemitism, outrageous in their accusations, and massively influential for decades to come.

In his popular book of 1846, *Les Juifs, rois de l'époque* (*The Jews, Kings of the Epoch*), Toussenel declared that the Jews were leading France down the path of "financial feudalism." To Toussenel, a respected figure in naturalism and animal studies to this day, Jews were contaminating finance, and finance was contaminating France—particularly through the destruction wreaked on French forests by "Rothschild's railroads." "The motto of the new revolution" should be "death to parasitism! War on the Jews!" he thundered in advocating for the French people to take control of the railroads. Toussenel goes on for hundreds of pages of invective, ranting at length about how Jewish influence has turned France into a backwater. "I call by the despised name of Jew every dealer in money, every unproductive parasite living off the work of someone else," he wrote. "Note well that not one Jew has done anything useful with his hands since the beginning of time."[9]

Toussenel was also one of the first of many subsequent authors and thinkers, some antisemitic and some not, to put the blame on the Rothschilds for Europe's constant internal warring. He wrote in *Kings of Epoch* that "the Jew speculates on peace, that is on a rise, and that explains why peace in Europe has lasted for fifteen years."[10] Essentially, it was currently better for Jewish business for Europe to be at peace, and when it was better for Jewish business for Europe to be at war, there would be war. Notably, the idea that armed conflict only takes place when the Rothschilds want it to would find its way into a great deal of future mythology about the

Rothschilds, including an apocryphal deathbed quote from family matriarch Gutle: "if my sons did not want wars, there would be none."[11]

Toussenel's mentor, the socialist Charles Fourier, was a hugely influential figure in the growing utopian communal living movement. He was also a prolific antisemite who portrayed Jews as financial pirates with no home port, moving from country to country while pillaging the common folk and taking what they wanted—a variation on the "rootless cosmopolitan" slur employed to this day. To Fourier, Jewish prosperity came not through hard work but at "the expense of the citizenry," echoing the common attack that Jews don't "work hard" and only profit off usury. The emancipation of the Jews in France was "shameful" to Fourier, who believed them to be devoted only to "mercantile depravities."[12] Fourier would later join a number of other nineteenth century thinkers in advocating that the Jews be forcibly returned to Palestine, with the bill sent to the House of Rothschild.

Similarly, it's been a constant subject of debate among academics and activists whether the founder of anarchism, Pierre-Joseph Proudhon, was actually antisemitic. But in his private writings, much of which were published a century after his death, he attacked French Jews with almost genocidal fervor. In one particularly incendiary diary entry in 1847, Proudhon referred to Jews as "the race that poisons everything" and admonished himself to publicly "demand [Jewish] expulsion from France with the exception of those individuals married to French women. Abolish synagogues and not admit them to any employment. Demand its expulsion. Finally, pursue the abolition of this religion. It's not without cause that the Christians called them deicides. The Jew is the enemy of humankind. They must be sent back to Asia or be exterminated." As for the Rothschilds, Proudhon privately denigrated them as "wicked, bilious, envious, bitter, etc. etc. beings who hate us."[13]

And for economic theorist and philosopher Pierre Leroux, writing in his own 1846 book called *Les Juifs, rois de l'époque* (the market for antisemitic books was apparently so fertile it could support two different tomes with the exact same name), Jewish spirit represented the "greed and cupidity" of feudal plunderers who made war with force of arms that was monetary, not physical. France's financial imbalance, with more and more wealth concentrated in fewer people, was simply the end result of Jewish economic vengeance for the repression and slavery of the Middle Ages, with Leroux writing in the voice of a vengeful Jew, "'I shall invent a weapon that will pierce your armor [. . .], a weapon of new invention, stronger than those guns with which the monarchy is beginning to overthrow your towers.' And the Jew kept his word: he invented the banks."[14]

There is a case made by some scholars of the period that the Jew hatred of French and other European socialists was much more economic in nature than religious—a term literally called "economic antisemitism." "Their anti-Juif terminology amounted to a misguided vehicle for the propagation of an ideology that was fundamentally anti-capitalist and not anti-Semitic," wrote the civil rights attorney Victor M. Glasberg in 1972, drawing a historical line between "Juifs"—the Kings of Epoch—and Jews in general.[15] The extent to which many thinkers of the time, both left and right, actually hated Jews, and how much Judaism and wealth had simply become bound together to the point where attacking one necessitated attacking the other, is debatable.

But if there's a potential historical debate to be had over whether Toussenel and his compatriots hated all Jews or just wealthy Jews, no such debate is possible when it comes to the man behind "Satan"—the virtually unknown French journalist and tract writer Mathieu Georges Dairnvaell.

His 36-page pamphlet *Histoire édifiante et curieuse de Rothschild Ier, Roi des Juifs* (*The Edifying and Curious History of Rothschild the First, King of the Jews*) is the first known example of the specific canard that Nathan Rothschild made a fortune off advance knowledge of Waterloo and connected Nathan's "scoop" to the growing discontentment over Jewish wealth that was brewing in France. "Satan" claimed that the penny-pinching James de Rothschild had neglected the safety of the passengers on the Nord Line to save a few francs, with the Fampoux disaster as the bloody, inevitable result. His pamphlet has long since been eclipsed in importance and infamy by other works attacking Jewish wealth, but it might be the locus of modern conspiracy theories about the Rothschild family.

"IS THERE ANYTHING IMPOSSIBLE FOR GREED?"

The Edifying and Curious History is obscure enough that it's virtually impossible to find a commercially available English translation, and little is known about its author. It's not clear where Dairnvaell came from, what he actually believed in, or even when he died. Writing in English Chartist paper *The Northern Star* in 1846, Friedrich Engels praised "Satan" as "a working man" and "a man nobody knows" whose "property consists of the suit of clothes he wears." But subsequent writing on the author of the pamphlet isn't quite so charitable. More modern scholarship points out that Dairnvaell was no simple poor laborer, but a prolific pamphlet, newspaper, and magazine writer able to make a living off his often-scabrous work, and that neither this pamphlet nor his other works denigrating the Rothschilds "show the slightest trend towards communism" or socialism. Instead, they invoke the language of declarations used to enrage local mobs in the leadup to pogroms.[16] As for Dairnvaell's view of himself, he wrote that he was merely "a writer without name, position, title or rank." Even what we think of as his real name may have been a pseudonym.[17]

Certainly "Satan" didn't invent the idea of Jews as a kind of self-crowned royalty. Both Toussenel and Leroux had written identically titled books castigating the Jews as "kings of the Epoch." And there was already a market for anti-Rothschild pamphlets, including a popular one coming out of Stuttgart in 1844 by the French writer Alexandre Weill—a fellow Jew who nonetheless attacked the family's apparently outsized control over critical aspects of French society. The "Satan" pamphlet was so harsh that many observers of the time assumed that Weill had written it—an accusation Weill denied, instead pointing to the still-anonymous Dairnvaell as the author.[18]

Given that Weill's attacks on the family weren't all that out of step with other French criticisms of the Rothschilds, it's easy to see why he disavowed *Edifying and Curious History*. Dairnvaell indeed took the attacks substantially further, into paranoia that was both cruel and deeply based in Jewish tropes. If Jews were indeed kings, then James de Rothschild was *their* king—a tyrant who ruled over all of creation, bestowing favors on those he favored and destruction on those he wished to be destroyed. And to find proof of the cheap and depraved cruelty of "James, King of the Jews," a good Frenchman didn't have to look particularly hard. Fampoux, after all, wasn't that far from Paris.

Like other accidents of the time, the Fampoux derailment was covered in graphic, lurid detail by French and English outlets. That wasn't unusual. Nor was the graphic coverage of the allegations behind the Damascus Affair, with its links to several of Mayer's sons. But the involvement of the Rothschilds gave Fampoux an extra layer for cranks to glom on to when combined with the growing scrutiny of Jewish wealth in France and the aftermath of the Damascus debacle.

Toussenel's attack on French Jews had come out a year earlier and sold briskly, but with Fampoux in mind, "Satan" focused specifically on the Rothschilds and made history. Published shortly after the crash, *Edifying and Curious History* viciously attacked James and his ownership of the Nord Line with the full arsenal of Jewish money tropes—greed, cheapness, cruelty, and pathological disdain for Gentiles. To "Satan," the disaster was yet another bloody Jewish insult against the good people of France—an unbroken line of hate and greed that began in 1815, "the year of grace of the Rothschilds."[19]

Virtually every iteration of the Waterloo canard, from John Reeves in the 1880s to Goebbels in the 1940s to Alex Jones in the twenty-first century, is built at least in part on the lie that Dairnvaell scrawled in 1846. Providing no substantiation for his claims, Dairnvaell launched the idea that not only had Nathan profited from the news about Waterloo, he was *there*, manipulating the news of the battle's outcome to his own ends and making so much money off the end result that he and his progeny would forever dominate world commerce. The author had no secret or undiscovered knowledge of the battle, spoke to nobody who was there, offered no proof, and likely wasn't even born until three years after Napoleon's defeat.

Indeed, the most widely used words employed by contemporary authors about Dairnvaell and his work are either "scurrilous" (spreading false rumors) or "hack." But like with conspiracy theories of today, the charge that Nathan leveraged Waterloo for total domination didn't need proof or testimony or citations. All it needed was a creative lie about a powerful figure that was told in an appealing way. In exploiting the strands of rumor about Nathan that had been fictionalized by Balzac in *The House of Nucingen* a decade earlier, this "obscure hack" would imprint his name on two centuries of Jewish history, even if history has mostly forgotten him and his self-described "scribblings."

"Nathan Rothschild was in Belgium with his eyes fixed on Waterloo," Dairnvaell wrote of the deceased Rothschild patriarch, instantly inventing a legend. Upon seeing the carnage being inflicted on both sides, Nathan saw an opportunity and "himself went to the stirrup. Arriving in Ostend, he saw the storm's muzzle, the sailors declared the crossing impossible; but is there anything impossible for greed?"[20]

In just a few short paragraphs of hyperbole, the Waterloo canard was born, the same one that would be reproduced with the same details for decades to come. Nathan watching the battle, the midnight ride across Belgium, the Channel storm and the reluctant sailors, the gargantuan amount of money he made—they all came from or were substantially fleshed out in *Edifying and Curious History*. Just how big was that score? Dairnvaell claimed, again without evidence, that Nathan "arrived in London, 24 hours before the arrival of the news; he won in one fell swoop twenty million [francs, about one million pounds], while his other brothers assisted him, the total profit made in this fatal year amounted to 135 MILLION! [sic]"[21] As we've already seen, Nathan made nowhere near that much money from the immediate aftermath of Waterloo, and while the family had major success in the months after Waterloo, the profit wasn't even close to what "Satan" claimed.

But Dairnvaell either believed it was true or wanted it to be true. So it was true. "Before 1815, the Rothschilds were very strong bankers, [but] after 1815 they were the masters of the bank," the writer taking the name of the Dark Lord continued, thundering that "they have enriched themselves with our impoverishment and our disasters." France being "impoverished and defeated" while forced to sign an "odious treaty" after their loss gave the Rothschilds even more money by putting them in control of collecting French war reparations, punishing France and bloating Rothschild profit margins even more. The family members were "vampires of commerce," "scourges," and "leeches" sucking at the neck of French pride. And as "Satan" makes clear in unending detail, they were only just getting started with their domination of world finance.[22]

After concocting the Waterloo canard, "Satan" effortlessly shifts from attacking Nathan (who was dead and couldn't defend himself) to attacking James. To Dairnvaell, the Nord Line hadn't been built thanks to French ingenuity but by Jewish exploitation, with James gaining the concession from the government through corruption and exploitation of the king's good graces—a point Toussenel, a naturalist, had also argued while blaming James for the ruining of pristine French land.[23] Again, Dairnvaell took it a step further, accusing James of blatant corruption by distributing tens of thousands of shares to his agents, then crashing their value by issuing even more without governmental consent, defrauding good, honest French citizens who clamored for their own shares of the Nord Line, and getting away with it because he'd bought off everyone who could stop him.[24]

Finally, on June 14, 1846, in a star-studded gala attended by the royalty of French society, James opened the Nord Line and crowned himself "king of Europe, Asia, Africa, America, Oceania and other places, and especially the Jews!" Even here, describing the largesse and pomp of James's "coronation," Dairnvaell can't resist cheap shots at Jewish frugality, writing that the generals and barons invited by James gorged themselves, while the common folk "found barely fifty buns and a few rare decanters of lemonade" on the hot day, grudgingly provided by "a capitalist who gets richer and richer when fathers lose even their last piece of bread."[25] Here Dairnvaell references France's extremely bad harvest in 1846, with numerous papers of the time blaming the possibility of mass famine on James and his greed.

Less than a month later, the Fampoux derailment took place, an event "Satan" squarely pinned on James and his boundless greed. The deaths of dozens of French citizens due to Jewish callousness symbolized the corruption and mendacity of capitalism and the government, and how both were controlled by Jews—with James acting as the puppet master of it all as self-crowned "king." "Satan" attacked James for the poor quality of the Nord's rails (they were "sagging, broken, or disjointed"), his supposed orders that service continue even as bodies were being pulled out of the wreckage, its improperly working signals, its trains driving too fast, and James ignoring pleas from his engineers to shut the line down—deeming them lies. To enact repairs before Fampoux, "it would have been necessary to spend a few hundred more francs," but to James, "the life of men is not worth it."[26]

In recounting the derailment, Dairnvaell relied on the same traumatic descriptions that readers of the continent had gotten used to, possibly even copying them outright from other sources. The details are so bloody they verge on pornographic—wagons full of humans crushed on top of each other, uncountable cries of despair, ten people locked in a submerged carriage fighting with each other to be rescued, an Englishman with a shattered arm trying to hide his wound from his wife, "a man in his thirties trying to revive his mother's corpse," an injured general's aide eviscerated by the accident and begging for death, "the scattered limbs and the bloody entrails" . . . on and on the misery went. And James's response to this horror, according to "Satan"? To deny that the accident happened, downplay the number of dead, and demand business go on as usual.[27]

Finally, Dairnvaell made one last broadside: he demanded punishment for the "king of the Jews," writing in the final paragraph, "we call for justice against those men who sacrifice human blood to the Golden Calf."[28]

And that call was heeded by countless French citizens. Despite entering into a market overcrowded with scurrilous and antisemitic literature, *Edifying and Curious History* was a hit. It sold as many as sixty thousand copies, being reprinted multiple times just in 1846 (Engels claims it went through "twenty editions") and translated into numerous other languages.[29] Clearly at least some part of the French public was looking for a distilled manifestation of their unease over Jewish emancipation and the perceived control of European commerce by the Rothschilds. "Satan" provided it and, in the process, fired the loudest shots in what quickly pitted anti- and pro-Rothschild forces against each other in an all-out Parisian pamphlet war that would have dire consequences for the future of how the Rothschilds were perceived in popular media.

SATAN'S CHILDREN

Edifying and Curious History wasn't the first anonymous attack pamphlet written about Nathan Rothschild. Appearing with an anonymous byline ten years before the Dairnvaell screed, *The Hebrew Talisman* worked off the idea that Nathan's success wasn't because of hard work, but thanks to a mythical object that brought him the ability to literally conjure gold out of nothing. Its author has never been discovered, but it serves as a kind of prequel to many of the most fantastical allegations about Nathan and the Rothschilds.

A mostly unfollowable ramble, the story is narrated by what appears to be a manifestation of the Wandering Jew trope who detests "the followers of the Nazarene" and was given a gold Talisman in order to "prepare the people of God for the dominion of the whole earth." The narrator spends pages teasing that he gave the Talisman to a pitiful young man in the looted ruins of Frankfurt, only to reveal that the now-wealthy man (who was handed a bag of gold after using the Talisman to wish for it) was none other than "NATHAN MEYER ROTHSCHILD! [sic]." He had used the luck brought by the Talisman and, now "more wealthy than any who had gone before him, his riches astonished the gentiles, and very justly they said, such amazing wealth could not be amassed by one man, in so short a time by any human agency." Then the narrator snatches the Talisman from Nathan, who returns to Frankfurt a broken man and dies in the *Judengasse*.[30]

The Hebrew Talisman cross-pollinates with early and later myths about various Rothschilds. Its author claims their wealth was the result of divine intervention, and that Nathan hid the Talisman "beneath a tree in his little garden, while the murderous and plundering French vexed the city with their presence" in an echo of both the myth of the Elector's Treasure and Mayer's actual hiding of valuable items belonging to the Elector. Like other anti-Rothschild works, the accusations get more and more hyperbolic, as the narrator claims the Talisman's riches helped Nathan bring down Napoleon and make the Rothschilds a fortune of as much as five million pounds. And without it, he was nothing—implying that Nathan wasn't a skilled banker, but a lucky wealth hoarder. It's clearly a fantastical story meant to exploit myths about Nathan's unimaginable wealth, and isn't to be taken seriously. Even the Rothschild Archives label it simply as "a satire of Nathan Rothschild."[31] But its rambling narrative linking the Rothschilds to world events both related and unrelated would be copied again and again, first by French pamphleteers trying to build on the success of "Satan's" work, and by generations of later propagandists.

Pamphlet wars weren't brand new to France in the 1840s. They'd been going on for several hundred years, as sides for and against a contentious social issue blasted each other in cheaply produced, hastily written broadsides meant to shock and horrify. And "Satan" kicked off another one. At least half a dozen attack tracts followed in the wake of *Edifying and Curious History*, with Engels later writing in *The Northern Star* that there were at least thirty pamphlets written for and against the family as the public followed the drama "with the greatest interest."[32]

Several more were written by Dairnvaell himself, including the unsubtly titled *War on the Swindlers*, which continued the attacks on James's control of the Nord Line and the allegations of bribery of French officials to get the railroad concession.[33] Anonymous pamphlets like *Letter to M. Baron de Rothschild* and *Judgement Passed Against Rothschild and Georges Dairnvaell* had the decency to allow that many of the claims against James were false, but that James himself was the product of a sick system that allowed Rothschild to "exploit all that is exploitable" while "millions of men" suffered in "misery and desperation."[34]

As the "pamphlet war" went on, additional attack pamphlets like *Guerre aux Juifs! Ou la vérité sur MM. De Rothschild* (*War on the Jews! And the Truth about Mr. Rothschild*) and *Dix jours de règne de Rothschild I er, roi des juifs* (*Ten Days in the Reign of Rothschild I, King of the Jews*) were published, to hungry audiences.[35] But James also had defenders, and at least one prominent tract supporting James came from followers of the Saint-Simon movement, a socialist thought collective that had, at one point, included several prominent anti-Rothschild writers. A Saint-Simonian article that got traction around Paris said of James, "there is no one today who better represents the triumph of equality and work in the nineteenth century than M. le Baron de Rothschild," who became wealthy at a time when to be a Jew "was to be a dog that children chased in the street, hurling insults and stones."[36]

Some pro-Rothschild pamphlets even claimed to be rebuttals *from* James, supposedly making one of the family's still rare public statements about the various theories swirling around them. One, *The First Official Response of M. Baron James Rothschild*, claimed to be an account personally written by the baron himself (hence "official"), revealing that Dairnvaell had demanded 5,000 francs from James not to publish *Edifying and Curious History*. When James, ever the cheapskate, offered only 1,000 francs, Dairnvaell went ahead with a mass printing; even in attacking James's attacker, it apparently was irresistible to not include a petty jab at the man.[37]

There is some evidence that someone was actually attempting to blackmail James found in a letter written by Anselm Rothschild, son of Vienna house founder Solomon, to the Austrian emperor that claimed that the pamphlet's "vulgar abuse [. . .] emanated principally from a despicable person, to whom our Paris House had quite rightly refused a loan."[38] But Anselm's letter doesn't mention details about the blackmail attempt, and there's no record of Dairnvaell attempting to get a loan from the Paris house. Another pro-James pamphlet attributed to him, *Response by Rothschild, First King of the Jews, to Satan the Last, King of the Impostors*, thundered that "Satan" should "go to all the banks and exchanges of Europe, [and] I defy you to discover a single operation of the house of Rothschild that lacks honesty and integrity."[39]

"ENTIRELY UNFOUNDED IMPUTATIONS"

By this point, the Paris pamphlet war was confined neither to Paris nor pamphlets. Just two weeks after Fampoux, the long-running French satirical magazine *Le charivari* blamed James for the disaster and attacked him as a kind of Charlemagne of the railroads, "seeking to join people and continents in a universal alliance."[40] And French revolutionary writer Emile Barrault wrote the scabrous *Letter to M. Rothschild* attacking

James as "the Jew, king of the Epoch [...] standing firm" amid the ruin of the 1848 Revolutions while "shareholders, shopkeepers, manufacturers, [and] pensioners tumble down in a mass of people, grand on petty, crushing the crushed."[41]

Attacks on the Rothschilds and their wealth in French papers like *Le National* and English language papers like *The Northern Star* began ratcheting up at the same time as the crude claims in pamphlets. And anti-Rothschild sentiment was also spreading in Europe, fueled by the growing political and economic upheaval. It produced countless crude caricatures and attack pamphlets around the rest of the continent, works like Jewish Rothschild critic Alexandre Weill's German-language pamphlet *Rothschild and the European States*, the same 1844 pamphlet that led observers to claim *Edifying and Curious History* was his work. While it wasn't, Weill had nothing good to say about the family, claiming Rothschild had become the only power of note on the continent.[42]

The public sentiment toward the family had curdled to the point where Anselm Rothschild wrote his letter attempting to suppress similar pamphlets in Prussia. He complained to the emperor about the "scurrilous attacks against my uncle, Baron James" that linked James to the "unfortunate accident on the Northern Railway of France" with "the foulest and entirely unfounded imputations upon the character and morality of our business with an impudence such as I have never before experienced." Anselm called on "the special claim" the family had over business with the emperor "to prevent any recurrence of this nuisance."[43] If the Austrian emperor took any action to censor these pamphlets, it's not recorded by history.

The volume of attacks on the Rothschilds begs the question of what exactly the family did to fight back, beyond Anselm's letter. Based on both the historical record and how the Rothschilds have handled subsequent smears and attacks, the answer is likely that they didn't. There's no record of James publicly refuting the allegations about either Waterloo or Fampoux, though he seethed in a letter to his brothers in 1846 about the Fampoux backlash that "the world can no longer live without the railways and the best answer one can give to *Le National* is that if France should opt to exclude herself from the railway developments [...] then the result will be that all the travelers will make use of the other railway routes."[44]

Certainly, none of the pamphlets attributed to James have any known connection to him. In *The Rothschilds: A Family Portrait*, Frederic Morton goes out of his way to make it clear that not only did James not commission these responses, when James was approached by the creator of *Response by Rothschild, First King of the Jews*, "he did not pay the author" because "petty graft disgusted him."[45] Again, even in complimentary accounts of the family, the trope of the cheap Jew can't help but creep in.

Beyond those few private letters, the Rothschilds greeted the explosive growth of the Waterloo canard and the attacks on their wealth in general with silence, as even Anselm's letter to the Austrian emperor allowed that it was "beneath our dignity to defend ourselves against such vulgar abuse."[46]

It wasn't until 1903 that Nathan's grandson Leopold de Rothschild addressed the tale in a speech to British newspaper editors, purporting to finally give "the authentic story" of Waterloo, nearly 100 years after the fact. As Leopold told the story, Nathan got the news through a courier based in Amsterdam and took it straight to the British government—with no chicanery or fraud, and certainly no trace of Nathan near the Waterloo battlefield.

That version was duly picked up by the British journalist and Rothschild supporter Lucien Wolf, who formalized it by removing any notion of Nathan being at the battle, and instead offered the version told by many later biographers of the family that featured a network of couriers, a Rothschild fast boat berthed at Dunkirk, and midnight horse rides.[47] Ten years later, the family would finally take formal action to suppress the false version of the story. They went to court in London, unsuccessfully suing the publisher of Ignatius Balla's 1913 book *The Romance of the Rothschilds* due to its reliance on the story that Nathan was at Waterloo, and tasked Lucien Wolf with writing an article for the *Daily Telegraph* claiming that Dairnvaell made the story up in an attempt to blackmail James.[48] It put another version of the Waterloo story in the public eye but didn't erase all the other ones, merely confusing the issue.

Virginia Cowles's bestselling biography of the Rothschilds, *A Family of Fortune*, would later echo Wolf's story, claiming that "Dairnvaell submitted the unpublished version [of *Edifying and Curious History*] to James Rothschild in Paris, demanding a large sum of money for its suppression," but that James refused and instead publicly refuted the allegation that Nathan had been at Waterloo.[49] But it's not clear if this blackmail attempt actually happened, as the story differs from what Anselm wrote in his letter to the Austrian emperor. And there's no record of James publicly pushing back against the Waterloo canard, or of publicly acknowledging the "response" pamphlets written in his name.[50]

But no matter how the details varied, the story itself would prove to be virtually unkillable. By the time the Revolutions of 1848 had died down and anti-Rothschild sentiment in France cooled, the picture of the Rothschilds as uncrowned kings and puppet masters was cemented for all time. France would endure wave after wave of antisemitic hysteria in the late nineteenth and early twentieth centuries, highlighted by the chaos of the Dreyfus Affair and continued distrust of Jewish wealth and control.

The Waterloo canard wasn't just the stuff of forgotten pamphlets and hopelessly arcane attacks. It powers antisemitism to this day and is embraced by legions of cranks and fascists, including spawning some of the most important anti-Jewish pieces of art of all time. By the time of James's death in 1868, a new generation of European, English, and American opponents of "Jewish power" were ready to pick up the gauntlet dropped by Dairnvaell, Toussenel, and their contemporaries. Rothschild conspiracy theories and hoaxes, exploding into the public consciousness as the family entered the twentieth century, would be exploited by some of the worst people in history and monetized by an entire industry devoted to promulgating antisemitism.

RISES AND FALLS: A BRIEF HISTORY OF THE ROTHSCHILDS, PART 2: 1868–1933

When James de Rothschild died on November 15, 1868, he was one of the richest men in the world. He had outlived his competitors, his brothers, and the vagaries of the business cycle. As part of his estate, he left a massive railway empire, a huge collection of art, numerous palaces and estates, and an almost uncountable amount of money. Just like cranks and conspiracy theorists do now, rumors and newspaper reports of the time would grossly exaggerate his net worth—one German-language paper gave a number so high that it would have represented over four percent of France's entire gross national product.[1]

But even with Mayer's five sons gone, the family continued to take the founder's ethos of the primacy of family unity over all else into another wave of expansion. Nathan's son Lionel took over as its new "king" and point man for its business ventures. But while the Rothschilds would find vast riches in new frontiers in Europe, Asia, the Americas, and elsewhere, the world was changing. Banking, communication, social norms, and society's perception of the rich were all radically transforming as the new century beckoned.

What changed most of all was that the Rothschilds' legendary skill at peacemaking would fail under this new generation as long-simmering feuds boiled over into open war and vast bloodshed. France was pushing for rearmament, and, led by Bismarck's fervent nationalism, the North German Confederation was marching toward unifying all the German states under one flag. There could be only one most dominant power in Europe, and despite the Rothschilds' constant communication with Bismarck's banker, the Rothschild ally Gerson von Bleichröder—who himself was acting as a back channel to the French government in an attempt to avoid war—large-scale armed conflict seemed inevitable. Sure enough, the Rothschilds' attempts to defuse the tension through diplomacy and lending failed, and France invaded Prussia in 1870, attempting to win before Bismarck's forces could fully mobilize. The invasion stalled, and a brutal, often house-to-house war began between the two great powers, with casualties high on both sides.

The Rothschilds found their family unity tested in a way it never had been before, with some family members backing Bismarck and others getting behind France's new emperor, Napoleon III. Unwilling to accept Prussian peace terms after their initial invasion failed, France fought on. In retaliation, Bismarck ordered Paris besieged and moved his headquarters to James's enormous palace, Château de Ferrières, about twenty miles to the east of Paris, which had been captured by German forces. But even with French Rothschilds forced to cooperate with Bismarck, the London branch attempted to alleviate the plight of starving Parisians by sending massive amounts of food across the English Channel.[2] After just six months of fighting, France collapsed at the hands of the technically and numerically superior German force. Emperor Napoleon III was captured, and the German Empire emerged with Kaiser Wilhelm I at the top and Bismarck as its Chancellor. Like after Napoleon's defeat at Waterloo, France was forced into paying another crushing war indemnity, with the Rothschilds advancing much of the money to the defeated at low interest rates.[3]

But the 1870s didn't just bring the rise of the German Reich—the decade brought a fourth generation into the business. Not only were Mayer's sons gone, but his grandsons were beginning to die off. This new generation had known nothing but wealth and privilege, and many seemed more interested in obtaining advanced education, reveling in decadence, and practicing social climbing through assimilation than in being "Kings of Epoch." The family also had surprising difficulty producing male heirs to the houses, with the Frankfurt house especially in peril because Mayer's oldest son Amschel Rothschild died without having children. As business continued to grow, Rothschild luxury and consumption exploded; they bought and built expansive country houses with vast gardens, introducing a scale and decorative style of thick tapestries and gold gilding—*Goût Rothschild*—that the superrich of that era emulated. Conflicts of interest and business disputes between the Rothschild houses also began appearing at a scale the family hadn't seen before. As if to symbolize the unraveling of the unity that Mayer and his sons had urged, the practice of cousin marriage began to decline due to its increasing social unacceptability, ending for good in the mid-1870s.[4]

But even with some descendants of the family spinning off into a life of the idle rich and the family's share of the capital market declining after 1880, the Rothschilds were still a powerful force in European banking and economics. This primarily took the form of backing various European imperial forays, particularly those of Britain. With the so-called "Scramble for Africa" kicking off in 1881, the Rothschilds had opportunities to expand their already considerable foreign operations and exploit the rapidly growing need for major nations to finance their colonial expansion through the issuing of new bonds—still an area in which the Rothschilds had no equal.[5]

Presented with opportunities to assist in this redrawing of the map of the world, the Rothschilds participated in some of the biggest colonial expansions of the era—with both positive and deeply negative connotations. Rothschild funding helped create massive engineering and transportation projects across the continent, particularly in South Africa, and was a critical part of mining the resources that would usher in the modern age. They were also complicit in, or at best ambivalent toward, many of the worst abuses against the people already living in these lands.

THE ROTHSCHILDS AND THE SUEZ

It's yet another misconception played up by conspiracy theorists that the family financed the actual construction of the Suez Canal. The canal had opened in 1869, with its construction taking eleven years, funded mostly by the French government, and carried out at least partly by forced laborers who died by the thousands. The canal was seen by England as a threat to their geopolitical dominance and dismissed as too risky by other major players like Russia, Austria, and the US, none of which invested in it.[6]

But by 1875, debt from the canal's massive construction cost, the bankruptcy of the Ottoman Empire (another shareholder), and the profligate overspending of the Egyptian *Khedive* (viceroy) forced Egypt to sell their share in the Suez Company. In one of the most daring financial moves of that era, Lionel de Rothschild quickly financed the four million pounds needed for England to bail out the *Khedive*. Without the consent of Parliament, Prime Minister Benjamin Disraeli swooped in and made England an instant shareholder. Even for the Rothschilds it was an enormous sum, equivalent to more than eight percent of England's entire budget for the year.[7] The loan was repaid within five months at an extremely steep interest rate, and Britain's massive investment in the region would tie them to Egypt's internal strife for decades to come, until Nasser nationalized the canal in 1956.[8] In one stroke, the Rothschilds had cemented Britain's status as the preeminent global power just as Germany was on the road to empire.

While the Suez purchase could be seen as both a personal favor to Disraeli and a shrewd business move that would benefit the British Empire, other Rothschild adventures in the Middle East and Africa around the 1870s and 1880s had no such altruistic motive. The expansion of European colonization in Africa and the relentless thirst for new natural resources precipitated a massive expansion of the Rothschild's business interests, particularly with mining. They already owned exclusive leases on the lucrative mercury mines of Spain but expanded even further—buying the enormous Société Le Nickel mining company in the South Pacific, establishing ruby mines in Burma, drilling for oil in Russia, founding a slew of international railways, and taking control of the massive Spanish-based Rio Tinto mining company in 1880, a purchase that made the family the world's largest supplier of copper.[9]

Many of these moves would fuel conspiracy theories and antisemitism for decades to come, often based on misconceptions or outdated information as well as principled anti-imperialist critique. But if there is one area of the Rothschilds' massive expansion into mining and drilling that hasn't gotten the scrutiny it deserves, it's their involvement with Cecil Rhodes and the De Beers company.

Born in a small English market town, a sickly Rhodes was sent at age seventeen to what was then known as the Cape Colony, encompassing parts of modern South Africa, Namibia, and Lesotho. Within a year he had already entered into the hugely expanding diamond and gold trade based on the seemingly limitless finds in South Africa's mines and fields. Rhodes soon sought 1.4 million pounds to merge his existing diamond business with that of another firm and monopolize the market. There was only one name that could lend such an extraordinary amount of money that quickly—the Rothschilds. By then controlled by Lionel's son Nathan—usually referred to as Natty—N. M. Rothschild made a million-pound loan to Rhodes, who formed the De Beers company in 1888. With the ability to outspend their potential rivals, the partnership between Rhodes and Natty quickly gained a stranglehold on the South African diamond industry.[10]

Fueled by the enormous wealth he was quickly accumulating, Rhodes would become prime minister of the Cape Colony in 1890 and set about a rapid expansion of British control of South Africa, expropriating native land for the purposes of gold and diamond mining while disenfranchising Black natives and violently suppressing resistance to British imperialism. While the Rothschilds weren't ardent expansionists, they recognized the economic potential of South Africa and therefore generally supported Rhodes's auto-cratic control of the Cape Colony. Rothschild loans helped De Beers refine its mining process and expand into new areas for exploitation, while family members excitedly wrote in letters about the carnage of British military en-gagements with rebels and Natty served as a shareholder and advisor for the British South Africa Company.[11]

But the Rothschilds weren't interested in funding De Beers's limit-less expansion and made loans to other governments operating in the same area—including to Britain's rivals in the Dutch-speaking Boer Republics. Within a few years, the relationship between Natty and Rhodes fell apart over disagreements about the expansion of De Beers, the governance of the Cape Colony, and the family's business with the Boers. The entire family was appalled in December 1895 when Rhodes used what was essentially a private army of British South Africa Police in a botched attempt to raid the Boer-led South African Republic.[12]

What became known as the Jameson Raid caused nearly two dozen deaths and helped spark the Second Boer War between the British Empire and the Boer Republics, killing more than eighty thousand soldiers and in-nocent civilians from 1899 to 1902. More immediately, it spelled the end for both Rhodes as prime minister of the Cape Colony and his easy access to the Rothschilds and their money. But even after Rhodes died in 1903, the London and Paris houses would retain a major share of De Beers well into the twentieth century.[13]

Natty Rothschild would have one more link to what is now a hotly de-bated aspect of Rhodes's legacy: he was the executor of the estate Rhodes left behind and was given instructions to use the funds "to encourage and foster an appreciation of the advantages [that] will result from the union of the English-speaking peoples throughout the world." Conspiracy theo-rists would later link the Rhodes Trust to another statement of Rhodes, his "Confession of Faith," written in 1877 when Rhodes was twenty-four. In the "Confession," Rhodes sought to end armed conflict by bringing "despicable specimens of human beings" in Eastern Europe and elsewhere under British control and enumerated his desire to "form a secret society with but one object: the furtherance of the British Empire and the bringing of the whole uncivilized world under British rule."[14]

By the time of his death, though, Rhodes had rewritten his will numerous times, removing much of the language of the "Confession." Far from taking the money and using it to create some kind of ultra-nationalist secret society, as future conspiracy writers would allege, Natty instead used it to establish the famed Rhodes Scholarship at Oxford University, with Rhodes's final will stipulating that "no student shall be qualified or disqualified for election [...] on account of his race or religious opinions." Over a hundred years after Rhodes's death, debate still rages as to what it means to "take money from the 'godfather of apartheid'" and how to reckon with past imperialism in a society slowly coming to terms with the role of systemic racism in European expansion.[15]

The Rothschilds' continued investment in De Beers would become more of an exception as the family went into the new century. While the family once monopolized the mining and refinement of copper, mercury, bauxite, nickel, and other common metals, those holdings would eventually be sold off or consolidated. Naturally, that doesn't stop conspiracy theories about the Rothschilds and their dealings from making it into countless publications—everything from a groundless theory in Eustace Mullins's conspiracy classic *Secrets of The Federal Reserve* alleging that future president Herbert Hoover was a secret Rothschild agent who was handed directorship of the Rio Tinto mines[16] to the Rothschilds owning "the gold and diamond mines of S. Africa and major extractive industries such as Rio Tinto and British Petroleum," as alleged by a letter to the editor of Ohio's *The Athens News* in 2013.[17]

By the beginning of the twentieth century, the family's wealth was truly enormous, even if more members were eschewing the family business for individual pursuits. The numbers are staggering—one newspaper report held that the family had lent over $450 million just in the last decade of the 1800s, and that they'd lent more money to individual nations than comprised the entire fortunes of American titans like J. P. Morgan and others.[18] And they spent money just as quickly as they made it. The family built or renovated dozens of country houses and palaces, acquired truly massive collections of paintings by old masters and new talents alike, and went on massive shopping sprees for clothing and jewels. They gave lavish bonuses to employees, routinely dined with prime ministers and the Royal Family, subsidized music and theater around Europe as patrons of the arts, and established charity hospitals in England, France, Germany, and elsewhere.

But for everything they'd accomplished in business and culture, they were still Jews. When a new wave of antisemitism and anti-Zionist violence crashed down on Europe in the 1880s and '90s, they were positioned as ever to take a larger than average share. And many of the crackpot theories and accusations that took hold in France in the first half of the 1800s would fully bloom in the second half of the century, with catastrophic results for international Judaism.

JEWISH FRANCE AND *JEWISH FRANCE*

Like the Damascus Affair in the 1840s, another French scandal linked to Jewish "otherness" would play a major role in the rebirth of anti-Rothschild tropes in the last decade of the nineteenth century. The 1894 arrest and trial of Jewish French artillery officer Alfred Dreyfus on charges of giving secret military documents to Germany launched a scandal that bitterly divided French society for over a decade. Sections of France's intellectual class increasingly supported Dreyfus—they called themselves Dreyfusards—believing the evidence actually pointed to a different, non-Jewish French officer. It was a time when both nationalism and popular antisemitism were on the rise again, fueled by a new wave of polemics attacking Jewish wealth in much the same way as Toussenel, Dairnvaell, and their compatriots had two generations earlier. But by now, the socialist movement had abandoned antisemitism as Jewish workers' movements rose up around Europe, and as newer cohorts of far-right antisemites saw Jews and socialists as different versions of the same parasitism.

The Rothschilds tried to stay out of the Dreyfus Affair, given the negative attention it was bringing to Jewish wealth. Nonetheless, rumors swirled in French salons that the family was part of a "Syndicate" that pulled the strings on French society and commerce, with right-wing antisemitic writers and Dreyfus opponents obsessing over the family's wealth and its historic symbol of five arrows, representing the five sons of Mayer Amschel.[19] These attacks would continue in a slew of newspapers and pamphlets and spark numerous acts of violence against Jews, until Dreyfus's exoneration and reinstatement in the French Army in 1906.

While it's not outlandish to see the family's monopolistic control of raw materials, diamond mining, and railroads as deeply problematic and syndicates of a sort, the organization described in antisemitic materials of the time is distinctly a single entity—a supposed cabal of influential bankers, military officers, and politicians trying to exonerate Dreyfus and blame a Christian officer for his treason. The concept of such a French "syndicate" is rooted in one of the most important documents in the history of Jew hate: an unhinged and operatically antisemitic 1,200-page, two-volume tome published in 1886 and called simply *La France juive* (*Jewish France*). Both the Dreyfus Affair and the titanic success of *Jewish France* and its copycat works were hugely responsible for the transformation of antisemitism from a religious and financial philosophy to a political one, as leaders on both the far left and far right sought to harness perceptions of Jewish power to further their own personal struggles against the upper class and their financial controllers.[20]

Writing what was part political diatribe and part gossipy rant, *Jewish France* author Edouard Drumont set out in exhausting detail how the Jews were a racially inferior, physically revolting, endlessly greedy race of swindlers, traitors, spies, cowards, and disease vectors who were destroying France from within, and how, despite offering nothing of value, they possessed "half the capital of the world."

Borrowing from Georges Dairnvaell, much of the first part of *Jewish France* is an unabated attack on the Rothschilds and their political influence. Mentioning the family several hundred times over the course of *Jewish France*, Drumont pillories the Rothschilds as having "escaped from the ghetto" to hoard wealth while "so many French people are dying of hunger," claims they "live outside the law" as ministers and kings, compares Rothschild women to "vendors in the bathroom" selling cigarettes and the men to vultures and "second hand clothes dealers," attacks them for their role in administering French war reparations after Waterloo as "helpful Shylocks" extracting every franc possible, and calls their legendary philanthropy "absolutely a myth," with the family giving away less than a man who tosses a few coins at a pauper. The Rothschilds, Drumont rants at one point, are "reviled, ridiculed, and despised" for their "gross impudence [and] insolent splendor" as they destroy the glorious history of France.[21]

Drumont considered himself a disciple of Toussenel and mentions *Kings of Epoch* in his own text. And like Dairnvaell, he firmly embraced the Waterloo canard and the Rothschilds' domination of the Nord Line, attacking both Nathan and James numerous times with the same libelous accusations as his mentors. And like in those past works, Drumont's hatred turned out to be extremely lucrative. After sluggish initial sales, the notoriety from disparaging reviews and Drumont's knack for getting publicity (he was involved in several high-profile duels at the time it was published) made it a huge success. *Jewish France* sold one hundred thousand copies just in 1886, when France's population was less than forty million. Printing presses worked day and night to churn it out, while industrialists and newspapers bought bulk copies and gave them away. The book quickly became the most widely read in the entire country. In 1887, Drumont published both an expanded and illustrated edition and an abridged half-price edition for peasants who wanted to know more about the vile cabal keeping them in poverty. All told, it was reprinted over a hundred times over the next few decades.[22]

When the Dreyfus Affair exploded a few years later, Drumont was in the thick of it, publishing nearly six dozen books and pamphlets along with his own anti-Jewish newspaper. Much of this was simply crudely packaged lists of grievances sold to a Drumont-obsessed French public. Toussenel's *Kings of Epoch* was republished alongside new works, and a slew of copycats published their own takes on Drumont's hate and conspiracy theories about the Rothschilds.[23]

French authors like the journalist and playwright Auguste Chirac viciously attacked the Rothschilds, with Chirac finding huge success with his books *Kings of the Republic* and *The Speculation of 1870–1884*. Catholic-leaning papers put the Rothschilds at the center of vast conspiracies against their religion. And French cartoons depicted them as pigs and decrepit ghouls literally hoarding the world.[24] Anti-Rothschild sentiment ran hot in Germany as well, beginning with Frederich von Scherb's influential 1893 biography *The History of the House of the Rothschild*—which itself played off the wildly popular books of anti-Jewish German author Wilhelm Marr from the 1840s. Like his French counterparts, von Scherb attacked the Rothschilds for monopolizing the bond market, the railroads, and the mining of raw materials. And echoing other familiar tropes, von Scherb claimed the family had "become great and mighty from wars. The misfortune of states and peoples has been its fortune."[25] A slew of works followed by other German and Austrian authors and pamphlet writers castigating Jews as parasites and financial string pullers—with the Rothschilds at the top.

Drumont's success was so ubiquitous that it inspired American writers to take up his cause, usually with dollar signs in their eyes. One, the little-known Greek American author Telemachus Timayenis, became the "father of American antisemitic publishing" thanks to wholesale lifting of long stretches of *Jewish France* for his first anti-Jewish book *The Original Mr. Jacobs: A Startling Exposé*, which sold two hundred thousand copies upon its publication in 1888. Its sequel, *The American Jew: An Exposé of His Career*, saw Timayenis tell, among other lurid tales, the real and scandalous story of a man named Abraham Rothschild of Cincinnati accused of robbing and murdering his mistress, nicknamed Diamond Bessie, only to walk free when his conviction was overturned and he was acquitted in a second trial. Naturally, this Rothschild is often erroneously referred to as a member of the famous family, despite there being no reason why the European Rothschilds would be involved in such a sordid and local matter.[26]

Even legitimate writers not generally known as anti-Jewish got in on the lucrative act of attacking the Rothschilds, with literary legends like the

English novelist Anthony Trollope and social scientist J. A. Hobson using thinly veiled Rothschild or Jewish banker caricatures as financier villains and scapegoats. Hobson, in particular, joined many other intellectuals of the time when he blamed the outbreak of the Boer War on "a small group of international financiers, chiefly German in origin and Jewish in race"—a clear reference to the Rothschilds.[27]

And as evidenced by the popularity of works like those of Telemachus Timayenis, antisemitism was taking hold in the United States to the point where the loathing of the Rothschilds far outstripped their actual impact in that country—to an extent which will be fully explored in the next chapter. Ultimately, conspiracy theorists and cranks of the next century would find rich veins to mine in these unhinged diatribes putting the family at the head of a vast pyramid of exploitation and profiteering. And the consequences for Jews would be immediate.

In the short term, it was a terrible time for the Rothschilds, with members of the family victimized by crude assault attempts, a letter bomb, and an assassination attempt against Leopold de Rothschild, the youngest child of Lionel, by a mentally disturbed man who fired at Leopold as his car was leaving the family office in London.[28] But for Jews across Europe, the danger was far more evident than just a botched shooting. Fueled by working-class resentment over the growth of Europe's middle class and the continent's seemingly endless influx of Jewish immigrants from Eastern Europe, systemic antisemitism and discriminatory laws rose up all over countries where the family had deep roots. There were also more immediate physical dangers—a sharp increase in riots, threats, vandalism, and assaults on Jews in the decades leading up to the rise of the Nazis. It was at its worst in Germany, but evident in England, France, and Eastern Europe as well—sending Jews fleeing from nations they were hated in to other nations that, increasingly, also didn't want them.[29]

As in the past, the family's response was not to publicly refute the attacks but to increase their philanthropy to Jewish relief organizations and hospitals. But some Jewish thinkers sought a more long-term solution: leave Europe and return to the Holy Land. And for decades, authors and thinkers, both for and against Jews, openly wondered why the Rothschilds couldn't use their limitless wealth to simply move their coreligionists from countries that didn't want them to one where they could live according to their own customs.

Considered the father of the modern Zionist movement, Austro-Hungarian writer Theodor Herzl made his initial proposal for a *Judenstaat*—a Jewish state—to the Rothschilds, even originally subtitling his 1896 pamphlet of the same name "Address to the Rothschilds."[30] Herzl believed that only the Rothschilds could supply the billion marks needed to repatriate Europe's harried Jews to either Argentina or Palestine, where they could establish their own nation. But Natty and Leopold in London, along with Baron Albert von Rothschild in Vienna, all rejected Herzl's proposal, seeing his embrace of a Zionist form of socialism as a threat to their own financial interests and attempts to found settlements in Palestine. Moreover, they didn't support the idea of a Jewish state in general—they couldn't imagine a scenario where the people of modern Europe took their generalized distrust and dislike of Jews to a level that ended in expulsion or extermination.[31]

DISSOLUTION AND CALAMITY

Despite the family's monopolies on raw materials and their continued success in the international bond market, the twentieth century saw the beginning a slow, general downturn for the Rothschilds. In August 1901, the original pillar of the House of Rothschild, the Frankfurt branch, closed after a lengthy liquidation process. This was more symbolic than indicative of declining business—branch head Wilhelm Carl von Rothschild, the son of Mayer's youngest son Carl, had died without a male heir, and nobody else in the family wanted to move back to a city that had been usurped by Berlin as Germany's financial capital.[32]

The family was also continuing to struggle in establishing a permanent business in the United States. Because of both exclusion by established American bankers like J. P. Morgan and John D. Rockefeller and the

Rothschilds' own doubts about the fragility of the American economy, the family wasn't positioned to profit from the explosion of railroad expansion, mining, and urban construction after the Civil War. Beyond that, there was simply a lack of interest by many of the next generation of Rothschild men in growing the business. This left many of the houses with a number of "silent" partners who did little but withdraw money to spend on personal interests, and others whose idea of "bankers' hours" was coming in around ten and leaving at two.[33] In 1905, the formal partnership between the Vienna, Paris, and London houses wasn't renewed. The Rothschilds simply weren't dominant enough in the new ways of banking and moneylending to warrant such a formal link to one another at this point.[34]

But none of these blows compared to what was looming with the First World War.

Contrary to a century of traditional teaching, war between the great European powers was not inevitable. Even in early 1914 it looked far from certain that Germany's increasing militarism and England and France's rising trepidation would collide. In the aftermath of Archduke Franz Ferdinand's assassination in Sarajevo in late June, events moved far too quickly for the Rothschilds' legendary diplomatic skill to have any impact on the march to war, as decades of treaty obligations activated and the crisis took on a life of its own.

In early August, German troops invaded France in an effort to knock them out of the war before Russia could mobilize and invade from the east. Germany's failure to execute its daring plan to get France out before Russia could get in led to four years of bloodletting both west and east of Germany, with millions of young men killed or wounded on all sides. Like all wealthy families of the time, many Rothschild men joined the armed forces of their respective nations, desperate to avoid the traditional canards of Jewish disloyalty and "rootless cosmopolitanism." Far from the reputation as "cowards" that hacks hung on the Rothschilds, members of the family fought with distinction in the endless trench warfare that followed 1914. Leopold de Rothschild lost one son and had another badly wounded fighting for England, while Baron Albert's son nearly lost a leg fighting for Austria—England's enemy.[35]

Naturally, the truth about what the family did and didn't do during the Great War has little impact on the deluge of conspiracy theories. Generations of future cranks would write that the Rothschilds spent the war profiting off all the misery through outrageous interest rates on loans and weapons sales made to both sides. A typical version of these claims can be found in Alex Jones's movie *Endgame: Blueprint for Global Enslavement*, where the conspiracy influencer gravely intones that "armaments companies financed by Rothschild controlled banks in Germany, France, England, and Austria bankrolled all the factions."[36]

Nothing could be further from the truth. The Great War was extraordinarily tumultuous and unprofitable for the family, and may have done more than any other event before the rise of the Nazis to contribute to the decline of the Rothschilds as "the world's bankers." Far from their almost single-handed funding of the effort against Napoleon, or of Prussia in the Franco-Prussian War, the Rothschilds lent virtually nothing to support the enormous war effort.

Instead, in 1914, the French Rothschilds had to look outside the family for help, going to their American rival J.P. Morgan & Co. to help establish a line of credit for France. It would be Morgan that served as the purchasing agents and principal lenders to Great Britain and France in the time leading up to the United States's entry into the war in 1917. It was a syndicate of banks led by Morgan that made the massive Anglo-French Loan of 1915, a $500 million boost to the Allied war effort. And it was firms like Morgan that were accused of steering the United States into the war in order to maximize their own profits, though American entry into the war was likely inevitable. Other than early connections between the French house and Morgan, the Rothschilds played no role in any of these transactions.[37]

Many of Mayer's grandsons died of old age during the years of the Great War, including all three brothers running the London branch passing in just two years. Among the remaining branches, there were conflicts over Zionism, bad press from spending too lavishly during years of austerity, and the same old struggles with new technology and types of lending. Banking around Europe was a shambles once the guns fell silent, and the situation was especially bad for the Rothschilds thanks to a new wave of small joint-stock banks that relied on lending the money of investors, not of their wealthy owners. Cooperation between the Vienna, London, and Paris houses all but ceased, the family lost its connections to German banks and industry, and Europe's governments drastically raised taxes to fund the war. N. M. Rothschild took a particularly massive hit from British tax increases, as the London family had to pay millions on the estates of the three brothers who died during the war years.[38]

During the years between the World Wars, the Rothschilds found themselves left behind. It would be American money that would fund the rebuilding of Central Europe's broken empires, not British money supplied by the Rothschilds. And while Weimar Germany struggled to pay off its crushing war reparations, the Rothschilds didn't assume their other familiar role of administering and making interest off those payments.

In fact, N. M. Rothschild was shut out from attempts to make loans to both Austria and Hungary as the two nations struggled to get on their feet after the breakup of the Austro-Hungarian Empire. The world was moving on from the traditional strengths of the Rothschilds, which had been the loaning of gold and private bond issues. The family was increasingly inflexible and orthodox even as Europe's struggling new nations desperately needed new solutions to their problems, and the bond issues the family did make tended to go to unstable regimes in Latin America, Asia, and Central Europe, where political upheaval and economic distress meant their bonds consistently lost money.[39]

The few loans that N. M. Rothschild was able to float in the US did little to alleviate the economic catastrophe looming with the crash of the American stock market in 1929. With the Depression in full swing in the US, the European economy began to teeter on the edge of calamity, and in May 1931, disaster finally struck—a disaster in which the Rothschilds were deeply involved.[40]

DISASTER IN VIENNA

Anselm von Rothschild, the son of Vienna house founder Solomon, had established the *Creditanstalt* in Vienna in 1855, and it would quickly become the largest bank in Austria-Hungary. By 1931, it held over half of all the bank deposits in the nascent country of Austria. Its board was made up of luminaries like Baron Louis de Rothschild, representatives from the Bank of England, and board members from some of the biggest banks in Germany and the United States. It was, to use the term applied to modern banks, too big to fail. And like our more recent banks, it failed. On May 8, its executives informed the Austrian government that it had lost $20 million in 1930 due to bad debt from merging with another bank, essentially wiping it out and putting all of its investors at risk.[41]

Austrians responded the same way Americans responded to the wave of financial disaster brought about by the stock market crash of 1929: by frantically withdrawing money from wherever they had it. In early May bank runs, 10 percent of all of Austria's deposited money was taken out, sparking an instant financial crisis that sent Austria's economy spiraling. With dozens of banks connected to *Creditanstalt*, and so much capital tied up in its holdings, the failing bank had to be propped up immediately. Government bailouts, funded in part by the Vienna and Paris houses, were quickly made to stem the run, with even more danger looming due to an Austrian law that required any bank losing half its assets to immediately close.[42]

The Rothschilds took an active role in trying to rescue the crippled bank, with the Vienna house optimistically writing to another bank that "the capital reconstruction adequately covered all losses."[43] It did not, and *Creditanstalt* collapsed, with the financial contagion quickly spreading to Hungary and Germany. France secretly encouraged its banks to pull their deposits out of Austria, and with German money starting to flee as well, rumors swirled that the struggling Weimar government would suspend paying reparations to France. Such drastic action would, in turn, imperil the French economy, which depended greatly on the payments mandated by the Treaty of Versailles.[44]

US officials begged London bankers not to pull money out of Germany, while a run on the Bank of England forced the country to abandon the gold standard—as did every other European nation dealing with the banking contagion. Germany would lose half its gold reserves in the first weeks of June, forcing it to forbid the flight of money outside the country. With the crisis expanding, the already-beleaguered US was forced to demand a one-year pause on repayment of Allied war debt, essentially demanding the Allies suspend German reparations at a time when their own financial systems were in peril. As the largest holder of reparations, French officials were enraged and hamstrung the deal while Germany bled out.[45]

By July, the Reichsbank needed $1 billion to stave off economic collapse. They couldn't get it, refused by other nations struggling to maintain liquidity, and by French Rothschilds head Edmond de Rothschild, who was too anti-German to make any kind of deal.[46] Later in July, Germany declared a two-week bank holiday, bringing the Weimar economy to a complete stop. Banks in Austria, Hungary, Yugoslavia, Czechoslovakia, and Poland all closed down. German banks in the Middle East faced riots by depositors desperate to get their money, and the contagion spread to Central and South America. Chile saw four governments installed and overthrown in a few days that July, while Mexico's largest bank closed. And banks all over London, including the Bank of England, faced their own collapse with as much as three billion pounds tied up in bad debt, much of it owned by Germany.[47]

Riots broke out all over the world, factories and mills closed, unemployment lines stretched across the horizon, suicides skyrocketed, encampments of the homeless sprung up in every conceivable public space, and power-hungry leaders conspired to use the crisis for their own advancement. Germany in particular was crushed under the weight of reparations (which wouldn't fully be forgiven until June 1932), hyperinflation, continued capital flight, business failures, and unemployment. And as incomes declined, support for the National Socialist Workers Party (NSDAP), led by Adolf Hitler, increased. The NSDAP found ready converts in towns where industries depended on significant capital lent by Jewish banks, and where unemployment was rampant.[48]

By the time Nazis and their supporters rallied at a mountain spa town in late 1931, a third of the German labor force was unemployed, including millions of Great War veterans, who stood shoulder to shoulder with angry young brownshirts looking for someone to blame their woes on. The situation was so bad that the former head of the Reichsbank had thrown in his lot with Hitler, declaring at the same 1931 meeting that the country was broke.[49]

Nazi militarism was deeply alluring to these men, roping in legions of embittered veterans and their former commanding officers by taking advantage of Hitler's accusations of "November criminals" in the Weimar government stabbing the German fighting man in the back in 1918, giving victory to a Jewish-funded enemy that had never set foot on German soil. In the July 1932 federal elections, the NSDAP—backed by armies of street fighters—won enough seats to become the dominant party in the Reichstag, benefitting from the refusal of socialists and communists to ally with each other, even though their total numbers in the parliament exceeded the NSDAP's.

Six months later, Hitler would seize power on a wave of violent grievance against the Jews who had brought Germany down so low. And the Nazis and their collaborators readily embraced the hysterical antisemitism, fear, and paranoia of past Rothschild enemies like Eduard Drumont, Georges Dairnvaell, and countless others in Europe and the United States alike.[50]

The Rothschilds can't solely be blamed for the banking crisis of 1931 and its aftermath. The Depression was already in full swing, and Europe's economy was too fragile (and too dependent on reparations) to stand up to such a grave financial shock. But among Germans, the Rothschilds and other wealthy Jews made easy scapegoats. Once Hitler had taken power in the ashes of Europe's banking disaster and Germany's near collapse, the family would find itself the most high-profile victims of an organized spasm of violent hate and conspiracy theories that would spell disaster for Jews around Europe.

"A COUNTRY THAT DEFIES ALL CALCULATIONS": ROTHSCHILD MYTHS IN AMERICA

It's not a surprise that conspiracy theories powered so much of the discourse about the Rothschild family in Europe—they were "kings of epoch," with their limitless power and wealth touching every aspect of business, culture, politics, and style. Their influence was measurable and visible to everyone.

But in the United States, the family was much more a myth than a growing concern, something between a clannish group of outsiders to gawk at and an unimaginably wealthy family to aspire to be like. The legend of the Rothschilds was greatly out of proportion with their presence in the United States—a country that many family members continued to see as a backwater with an impenetrable Christian culture that didn't want them. Or, as James de Rothschild put it in a letter, "America is a country that defies all calculations."[1]

As conspiracy theories about Jewish wealth and power became more acceptable in mainstream publications and speeches, many Americans began to see the Rothschilds as alien outsiders who exerted too much control over domestic affairs, manipulating them for their own gain. Like their European counterparts, American cranks and antisemites would spend decades linking world events to Rothschild-funded Jewish machinations in books, pamphlets, speeches, newspaper articles, and eventually films. Ultimately, these tracks would converge in the leadup to World War II. European fascists and their American counterparts would come together to make the house of Rothschild a target for some of the most unhinged hate uttered in a decade full of unhinged hate, stoking American distrust of Jews just as Jewish refugees desperately needed somewhere to run to.

But whispers about the Rothschilds' involvement in the United States are bound up in some of the earliest epochal events in American history, even if the family had nothing to do with them—or barely existed when they took place. The Rothschilds may not have understood the United States, but the United States truly believed it understood the Rothschilds.

ALEXANDER HAMILTON: ROTHSCHILD AGENT

Conspiracy theorists constantly claim to "question everything" and that this unwillingness to simply go along with what they're being told makes them smarter than the rest of us. Yet they also believe virtually anything that any guru or "researcher" tells them as long as it fits in with their preexisting ideas.

This tendency is apparent in American myths about the Rothschilds. Because the Rothschilds have such a reputation as global string pullers, many outlandish conspiracy theories and accusations about them are accepted as truth without being plausible—or even possible. Many of these concern Mayer and his supposed involvement in the earliest days of the United States—at a time when no such business would have been anywhere near his bailiwick.

Mayer Amschel Rothschild spent the years of the American Revolution building his rare coin business while working as the court Jew for the crown prince of Hesse. Part of this involved selling soldiers to England for use in the Colonies—the Hessians are referred to as "large armies of foreign mercenaries" in the Declaration of Independence. But since conspiracy theorists also believe that the Rothschilds have funded both sides of every war since Napoleon, there's little stopping them from going back in time even further and linking Mayer to not only the British side in the American Revolution but the American one as well. After all, Hessians killed in battle brought the crown prince a higher price than those who lived or were merely wounded—and the Rothschilds are renowned by their mythmakers as believing the value of money far outstrips that of human life.

It's true that the system of Hesse selling troops was extremely lucrative, with England paying about seven pounds for each man sold, and double that if the man was killed in combat.[2] But the vast majority of this windfall went directly to the Elector, with Mayer seeing little, if any, of it. Funds from Hessian mercenaries would go on to form a large part of the Elector's Treasure that Mayer and his sons were tasked with hiding—and it wasn't their money. But facts, logic, and historical evidence don't dissuade conspiracy theory content creators; they only encourage them.

In *The Suppressed History of American Banking*, author Xaviant Haze (whose bio on Amazon calls him "an author of conspiracy theories, lost civilizations, ancient aliens, ancient giants and the globalist plans of the New World Order") rolls the family into even further chicanery by accusing "the dastardly Alexander Hamilton" of being a "friend to the Rothschild family," and of setting up the First Bank of the United States with Rothschild financial backing.[3] The link between Hamilton and the Rothschilds likely stems from another, even more prolific avatar of bunk: the popularizer of the "reptile elite" conspiracy theory and former Coventry City goalkeeper, David Icke. In his book *The Robots' Rebellion*, Icke writes without citation that "Hamilton's backers [in creating the First Bank of the United States] were reputed to be the Bank of England and the Rothschilds."[4] They were not.

In reality, there *was* a Jewish banker who funded much of the American side in the Revolutionary War—the Polish-born Haym Salomon, whose loans were particularly critical to Washington's decisive victory in the Yorktown campaign. Naturally, this inconvenient fact is simply worked into more conspiracy theories, with at least one book incorrectly asserting that Salomon, whose loans were made both from money he made as a broker in Philadelphia and through fundraising from other sources, was himself a Rothschild agent.[5] Mayer had no "agents" at the time and would have had no way to funnel money to the nascent United States.

Beyond that, there's no evidence Mayer Amschel Rothschild and Alexander Hamilton knew each other. There are other rumors that Hamilton married into the Rothschild family, which also aren't true, since Hamilton's wife, Elizabeth Schuyler, was born in New York to a family that had left Holland a century earlier. And the Rothschilds played no role whatsoever in the launch of the First Bank of the United States.

The Rothschilds started doing business in the United States in Philadelphia in 1821, and later expanded into Baltimore and New York City, in keeping with their tradition of working with local banks as intermediaries. The London branch soon won the concession to handle American governmental business in Europe, taking the role away from their bitter rivals the Baring family.[6] But the family quickly found itself struggling to deal with the United States's federalist system, having long been used to a strong central government that they could loan to without anyone else interfering. Beyond that, Americans were generally distrustful of foreign bankers, and of central banking in particular.

Attempts by the family to work with the First Bank of the United States, as well as its successor, the Second Bank of the United States, fell through for a number of reasons, primarily President Andrew Jackson's determination to "kill it," along with the distrust of states toward the federal government universally handling monetary policy.[7] Naturally, the failure of central banking in the United States before the Civil War would be tied in with the Rothschilds, with accusations later arising that the family supposedly hired the mentally disturbed housepainter Richard Lawrence to shoot

Jackson in a botched assassination attempt in January of 1835.[8] This would be the first of many presidential assassinations and attempts falsely linked by cranks to the Rothschilds, and the family being the "real" power behind these killings would become a constant theme in the conspiracy theories about them.

MORE WAR, MORE DOUBLE-DEALING

Between the Revolution and the Civil War, there would be another war for the United States to fight, and another war supposedly funded on both sides by the Rothschilds. While the War of 1812 was a conflict involving England, whose efforts against Napoleon were being funded in large part by Nathan Rothschild's gold, there's no evidence that Nathan played any role in directing money toward this particular conflict. As always, that doesn't stop conspiracy theorists from claiming that Nathan essentially ordered England into war to load the United States up with public debt, which he could then make loans to pay off. There's even a fake quote to go along with the fake orders: Nathan supposedly bellowing to his agents that they must "teach these impudent Americans a lesson. Bring them back to colonial status."[9] The outcome of the war was essentially a draw, but it didn't matter; to their detractors, the Rothschilds made money off selling arms to England and off the debt the United States accumulated through the conflict.

There are a slew of other post-hoc conspiracy theories about the family's supposed involvement in pre–Civil War affairs: James de Rothschild secretly causing the Panic of 1837 as revenge for Andrew Jackson subsequently taking down the Second Bank, and causing yet another panic twenty years later, and James working with his brothers to ensnare the still-young nation in an endless cycle of booms and busts driven by tyrannical central banking.[10] None of these are supported in any correspondence written by the family or in any surviving financial records. They don't even make sense, given the actual history of the family—why would James cause the Panic of 1837, when said panic left the Rothschilds unrepresented in New York until August Belmont's arrival?

Regardless, their almost inconceivable wealth made for good media fodder. Newspapers and magazines depicted the family with the same myth-drenched patina that the European public had, speculating about their fabulous wealth and style and marveling over their riches. Many Americans had no familiarity with Jews or Jewish culture, and accounts of the time often used the Rothschilds as avatars for wealthy European Jews in general.

The Middle Ages expression "rich as a Jew" migrated across the Atlantic along with millions of Europeans, and was often applied to the Rothschilds by people who knew nothing about them. An 1836 article in the influential Baltimore magazine *Niles' Weekly Register*—the most widely circulated weekly publication of the era—fawned over them as "the wonders of modern banking," with James cast as "the king of Judah [. . .] the messiah so long looked for by this extraordinary people" and "brokers and councilors of the Kings of Europe and of the republican chiefs of America."[11]

They were seen by other complimentary accounts of the time as wise givers of advice and maxims, were lauded for their "enormous wealth" and "colossal fortune," were viewed as a cut above the bawdy American rich of the time, were rumored to give away vast sums of money to anyone who knocked on their door after a family member's death, and were the subjects of countless arcane bits of folklore about their customs, decorum, longevity, and good luck. American writing about the family even echoed Thackeray's praise of the Rothschilds, seeing people like James and Nathan "not [as] the 'King of the Jews' but the 'Jew of the Kings.'"[12]

Still, like European writing of the time, many of these accounts relied on classic tropes of the family as cold, snobbish, and devoted to their religion above their country. The ugly linkage to usury sometimes wasn't far behind. Stereotypes of the "wandering Jew" and the Hebrew Talisman were used by American writers as much as they were by European writers. And there was a vague, menacing air of the family being "too wealthy," with publications writing that they "sleep free from the annoying dreams of poverty-stricken humanity" as "former high priests of Mammon" without a care in the world.[13] Antisemitism crept in as well, as the young nation's many financial panics and individual states defaulting on loans were consistently blamed by American politicians on the "Shylocks" and "Judases" like Rothschild "and other large money dealers."[14]

Somehow, in a country where the only limits on success were your own dreams, the Rothschilds had accomplished too much—and couldn't be trusted because of it.

The American public's veering between irritated tolerance and gawking fascination at the Rothschilds would be severely tested during the Civil War. The war between the states would spark countless conspiracy theories about the family's links to the combatants, both during and long after the conflict. But like everything else with the Rothschilds, the reality is more complicated than the cartoonish villainy of the conspiracy theories about them. What stands out most about the Rothschilds and the Civil War is not what the family did, but what the family didn't do.

THE INVISIBLE GRASP OF "THE HIDDEN HAND"

A trawl through conspiracy theorist materials about the Rothschilds and the American Civil War reveals an alternate history in which the family schemed in its luxurious mountain palaces as to how they could best cripple the United States and end it as a threat to European power. They supposedly sold bonds and made loans at bloated interest rates and sent arms flooding to both sides. The Rothschilds, as the stories go, raked in the profits while American boys killed each other in a war that history says was about slavery but was *really* about the Rothschilds consolidating their total control of the global banking system.

The details always vary when the story is told. Some have the Rothschilds only funding the Confederate side so they could profit off the African slave trade or steal the South's agricultural bounty. Others have them more devoted to the Democratic Party in the North, locked in battle with Republican Abraham Lincoln over the fate of American banking, with the Rothschilds hiring John Wilkes Booth to assassinate the sixteenth president when he wouldn't give in to their demands.[15]

Many of these tales put August Belmont as the family's contact with the Union, and Jewish American lawyer (and supposed Rothschild agent) Judah Benjamin, who briefly served in the Confederacy's cabinet, as their link to the Rebels, with their goal being to divide the country in two between James and Lionel. The family's meddling in the war is often linked to one of the shadowy cabals of which they are charter members—the so-called "Committee of 300" written about in conspiracy books for decades as untouchable Jewish power brokers.

Or, as one meme frequently seen on places like 4chan puts it, "the American civil war [sic] was engineered by the Rothschild Banking Elite" who created a conflict between the North and South with the intention of giving the North to Canada under Lionel Rothschild, and the South to France under the control of James de Rothschild. The meme helpfully notes that "'slavery' [sic] was not the driving force of the war," but instead it was "who controlled the bank and the money supply."

Like the Waterloo canard, the vast majority of this inflammatory material was written long after the guns fell silent, by people with no access to the Rothschilds. It certainly wasn't a contemporaneous reaction to any actual news item. Books and pamphlets written about the family during and shortly after the Civil War make no attempt to tie them to the outbreak of the conflict. *The Rothschilds: Financial Rulers of Nations*, published in 1887, doesn't note any link between the family and the war, nor do the European anti-Rothschild works of the time. The closest mention is in Mary Hobart's 1898 pro-silver tract *The Secret of the Rothschilds*, and while that book excoriates "foreigners who [came] into our country and bought up our money at a depreciated price and converted it into bonded indebtedness," it barely mentions the Rothschilds.[16]

Even the idea of the "Committee of 300" was a post-hoc invention, taken from a remark by German Jewish politician Walther Rathenau in 1909 referencing the interconnected industrialists who "direct the economic destiny of Europe." That idea would go on to fuel innumerable other conspiracy theories about Rothschild/Jewish control of Europe's economy and would be wholeheartedly embraced by the nascent Nazi movement, which assassinated Rathenau in 1922 for good measure.[17]

The Rothschilds' supposed machinations to pit the North and South against each other were created in the mid-1920s to explain the "stranglehold" of Jewish banking on the rest of the world. The earliest fleshed-out iteration of the theory likely came from the poison pen of exiled Russian monarchist and naval officer Major-General Count Arthur Cherep-Spiridovich in his 1926 tract *The Secret World Government, or, "The Hidden Hand."* That book was, in turn, inspired by the considerable success of *The Protocols of the Elders of Zion*, which had circulated widely in English in 1920 in a series of articles in Henry Ford's *Dearborn Independent*, later printed in a book titled *The International Jew: The World's Foremost Problem*.[18]

First published in 1903 and exposed as a Russian hoax about two decades later, the *Protocols* continue to be passed around as a document that "patriots" and Christians "must read" to learn the truth about the ancient Jewish plan for world domination. Ford's initial publication alone would sell half a million copies when published in book form.[19] But the text of the *Protocols* itself never mentions the Rothschilds. Their name only appears in ephemera added before and after the supposed utterances of the "wise men of Zion" in various historical versions. One of the earliest of these was a 1923 translation credited to British journalist Victor Marsden, who had died three years earlier, which claimed "Rothschild journals" had printed earlier iterations of the Protocols going back to the 1400s.[20]

While the *Protocols* seemed to spare the Rothschilds, the authors of their successor works, many of which directly quoted from the original fraud, had no such qualms. Cherep-Spiridovich's incomprehensible tract refers to the Rothschilds over two hundred times alone. In particular, the Rothschilds are a critical part of the three hundred "Judeo-Mongols" who controlled world events, funding a shadow government called "The Hidden Hand." With popular antisemitism stoked by the *Protocols* and the worsening Depression, the tract unleashed countless accusations about the wealthy "Satanic-mankillers" who lived on a fortune of $300 billion while funding a secret world government, organizing "every bloodshed since 1770," and keeping it all silent by controlling "90 percent of the press."[21]

In particular, Count Cherep-Spiridovich (whose title of "count" was a papal title not recognized by the Russian government, and who had fled the Bolshevik Revolution for New York with the dream of founding a nation of Slavs) writes of an 1857 family wedding where James de Rothschild, his nephew Lionel, and British prime minister Benjamin Disraeli hatched a plan to destroy the United States by fomenting the Confederacy, then landing British troops in Mexico and dividing the country between England and France.

"Though since 1812 disputes had existed between the South and the North," Cherep-Spiridovich wrote, "the Civil War would have been postponed for 50 years or might never have happened, if the Hidden Hand had not decided to divide the United States at the Rothschilds' wedding in 1857."[22] It's not recorded what, if anything, Mexico thought of the supposed plan for the Hidden Hand to use it as a launchpad for an invasion of the Confederacy.

According to the "count," the plot only failed because of the intervention of the heroic Russian tsar Alexander II—who Cherep-Spiridovich wanted restored to his rightful place. Supposedly, the monarch sent his fleets to New York and San Francisco to head off the Hidden Hand's attempt to take control of the United States's ports—a near disaster for the cabal, which was subsequently suppressed by the Jewish-controlled media. In reality, Russian fleets did land in New York and San Francisco in September and October 1863, but they were massively publicized events, and the ships offered no assistance to the North other than showing moral support—though rumors of the time claimed they warded off a Confederate raid on the West Coast.[23]

Cherep-Spiridovich didn't live to see his bizarre accusation catch on in the wider fringe world—he asphyxiated himself in a Staten Island hotel room the same year his book was published, depressed that his "United Gentiles League" and dreams of restoring the tsar had failed.[24] But with sentiment against Jewish banking growing as the Great Depression worsened, his idea that the United States's various problems were the result of wealthy European plotting became more and more appealing to a diverse group of cranks.

The notoriously antisemitic radio preacher Father Charles Coughlin would adapt the Rothschild link to the Civil War in his 1933 book of sermons *Driving Out the Money Changers* and repeated it in a later pamphlet called *Abraham Lincoln and the Rothschilds*.

"Today as in the year 1862, we are being terrorized and tyrannized by the philosophy which then was spoken by the House of Rothschild to the American bankers," Coughlin thundered in *Money Changers*, going on to cite a letter supposedly written by the Rothschilds that claimed "the great debt that capitalists will see to it is made out of the war must be used as a means to control the volume of money. To accomplish this, the bonds must be used as a banking basis."[25] The document Coughlin quotes from, often called "The Hazard Circular," purportedly laid out exactly how the Rothschilds had taken control of the world's economy and is often used as a source for apocryphal quotes about the family and their power. It can't actually be fact-checked, though, because it doesn't appear to exist as a complete document, only as a few quotes in various conspiracy materials of the nineteenth and twentieth centuries.[26]

After World War II, the accusation that the Rothschilds had started the Civil War to divide the United States for themselves would be repeated by countless various fringe characters. It was embraced by Major General Ulysses S. Grant III, grandson of the former president, who mailed thousands of copies of *Abraham Lincoln and the Rothschilds* to friends and reiterated Cherep-Spiridovich's claim of an agreement between the Rothschilds and Disraeli.[27] Decades later, conspiracy author John Coleman, who prominently included the Rothschilds in his 1991 book *The Conspirators' Hierarchy: The Committee of 300*, would write in his 2006 book *The Rothschild Dynasty* that "the Rothschilds used slavery as an excuse to foment the American Civil War," among many other tropes and hoaxes.

"The idea was said to have come from Benjamin Disraeli, Lionel and James, who sat down to dinner after the wedding of Lionel's daughter," Coleman wrote, linking them to a vast mythology of moves and countermoves that was mostly created by Coleman himself and has no basis in reality.[28] And internet message boards are full of conspiracy theories that the Rothschilds used Abraham Lincoln as a pawn to take control of the

United States's banking system, then assassinated him when he tried to break free—an idea that goes all the way back to Mary Hobart's tract referring to "our martyred Lincoln" when discussing his assassination.[29]

"FOREIGN JEW BANKERS"

For all of the conspiracy theories about the Rothschilds and the Civil War, there definitely was ire directed at the family for what Americans saw as foreign meddling in a homegrown conflict. But with the Rothschilds seen as a distant and untouchable power, the bulk of these attacks were directed at a more immediate, though no less alien figure—their New York agent, the Jewish banker August Belmont.

Belmont wasn't intended to become the Rothschild's point man in the US—he had been tasked with sailing to Havana to keep watch on Rothschild interests in Cuba. As such, his relationship with the family was extremely complex. The Rothschilds were initially irritated at Belmont for defying their orders, with James declaring him to be "a stupid young man [who] needs to be kept on a short leash." Eventually, once it became clear that nobody else in the family wanted to go to New York, the Paris and London houses began working through him to grow their interests in the US. But the relationship was always more one of mutual interest than anything resembling a formal plan to launch another branch of the family, and they would work through Belmont's firm until well into the 1920s.[30]

Using the Rothschild name for his own ends as much as for theirs, Belmont began climbing the ladder of New York society, and by 1850, he had married a daughter of the famed naval officer Commodore Perry and had carved out a lucrative niche on Wall Street. He was also getting involved in the Democratic Party, starting with managing the party convention of Democratic nominee and eventual election winner James Buchanan in 1856—often seen as one of the United States's worst presidents for his failure to ward off the Civil War.[31] Belmont was only one of many German Jewish bankers who left Europe and headed for Wall Street in the mid-1800s, and many of their firms would eventually eclipse the Rothschilds.

But as an agent for the Rothschilds at the height of their powers, he was in a unique position to keep the family informed about the chaos in his adopted homeland, and it was his information that guided the family as they tried to make sense of the United States's descent into civil war.

In numerous letters back and forth with his bosses in Europe, Belmont went into painstaking detail about the status of the war, the gains and losses of various American commodities markets, and how Rothschild-held tobacco and cotton crops in the South were faring as the Union blockade drove prices up. Belmont seemed supportive of a negotiated peace and Confederate reentry into the Union, largely to restore agricultural trading. Crucially, while Belmont never expressed sympathy with the Confederacy or approval of slavery, he was deeply critical of Abraham Lincoln, and supported his Democratic electoral opponents in both 1860 and 1864. He also alluded to blaming Lincoln for the war, citing the president's "fatal policy of confiscation and forced emancipation" of slaves, while consistently expressing a wish that the war would end and everything would go back to business as usual.[32]

With so much at stake economically, the family took the rare step of sending one of their own to the US to gather information, settling on James's son Salomon. And if any Rothschild can be seen as supportive of the Southern cause, it was Salomon. The 24-year-old saw the South as an orderly, Old World place that did business the right way, as opposed to the chaotic North, led by Lincoln, who Salomon disdained as having "the appearance of a peasant [who] can only tell bar-room stories." In his final letter back home before leaving in April 1861, just as the war was starting, Salomon urged the continental powers to recognize the Confederacy as a nation and nip the war in the bud.[33]

But Belmont also feared that other European nations might support the Confederacy, or at least recognize them as a nation, drawing Rothschild interests into a war that could expand across the ocean. And James had the final say. While anti-Rothschild writers would continue to accuse the family of financially supporting the Confederacy, it's clear from Belmont's letters and the Rothschilds' actions that the heads of the family had no intention of getting involved on either side and felt the risks outweighed the potential rewards. Belmont often reiterated that the Union would win, writing in a letter shortly after the war broke out that "we have three times as large a population as committed and as brave as theirs, we have a navy and have money and credit, in which latter they are most sadly and justly deficient."[34]

With risks to supporting either side, Belmont advocated for the family to use their influence to get the British involved in the conflict as peacemakers—though tensions between the Union and Britain became inflamed due to British ships running the Union blockade. Ultimately, the family was well-informed enough to regard the Union as not needing their help, and supporting the Confederacy as both a moral nonstarter and as an unacceptable credit risk. It was a hunch that paid off when the Union refused to honor Confederate debt after the war.[35]

Despite his ambivalence toward Lincoln, Belmont and the president wrote each other a series of letters in 1862. In these correspondences, Belmont takes the same tack he did with his letters to the Rothschilds, telling the president that he favored a negotiated peace that brought the Southern states back and kept the war from becoming a global conflict. In one example, Belmont warned Lincoln in May 1862 that France and England "will ere long find themselves obliged to have recourse to an armed intervention having for its object the opening of the Southern ports & the consequent recognition of the Confederacy."[36] Accordingly, the animosity between the Union and Britain cooled, and foreign powers stayed out of the war.

Still, a famous Jewish family not throwing in its lot with Lincoln was an obvious thread for abolitionist papers and politicians to enrich with their own antisemitism. Northern newspapers and pamphlets claimed that the Rothschilds were funding the South by selling them bonds, that they supported European intervention in favor of the Confederacy, and that the treasonous and un-American Democratic Party sought a leader "in the agent of foreign Jew bankers."[37] A *Chicago Tribune* op-ed published just before the 1864 election made it clear what the stakes were, calling Belmont the "owner" of Democratic candidate George McClellan, with Belmont himself "owned" by the Rothschilds—who in turned owned incalculable Confederate debt.[38] None of it amounted to much, as Lincoln easily won the election, and the war ended the next year with the collapse of the Confederate economy and military.

Anti-Rothschild sentiment, much of it aimed at Belmont's role in Democratic politics, would continue after the war, even as the family made multiple bond sales and loans to help the Grant administration get the country back on its feet.[39] No matter what the family did financially, the antisemitic attacks continued, as the family was denounced by the press as "European shylocks" who would "get their pound of flesh" in return for helping the postwar United States climb out of its billions in war debt. Political resentment toward the family lingered as well, with speeches on the floor of the House demanding that the Rothschilds and their Jewish banking brethren "no longer have the entire control of our financial legislation."[40] Sentiment against Jewish banking in general would curdle in the US as the twentieth century dawned and modern concepts of central banking took hold in the United States.[41]

FROM FREE SILVER TO CENTRAL BANKING

After the Civil War, press coverage of the Rothschilds began to take on a more sinister tone. In particular, the Rothschilds' long-held insistence on trading physical gold put them at odds with the growing anti–gold standard "free silver" movement of the late nineteenth century, leading to a slew of tracts, letters, and articles in the same league as Mary Hobart's *The Secret of the Rothschilds*—many of which were blatantly anti-Jewish, anti-Rothschilds, and anti-German. The silver versus gold debate, powered by the demonetizing of silver by the Coinage Act of 1873 (which the Rothschilds were wrongly blamed for and had nothing to do with), drove two extremely contentious presidential elections in 1896 and 1900. As some of the wealthiest and most well-known "goldbugs," the Rothschilds were viciously attacked by the free silver movement and used as props to rally an almost frenzied hatred of gold.

Despite the Paris and London houses' continued ambivalence toward

American finance, newspaper articles of the 1890s blasted the Rothschilds as carrying out a grand conspiracy to "[be given] a firmer grasp upon the finances of the world."[42] "Rothschild and other Jews who are oppressing mankind" were running a "great international Jew conspiracy to demonetize silver."[43] Some pro-silver papers even ran a syndicated poem called "Emperor Rothschild's Soliloquy," which declared "I am Rothschild / king of the gold world / hater of silver / and all around manipulator of finances / I own the world! / Its people are my / slaves."[44]

And these vicious attacks weren't limited to agitating op-eds and bizarre poems in silver-backing papers. Major politicians, authors, and business figures had no problem whatsoever with putting their utopian dreams of silver and socialism up against the stranglehold of British Jewish financial control—with the Rothschilds gripping tighter than anyone else.

Telemachus Timayenis had already found considerable success in the late 1880s with his antisemitic books, which had directly cribbed much of their content from Edouard Drumont. Numerous other major figures in US politics and culture would soon join in. The famed silver evangelist and People's Party agitator "Coin" Harvey wrote of an English "Baron Rothe" who sought to destroy the United States through demonetizing silver in his 1894 novel *A Tale of Two Nations*. That same year, Harvey included an antisemitic cartoon of a giant octopus labeled "Rothschild" dominating a map of the world with its tentacles in his million-selling investment pamphlet "Coin's Financial School."[45] And renowned suffrage leader and labor union advocate Mary Elizabeth Leese used the occasion of a speech at the Cooper Union, the same New York City venue where Lincoln launched his presidential campaign in 1860, to blast interest-bearing bonds as "the curse of civilization," while announcing to the enthusiastic crowd that the US was "paying tribute to the Rothschilds of England, who are but agents of the Jews."[46]

One of the most legendary speeches in American political history, Democratic presidential candidate William Jennings Bryan's "Cross of Gold" convention speech, given a month before Leese's attacks on the "tyranny of British gold," equated demands for the United States to go on the gold standard to the crucifixion of Jesus. The thunderous address was said to have been duly met with whoops of "Down with gold! Down with the hook-nosed Shylocks of Wall Street! Down with the Christ-killing gold bugs!" though actual existence of such shouting has never been proven.[47] And Henry Ford's antisemitism was likely inspired at least in part by early pro-silver "Greenback" supporters who blamed Jewish bankers and "the Rothschilds across the water" for the United States's post–Civil War economic woes.[48]

The free silver movement fell apart after Bryan's second consecutive election loss in 1900 (he'd lose one more time in 1908), and the US formally moved to the gold standard in the same year. But the conspiratorial hatred of the Rothschilds simply got shuffled to another American banking upheaval—the founding of the Federal Reserve in 1913. And while the silver versus gold debate is mostly forgotten, the Rothschilds' supposed role in the rise of American central banking continues to spark conspiracy theories, hoaxes, and memes about the family owning "every central bank" in the world except for a few nations that the West is in constant conflict with. Along the way, they supposedly sank the *RMS Titanic* to eliminate opposition to the new central bank, created a "core of Jewish families" that controlled the Fed, and added more money to their already boundless coffers in service of starting more wars and selling weapons to both sides.

While virtually all of this is nonsense, the later twentieth and twenty-first century iterations of these Rothschild/Federal Reserve conspiracies are at the heart of some of the most important touchstones of conspiratorial thinking. They form the core of books and videos that have been relied on as "research" tools by "free thinkers" for decades. And they're all over the internet, which even a simple search for a term like "Rothschilds federal reserve" will reveal. But unlike the Jew-hating hysterics over free silver by anti-gold press and politicians, the Rothschilds' role in founding the Federal Reserve wasn't discussed in the papers and books of the time, for a very good reason: they didn't have one.

Certainly, there was a need for the United States to centralize its banking. The volatile American economy was prone to wild swings in Treasury bond prices, bank reserves, and cash liquidity. In particular, the Panic of 1907, when the New York Stock Exchange lost half its value in three weeks and triggered a cascade of bank runs and bankruptcies, forced US lawmakers to act decisively to make sure an even worse crisis couldn't happen—which, of course, it did anyway a few decades later.

While brief, the Panic of 1907 went global in a preview of the crisis to come. And as they had so many other times, the Rothschilds stepped in to shore up Europe's finances, with Natty in London and Edouard in France helping to balance out their respective nations' gold reserves.[49] But the American rescue from the panic was just that—an American affair, led by J. P. Morgan, who personally pledged his own wealth to prevent the panic from wiping out New York's economy.[50] Rothschild activity in the US was so limited that it was noteworthy enough for *The New York Times* to write about N. M. Rothschild joining their British rival Baring and New York firm Kuhn, Loeb, & Co. on a $40 million bond issue for the Pennsylvania Railroad, with the paper hinting it might "possibly [indicate] the establishment of a new connection between New York bankers and the Rothschilds."[51]

Instead, the elite of New York banking met in secret in late November 1910 at the Jekyll Island Club on the Georgia coast (a favorite vacation spot of American "kings of epoch" like Morgan and Vanderbilt) to discuss the creation of a European-style central bank in the United States. That meeting included some of the most legendary names in American finance. There was Kuhn, Loeb, & Co. partner Paul Warburg; J.P. Morgan senior vice president Henry Davison; National City Bank of New York president Frank Vanderlip; and the group's link to the US Congress, Republican Senator Nelson Aldrich, along with Aldrich's secretary and a senior Treasury Department official.[52] Working over ten days in secrecy and isolation under the auspices of a winter duck hunt, the six men hashed out the apparatus that would become the Federal Reserve, an independent system of regional feeder banks printing paper currency that each had one vote over central monetary policy, with a chairman at the top.

The Jekyll Island meeting would become the subject of innumerable conspiracy theories and books about what was "really" discussed at the retreat. Was it the enslavement of the masses through debt and taxes? The planning of future wars against those who resisted the crushing power of the dollar? The horrid details of an international banking conspiracy that would rule the world? The details of the meeting, carried out next to a fireplace and through thick cigar smoke between horseback rides and lavish meals, were far less interesting, mostly focused on dividends and reserve notes. But through all of the myth and misinformation about what the group did and didn't talk about, it's clear that the meeting had a distinct lack of Jews in general (only Warburg was Jewish among the Fed's founders) and Rothschilds in particular. The family simply had no role in the founding of the Federal Reserve, and there's no evidence they were even considered to take part in its creation.

Jewish control of the Federal Reserve didn't become a subject of debate until at least several decades after the Jekyll Island meeting, likely starting when New Zealander journalist Arthur Nelson Field published his 1934 book *The Truth About the Slump*, which blamed a cabal of German Jewish bankers for manipulating American central banking into causing the Great Depression.[53] Even that book only mentions the Rothschilds a few times, seemingly finding more inviting targets to attack with hateful tropes. And while the Rothschilds had made loans with some of the participants of the meeting, they had long since been eclipsed by these bigger, mostly homegrown firms made up of mostly Christians, and a few Jews from Germany who had made the long, one-way trip that no Rothschild heir wanted to make.

But those firms didn't have the outsized reputation as "kings of epoch" and "financial rulers of nations." The Rothschilds did. And with the global economy in upheaval, they were easy targets for the masses of angry and unemployed men looking for someone to blame, and for the demagogues who had the tools to do something about it.

TO LIVE WITH DIGNITY: THE ROTHSCHILDS AND WORLD WAR II

As the Nazis prepared to unleash their "final solution" on Europe, it was critical for the German people and their allies to be convinced that Jews weren't just greedy or cheap, but rootless, backstabbing, Christ-killing parasites who ruined Germany and sent the world's economy into a spiral to increase their wealth. And it couldn't happen all at once—it had to be done methodically, layering level after level of hate onto extant prejudices, until there was nowhere left for the animus to go except bloodletting.

The ground was fertile for an organized spasm of violence against the Jews and their British money lords, the Rothschilds. Centuries of conspiracy theories, hoaxes, myths, and tropes would be methodically and cynically updated to create a murderous fever in people already desperate for someone to blame for their economic woes. What began with ranting and speechifying transitioned into art, literature, and film, all carefully created to maximize revulsion and dehumanization. And while the Rothschilds were able to survive the horror mostly unscathed physically, their prominent profile meant they were singled out for all manner of crimes. The family's properties were seized by the German military, their art collections were looted to benefit Nazi officials, family members were sent fleeing into exile, and their industries were transformed into cogs in the Axis war machine.

And it wasn't just a German phenomenon. The leaders of German and Austrian antisemitism had allies in fascists and anti-communists in both the Axis and the Allies. Over the 1920s and 1930s, these groups, working both together and on their own, took extant myths and weaponized them to create a singular storyline: Jews controlled the world, the Rothschilds controlled the Jews, and something had to be done to end the nightmare.

THE PROPAGANDA WAR

Völkisch activist and journalist Dietrich Eckhart, lauded by Hitler as a spiritual mentor and guiding light, cofounded the German Worker's Party on an expressly antisemitic platform and specifically targeted the Rothschilds in his scabrous writings. In his 1919 pamphlet *To All Working People!* Eckhart attacked the family for its reliance on interest over hard work, bellowing in capital letters "THE HOUSE OF ROTHSCHILD OWNS 40 BILLION!," a number that he claimed was more than three times the entire industrial capital of Germany, and declared that if they weren't stopped "they will own 160 billion in 1950 and 320 billion in 1965."[1]

Likewise, in early speeches and articles printed under Hitler's byline in Nazi daily paper *Völkischer Beobachter*, the burgeoning dictator singles out the Rothschilds as one of the "socialist" families that controlled the world press, and contrasts their "rapacity" and "[bringing] the people into interest-servitude through loans" against good-hearted German industrialists like future war criminal Alfred Krupp.[2] And in his 1930 book *The Myth of the Twentieth Century*, *Völkischer Beobachter* editor Alfred Rosenberg attacks "Rothschild bankers" for infecting Western European nations with "the germ of bastardization" as Africans began to settle in French port cities and "negroes and mulattos stroll about on arms of white women."[3] That supposed link, between Jews and their "Asiatic" or "Mongol" minions, became more prevalent in both US and European intellectual circles due to the growing popularity of the eugenics movement. And German propagandists took notice.

As Hitler and his inner circle consolidated their control over German society, they combined conspiracy theories of the last century with cutting-edge propaganda techniques and new technology to focus state-sponsored art on the "kings of the Jews." Playwrights, authors, filmmakers, and artists all blamed the Rothschilds specifically for bringing on Germany's military humiliation and financial destitution, and linked them to a vast Judeo-Bolshevik conspiracy that controlled every aspect of global finance and politics.

It's an attitude epitomized by the work of Nazi playwright and drama critic Eberhard Wolfgang Möller. As part of a prolific rush of National Socialist hokum, Möller repurposed Dairnvaell's Waterloo canard in his 1934 play *Rothschild Wins at Waterloo*, casting Nathan as a cowardly parasite who eagerly watched the clash between Napoleon and Wellington at a safe distance, to the point of refusing to help a wounded Frenchman crawling toward him while bribing a sailor to take him across the Channel in a violent storm so he could make untold millions. *Rothschild* was one of six explicitly anti-Jewish plays Möller wrote between the Nazi takeover and the onset of war with Poland, making him a rising star in German theater and film.[4]

The Nazis stepped up their attacks on the Rothschilds through academic channels as well. In 1937, *The New York Times* breathlessly covered a conference of Third Reich historians as they "got down to grips with the Jewish question." Among them were Professor Wilhelm Grau, who called the Rothschilds "servants of money" who held Europe in a vice-like grip of debt and were "brothers in blood and in spirit" with Karl Marx—despite Marx himself being extremely anti-Rothschild.[5] Infamous Nazi publisher Julius Streicher paid particular attention to the Rothschilds in his antisemitic newspaper *Der Sturmer* and devoted an entire room of his 1937–38 exhibition *The Eternal Jew* to the Rothschilds that included forged letters from Mayer Amschel claiming he was sending his five sons to take control of banking on the continent.[6] And German lawyer and author Peter Deeg's 1939 book *Hofjuden* (Court Jews) was a 500-page attack primarily on the Rothschilds, published by Streicher with a forward by Adolf Hitler himself, that could be found on the shelves of the prison library at Nuremberg as the leading Nazis awaited trial and execution—including Rosenberg and Streicher themselves.[7]

Still, many German people were essentially apathetic toward the Jews, too busy trying to survive Germany's worsening economy to spend much time scapegoating. But as the Nazi propaganda machine sharpened its message, that apathy would slowly curdle into hate. And as Nazi attacks on the Rothschilds increased, so too did the attacks on the family in the rest of the world.

NEW GENERATIONS, OLD PARANOIA

By the 1920s, Rothschild myths had supplanted history as the primary source of information about the family. In particular, the success of *The Protocols of the Elders of Zion* and *The International Jew* inspired countless hacks in the West to take their shot at writing long, rambling screeds about Jewish control of finance and politics, with the Rothschilds at the top.

Among the most popular of these early works was English fascist Nesta Helen Webster's 1921 book *World Revolution: The Plot Against Civilization*. The daughter of a wealthy British banker, Webster first gained fame among western antisemites for contributing to *The Jewish Peril*, a series of widely read editorials in *The London Morning Post* that helped bring the *Protocols* to a larger audience. She would repurpose that work for *World Revolution*, in which she liberally quoted from a host of other antisemites, while casting the Rothschilds, the Freemasons, and the Illuminati as the heads of a "gigantic plan" to take over the world through debt and war. But even Webster, quoting British socialist and antisemite Henry Hyndman, conceded that the Rothschilds were "but the leading name in a whole series of capitalists [who are] beyond dispute the leaders of the plutocracy of Europe."[8] Hyndman, it should be noted, was another British intellectual who blamed "Jewish bankers" like the Rothschilds for the carnage of the Boer War.

British antisemitic material like that of Nesta Webster was mostly focused on Jewish control of European banking and press, and in particular on evangelizing the *Protocols*, which Webster refers to as an "amazing" and "never refuted" "revised program of illuminized Freemasonry formulated by a Jewish lodge of the Order."[9] Webster's legitimizing and academic analysis of the *Protocols* would have a profound impact on the forged document's spread over the next century and help give their antisemitic conspiracy theories a respectable sheen for generations to come.

American antisemitism had a much sharper focus on immigration, particularly on recently emigrated Jewish bankers based in New York like the Lehman Brothers, Federal Reserve cofounder Paul Warburg, financier Bernard Baruch, the wealthy Guggenheim family, and other prominent names. Because the Rothschilds had never actually emigrated to the US, they were spared some of the worst of prewar antisemitism. But even without their name on a building on Wall Street, the Rothschilds were well-known enough that anti-Jewish writers and politicians could fall back on hitting out at their largesse when they needed to link Jewish power in the United States to its European counterpart, or if they just ran out of other targets.

A key example can be found again in the *Dearborn Independent*, as the week after Henry Ford's Saturday weekly paper finished printing *The International Jew* it started another series collectively called *Jewish Activities in the United States*. Despite the Rothschilds having a fairly limited role in said "activities," the *Independent* attacked them as the vessel through which "Jewish high finance first touched the United States" due to the Elector William's leasing of mercenaries to England, which netted the family their "first twenty million dollars [sic]." It also accuses them of being rootless, unpatriotic, part of a cabal of "International Jewish Finance," and of deliberately postponing the start of the Great War to better deploy their propaganda assets against Gentiles who didn't want conflict.[10]

Apparently not content to blame the Rothschilds for starting the Civil War, Father Coughlin ranted against the family in 1936 campaign speeches on behalf of longshot Union Party presidential candidate William Lemke, claiming that the cancellation of war debt would be a gift to his long-hated "international bankers" like the Rothschilds, and that Congress's right to coin money benefited only "the Rothschilds of Wall Street." But Coughlin also employed a crutch that antisemites would lean on time and time again: claiming that not *all* Jews were responsible for the evils of the banking system, just *these* Jews, and later urging Jews to "accept Christ's principles of brotherhood."[11] The United States's Jews politely declined the invitation.

Pro-fascist and antisemitic ideologies, much of which was open in its admiration for Adolf Hitler and eugenics, were catching on across the country. And these attitudes weren't on the fringes of the fringe—they remained remarkably popular even as war loomed in Europe. Twenty thousand people filled Madison Square Garden on February 20, 1939, for an anti-interventionist "pro-Americanism" rally hosted by the pro-Nazi German American Bund. With huge swastika banners flanking a massive portrait of George Washington, Nazi-uniformed Americans screamed to the crowd how Washington would have been friends with Hitler, Jews controlled the media and Hollywood, and it was time to "Wake up! You, Aryan, Nordic and Christians, to demand that our government be returned to the people who founded it!"[12]

The unabashed pro-Hitler stance of anti-interventionists goose-stepped right alongside similar antisemitic sentiments from both American politicians and the public at large. The prewar years were something of a high watermark for American antisemitism, based on a deeply rooted belief that American Jews were pushing the West toward a new war with Germany that would be as devastating as the last one.

Polling taken in both 1940 and 1942 showed that significant percentages of Americans believed that Hitler was "doing the right thing" in regard to German Jews, saw Jews as a national menace to the United States due to their perceived desire for war, and would even have supported a widespread "campaign against the Jews" in the US should one ever start.[13]

As always, proponents of the new wave of antisemitism pumped out an endless stream of content to keep followers fearful and angry. Locally produced anti-Jewish tracts circulated to small but enthusiastic followings who met in person to discuss what they could do to push back against communist infiltration and Jewish control. They could be found on both coasts. A Los Angeles pamphlet dubbed *Christocracy* demanded that the "Jewish Rothschild Talmudic system" be demolished to give each unemployed man $25[14]; meanwhile, issues of the New York–based pro-Nazi newsletter "American Bulletin" (offering "the White Man's Viewpoint") heaped praise on National Socialism and the *Protocols* while attacking the "Jewish Super-Government" and those who funded it. Issues of the crudely illustrated rag singled out N. M. Rothschild as "one of the quintuplets of world finance [who] have boasted that they control the world's gold supply"[15] and claimed without evidence that "Mussolini's son-in-law Count Ciano, Minister of Press and Propaganda, is an intimate friend of the Rothschilds."[16]

These newsletters would often advertise popular anti-Rothschild books such as *The Secret World Government, The Rothschilds: Financial Rulers of Nations*, and *World Revolution*, among others. The German invasion of Poland set off another wave of explicitly anti-Rothschild books and pamphlets, many liberally quoting both the *Protocols* and the works inspired by that falsehood, all seemingly devoted to keeping the US out of the conflict. Their authors each put their own spin on the story, but they tended to share a few traits—they were deeply isolationist, openly supported Hitler and Mussolini, decried communism, and blamed a deeply rooted and ancient Jewish plan for the current economic crisis and march toward global conflict.

FASCISTS HERE AND ABROAD

Elizabeth Dilling had already made a name for herself with her books *The Red Network* and *The Roosevelt Red Record*, purporting to expose thousands of communists in the upper reaches of American politics and industry—to the point where she'd inspired a character in Sinclair Lewis's 1936 dystopian novel *It Can't Happen Here*. In 1940, Dilling self-published her next book,

The Octopus, under the pseudonym "Rev. Frank Woodruff Johnson," fully turning her attention to Jewish power in the United States. Dilling posited that the Rothschilds were part of a Jewish alliance with J. P. Morgan (who was not Jewish) "to prevent the shipment of gold from [the US] to Europe," while being linked by marriage or investment to countless other major German Jewish banking figures. The result was a kind of mythical creature with total control over world finance—akin to "Coin" Harvey's 1894 cartoon of an English Rothschild octopus grabbing control of every other nation. Like Harvey's bestselling pamphlet, *The Octopus* was popular enough to be reprinted long after Dilling's death, with new editions sold well into the 1980s.[17]

Initially published anonymously because its author feared indictment, George Washington Armstrong's 1940 book *Rothschild Money Trust* was one of many tracts in which the former Texas judge "expressed his frequently controversial views, which included advocacy for the repeal of the Fourteenth and Fifteenth amendments, anti-Zionism, anti-Communism, and strong support for segregation and the doctrine of White supremacy," as one biography put it years later.[18] Armstrong had been a wealthy oilman in the first decades of the twentieth century but went bust after the Great War and blamed it on the machinations of Nathan Mayer Rothschild, who had been dead for a century.[19]

In *Rothschild Money Trust*, Armstrong joins other contemporary writers in tying various strands of conspiracy together to form a narrative that seems both cutting edge and deeply rooted in the past. He rehashes the old tropes about the partnership that "First King of the Jews" Mayer Amschel entered into with his sons and claims the family wants nothing less than a "Jewish world empire" through "subjugation" and "debt slavery of the goyim."[20] But he also attacks contemporary Jews for changing their names and makes ludicrous claims like the family having $500 billion in wealth—a number that would be repeated later in countless internet memes, with a few zeroes added on.[21]

And after helping to establish the America First Committee, journalist John T. Flynn wrote the 1941 book *Men of Wealth: The Story of Twelve Significant Fortunes from the Renaissance to the Present Day*, in which he spent an entire chapter calling the Rothschild sons "coarse, unlettered, graceless, [...] vulgar, ignorant Jews" who "sought money not to enjoy power; but power in order to make money."[22] But even while savaging the Rothschilds, Flynn simultaneously attempts to downplay their wealth, writing that by 1940, no Rothschild had any major role in any prominent London bank, and that their railroad and mining empires were vastly exaggerated.[23] Despite his isolationist proclivities, Flynn immediately abandoned the America First Committee after the Japanese attack on Hawaii, fully embracing anti-communist and anti–New Deal hysteria. He later wrote *The Truth About Pearl Harbor*, alleging a conspiracy theory that the Roosevelt administration provoked Japan into attacking the Hawaiian naval base, which he believed had deliberately been left defenseless, to get the US into the war.[24]

On the other side of the Atlantic, British fascist and *Protocols* devotee Arnold Leese wrote *Gentile Folly: The Rothschilds*, a self-published pamphlet written to "expose a small fraction of the total evil done by certain members of this Jewish family in the past."[25] Readers of *Gentile Folly* would find the same repackaged tropes along with the deranged accusation that "one of the saddest reflections that Aryan patriots must suffer is in the recognition that Royalty in Europe has gradually succumbed to the influence of the money of the Rothschild family."[26] Shortly after publishing his pamphlet, Leese would be arrested.

But there may be no better-known World War II–era Rothschild conspiracist than the poet Ezra Pound. Already famous as a pioneer of modernist poetry and his editing and championing of contemporaries like James Joyce and T. S. Eliot, a disillusioned Pound blamed the carnage of the Great War on Jewish usury. Moving to Italy, he enthusiastically supported both Mussolini and Hitler, wrote countless articles, made numerous pro-fascist radio broadcasts, and published rambling diatribes holding Mussolini up as a paragon of virtue. Pound began to see Jews less as individuals and more as a race who "deserve all the kicks they get."[27]

As Pound's support of fascism hardened, his poetry and letters became full of references to Jewish power, greed, control of the media, physical deformities, diseases and sexual depravity, and the undue influence Jews had over finance and politics. He wrote hundreds of letters trying to keep the US out of the war and targeted the Rothschilds as the chief usurers of Europe who had kept the English as a "slave race" since Waterloo, were plunging Europe into war to keep their gold monopoly and get revenge on Germany, and employed a senile Churchill as their public front. At one point, he even exchanged letters with fellow antisemite Arnold Leese.[28]

But it was in Pound's never-completed *Cantos*, the series of poems he'd write on and off for his entire life, that the poet truly savaged Jews and the Rothschilds. Pound used the *Cantos* to accuse the Rothschilds of starting the Civil War by tricking the American people into endorsing the country's division, focuses on them as the kingpins of Jewish war profiteering and usury, refers to the family name as "Stinkschuld" who are "paying for a few big jews [sic] vendetta on goyim" ("schuld" roughly translates as "debt" in German, which some scholars see as Pound approving of the blood libel), and attacks the "spawn of Mayer Anselm" [sic].[29]

Pound's attacks on the Rothschilds were so acidic that even T. S. Eliot was concerned about the poet's potential exposure for a libel suit, writing "if you remain keen on jew-baiting [sic], that is your affair, but that name of Rothschild should be omitted." Pound's publisher did censor references to the family in his works until the late 1960s.[30] Pound was arrested for treason at the end of the war but proclaimed that he was not an antisemite, only deeply opposed to Jewish usury (a sentiment many Pound scholars agree with), and spent the next decade in a mental hospital. A slew of biographies would later attempt to reconcile Pound's seemingly boundless support of fascism with his literary genius. In an ironic twist, one of these revisionist biographies was the 1960 book *This Difficult Individual, Ezra Pound*, written by antisemitic conspiracy theorist Eustace Mullins, whose *Secrets of the Federal Reserve* was a postwar touchstone linking the Rothschilds to global financial control through central banking—and which was essentially commissioned and financed by Pound himself.

THE *HOUSE OF ROTHSCHILD* FIASCO

The first motion picture specifically about the Rothschilds was likely the 1922 German biopic *The Five Frankfurters*. That film, in turn, was adapted from a 1912 play of the same name deemed "a cruel satire on that famous banking family" by *The New York Times*.[31] The year 1934 would see two films that touched on the Rothschilds. One was a mostly forgotten French comedy called *Rothchild* about a vagrant who exploits his coincidental last name to enjoy the good life that real Rothschilds were seen as living.[32] The other was the Oscar-nominated Hollywood biography *The House of Rothschild*, which would become one of the most important and infamous films in prewar Hollywood history.

When upstart producer Darryl F. Zanuck launched Twentieth Century Pictures, he enticed a number of stars to join him, including the veteran British actor George Arliss. Together, they saw an opportunity to tell a dramatic and affirming Jewish story just as the rest of the film industry backed away from dramatizing the growing persecution of German Jews. In particular, studios had balked at producing a script called *The Mad Dog of Europe*, written by future *Citizen Kane* scribe Herman J. Mankiewicz and brutally depicting Hitler's rise to power—and which would have portrayed the dictator himself onscreen for the first time. Hollywood particularly feared the loss of the critical German film market, remembering that Nazi brownshirts had rioted and ransacked theaters in 1930 when the Hollywood adaptation of *All Quiet on the Western Front* had been released, with the film quickly banned in the Reich. There was also growing antisemitic backlash and the open embrace of the Nazis in general and fascism at large in the US. So the Mankiewicz script was never made, and both the tumult of rising fascism and the danger it presented to European Jews started becoming off-limits for storytelling.[33]

Arliss, who had just come off playing Benjamin Disraeli in an Oscar-winning performance, had discovered a play about the rise of the Rothschilds, and Zanuck saw it as an opportunity to make an explicitly anti-Nazi, pro-Jewish statement. While Zanuck had produced Jewish-themed films like *The Jazz Singer*, neither he nor Arliss were Jews, which seemingly put them in the right position to make such a film without risking angering either German interests or the Jewish advocacy group the Anti-Defamation League, which had opposed producing *The Mad Dog of Europe* on the grounds that Gentiles should be the ones leading the Hollywood fight against the Nazis.[34]

Zanuck, Arliss, director Alfred Werker, and screenwriter Nunnally Johnson all took pains to tell an affirmational story about the tenacity of Jews in the face of overwhelming antisemitism. But looked at today, their efforts come off as deeply rooted in generations of tropes. Mayer (played by Arliss, who also played Nathan later in the film) is shown as both a victim of organized persecution and as a conniving schemer, with his first lines in the film seeing him rub his hands together, whispering, "If anything should happen . . . all that money . . ." when told that a shipment of coins is running late. Later, Mayer fumes about a cheating customer who'd given him a fake coin (revealed as phony when Gutle bites on it) being provided "some of the *good* wine!" The family then learns the crooked Frankfurt tax collector is coming and goes through a frantic rush to hide the trappings of their wealth so as to not be extorted, only to be extorted anyway.

To play Mayer, Arliss had studied the Rothschild biographies by Egon Caesar Corti, which were full of inaccuracies and exaggerations.[35] And those exaggerations make their way into the film. After Mayer learns his shipment has been intercepted by the scheming Frankfurt tax collector, he pounds on a table, exclaiming, "Money is the only weapon the Jew has to defend himself with," before collapsing. On his deathbed, Mayer tells his sons to go to the five financial capitols of Europe and ensure warring nations have safe access to gold, while emphasizing loyalty, unity, and, above all, dignity. "To trade with dignity, to live with dignity, to walk the world with dignity," a dying Mayer gasps to his young sons, with his five daughters omitted from the script.[36]

The film then skips several decades and quite a bit of history. It invents a schmaltzy romance between Nathan's daughter Julie and one of Wellington's officers, a Captain Fitzroy. Meanwhile, Nathan purposefully creates a panic on the London Stock Exchange *before* Waterloo to bankrupt his business rivals, chiefly a fictional antisemitic count (played by horror legend Boris Karloff, a few years removed from his star-making role in *Frankenstein*) who laughs at the news of pogroms reducing Jewish communities to ashes, and who demands Nathan be arrested.[37]

But when Napoleon escapes exile and returns to the continent, the leaders of Europe must beg Nathan to fund their war—and Nathan demands total emancipation of the Jews as his price. Faced with the near collapse of the British economy and anti-Jewish riots due to Napoleon's rampage, Nathan singlehandedly props up the Stock Exchange with his money, even as rumors of Wellington's defeat at Waterloo send the Exchange into a panic. Ultimately, Nathan gets the news of Napoleon's defeat first, brought by pigeon post and delivered by his trusty agent Rothworth, naturally. He triumphantly announces it to the Exchange, thunderous applause ensues, and, as a reward, Nathan is made a baron, and the Rothschilds become the richest family on earth. The heroic Jew has saved Europe with his courage and business acumen, as the film subtly hints that money can buy peace, if you have enough of it.[38]

Almost none of this actually happened in the way the film presents. Just in one example, Nathan's *sister* was named Julie, and while Nathan did have a daughter who married an English politician named Henry FitzRoy, he was eight during the Battle of Waterloo and did not serve in Wellington's army. But Zanuck didn't intend to accurately portray the Rothschilds—he intended to tell a story about the dignity of Jews, the truth about their reputation as financial savants, and the danger they faced from the Nazis. The Anti-Defamation League saw it differently. They deemed that the film's depiction of Nathan and his brothers as conniving Jewish bankers making Christian leaders beg for money to fight a righteous war could imperil Jews both in the United States and Germany. And they were rightly concerned about the film's first scenes, in which Mayer is played as a miserly trickster.[39]

Even with their concerns, the Anti-Defamation League never publicly protested the film. *The House of Rothschild* opened in March 1934, and its box office success helped Zanuck get Twentieth Century Pictures off the ground, propelling it to merge with Fox Studios the next year. Reviews and audiences seemed to understand the true purpose of the film, even with the unfortunate portrayal of Mayer, with *The Hollywood Reporter* singling out Nathan's demands as "[bringing] about the treaties whereby his people were to be recognized as human beings with human feelings for humanity."[40] It even received an Academy Award nomination for Best Picture the next year, losing out to Frank Capra's *It Happened One Night*.

Hollywood didn't view this success as the impetus to make more explicitly pro-Jewish, anti-Nazi films, though. Instead, still hoping to hang on to the German market and avoid potential domestic unrest, portrayals of Judaism were drastically reduced in Hollywood product for the rest of the decade—to the point where Jewish themes, humor, stories, and characters were censored for German versions of films, removed from scripts, or outright banned in Hollywood. Jewish actors struggled to find work, and Jewish screenwriters openly wondered where the portrayals of their coreligionists had gone.[41]

It was simply too important for Hollywood to have access to German audiences, and too difficult for Jewish artists to have their concerns taken seriously. While many individual filmmakers and artists were vocally anti-Nazi, and several explicitly Jewish-themed films were made in Britain over the next few years, it would be 1939 before the United States produced what could be considered its first explicitly anti-Hitler film, Warner Bros.' *Confessions of a Nazi Spy*. Less than six months later, Nazi Germany invaded Poland, and the film industry's opposition to dramatizing the danger of the Third Reich was rendered moot.

"THIS JEWRY MUST BE ANNIHILATED"

The success of *The House of Rothschild* actually *did* inflame American antisemitism, particularly of prolific American fascist William Dudley Pelley. Once a respected author and screenwriter, Pelley's career had stalled, with him believing it was due to Jewish interference. Like Nesta Webster, Pelley would be mentioned in *It Can't Happen Here* as a producer of the "grand literature" favored by the book's burgeoning American dictator

Buzz Windrip, and was an avowed fascist and occultist. Pelley founded his pro-Nazi paramilitary organization the Silver Legion of America just after Hitler took power, and went to work pumping out an inexhaustible stream of newsletters and other written content. Writing with a strong bent toward combining the baser aspects of patriotism with concerns of the metaphysical realm, Pelley was an advocate of everything from secret Jewish bankrolling of the Bolshevik Revolution to Jewish control of Gentile minds through vaccines and illegal drugs.[42]

Pelley made it clear that he was no fan of the Rothschilds, linking them to the proposed dividing of the United States during the Civil War, and finding an admirer in Ezra Pound, who espoused a version of the Rothschild/Disraeli theory in the *Cantos*.[43] Writing about *The House of Rothschild* in his periodical *Liberation*, Pelley attacked not just the Rothschilds but their biographers, chiefly George Arliss. Pelley deemed "poor old" Arliss a "Jewish propagandist" for playing Mayer and Nathan, and claimed he had thrown his lot in with the "fur dealers from Grand Street and the pants pressers from Milwaukee" in a plot to corrupt Christian American morals by using subliminal messages on moviegoers whose "defenses are down" to show Jews as humans worthy of dignity.[44] Ironically, Arliss would go on to portray the main character in an English remake of the French comedy *Rothchild* that same year, retitled *The Guv'nor*.

But if Pelley was distraught about *The House of Rothschild*, his counterparts in Germany were ecstatic. Nazi consuls in the US and London were especially enthusiastic, seeing its portrayal of Mayer's life in the *Judengasse* as "the truth" about Jews—they were greedy, sniveling rats who had taken control of European finance through duplicity and warmongering.[45] With the Nazi government surprised by public indifference to the *Kristallnacht* pogrom of November 1938, propaganda minister Joseph Goebbels demanded a new type of film that would combine historical antisemitism with Nazi politics, using the Hollywood films that Hitler loved so much as their guide.[46]

Like with the explosion of anti-Jewish, anti-Rothschild books in the US in 1940, the year was a banner one for the German film industry pushing Jew-baiting hate. In particular, Nazi studios released three films that year that have been deemed among the most antisemitic ever made, all rooted in classic anti-Jewish conspiracy theories that at least touch on the Rothschilds. And they were immeasurably helped by the 1934 film that they believed exposed the family's true nature.

The first and most impactful was a Nazi-fied adaptation of *Jew Süss*, with screenwriter Eberhard Wolfgang Möller turning Joseph Süss Oppenheimer's misfortune into a repulsive, Jew-baiting box office hit. Goebbels intended the film as a response to the 1934 British film of the same name starring Conrad Veidt, turning Oppenheimer into a greedy rapist who almost singlehandedly plunges his hapless duke's land into civil war. And the Nazi propaganda chief got what he wanted—as many as twenty million Germans saw the film, it caused immediate spasms of antisemitic violence in territories under Reich control, and it was screened as a morale booster for SS troopers and concentration camp personnel.[47]

The others, *The Eternal Jew* and *The Rothschilds' Shares in Waterloo*, would take the successful Zanuck production and mutate it for their own purposes, one by twisting its story into a negative of itself, the other simply by stealing footage from it—a copyright violation that surely ranks as one of the Nazi regime's lesser crimes. They didn't have the financial success or cultural impact of the Nazi take on Oppenheimer's story, but together they formed a core of works that clearly show Nazi Germany in transition from simple oppression of Jews to outright dehumanizing, particularly against Jews in newly conquered European nations.

The Rothschilds' Shares in Waterloo inverts the 1934 film and makes Nathan the villain, akin to telling the story of the *Titanic* from the point of view of the heroic iceberg. It begins with a text crawl describing how the "international Jewish House of Rothschilds" made its fortune off the Landgrave of Hesse and used it to "pave the way for the Jewish overtaking of England." From there, it creates a funhouse mirror version of the Rothschild rise to power, with Jews portrayed as devious and greedy schemers, and Nathan singled out as a thieving weasel who shamelessly attempts to romance another banker's wife, concocts a scheme to steal the Elector's gold meant to finance Wellington's army, is chased out of a room by a dog, and at one point declares "dignity costs money," directly rebuking the George Arliss portrayal of Mayer.[48]

With Napoleon's escape leading to the Battle of Waterloo, Nathan bribes his sniveling agents to get him the news of the outcome first. Sure enough, Rothworth (played here as a hapless drunk) crosses the Channel and brings news of Napoleon's crushing defeat—and gets cheated out of his prize for his trouble. Nathan then creates panic at the Exchange with a fake story of Napoleon smashing Wellington's forces, sparking a massive sell-off, which Nathan's agents greedily exploit. Nathan makes 11 million pounds, "enough to buy England!" he exclaims, his eyes bugged out with greed, with his rivals left either wiped out or dead of heart attacks. With his ill-gotten fortune made, Nathan draws a map of his brothers in the financial centers of Europe, all connected by a Star of David that bursts into flames, augmented by text that while the last of the Rothschilds have fled Europe as refugees, the struggle against their compatriots in "the British plutocracy" goes on.[49]

The film was a middling success financially, but missed the mark in attempting to fuse the Rothschilds and the English as one entity. One German reviewer, who gushes over the film's historical accuracy as painting the Rothschilds as a "rash [that] covered all of Europe," allows that even the other English bankers detest Nathan, showing a disunity in Jews that wasn't pleasing to German audiences used to propaganda presenting Jews as a monolithic block.[50] But even the obvious antisemitism of *The Rothschilds* paled in comparison to *The Eternal Jew*. Billed as a documentary and fusing footage taken in actual Jewish ghettos in newly conquered Poland with a fusillade of attacks on worldwide Jewry, *The Eternal Jew* was so important to the Nazi propaganda effort that its production was personally supervised by Goebbels in response to a rebuke by Hitler that Germany hadn't made a proper antisemitic film. It became the enduring symbol of the Nazi drive to purge Jews from the Earth.[51]

The film was named after the legend of the immortal wandering Jew who taunted Christ on the road to the Crucifixion and was doomed to

roam the world until the Second Coming. The legend has been a part of antisemitic lore since the thirteenth century, and had been used as the title of
Goebbels's "degenerate art" exhibition of just a few years earlier. It would
have been as familiar to Reich filmgoers as the conspiracy theories about
both Oppenheimer and Nathan Rothschild's big score at Waterloo. But
even Nazi audiences likely weren't entirely ready for *The Eternal Jew*'s onslaught of racism, disgusting and shocking images, and white-hot hate.

The Eternal Jew is sixty-five minutes of relentless visual and verbal violence against the Jewish people—a race it deems "a plague on the Aryan
people." In cold, detached narration, Jews are presented as uncivilized demons, corruptors, and hoarders of wealth who dwell in "filthy and neglected"
homes passed down from generation to generation. Their physical labor is
useless, as Jews "don't want to work, but barter" because their "religion makes
cheating and usury a duty" and only money has any value to them.[52]

The film then tells a distorted history of the Jews wandering and plundering their way from Egypt through Europe, race mixing with "Orientals
and negroids," cheating and looting everywhere they went, until they found
Eastern Europe and eventually the rest of the world—much like the plague
rat, carrying its filth and disease with it. Finally, after twenty minutes of relentless attacks on the Jews, *The Eternal Jew* introduces some of the only
Jews it mentions by name—the Rothschilds.[53]

"Here we show a scene from a film about the Rothschild family," the
narrator intones. "It was made by American Jews [sic], obviously as a tribute to one of the greatest names in Jewish history"—then cut right to scenes
from *The House of Rothschild*, showing Mayer scheming, his family hiding
their wealth from the tax collector, and the patriarch plotting to send his
sons to the financial capitols of Europe. They were the same scenes that the
Anti-Defamation League had decried a few years earlier, and sure enough,
they were being used to inflame anti-Jewish hatred.[54]

But that's only the start of *The Eternal Jew*'s hatemongering. The film
continues by claiming that the House of Rothschild "is only one example of
the Jews' tactic of casting their net of financial influence over the working
man." It attacks every aspect of Jewish culture, art, religion, family, science,

education, and hygiene and even claims Jews are incapable of sympathy to animals, bolstered by graphic footage of Jews ritually slaughtering animals—footage that reportedly horrified Hitler when he saw it.

Naturally, the cure for this plague can only be the leadership of Adolf Hitler, who has "raised the battle flag against the eternal Jew," a statement punctuated with shots of lantern-jawed, Aryan young men staring off into the distance.[55] And as Hitler makes clear in a January 30, 1939, speech shown in the film, if international Jewish finance pushes the world into another war, the result will be "the annihilation of the Jewish race in Europe," with the crowd lavishing him with applause. In that same speech, Hitler takes aim at Hollywood's first attempts to truly address the Nazi menace, films like *Confessions of a Nazi Spy*, declaring that German filmmakers would only be creating "antisemitic films in the future."[56]

Despite its release in cinemas across the Reich, *The Eternal Jew* was a box-office flop. Apparently, it was too much even for German audiences. But its legacy endures—not in other films it inspired or any kind of affection from viewers, but in the effect it had on Nazi leadership. When Goebbels, who oversaw the production of *The Eternal Jew* and personally gave director Fritz Hippler notes and ideas, saw thirty minutes of staged ritual slaughter shot for the film in October 1939, he was shocked. The next day, he wrote in his diary of "scenes so horrific and brutal in their explicitness that one's blood runs cold. One shudders at such barbarism. This Jewry must be annihilated."[57]

On May 20, 1940, Hitler, who had seen multiple cuts of the film and was also shocked by its "frank" depictions of Jewish life, signed paperwork allowing it to be publicly screened. Apart from any single document from the Fuhrer ordering the Holocaust, that approval served as his written endorsement of the idea of Jews as vermin who must be exterminated for the Aryan race to survive.

A few months later, *The Eternal Jew*, featuring both that "horrific" footage and Hitler's declaration that another war would mean the annihilation of the Jews of Europe, hit German cinemas. At the same time, Germany was dealing with an influx of Jews as it conquered territories while planning even further invasions of countries with large Jewish populations—chiefly the republics of the Soviet Union. Something needed to be done about these people, and the German people were coming around to it, so the lack of box office receipts for *The Eternal Jew* is beside the point. Taken with the other blatantly Jew-baiting films of that year, along with the great mass of newspapers, art exhibits, plays, and books relentlessly attacking the Jews—and the Rothschilds in particular—the German people had their orders, knew their enemy, and understood what they had to do and why they had to do it.

THE ROTHSCHILDS DURING WORLD WAR II

Contrary to the deluge of propaganda unleashed by the Nazis, the Rothschilds were not annihilated, nor did they all flee Europe as refugees—though many did leave Europe, having the means to run that so many other Jews didn't. But murder was just one part of the Nazi repression of the Jewish people; theft was another. As the most visible Jewish family in Europe, they were a prime target for the regime's sticky fingers. So while the family escaped the industrialized murder machine, they did suffer incalculable losses in property and possessions thanks to wholesale Nazi plundering of their estates and business holdings, many of which have never been made good.

The looting reached a fever pitch once Germany annexed Austria in March 1938. Institutions in both nations that had been named after the Rothschilds were renamed in a process of "Aryanization," their charitable foundations were wound down or stolen, and their ancestral lands and homes were seized. The family's five mansions in Vienna were taken, with one used by infamous Holocaust perpetrator Adolf Eichmann's Office of Jewish Emigration and another employed as a Gestapo interrogation center before being damaged beyond repair by Allied bombs—the same fate that befell most of the old *Judengasse*. The vast hunting ground of the Austrian Rothschilds, a parcel as big as Manhattan, was taken as well, as were countless offices, industrial buildings and machines, artworks, jewels, and priceless possessions. Some were "bought" by the Nazis for far less than they were worth, with "atonement payments" tacked on by the Nazi government to make Jews pay for the damage done by Nazi looting. Most was just taken, and much of the plunder was lost for good.[58]

When the German army invaded France in May of 1940, the same situation played out for the French Rothschilds. German troops entering Paris were ordered to confiscate Rothschild possessions, French Rothschild homes were used as military installations, and high-ranking SS men were personally put in charge of finding priceless artworks that family members had managed to hide. The Nazi looting of Rothschild collections was part of one of the biggest and most organized thefts of art in history—nearly four thousand Rothschild paintings and sculptures were taken, with many personally selected for plunder by *Luftwaffe* head Hermann Goering, who kept many and gave others to Hitler himself. And like the losses incurred by the Austrian Rothschilds, some of it was never found.[59]

At a time when international Jewry needed the resources of the Rothschilds more than ever, the Rothschilds needed what they had simply to survive. A number of them were forced to sell or leave behind everything they owned, essentially becoming destitute. Many family members saw the danger looming and got out early, emigrating to the United States, the UK, Canada, or neutral nations. But those who stayed behind were subject to the same constant danger and oppression as any other European Jew, even if few were directly imprisoned. The Nazis' worst treatment was reserved for Louis Nathaniel de Rothschild, great-grandson of Vienna branch founder Salomon and former president of the now infamous *Creditanstalt* bank— the place where the banking contagion that took down Europe began.

After transferring his Austrian assets to various trusts, including a controlling stake in the massive Czech-based Witkowitz Ironworks, Louis attempted to flee Vienna as German troops marched in on March 11, 1938. Instead, he was arrested and taken to the local Gestapo headquarters, with SS men immediately descending on his Palais to pick it clean.[60] Thus would begin a lengthy and expensive hostage negotiation, as the Nazis attempted to seize control of the ironworks through Louis's stake. Public demand for Louis to be punished for his role in the banking crisis was high, with a

Vienna *Völkischer Beobachter* article a week after the arrest demanding that Louis be held captive until he personally made good on the losses suffered by *Creditanstalt.*[61]

After nearly fourteen months in captivity, at least some of which was personally supervised by SS head Heinrich Himmler, Louis finally secured his release by paying the equivalent of $21 million—over $400 million adjusted for inflation—in what's likely the largest hostage ransom ever paid. He was able to "sell" the ironworks to the Nazis, but the payment was never made, and the Germans simply seized its shares and incorporated it into their industrial machine. Louis left Austria for the United States, and it wasn't until 1999 that the Austrian government finally returned the remains of his looted art collection to his descendants.[62]

With the Rothschilds on the run and their banking empire in tatters, the family played no role financing the war—and certainly didn't finance "both sides" of the conflagration, as future conspiracy theories would allege. But many Rothschilds served in uniform and saw active combat, while Rothschild properties in England were used in service of the war effort. And while no blood relative of Mayer died during the Holocaust, two members of the extended Rothschild family fell victim to the killing machine. Élisabeth de Rothschild, the estranged (and once Catholic) wife of French winemaker Philippe de Rothschild, was the only actual holder of a Rothschild name to die, killed in Ravensbruck concentration camp in 1945 after her arrest for a forged passport.[63] And Aranka von Werthemstein, the sister-in-law of N. M. Rothschild partner Charles Rothschild, was beaten to death by SS guards as she stepped off the train upon her deportation to Auschwitz in May 1944.[64]

The rest of the family would spend years or decades trying to get back what it had lost. And the Rothschild name entered a postwar world where the myths about its wealth and power far outstripped their actual wealth and power—not that the mythmakers would notice.

CALLING ALL CRACKPOTS: ROTHSCHILD CONSPIRACY THEORIES IN THE POSTWAR WORLD

After the war, the fight against fascism quickly transformed into a struggle against a different kind of world domination: communism. Both the Western public and their political leaders were rightly concerned about the expansion of the Soviet sphere of influence into Eastern Europe and the danger of Soviet proxy governments in once-occupied nations like Poland and Hungary. There was also legitimate fear of the growth of communist parties in France, Italy, and Greece. But for a certain type of Western anti-communist politician, preacher, and writer, the battle was seen not as a clash of economic or social philosophies, but in entirely apocalyptic and cosmic terms.

The Cold War was a life and death struggle to save the United States (and, to a lesser extent, the rest of the world) from the Red nightmare of "one world government," which would mean forced wealth distribution, the elimination of freedom, and the mass murder of dissenters. Inevitably, this fear of Bolshevism curdled into a fear of Judeo-Bolshevism, since the two were inextricably linked for so many. The postwar years would see anti-communist paranoia walk hand in hand with Jewish scapegoating, leading to an almost unrelenting hysteria over Jewish intellectuals "given orders by Moscow" to infiltrate the US government, entertainment, and academia. Nobody was safe, and "they" were everywhere.

Like before, this menace had many names: the "unseen hand," the "insiders," the "Round Table," the "Jewish super-government," "the Illuminati," "the New World Order," and countless others. It was run through a slew of interlocking front groups and think tanks: the Council on Foreign Relations, the Trilateral Commission, the Bilderberg Group, and so forth. And it was funded by the very top of the Jewish wealth pyramid: the Rothschilds and their allies.

As always, where hate grew, grift blossomed. Some new conspiracy pundits were more focused on secular "economic antisemitism," while others explicitly pushed Christian nationalism, espousing religious authoritarianism in the guise of defending liberty. But they had common themes: the ever-approaching takeover by the global government, the pollution of American values with leftist godlessness, and the penetration by communist agents into the upper reaches of Western life. And the Rothschilds were always there, silently pulling the strings in the shadows, pitting everyone against everyone else, and driving the world ever closer to a final Satanic/Illuminati takeover.

REBUILDING FROM THE ASHES

Despite the horrors of the Holocaust, there was no immediate postwar "era of good feelings" for the Jewish people.

For one, even with the depth of Jewish suffering revealed with the liberation of the camps, many Europeans still distrusted Jews. Even though Germany made Holocaust denial and the displaying of Nazi symbols illegal, polling of Germans in 1947 revealed that as many as three-quarters still believed Jews were of a different and lesser race, while a sizable minority still believed their nation would be better off without its Jewish population. And not all nations were willing to go as far as Germany did in the immediate aftermath of the war to denounce totalitarianism. Mussolini's fascist legacy was immediately carried forward by a new far-right Italian political party, while Austria dragged its feet for decades about returning Jewish property to Holocaust victims.[1]

Antisemitism didn't disappear within the Allied nations, either. French society continued to question Jewish loyalty, while the August bank holiday in 1947 saw violent riots and organized vandalism against Jewish businesses and synagogues in Liverpool, Glasgow, and London after a Jewish resistance movement killed two British officers in Palestine. But the most perilous moment for Jews in the immediate postwar years was when Stalin embarked on a vicious campaign against "rootless cosmopolitanism"—the same "crime" the Rothschilds were often accused of. It began with the mass arrest of Jewish physicians in Moscow who were baselessly accused of plotting rebellion, and it might have gone even further, into potential genocide. According to multiple scholars, Stalin was making plans to use the "Doctors' Plot" as the "crisis" he needed to deport the USSR's entire Jewish population to Siberia. Only his death in 1953 halted the organized repression of Jews in the Eastern Bloc.[2]

The popularity of US anti-Jewish sentiment mostly faded once the war started, as American isolationists found that parents who'd sent their boys off to fight Hitler weren't interested in being ranted at about the economic advantages of National Socialism. The war silenced many of the most prolific antisemitic thinkers of the time, who were either arrested or almost instantly lost their followings.[3] And Hollywood's moratorium on Jewish themes ended with the declaration of war against Germany and Japan as the entertainment industry fully joined the war effort. In particular, *House of Rothschild* producer Darryl Zanuck would take his rejection from a Hollywood country club for being Jewish (which he wasn't) and use it as the inspiration for the 1947 film *Gentleman's Agreement*, a blunt examination of the banal nature of antisemitism in upper-class America, which won him a Best Picture Oscar.

The time, it seemed, had finally come for the United States to "look at that curious, archaic aberration, anti-Semitism—as it exists not in darkest Naziland, nor among our own lunatic fringe, but among Americans of good will—the nice lady in the next seat—yes, one suspects uneasily, even oneself," as a contemporary review of the film in the once-leftist Jewish cultural magazine *Commentary* put it.[4]

As for the Rothschilds, life went on, though much diminished in both business and status. Contrary to countless conspiracy theories that the Rothschilds profited off both sides in the Second World War, the three remaining centers of Rothschild activity—Paris, Vienna, and London—had all suffered from either occupation or sustained bombing. The Paris branch would successfully resume business, but the Austrian house was forced to close for good, with most of its assets never returned. In London, N. M. Rothschild hung on but was severely hampered by the continuation of wartime restrictions on capital exports, particularly gold. The firm finally would do the unthinkable in 1960—admit non-Rothschilds into the partnership and focus more on domestic banking and acquisition.[5]

The Rothschild surname still evoked connotations of wealth and opulence, and would still serve as a stand-in for wealthy, powerful Jews in both legitimate art and crank nonsense. But their days of influencing global politics with their loans and gold shipments were long over—except to those determined to live in the past and apply it to the present.

As the American far-right ascended in the 1950s, Rothschild conspiracy theories continued to be a powerful driver of antisemitism and regressive politics. In particular, the unevidenced idea that the Rothschilds "owned" the Federal Reserve, and therefore dominated American monetary policy, would become especially lucrative for postwar cranks. The works centered on that conspiracy theory remain deeply influential even to this day and set the stage for a new generation of rabid Jew-hatred, more popular than ever.

THE SECRETS OF EUSTACE MULLINS

Just as Bob Dylan's 1961 visit to an institutionalized Woody Guthrie would have profound reverberations in popular culture, so too would the 1949 visits of young conspiracy theorist Eustace Mullins to institutionalized "political prisoner" Ezra Pound for postwar paranoid culture. Mullins's book *Secrets of the Federal Reserve* would cement the idea that the Rothschilds were pivotal players in the vast plot to enslave the United States through central banking. And according to Mullins himself, it was Ezra Pound who directly commissioned Mullins to write what Pound suggested be crafted as a "detective story" of finding out who "really" controlled our money.

Born in 1923, Eustace Mullins began cultivating antisemitic conspiracy theories as a journalist, claiming that by 1947 he'd already "predicted that if the Zionists gained control of the U.S. Military, the world would be plunged into endless wars, culminating in worldwide control by Israel."[6] In 1949, after a chance meeting with the poet's wife, Mullins began exchanging letters with Pound. They drew on the one thing they had in common above all other: loathing of Jews. Mullins wrote on letterhead of the Aryan League of America about how "THE JEWS ARE BETRAYING US," and the two joked about burning a synagogue down, among other inanities.[7]

Institutionalized at St. Elizabeths Hospital in Washington, D.C., Pound was a figure of curiosity for characters on the fringe, receiving all manner of hangers-on and visitors. In turn, Pound continued to recommend they read *The Protocols of the Elders of Zion* as a vetted explanation for what was "really" going on. Mullins's version of how Pound opened his eyes is a classic conspiracy theory conversion story that wouldn't be out of place in a Facebook group today: Pound asked if the young man knew anything about the Federal Reserve System. Mullins said he didn't, then claims Pound "showed me a ten-dollar bill marked 'Federal Reserve Note' and asked me if I would do some research at the Library of Congress on the Federal Reserve System."[8]

Funded to the tune of ten dollars a week by Pound, Mullins began "doing his own research" and uncovered a shocking secret, hidden in plain sight: that an international Jewish cartel, led by the Rothschilds, controlled the United States's central bank, the Federal Reserve. The Fed, in turn, held the United States's debt to other nations—which was being "paid off" by illegally extorted income tax stolen from working men at the point of IRS guns. But instead of actually paying that debt or funding the government, the extorted blood money went right to the holders of the "debt"—the wealthy Jewish cabal in charge of global finance. It was, as Mullins would claim, a sick cycle of theft and debt, meant to keep the downtrodden down and enrich the already rich. And all of it was masterminded by the Rothschilds.

After two years of work and countless rejections by legitimate New York publishers, Mullins released what he then titled *Mullins on the Federal Reserve* on a private press founded by two other Pound acolytes. It was a smash hit. Multiple printings followed, and the general thesis of the book only became more refined with additional Mullins "discoveries."[9]

Because Mullins would update the text every time *Secrets of the Federal Reserve* was reprinted (it wasn't actually published with that title until 1983), its details tend to shift, working in world events that hadn't even taken place when the initial print run was released. But the core accusation never changed: a cartel of Jekyll Island meeting participants, paid-off US puppets, and international bankers pushed the unconstitutional Federal Reserve Act through Congress as a means to control the American money supply. The Federal Reserve System, as Mullins posits, "is not Federal; it has no reserves; and it is not a system at all, but rather, a criminal syndicate."[10] Its goal was the total control of global finance by yoking ordinary Americans to debt slavery, making hundreds of billions of dollars in annual debt payments to communist and Jewish puppet masters. And what Jews are more puppet mastery than the Rothschilds?

Citing everything from past Rothschild chroniclers to legendary outsider candidate and economic cult leader Lyndon LaRouche (himself a prolific Rothschild conspiracy theorist), Mullins calls the Rothschilds charter members of the cabal that "controlled our political and economic destinies since 1914." They operated in secret using J.P. Morgan & Co. as the façade for an unholy alliance with Rockefeller. They dictated American politics through strangleholds over key figures in American history like Hoover, FDR, and former CIA heads George H. W. Bush (who actually ran the Agency for less than a year) and Allen Dulles. They had financed both sides of the Civil War, both World Wars, the Bolshevik Revolution, and the Cold War. And they used various British banks to move their shares in the Fed around and escape public notice. Mullins would deem the arrangement of British banking controlling American finance "the London Connection" and made it his life's work to expose this cabal's "iron grip" on finance and the media.[11]

That life's work was lucrative, prolific, and deeply antisemitic—almost to the point of cartoonishness. In his pamphlet *Adolf Hitler: An Appreciation*, Mullins claimed that "Hitler, like Christ before him, was crucified on a Cross of Gold through the duplicity of his own Christian people. [. . .] Because Hitler drove the economic leeches of the Rothschild and Warburg families out of Germany."[12] Not content to blame the Jews just for the United States's money trouble, he transitioned into "scientific racism" with his book *The Biological Jew*. And he spent decades promoting vaccine denialism, demonology, quack cures, medical pseudoscience, and homophobic AIDS conspiracy theories, culminating in his 1988 book *Murder By Injection: The Medical Conspiracy Against America*.

Working well into the twenty-first century, Mullins bridged the gap between Ezra Pound and Alex Jones. He became a key figure in the Clinton-era militia movement, to the point where one day before the Oklahoma City bombing, Mullins was lecturing an anti-government conference in Idaho on the evils of the Fed while calling federal agents "kill-crazy" for perpetrating the "Waco Holocaust."[13] And his work massively influenced other seminal conspiracy theory thinkers. In a fawning 2005 radio interview, Alex Jones called Mullins "the great-grandfather of the movement against the Federal Reserve and the New World Order," while the two traded conspiracy theories about fluoride, "international bankers," and "Oriental despotism."[14]

Even as his existence descended into delusions about gangs of Jewish assassins trying to kill him,[15] Mullins continued to give speeches about the depravity of the Fed and the "London Connection," before his death in February 2010.[16] After his passing, Mullins's work continued to find new eyes, thanks in large part to Glenn Beck, who promoted *Secrets of the Federal Reserve* in late 2010 as part of his chalkboard conspiracy attacks on the Fed, George Soros, and Obama-era monetary policy.[17]

Through it all, Mullins remained resolute in his vision of the United States as a crumbling and demon-riddled puppet state controlled by Jewish money, with the Rothschilds controlling the controllers. "The world is now a Gulag Archipelago," Mullins declared in 1988, "run by the ruthless minions of the Rockefeller-Rothschild conglomerate. Its gods are money and power; its only enemy is the advocate of liberty."[18]

Liberty, as it would turn out, would be lousy with poor advocates.

PARANOIA, INC.

The late 1960s and early '70s were a lucrative time to be in the conspiracy business. The optimism of Woodstock and the moon landing had curdled into the chaos of the Manson murders and Watergate, creating a golden age of paranoia. Both fiction and nonfiction embraced the disillusionment and the suspicion that everyone was lying to us about everything. It wasn't all bad—this was the time of classic "'70s paranoia" thrillers like *The Parallax View*, *The Conversation*, and *Three Days of the Condor*. On the negative side, it gave us piles and piles of racist and antisemitic waffle alleging that the Jews were behind the financial hobbling and racial pollution of modern times, just like they'd always been.

The paranoia powered the growing body of anti-communist political agitation groups, through which an endless number of newsletters, tracts, pamphlets, and magazines made the Rothschilds featured players in the super-conspiracy to impose Jewish-Soviet control over the world. And they added their own twists and details—a choose your own adventure of racist hate where the path might wind in different directions but the end results were always the same: the Jews did it.

The *Liberty Letter* and other publications of Holocaust denier Willis Carto's ultra-conservative Liberty Lobby attacked all manner of

"Rothschilds and Rockefellers and Communists and Carter and Bankers and Rich People and the Tri-Lateral Commission," as *The Washington Post* put it in 1979.[19] John Birch Society founder Robert Welch also routinely beat up on the family, claiming a "Master Conspiracy" of the Rothschilds and the Council on Foreign Relations actually controlled both the US and the USSR, pitting them against each other and enacting a "Negro Soviet Republic" in the American south. Welch wasn't even the most prominent Birch executive to attack the family—and he wasn't in a small minority.[20]

When New Jersey–based publisher Conde McGinley launched his bi-weekly paper *Common Sense* in 1947, it was exclusively anti-communist. But you can't attack "Judeo-Bolshevism" by just attacking Bolsheviks, so McGinley soon went after the Rothschilds, calling the family "horny-handed toilers" with unfathomable power and influence, while printing articles by a slew of antisemitic, pro-Nazi, and neofascist guest writers. And it found a ready fanbase, reaching more than 82 thousand households just in 1964.[21] One particularly scabrous issue from 1970 declared "ROTHSCHILD BANK SYNDROME" was the cause of all modern woes, with a photo caption claiming that "Rothschild banks have financed both sides of every war. They have murdered 106,000,000 of God's humans in the 20th century alone."[22] McGinley's antisemitism was so blatant that he was investigated and condemned by the House Un-American Activities Committee, which did nothing to deter *Common Sense* from publishing until 1972 under the auspices of the "Christian Educational Association."

As *Common Sense* wound down, the Florida-based monthly journal *Instauration* (meaning renewal or restoration) launched in 1975, created by "intellectual racism" pioneer and white nationalist Sumner Humphrey Ireland. Writing under the name "Wilmot Robertson" in both *Instauration* and his more well-known book, 1972's *The Dispossessed Majority*, Ireland hit the usual world domination and race-mixing talking points, tying them into both historical and imaginary events, all with a pseudo-intellectual flair. In particular, Ireland seemed obsessed with the idea that the Rothschilds had funded the Union during the Civil War (as opposed to pro-Union theories that they had funded only the Confederacy), leaving the victors deeply in debt to England, and hailed Andrew Johnson for refusing "the repayment of war debts that Lincoln had incurred to the Rothschilds and other Jewish interests [which] could only be detrimental to the Joe Six-Packs of his day."[23]

In something of a printed version of an internet comments section, Ireland also opened his paper to letters to the editor, printed with only the first three digits of the zip code of the writer to preserve anonymity. In what he called "The Safety Valve," Ireland's readers freely ranted about whatever was getting their goat with the Blacks and Jews that month—a harbinger of the anonymous message boards so crucial to the development of modern conspiracy cult movements. Most of these newsletters didn't survive into the digital age, but Ireland kept *Instauration* going until his death in 2005.

And while the explosive growth of southern "White Citizens' Councils" after the *Brown v. Board of Education* decision was usually focused on restoring the glory of segregation, these organizations were never shy about scapegoating Jews as well. Publications of various Citizens' Councils are full of references to Jewish wealth and power, and especially the depravity and control of the Rothschilds. The Louisiana Citizens' Council newspaper *The Councilor* had a national circulation of two hundred thousand at its highest point, and in one March 1963 issue, it mentions the Rothschilds by name on sixteen of its first sixty-five pages. One especially bizarre reference is to the family supposedly funding both the US and Soviet-backed sides of the Korean War, making it a "profitable little police action."[24]

In an ironic twist of fate, when the Citizens' Councils started bombing places that promoted desegregation, synagogues were among their targets. One particularly infamous attack took place in Atlanta in August 1958, when fifty sticks of dynamite blew a hole in the side of the Hebrew Benevolent Congregation. Its rabbi was a Pittsburgh transplant named Jacob Rothschild—who survived the bombing and went on to preach equality and tolerance for decades to come.[25]

NAKED AND DARING

These newsletters, and many others like them, were extremely popular, circulating as many as half a million copies total per week just during the early and mid-1960s.[26] The bummer boom would continue well into the 1980s and be particularly lucrative for the acolytes of Eustace Mullins.

Merging classic John Birch paranoia with fringe Mormon eschatology, former FBI agent and small-town police chief W. Cleon Skousen was loathed even by his fellow cranks; he was thrown out of an ultra-conservative think tank for having "[gone] off the deep end" in the early '60s.[27] But the deep end isn't a bad place to be if you want to make a lot of money selling conspiracy theories. Skousen turned his books *The 5000 Year Leap*, *The Naked Communist*, and *The Naked Capitalist* into bestsellers by embracing virtually every unevidenced political and economic theory of the last two centuries and wrapping them in a cloak of patriotic hokum.

Selling over a million copies according to several accounts, 1970's *The Naked Capitalist* was itself a book-length review of historian Carroll Quigley's mammoth 1966 examination of nineteenth and early twentieth century economics, *Tragedy and Hope*. Quigley was something of a conspiracy theorist himself, and certainly no bleeding-heart liberal, but he wasn't an antisemite. Even as he made unevidenced claims that an international cabal known as "The Society of the Elect," supposedly a realization of the "secret society" fantasized about by Cecil Rhodes in his 1877 "Confession of Faith," played a major role in global politics and banking, he specifically disclaims Rothschild conspiracy theories. Of the supposed "financiers of both sides," Quigley correctly writes merely that "the Rothschilds had been preeminent during much of the nineteenth century, but, at the end of that century, they were being replaced by J. P. Morgan."[28]

While mainstream historians rejected it, Skousen folded the "Society of the Elect" theory into an alluring Rothschild-Rockefeller one world government plot. To Skousen, the Rothschilds were the power behind Morgan, who was, in turn, the power behind the Council on Foreign Relations, whose archives Quigley had based much of *Tragedy and Hope* upon.[29] But even Skousen allows that while the Rothschilds "and certain other Jewish families cooperated together in these ventures, this was by no means a Jewish monopoly."[30]

Skousen's interpretation of Quigley's "Society of the Elect" theory had its own detractors—including Quigley himself, who called Skousen "a political agitator" who violated his book's copyright to create a work full of "assumptions and preconceptions" and "fantastic ideas." It wasn't a compliment.[31]

But both the book and its author also had influential fans, including Ronald Reagan (apocryphally said to have told Skousen that *The Naked Capitalist* was "sad but true"), Reagan's Secretary of Education Bill Bennett, future Housing and Urban Development Secretary Ben Carson, longtime Utah senator Orrin Hatch, and, more recently, Glenn Beck.[32] Like with his promotion of Elizabeth Dilling and Eustace Mullins, Beck would drive up both his and Skousen's book sales with his Obama-era gushing about the author as "fantastic" and someone whose books will tell the truth after "the history of this country [will be] lost because it's going to be hijacked by intellectuals and communists."[33] And the Skousen name would continue to be associated with conspiracy theories after Cleon's death in 2006, as his nephew Joel is a regular guest on Alex Jones's Infowars.

Anyone looking for intellectuals and communists to scorn would find plenty in the mammoth 1978 book *Which Way, Western Man*, written by white supremacist and crank philosopher William Gayley Simpson. Over a thousand pages long, *Which Way* plods through endless paragraphs of monotonous babble about "the ennobling of man," "the necessity of an aristocracy" and "the effect of industrialism on human life" before getting down to who's really to blame for "western man's" peril. You can probably guess.

"A hard core within world Jewry [. . .] long ago set itself to gain control of all the nations of Europe, and eventually of all the other nations of the entire Earth," Simpson pontificates in an endless chapter asking "Is There a Jewish Race?"[34] Naturally, the Rothschilds were the hardest of the "hard core"—funding the South during the Civil War, using the Federal Reserve to take control of world finance, working "hand in glove" with the secretly Jewish Rockefellers (they were actually Baptist), and being one of the principal players in the encroaching one world government.[35] To reinforce his claims, Simpson liberally quotes from past cranks, the *Protocols*, and *The International Jew*. And all of it is wrapped in a cloak of mystical, high-sounding nonsense that would make the book at home on the shelf of a New Age guru with a slight fascist lean.

Likely because of its gargantuan length, *Which Way, Western Man* didn't sell all that well. But decades later, its title became an ironic internet meme in which two different choices, one "traditional" and therefore good, and the other "modern" and therefore bad, are pitted against each other, with the reader offered a choice of which to pick.[36] As with most memes, some racists post it seriously, but the majority of its uses are harmless or meant as an ironic joke. Except most of the people using it for laughs have no idea that the phrase originated in a book that called Jews "aliens [. . .] who must be put out and kept out" if the United States is to survive.[37]

Of course, some people know exactly what these phrases mean—they're usually the ones longing for tradition and white male supremacy at the expense of progress and inclusion. And a lot of them probably listen to Alex Jones. In between his own rants about the Rothschilds, Jones has extolled Eustace Mullins, and essentially adapted *The Naked Capitalist* for his own 2009 movie *The Obama Deception*. But there's one book from the Cold War that did more than any other to "wake up" Jones to "what was really going on"—1971's *None Dare Call It Conspiracy*.

Written mostly by John Birch Society spokesman Gary Allen (another Bircher, Larry Abraham, shares the byline), *None Dare* combines Mullins's Federal Reserve attacks with Skousen's Council on Foreign Relations paranoia. It even specifically cites Carroll Quigley, just as Skousen had (and, like Skousen, Quigley was not a fan of the interpretation), making relentless attacks on the nonexistent Rockefeller-Rothschild alliance to rule the world. To *None Dare*, they were charter members of the "Insiders," using illegal income tax to suck up the wealth of ordinary working men at the point of a gun and funnel it to international bankers who hold the United States's crippling national debt.

In hypnotic, rapid-fire prose, *None Dare* makes the bold claim that the relentlessly greedy Rothschilds should not only be despised by Gentiles, but by other Jews as well. "It is just as unreasonable and immoral to blame all Jews for the crimes of the Rothschilds as it is to hold all Baptists accountable for the crimes of the Rockefellers," the book thunders, apparently not believing *Which Way, Western Man* in claiming the wealthy industrialists were secret Jews. Later, the book accuses the Rothschilds of "sitting out" World War II in luxe Paris hotels alongside their fellow wealthy German Jews the Warburgs, and of being "power seekers" who have foisted uncountable suffering on other Jews—for whom they do nothing other than take for themselves.[38]

"A Rothschild has much more in common with a Rockefeller than he does with a tailor from Budapest or the Bronx," *None Dare* writes, intimating that it's not antisemitic to attack the Rothschilds because they aren't real Jews—a sentiment that's still hugely popular among internet cranks and conspiracy theorists.[39] In its "revelation" of the players behind the creation of a "World Super State of the elite" meant to enslave everyone else, *None Dare* boiled countless players and plots down to 140 pages full of alluring threads for grateful future "researchers" to run with. Inevitably, *None Dare* was a huge hit, selling as many as five million copies in the run-up to the 1972 election and being perpetually reprinted and reissued.[40]

One of its most important purchasers wouldn't be known until decades later.

Already a voracious reader soaking up conspiracy theories from his John Birch Society–aligned father David, a teenage Alex Jones found *None Dare* in his dad's library and immediately was hooked on its alternative explanations for how government and finance work.[41] In interviews and on the air over the next decades, Jones would extol its clairvoyance, mention or recommend it dozens of times, and say it did more than any other work to open his eyes to the evils of the secret global government. In a 2011 profile, Jones would call *None Dare* "the easiest-to-read primer to the New World Order" and claim he read it multiple times as a teenager, alongside history touchstones like Gibbon's *Decline and Fall of the Roman Empire* and Shirer's *Rise and Fall of the Third Reich*.[42]

Even as Jones's financial fortunes crashed as a result of lawsuits and social media deplatforming, he clung to *None Dare* and its message of impending global enslavement. He spoke admiringly of it in the 2022 documentary *Alex's War*, and, as if looking for a quick explanation for Jones's embrace of conspiracy theories, the film's director screen-grabbed a quote from the book: "In politics, nothing happens by accident. If it happens, you can bet it was planned that way"—a statement that skeptic and scholar Michael Shermer points out does not actually conform with a world full of coincidence, happenstance, and incompetence.[43]

CROSSES AND SWITCHBLADES

Most of the superstars of Cold War antisemitism didn't wrap their conspiracy theories around a cross. But other authors built theories around a highly questionable interpretation of Christianity, spreading a distinctly anti-Jewish, pro-America Christian nationalism that hijacked the Republican Party in the 1980s and still wields enormous influence today. The explicitly Christian popularizers of conspiracy theories now shared a common enemy with secular antisemites: the wealthy Illuminati who supposedly relied on Rothschild money to keep the working Gentile down.

Or, as the headline of the 1953 rag *The Coming Red Dictatorship*, published by *Common Sense* scribe Conde McGinley under his Christian Educational Association banner, blared: "ASIATIC MARXIST JEWS CONTROL ENTIRE WORLD AS LAST WORLD WAR COMMENCES: THOUSANDS OF PLOTTERS PLACED IN KEY POSITIONS BY INVISIBLE GOVERNMENT: FEW WERE EVER ELECTED." Naturally, the "invisible government" was the Rothschilds, working to execute the plan their coreligionists had meticulously laid out in the "definitely true" *Protocols of the Elders of Zion*.[44]

The rabidly antisemitic and pro-segregation preacher Gerald L.K. Smith did more to fuse anti-Rothschild conspiracy theories with Christian nationalism than anyone else in the immediate postwar years. Born in 1898, Smith spent decades mixing hate preaching with anti-Communism, Jew baiting, and doomed runs for office. Several accounts have him joining both the Ku Klux Klan and William Pelley's fascist Silver Shirts, though Smith denied membership in either.[45] It's hard to see why he'd bother with the denials. He preached alongside Father Coughlin, demanded Blacks and Jews be expelled from the US, openly supported Adolf Hitler, and, in 1943, founded the isolationist America First Party—not to be confused with fellow anti-Rothschildian John T. Flynn's America First Committee, which had had the good sense to dissolve once the US entered the war. And Smith fully embraced Holocaust denial, believing that Europe's Jews hadn't died, but illegally emigrated to the US to bolster the Roosevelt Red plot.[46]

By then, Smith was publishing the monthly hate sheet *The Cross and the Flag*, combining all of Smith's dark obsessions and selling them alongside fundraising solicitations for his dream project: a still-existing 65-foot-high plaster statue of Jesus, called "Christ of the Ozarks." *The Cross and the Flag* never had the circulation of other newsletters like the *Liberty Letter* or *The Councilor*, and Smith claims to have printed it at a loss for its entire 35-year run.[47] But the paper raised Smith's profile to the point where he is still a figurehead for Christian nationalism, with several high-profile 2022 Republican candidates echoing Smith's language in speeches decrying "wokeness" and "cancel culture."[48] And in both *The Cross and the Flag* and other publications, Smith frequently laid into the Rothschilds as the funders of the international Jewish plot to suppress freedom and mix the races.

Typical of these rambles is a 1967 issue revealing the tyranny of Rothschild-funded "International Jewish Bankers" who control every aspect of the media, finance, commerce, and politics in both the US and every other "banker nation." One particularly bizarre notion in this issue that's managed to catch on in crank culture is that the family financed the writing of the *Communist Manifesto*, and that author Karl Marx, whose father had converted from Judaism in 1817, was actually a Jew born "Moses Mordecai Levi."[49] Smith was obsessed with "Rothschilds started the Civil War" theories, including taking the speech supposedly given by Benjamin Disraeli at the Rothschild wedding in 1857, first transcribed in John Reeves's *The Rothschilds: Financial Rulers of Nations*, and adding the hokey proclamation "If you like, we shall divide the United States into two parts, one for you, James, and one for you, Lionel."[50]

As much reach as hate preachers like Smith had, their brand of Bible-thumping conspiracy mongering had become too square and stale as the '80s beckoned. So when evangelical Christianity began promoting a country-wide Satanic Panic with its witches, demons, and secret messages hidden on Led Zeppelin, AC/DC, and Black Sabbath albums, Rothschild conspiracy theories came along with it. Because what's better than the Rothschilds financially ruling nations and partnering with Satan? The Rothschilds "Ruling with Druid Witches," as one 2007 blog post claimed.[51]

Emerging out of the purple haze of occult conspiracy theories was John Todd, a preacher who claimed to have been born into the United States's first family of witchcraft and trained to be a druid priest, only to convert to Christianity after seeing the 1970 "Christian crime" movie *The Cross and the Switchblade*.[52] Speaking at churches and on self-produced tapes, Todd spun out an incomprehensible epic about total Satanic control of entertainment and politics, the depravity of the cabal, and the need to stock up on weapons and ammo for when Charles Manson's mind-controlled Illuminati army came for you. The details of Todd's story changed constantly, as did the identity of his version of the Antichrist and basic aspects of his own history. But the essential plot was always the same: the Illuminati were on the verge of taking over the world, and the Rothschilds ran the Illuminati.

Since Todd liberally borrowed from works like *None Dare* and *Secrets of the Federal Reserve*, it's only natural that he'd include the Rothschilds at the top of his conspiracy pyramid. Todd claimed that British-born "Illuminati leader" Philip Rothschild was running a complex plot to take over the United States, first through proxy leader Henry Kissinger, then through President Jimmy Carter. Christian citizens had no choice but to stock up on supplies to wait out the encroaching horror—and even possibly kill their own families if the need arose, rather than see them devoured by evil. Led by Philip Rothschild, the Illuminati were so powerful and omnipresent that they could lay down clues of their upcoming takeover decades in advance, knowing nothing could stop them.

Among other claims, Todd spoke on his tapes of how Philip had financed the writing of Ayn Rand's half-read college dorm room staple *Atlas Shrugged* as a public blueprint for what the Rothschild Witches would do during the Satanic takeover—and who besides the Rothschilds could simultaneously be accused of funding the works of both Ayn Rand and Karl Marx? Todd also said he had insider knowledge that the Rothschilds ran the Illuminati through a private priesthood of "Grand Druids" called the Council of 13—into which Todd had been initiated.[53]

Even Todd's conversion story, or at least one version of it, involved the Rothschilds. At several points, Todd claimed to have received a sealed Illuminati diplomatic pouch from the Rothschild office in London that included a "chart [that] listed an eight-year plan for world take-over ending in the December month of 1980" and the identity of the "son of Lucifer."[54] The oncoming approach of the Tribulation was apparently enough to get John Todd to embrace Christ and leave behind his sinning ways.

Or not, given his ultimate fate. While Todd would become an influential figure in the anti-Illuminati hysteria of the 1980s, his own story didn't end especially well: he was convicted of rape charges in 1988 and died in a psychiatric facility in 2007. As it turned out, Todd was an exceptionally gifted fraud whose real story was nothing like his pretend tales of druid initiation. Beyond that, there was no "Philip Rothschild," only French family scion Philippe de Rothschild, who did not fund the writing of *Atlas Shrugged*. Naturally, future conspiracy theorists would claim Todd was set up by the Illuminati to be taken out, but by the time the '90s rolled around, a more mainstream conspiracy book boom was underway. And the erratic former "Grand Druid" and his crimes were shunted aside for more palatable versions of the "one world government" story.

ANOTHER NEW WORLD ORDER

It's tempting to say that the conspiracy theory boom of the 1990s was kicked off by Bill Clinton taking office in 1993. But before many leading conspiracy figures hated Clinton, they hated his predecessor,

George H. W. Bush. "Pappy Bush" was a Skull and Bones man, part of that Yale secret society supposedly full of elite power brokers being trained on how to dominate the world. He was the former head of the CIA who knew where the bodies were buried and how they got there for some of the United States's worst globalist misadventures. And most unforgivable of all, he dared to approvingly use the name of the globalist controllers, telling a Joint Session of Congress in September 1990, just after Iraq's invasion of Kuwait, that "out of these troubled times, our fifth objective—a new world order—can emerge." He'd go on to use the phrase several more times in the speech, and would turn to it again in ensuing years.

If there was any further proof needed that the United States was under the thumb of the Rothschild-Rockefeller-CFR-Bilderberg-Warburg Illuminati, conspiracy writers didn't wait for it. Released a year after Bush's speech and freely referencing those remarks, Pat Robertson's book *The New World Order* took a century of crank nonsense and delivered it with the folksy, "aw, shucks" charm Robertson had perfected hosting *The 700 Club*. Freely citing *Secrets of the Federal Reserve* alongside Phyllis Schlafly, *Chariots of the Gods* author Erich Von Daniken, and "my friend" Cleon Skousen, Robertson lays out the "behind-the-scenes Establishment" plot to enslave the United States through "a one-world government where the control of money is in the hands of one or more privately owned, but government-chartered central banks."[55]

Naturally, the Rothschilds were part of that private ownership, and Robertson runs down the usual claims of the family "attempting to saddle the country with a private central bank" while loading working men down with trillions in debt.[56] But Robertson takes his paranoia considerably further by alleging that the Rothschilds, who Robertson claims "controlled" Frankfurt in 1782, are what he deems "the missing link" between the Bavarian Illuminati and the Freemasons. In a passage brimming with giddy discovery, Robertson breathlessly writes, "it is reported that in Frankfurt, Jews for the first time were admitted to the order of Freemasons. If indeed members of the Rothschild family or their close associates were polluted by the occultism of [Adam] Weishaupt's Illuminated Freemasonry, we may have discovered the link between the occult and the world of high finance."[57]

If the Rothschilds—or really just Mayer, given that the oldest of his sons was nine at the time—had "control" of Frankfurt in 1782, it would have been news to the Landgrave of Hesse. Beyond that, Jews were actually allowed to become Freemasons before then, though there was general resistance to Jews joining lodges in Germany. And while Frankfurt was a hub of Masonic activity, Mayer was never a Mason, and there's no evidence he wished to join a lodge.

But the much more troubling issue with Robertson's analysis of the Rothschild conspiracy is that it's lifted almost straight from Nesta Webster's 1924 book *Secret Societies and Subversive Movements*, the follow-up to her 1921 book *World Revolution*. And Webster, who Robertson cites by name in *The New World Order*, lifted the "Judeo-Masonic Conspiracy" idea almost directly from *The Protocols of the Elders of Zion*.[58] Once Robertson's sourcing was revealed, the connection caused a firestorm of controversy. Robertson defended himself as a devoted friend to the Jews, but liberal intellectuals pushed back by arguing that no matter his personal opinion, he was referencing one of the most antisemitic documents of all time and so maybe he wasn't. What followed was a long back-and-forth in Jewish journals and conservative magazines, during which editors and readers alike sought to determine whether you can accuse "European Bankers" of seeking to control global finance and simultaneously claim you have nothing against Jews.[59] *The New World Order* and Robertson were even called out by name in Umberto Eco's 1995 essay *Ur-Fascism* as "a prominent instance of the plot obsession" inherent to fascist movements.[60]

SILENT WEAPONS, ELECTRICAL ROTHSCHILDS

Of course, one step beyond quoting from a book that quotes the *Protocols* is simply including the entirety of them in your own book.

Such were the early printings of *Behold a Pale Horse*, still one of the most popular and influential books of the 1990s conspiracy boom. Cobbled together by conspiracy theorist and Navy veteran Milton William "Bill" Cooper out of supposedly secret documents, "a proposed Constitutional model for the Newstates of America," the texts of various congressional bills and executive orders, rambling personal recollections, letters to prominent UFO researchers, newspaper clippings, and transcripts of phone calls with fellow paranoiacs, *Behold a Pale Horse* presents the same encroaching one world government that Robertson does, but without Robertson's coherence or narrative throughline. The New World Order, according to Cooper, was dominated by occult secret societies and was making final preparations to imprison dissenters (i.e., gun owners), crush all opposition using secret alien technology gained from a 1954 treaty between Eisenhower and grey aliens, and suspend the Constitution in favor of martial law.

Like Robertson, Cooper firmly places the Rothschilds at the center of this world domination mechanism. He rehashes the Illuminati/Masonic conspiracy, claiming the family financed Illuminati founder Adam Weishaupt (they didn't), and that they shared Weishaupt's desire for the "abolition of all ordered national governments, abolition of inheritance, abolition of private property, abolition of patriotism, abolition of the individual home and family life as the cell from which all civilizations have stemmed, and abolition of all religions established and existing so that the Luciferian ideology of totalitarianism may be imposed on mankind."[61] Cooper lifts much of this language almost directly from Nesta Webster's *World Revolution*, which ascribed it to "the Bolshevik revolution," as Weishaupt never wrote anything like this.

Pale Horse is a scrapbook of conspiracy theories, incomprehensible plots, deep dives into the inner workings of organizations that don't exist, and Cooper's personal grievances. In one of the most bizarre accusations, Cooper implicates the Rothschilds in what he claims is a secret government plot revealed in a document written in 1979 that was "found on July 7, 1986, in an IBM copier that had been purchased at a surplus sale"— though other sources claim it was found by a Boeing employee in a Xerox machine.[62] Entitled "Silent Weapons for Quiet Wars," the "classified document" is the book's first chapter, and drops a bomb on the reader right away.

The "silent weapon" is said to be a vast computing system that can instantly analyze millions of socioeconomic interactions and control or punish individual people based on those interactions, acting as a monetary electrical grid. The brilliant mind who discerned the relationship between electrical systems and financial systems, the document claims, was none other than Mayer Amschel Rothschild, who found "the missing passive component of economic theory known as economic inductance."[63]

Even though the first complex electrical system wasn't developed until the 1880s, seventy years after Mayer's death, the document's anonymous author heaps praise on the Rothschild founder for putting together the connection between electrical energy and financial incentive. "What Mr. Rothschild had discovered," the document claims, "was the basic principle of power, influence, and control over people as applied to economics. That principle is 'when you assume the appearance of power, people soon give it to you.'"[64] Essentially, fake it until you make it, with "it" being total control of all money.

Except "Silent Weapons for Quiet Wars" was not a real government blueprint for world domination found by some random patriot in a surplus copy machine. Instead, it was likely written by a Pearl Harbor conspiracy theorist and sovereign citizen named Hartford Van Dyke. Responding to the document's printing in a 2003 issue of *Paranoia* magazine, Van Dyke wrote a letter to the editor claiming he wrote it in 1979 after being inspired by *None Dare Call It Conspiracy*, not as a "paranoid manifesto" but as "a politically biased technical instruction manual on how to justify, and how to selectively survive, human animal husbandry before the need for animal husbandry becomes unstably critical."[65] Notably, Van Dyke wrote to *Paranoia* from prison, where he was serving time for trying to pay his taxes with fake currency.

This wouldn't be the only authorship issue to dog *Behold a Pale Horse*. Cooper infamously devoted an entire chapter to printing what he called *The Protocols of the Wise Men of Zion*. But as if trying to prove he wasn't antisemitic, he included the helpful caveat that to obtain "clear understanding" of how the Illuminati wrote the document to deceive truth seekers, "the word 'Zion' should be 'Sion' [as in the Priory of Sion, a French secret society not founded until 1956]; any reference to 'Jews' should be replaced with the word 'Illuminati'; and 'goyim,' [a Yiddish term simply meaning "Gentile"] should be replaced with the word 'cattle.'"[66]

Cooper's weak attempt to recast the *Protocols* as not actually antisemitic didn't work, and future printings of *Behold a Pale Horse* simply omitted the chapter.

And there were *many* future printings—which Cooper didn't live to see, as he was killed in a November 2001 shootout with Apache County, AZ, sheriff's deputies who had a warrant for his arrest on charges of assaulting someone who went on his land. *Behold a Pale Horse* has sold at least three hundred thousand copies, and is still one of the most popular books on Amazon, where (as of this writing) it's #1 in the categories for UFOs, "Ancient and Controversial Knowledge," and "Radical Political Thought."[67]

The book is also a major hit in the American prison system and has influenced countless other conspiracy theorists along with a generation of rappers who see Cooper as telling the truth that the white establishment has kept hidden for so long.[68] Likewise, Robertson's *The New World Order* spent weeks on the *New York Times* bestseller list, mainstreaming one world government conspiracy theories in a way not seen since *None Dare*—the book which had, in turn, inspired portions of *Behold a Pale Horse*.[69]

There were innumerable other books and pamphlets of the early '90s that attacked the Rothschilds as part of their own version of the global government plot. G. Edward Griffin's 1994 attack on the Federal Reserve, *The Creature from Jekyll Island*, "theorized a strategy, dubbed the Rothschild Formula, in which the world's money cabal deliberately encourages war as a means of stimulating the profitable production of armaments and of keeping nations perpetually in debt," according to a 2015 profile from *The Daily Beast*. Ron Paul and Glenn Beck are big fans of Griffin's work, while Eustace Mullins claimed Griffin liberally plagiarized him.[70]

John Coleman's previously mentioned *Conspirators' Hierarchy: The Committee of 300* came out in 1991, full of accusations adapted from anti-Rothschild writers of the last century, while author William T. Still's 1990 book *New World Order: The Ancient Plan of Secret Societies* parroted

Nesta Webster's accusations that the Rothschilds "controlled half the wealth in the world" without any of Pat Robertson's need to equivocate.[71] And Fritz Springmeier's mammoth 1995 tome, *Bloodlines of the Illuminati*, purported to trace the thirteen families that have ruled the world for eons, mentioning the Rothschilds over six hundred times and making countless bizarre and unevidenced accusations about their dirty deeds—including the claim that an even wealthier and more powerful family known as "the Payseurs" actually controlled the Rothschilds and used them as agents for their own plans for enslaving the world.

These books were bestsellers, hugely influencing how millions of people thought about Jewish wealth and power. They're reprinted over and over, still finding powerful fans in high places. These converts extol their "truths" to massive audiences on the internet, where they're constantly referenced and shared. They helped set the tone for conspiracy theorists like Alex Jones leaving the dank gutters of fringe bookstores and shortwave radio and becoming media stars. They directly led to the United States electing its first conspiracy theorist president and were freely embraced by some of his biggest fans. And they would lay down theories about the Rothschilds that would be repurposed again and again against other wealthy Jews.

And their influence goes beyond just Western conspiracy culture. According to declassified files from the Office of the Director of National Intelligence, when Osama bin Laden was killed by US Special Forces in May 2011, he had thirty-nine English-language books on his shelf. Among them were *Conspirators' Hierarchy: The Committee of 300*, *Bloodlines of the Illuminati*, and the crowning work of Cold War anti-Rothschild conspiracy theories, *Secrets of the Federal Reserve*.[72]

DISINFORMATION SUPERHIGHWAY: ROTHSCHILD CONSPIRACY THEORIES TAKE OVER THE INTERNET

In 1990, computer scientists at Swiss-based research center CERN developed the rudiments of what would become the modern world wide web with still-foundational concepts like HTML, HTTP, and the URL. They also created the first website, info.cern.ch. You can still browse it, even though it's pretty crude by modern standards.

CERN made the software to create websites public domain in 1993, and the internet's first conspiracy theory site probably popped up seconds later.

When conspiracy theory culture moved online, it was following a pattern of early crank adoption of new technology, from easy duplication of photos fueling the Dreyfus Affair to home video equipment making it easier to make and distribute conspiracy films.[1] On bulletin board systems, email lists, Yahoo groups, blocky websites on long-gone providers, and text-based forums like USENET, conspiracy theories flourished. They grew so quickly that the USENET group alt.conspiracy was already getting nearly a hundred thousand monthly views as early as July 1994, making it one of the most popular parts of the early web.[2]

Within a few years, conspiracy theories would start their slow creep from the fringes to the mainstream, fired by right-wing talk radio and the adoption of the internet. And with it came the usual attacks on wealthy Jews, and their "kings," the Rothschilds. Overall, the Clinton years, the 9/11 attacks, and the Great Recession were all tremendous drivers of internet antisemitism. Once-fringe theories would become commonly accepted tropes, completely enmeshed with how we perceive history, finance, politics, and Judaism. What was shocking and scandalous in Paris in 1846, and genocidal in Nazi Germany a century later, was now so banal that tracking all of its variations would soon literally become impossible.

CONSPIRACY NATION

Much of the earliest internet is lost for good, so we may never know who posted the first Rothschild conspiracy theory online. The first discoverable reference to the family in searchable USENET archives, other than in posts about wine, might be an October 1994 post in, of all places, alt.sport.horse-racing. A user posted a short block of text called "Rothschild: The Head of the Beast" that claimed that "Rothschild agents are like cockroaches crawling around your home. These cockroaches crawl all over Europe—they are everywhere. [. . .] They are constantly maneuvering and working for the Rothschild purposes."[3]

It was new technology, but an old message. The rant was cut and pasted from an issue of the New Age newsletter "Revelations of Awareness," produced since 1977 by "Cosmic Awareness Communications" and devoted to interpreting and disseminating the messages of an apparently antisemitic Godhead figure.[4] But the anti-Rothschild hate didn't stay confined to Godhead-interpreting seekers. It steadily grew in places like alt.conspiracy on USENET, where threads liberally quoted *The Creature from Jekyll Island*'s "Rothschild Formula"[5] while decrying the ever-present "Rothschild-

Rockefeller Luciferian Conspiracy! [sic]" and demanding to know "How long is America going to put-up with David Rockefeller, and the rest of his peverted [sic] Establishment?"[6]

As websites became easier to create, the cranks moved from message boards to homemade sites full of clickable links and floating graphics against backdrops that can charitably be described as "garish." No matter what conspiracy you were into, someone would make a website for it, or you could make your own—delivering forbidden knowledge on "Secret Military Experimentation on Americans," blood purification, the evil deeds of the "rogue" ATF, alien bases on Mars, Freemasons, light energy, the atmospheric research array HAARP, the DEA framing OJ Simpson, the Hale-Bopp Comet's starship companion, the danger of electromagnetic fields, and, of course, *The Protocols of the Elders of Zion.*[7]

And if anyone could post someone else's conspiracy theories on the web, then anyone could create their own. As new avenues of paranoia opened up, there came a new batch of conspiracy theory authors and influencers ready to dictate those conversations, and maybe even make some money in the process.

Rothschild conspiracy theories were often featured in one of the earliest popular fringe internet newsletters, *Conspiracy Nation*. Launched in 1994 by Brian Francis Redman, *Conspiracy Nation* made it clear in its first issue that it would be devoted to the chestnuts of the genre: a JFK debate, an interview with "Clinton Body Count" creator Linda Thompson, and articles profiling conspiracy theorist and anti-Rothschild preacher Texe Marrs.[8] These were names that were all deeply familiar to the conspiracy community, and still are. In 2009, for example, Marrs released a video called *Rothschild's Choice: Barack Obama and the Hidden Cabal Behind the Plot to Murder America*, claiming that Jacob Rothschild, the fourth Baron Rothschild, had personally selected Kenyan Muslim usurper Barack Hussein Obama as the United States's next leader to oversee the ongoing financial collapse of the Western world. And it was a hit on early video aggregator sites.[9]

Over more than six hundred issues, Redman and his contributors took on the pressing topics that the media "wouldn't cover." They had a particular obsession with the Clintons, of course, along with "the truth" about the Oklahoma City bombing and the Waco siege. But there were also attacks on feminism and communism, examinations of Bigfoot sightings and bovine growth hormone, and even movie reviews and rants sent in by readers. Of course, there was the usual obsession with Jewish wealth. In one series of *Conspiracy Nation* issues, Redman liberally quotes from Iowa congress member and People's Party founder James B. Weaver's 1892 book *A Call to Action*, full of attacks on "European speculators" and their role in demonetizing silver.[10] Another extols Father Coughlin's fight against "internationalism" as "a recurring scheme favored by those wanting to hog wealth and power."[11] Numerous issues make vague references to "European funders" or "globalist bankers" as the power behind the power.

Regular *Conspiracy Nation* contributor Sherman Skolnick was already something of a fringe celebrity, having started the Chicago-based activist organization Citizens' Committee to Clean Up the Courts to rid the Windy City of its endemic graft and political corruption. He's also a tragic case study in how paranoia can turn a well-meaning and tenacious crusader into a crank—making more unhinged accusations while accomplishing less and less.

Though he was confined to a wheelchair because of polio, Skolnick's tireless reporting on real corruption in Illinois government helped bring down two state supreme court justices in 1969 and contributed to the legal case against one of the state's many imprisoned governors. But by the time *Conspiracy Nation* launched, he'd descended down the rabbit hole. Skolnick trafficked in bizarre claims about the Clintons, filed scores of frivolous lawsuits against the City of Chicago and Cook County, and ranted about the domination of a global government run by a Rockefeller-Rothschild alliance. It all culminated in his posthumously published book of columns *Overthrow of the American Republic*, in which, among other Rothschild-involved schemes, he bizarrely implicated the "French Rothschilds" in a plot alongside the Jesuits and the Japanese underworld to take over Bank of America and fund the 9/11 attacks.[12]

There would be many others who found audiences pumping out paranoia on the early internet, of course. And their influence began to creep into every aspect of the rapidly growing conspiracy theory/militia/antisemi-tism/New World Order nexus that blossomed with the botched raid on the Branch Davidian compound in Waco in 1993.

There were followers of the far-right survivalist and former Special Forces officer James "Bo" Gritz, whose acolytes at the off-the-grid sur-vival camp he founded in Idaho routinely claimed a Rothschild-run New World Order was about to strip them of their freedom.[13] There's Henry Makow, a Swiss-born conspiracy theorist whose website devoted to "expos-ing feminism and the New World Order" has archives going back to 2002 containing hundreds of articles attacking the Rothschilds, including a 2004 piece claiming the Iraq War was engineered to "[advance] the Rothschilds' program of world dictatorship as outlined in *The Protocols of the Elders of Zion*. These Lucifer-loving bankers and their confederates would like you to believe the *Protocols* is a forgery. It is not. It is the blueprint of the new world order unfolding before our eyes."[14]

Conspiracy theorist Jack Otto's mid-aughts radio show *Radically Right* pumped out a constant stream of crackpot theories about the supposed Rothschild-Rockefeller alliance while claiming the family were "fake Jews" descended from a lost central Asian tribe called the "Khazars" who con-verted to Judaism in the eighth century C.E. And Andrew Hitchcock's 2007 book *The Synagogue of Satan* claimed to tell "The Secret History of Jewish World Domination," invoking pretty much every extant Rothschild trope while adding a few operatically bizarre new ones like "on September 11, the attack on the World Trade Center and the Pentagon is orchestrated by Israel with the complicity of Britain and America, under the orders of the Rothschilds, which they in turn blame on so-called Muslim terrorists."[15] All it was missing was the Japanese underworld.

But even though the internet was bringing conspiracy theories to a much wider audience, most people still wanted nothing to do with this stuff or the people who cranked it out.

That changed in Austin, Texas, starting in the mid-1990s, when Alex Jones became a public access phenomenon. He took the scattered parts of conspiracy theory internet 1.0—the message board posts, the text-block newsletters, the technicolor-puke-looking websites—and put it all together in an entertaining and user-friendly package that could easily be monetized through the growing number of distribution channels opening up on the net. And he frequently took calls on his public access show, letting listeners and guests opine on their own conspiracy theories that he would then run with—Bill Cooper was a frequent early guest. Jones put a good-looking, well-spoken, deeply passionate face on a genre that was heretofore dominated by elderly cranks and street-corner shouters pushing shopping carts. And if there was one cabal he blamed more than any other for the ever-impending triumph of the New World Order, it was the Rothschilds.

"HANG UP, RED SHIELD!"

While promoting his book on climate change in 2007, London heir David Mayer de Rothschild—a swashbuckling adventurer and environmentalist with a six-foot-four frame, a history of dating Hollywood actresses like Cameron Diaz and more recently Angelina Jolie, and long flowing hair—made one of the family's few recent media appearances. For reasons that defy human understanding, it was on Infowars, talking to Alex Jones.

The Rothschild and the Rothschild conspiracy theorist spent an hour locked in a hostile, deeply awkward, and seemingly endless "debate" about both his family history and the dangers of climate change—which Jones believes is nothing but a globalist scam to enact carbon taxes and mind control. During the interview, Jones seems giddy to actually have the ear of an "heir of the House of Rothschild," and deluged de Rothschild with bad faith questions, bogus statistics, and off-topic rambles—before bringing up "the time of Waterloo, when your family was so active" and tying it to the myth of a massive Channel storm forcing Nathan Rothschild's messenger to bribe a terrified sailor.

The family might be press averse, but they know these theories have been around for a long time and decided long ago that the way they respond to them is to not respond to them. Sure enough, de Rothschild ignored the Waterloo mentions and the dog whistles about "your money-changing family," continuously going back to how we only have one planet and maybe we should stop treating it like a garbage dump. Likewise, Jones continued ranting at a level akin to the internet debate standard "if global warming is real, why is it cold outside," finally dropping any pretense of civil conversation and shouting, "I'm not your slave, Rothschild! And your scam's not going to work!"

With the Rothschild heir not taking the bait, Jones finally bellowed, "Hang up, Red Shield!," seemingly daring de Rothschild to abandon the call as music swelled, taking Infowars to a commercial break. Either because he was genuinely enjoying the experience, or because he was too polite to hang up, David stayed on the line, and the two grown men continued yelling over each other. Finally, mercifully, after forty endless minutes, the conversation wrapped up. Like any pointless debate involving a conspiracy believer, nobody's mind was changed.

"Lord Rothschild, you know that your house will fail in the end," Jones gravely proclaimed to David, who doesn't actually have that title. "And I want to let you know that anyone who supports the New World Order and dehumanization is going to go to prison, you just need to know that."

"Sure, thanks for letting me know," de Rothschild responded in his crisp English accent, practically smirking through the phone. "I hope you can visit and bring me some food." He finally hung up, and an outraged Jones mocked him some more before moving on.[16]

Because the Rothschilds so rarely give interviews, it's easy to look at the bizarre exchange between Alex Jones and David de Rothschild as a missed opportunity for Jones to get behind the locked door of one of the most secretive dynasties in the world. But Jones has no interest in the Rothschilds as anything other than what he perceives as the funders of the New World Order. And he never did, because nobody wants to listen to a show that tells you that the people you think run the world actually are okay, and maybe even trying to do some good for the world.

Jones's endorsement of the Waterloo canard in his 2007 film *Endgame* was yet another manifestation of an obsession that probably started the first time he grabbed *None Dare Call It Conspiracy* off his father's bookshelf and read its admonition to "remember that for over 150 years it has been standard operating procedure of the Rothschilds and their allies to control both sides of every conflict."[17]

Infowars shows as far back as 2003 are peppered with references to the Rothschilds "printing money," controlling central banking, and being "a major part of the New World Order."[18] By 2008, Jones was referring to the Rothschilds as part of a "Germanic death cult that believes they are the true Zionists" in an interview with conspiracy theorist author Jordan Maxwell.[19] In 2009, Jones included "European Rothschilds and Rockefellers" in a bizarre bit where he faked leaving a message on the voicemail of newly inaugurated president Barack Obama.[20] Ironically, a Rothschild did actually make a rare foray into American politics in that election, as Lynn Forester de Rothschild, wife of then–London branch head Evelyn de Rothschild (the father of David de Rothschild), flipped from supporting Hillary Clinton in the 2008 Democratic primary to endorsing Obama's opponent John McCain due to her belief that Obama was "an elitist" who "has not given me reason to trust him."[21] The endorsement didn't curry much favor with Jones, who loathed McCain as well.

Jones's obsession with the Rothschilds isn't just confined to his radio show. An un-bylined (and since deleted) 2010 article on Infowars referred to the Rothschilds and Rockefellers as "Trillionaires of The World," supported by a slew of fake quotes and debunked conspiracy theories. The piece was met with dozens of comments that the Rothschilds should die in a variety of horrible ways—not an uncommon reaction among anonymous internet trolls discussing the family.[22] Even the talk pages for Jones's Wikipedia entry, where editors discussed what should and shouldn't be included on his biographical page, became a battleground over whether Jones's constant references to the Rothschilds are actual antisemitism or merely "talk about certain corrupt individuals like Kissenger [sic] and the Rothschild family as well as hundreds of other people of all races and beliefs."[23]

Jones would continue making references to the Rothschilds being "broken and destroyed" and "rolling over for the ChiComs" (Chinese Communist Party) in episodes well into the 2020s as Rothschild power had long since waned. The Rothschilds are so omnipresent on Infowars that the family has been mentioned on more than 1,300 different episodes of Alex Jones's show, either by the host, one of his fill-in hosts, or a guest.[24] But even as Jones kept attacking the Rothschilds, he shifted much of his ire toward a different wealthy Jewish philanthropist—George Soros. Many of those coming up alongside Jones in the growing firmament of internet conspiracy theories would take Jones's deranged notions about the family down darker and stranger roads, leading to all manner of Jew-hating garbage.

WHERE THE NEW AGE MEETS THE THIRD REICH

When David Icke—the one-time Coventry City goalie, TV sports commentator, and Green Party spokesperson—reinvented himself as a turquoise-clad Son of the Godhead in March 1991, he seemed to genuinely be concerned about the fate of humanity, channeling his automatic writing binges into a slew of messages of love and warnings about upcoming disasters wiping England off the map. No disasters materialized, except for Icke being laughed at by befuddled British TV audiences. So he hitched his wagon to a familiar horse and transitioned into blaming the Jews for all of society's ills. Very quickly, the crowds stopped laughing and started cheering. Icke made himself a conspiracy superstar, speaking to massive audiences and making equally massive amounts of money, with the Rothschilds put at the center of a vast global "super-conspiracy" to purge the world and ruthlessly control anyone who survived.

Icke started theorizing about Jewish financial power with his 1994 book *The Robots' Rebellion*—see chapter 6 for Icke inventing a link between Alexander Hamilton and the Rothschilds. But that was a mere appetizer compared to the full meal of incoherent Jew-baiting in 1995's *And the Truth Shall Set You Free*. Dubbed by a columnist a few years after its publication as "where the New Age meets the Third Reich," *And the Truth Shall Set You Free* was deemed by Icke's publisher to be too antisemitic to actually release, leaving Icke to self-publish.[25] Icke mentions the Rothschilds over three hundred times in the book, liberally mixing giant blocks of text full of

New Age nonsense with hyperbolic attacks on every element of Jewish culture, history, and religion. He accuses a Jewish conspiracy of both funding the Holocaust and exaggerating its horror, of carrying out terrorist attacks against fellow Jews and blaming them on Gentiles, of running the Atlantic slave trade, of starting the KKK, of suppressing secret cures for disease and alien technology, and of being the masterminds behind countless other plots and conspiracies against Christendom.

Many of his attacks on Jews and the Rothschilds are retreads: Waterloo, the Elector's Treasure, founding the Illuminati and the Federal Reserve, and so on. But Icke seems to have a particular obsession with blaming the Rothschilds for funding the Nazi war machine—taking Gary Allen's line that nobody should hate the Rothschilds more than other Jews and making it an ethos.

"[T]he Allied and German bankers were on the same side," Icke writes in *And the Truth*, leaving out any sort of evidence. "They were connected by the same All-Seeing Eye cult; a force which goes back to antiquity. The short-term loans issued under the Dawes Plan went into specific German companies vital to rearmament. It was this money that expanded the pharmaceutical cartel known as I.G. Farben, which was, in reality, Hitler's war machine [. . .] These loans, which included some from Morgan and Rothschild companies, and the technology transfers from the United States to the German cartels, made the Second World War possible."[26]

Some of this is true enough—Allied and German officials *were* on the same side in 1924, when France had occupied the highly industrial Ruhr Valley in order to force Germany to make its latest reparations payment, sparking a diplomatic crisis in the process. The Dawes Plan used American loans to stabilize Germany's economy, rebuilding its mining and manufacturing industries, and curbing rampant hyperinflation—ending the French occupation in the process. But it was J. P. Morgan, not the Rothschilds, who floated the $200 million loan for Germany in the US market. Such distinctions don't matter to Icke, who accuses the Rothschilds not just of secretly funding the dictatorship that stripped them of their assets and sent them fleeing, but of profiting off said dictatorship's use of Jews as industrial slaves, as Icke rhetorically asks, "and who controlled I.G. Farben, a company that would use Jews and others as slave labour? The Rothschilds, via a stream of frontmen and companies."[27]

Not content to blame the rise of Hitler on the Rothschilds, Icke lumps them in with his next great conspiracy theory: the "reptilian elite" coming from distant worlds to take human form and enslave the masses. "Leading Brotherhood families like the Rothschilds and the Windsors are full-bloods, reptilians wearing human physical bodies like an overcoat in the full knowledge of who they are and the Agenda they are seeking to implement," Icke writes in 1999's *The Biggest Secret*.[28] He later adds, among countless mentions of the supposed reptile alien Illuminati elites, that "reptilian bloodlines like the 'Jewish' Rothschilds funded and supported the Nazis and allowed the rank and file Jewish people to reap the unspeakable consequences."[29]

Naturally, Icke rebuts claims that he's antisemitic because the Rothschilds aren't "real Jews." "There is no 'Jewish money,' you see, no Jewish billionaires funding both sides in US politics," Icke sarcastically writes in 2019's *The Trigger*. "It's all a myth, an 'anti-Semitic trope,' so it is outrageous to even raise the subject and most certainly 'anti-Semitic.' As for exposing ultra-Zionists like the Rothschilds for their serious involvement in the slave trade—you must be a Nazi to say that even though it's true."[30]

"There is not a single man, woman or child whose life is not affected, often disastrously, by the Rothschilds," Icke further declares in 2010's *Human Race Get Off Your Knees*, calling them "interbreeding global criminals and power-crazed genocidal maniacs" so obsessed with genetic perfection that they "actually have Rothschild sperm banks to constantly expand the bloodline."[31]

One article in particular, cited again and again by future conspiracy theories, takes a bit of historical arcana and runs with it in a shockingly antisemitic direction. In a now-deleted but archived 2003 article titled "Was Hitler a Rothschild?" Icke starts by announcing, "Official history is merely a veil to hide the truth of what really happened." And what "truth" would be more upsetting to the "accepted version" of history than Adolf Hitler not only secretly being Jewish, but having been spawned by a member of the Austrian Rothschilds?

Unlike many of his other claims, Icke is relying here on an actual document that reproduces a widely held rumor circulating at the time. He specifically cites a 1972 book by psychologist Walter C. Langer called *The Mind of Adolf Hitler: The Secret Wartime Report*. Langer's book, in turn, was an adaptation of a psychological dossier on the Nazi leader ordered in 1943 by the US Office of Strategic Services—the forerunner of the CIA.

Trying to pin down the identity of Hitler's paternal grandfather, which is still unknown, Langer writes of the Austrian police creating "a secret document that proved that [Hitler's grandmother] Maria Anna Schicklgruber was living in Vienna at the time she conceived [Hitler's father Alois]."

"At that time she was employed as a servant in the home of Baron Rothschild," Langer continues. "As soon as the family discovered her pregnancy, she was sent back to her home in Spital where Alois was born."[32] Note that this is incorrect, as Alois was born in the town of Strones, 45 kilometers east of Spital.

Icke's article adds some of his own "research" pointing to Austrian branch founder Salomon Mayer Rothschild as living alone in his Vienna mansion in 1836, around the time Alois would have been conceived, and therefore being Alois's "real father" and, by extension, Adolf Hitler's grandfather.

As Langer's book hints, the rumor that Hitler had Jewish blood by virtue of his paternal grandfather was rampant in Germany in the 1920s, particularly in the cafés of Munich and among foreign journalists. The rumor became even more entrenched after the war, when Nazi lawyer Hans Frank claimed in his jail cell memoirs, dictated as he was waiting to be hanged at Nuremberg, that Hitler had ordered him to look into Alois potentially having a Jewish father, allegedly due to a letter Hitler received from his nephew attempting to blackmail him.[33]

Icke didn't even invent the idea of a Rothschild specifically being the father of Alois Hitler, as a very similar passage had appeared in Fritz Springmeier's *Bloodlines of the Illuminati* in 1991—and Icke acknowledges *Bloodlines* at the end of his article. But that was a fairly obscure book, while Icke was a full-blown celebrity—endorsing one of the most repellent conspiracy theories one could imagine.

Historians have generally settled on one of two men to be Adolf Hitler's paternal grandfather: either journeyman miller Johann Georg Hiedler, who married Maria Schicklgruber five years after Alois was born and whose name Alois would adopt (though he changed his last name from Hiedler to Hitler for unknown reasons), or Johann Georg's brother Johann Nepomuk Hiedler, who raised the boy after his brother's death in 1857. A third possibility for Hitler's grandfather, a Jewish man from Graz named Frankenberger, who supposedly employed Maria as a maid or cook, was put forth by Hans Frank. But the Frankenberger hypothesis is generally discounted by historians, pointing out that no Jews were allowed to live in Graz at the time Alois would have been conceived, and that Hans Frank was likely in the midst of a mental breakdown while waiting for the gallows.[34]

Notably, none of these men are Rothschilds. Maria Schicklgruber never worked as a maid for Baron Rothschild and, like most peasants of the time, lived most of her life in the place she was born: Strones, the tiny town 100 kilometers northwest of Vienna where both she and Alois were born. The name "Salomon" being linked to Hitler's lineage was the result of an error in an article in a German paper in 1932, according to research by Hitler biographer Ian Kershaw.[35] Even Langer's study of Hitler allows that the link between the dictator and the baron is merely a story, while the "secret document" supposedly developed by the Austrian police turned out to be written by a former Nazi streetfighter and known plagiarist who had had no access to such secrets.

And in one final, ironic twist, while Hitler wasn't a Rothschild, his archrival Joseph Stalin *did* have a direct connection to the family. In late 1901, the young Stalin bragged to his comrades that he was "working for the Rothschilds" after he got a job at a refinery owned by Edouard de Rothschild in the port city of Batum, now in Georgia. After the refinery caught fire, almost certainly due to arson, and refinery managers refused to pay the employees a bonus, Stalin led a strike against the company. The strike was violently broken up with numerous workers killed, and Stalin was arrested and exiled to Siberia as punishment.[36]

But for Icke, both the details of Hitler's mother's birth and the much more interesting story of Stalin fighting the Rothschilds are irrelevant. All that matters is that his bizarre tale *could* be true—therefore, it's true. It's a faulty logic that infects conspiracy discourse over and over, getting worse with each iteration, each share, and each new adaptation of an old trope. And never worse than on social media.

"I CARE NOT WHO MAKES THE LAWS" AND OTHER BUNK

By the time sites like Facebook and Twitter emerged as the principal vector by which strangers yelled at each other, it had become trivially easy to connect the Rothschild name or a company they once owned to a world event—any world event—and spread the story around to your followers as if it were true. If you got lucky, it could go viral and get you internet clout.

Memes, viral videos and Twitter threads, podcasts, foreign blogs posting fake stories, and Facebook groups full of people "just asking questions" became as important to the Rothschild myth in the twenty-first century as pamphlets and self-printed newsletters were in the past.

Some new Rothschild conspiracy theories bubbled up and popped quickly, but others continue to dominate search results and social media discourse to this day. The most durable of these are everywhere, easily accessible with a Google search, and have pervaded every aspect of how we talk about Jews and money. Cataloguing them all is impossible, but some are more important than others:

"Rothschild central banks": If the Rothschilds are going to "own" the US Federal Reserve and the Bank of England, they might as well own every other nation's central bank, too, at least according to a variety of popular memes claiming the Rothschilds "own" the central banks of all but an ever-changing list of five or seven or nine countries that we are "always at war with."

One hallmark of conspiracy theories is that they're both extremely detailed and extremely inconsistent. So it doesn't matter to believers that one list names these countries as "Abkhazia [a breakaway republic in Georgia that's not generally recognized as a country], Bolivia, Cuba, Iran, North Korea, Russia, and Syria," while another lists them as "Russia, China, Iceland, Cuba, Syria, Iran, Venezuela, North Korea, and Hungary," while another claims merely "Iran, North Korea, and Cuba" are the nations who have boldly refused a Rothschild central bank.

This is a basic and willful misunderstanding of how central banking works. Some state banks do have privately owned shares; the Federal Reserve's twelve feeder banks have shares, but they're only owned by other banks. And while the Bank of England did once have private shareholders, it hasn't since it was nationalized in 1946. Most of these lists are simply nations where the government has taken control of private financial institutions—or who never had private banking at all. Iceland isn't on these lists because "we've always been at war" with them, but because their government nationalized the country's biggest private banks in 2008 as the financial crisis deepened.[37]

As previously written, the canard that the Rothschilds "own" various central banks dates back to their bailout of the Bank of England in 1825. But two centuries haven't dimmed the enthusiasm for this particular trope. In December of 2005, a conspiracy theorist named Daryl Bradford Smith wrote a timeline of supposed Rothschild abuses, including planning the 9/11 attacks as a pretense for the US invading Afghanistan and installing a Rothschild central bank, a baseless charge that would later be repeated with Iraq in 2003 and Israel in 2005—thanks to the London bus bombings, of all things.

"There are now only 5 nations on the world left without a Rothschild controlled central bank," Smith wrote on his now-dead website I Am the Witness: "Iran; North Korea; Sudan; Cuba; and Libya."[38] Given the disastrous attempts by the US to install stable governments in both Afghanistan and Iraq, it would seem that the plan for Rothschild banking colonization should have gotten one more look before being implemented.

Malaysia Airlines Flights 370 and 17: The crash or disappearance of jetliners is exceedingly rare, which is why it was so shocking when Malaysia Airlines lost two planes in four months in 2014. First, MH370 disappeared on March 8, vanishing off radar somewhere over the southern

Indian Ocean. Then on July 17, MH17 was shot down over Donetsk by a missile fired by pro-Russia separatist forces fighting against Ukraine. Both incidents spawned extensive investigations—one to find out what happened to MH370, the other to find out why MH17 was downed. And the Rothschilds were somehow linked to both—proof that the family was so powerful, it thought nothing of wiping out an entire plane full of innocent people just to advance its aims.

For MH370, the conspiracy theory was that Lord Jacob Rothschild, through investment firm Blackstone, owned 20 percent of the patent of a mysterious technology known as KL03, supposedly a tiny semiconductor that could deliver enormous power to devices hooked up to the internet. Who owned the other 80 percent? Four Chinese-born employees of the Texas firm Freescale Semiconductor—who all happened to be on MH370 when it vanished. With those four employees out of the way, Lord Rothschild would own the entire patent—and be poised to make limitless money off "the internet of things."

KL03 is a real chip developed by Freescale Semiconductor, but that's about the extent of this conspiracy theory's veracity.[39] According to multiple fact-checking sites, the four men supposedly owning the other 80 percent were employees of the company, but the company itself was the patent holder. They were also not actually on the plane in the first place, and weren't listed on the passenger manifest. Finally, Jacob Rothschild didn't "own" part of the patent; he merely had shares in Blackrock, an investment firm that held shares in Freescale. The flight's disappearance made him no money whatsoever, but the conspiracy theory was explored in multiple high-profile books about the incident.[40]

With MH17, the mystery was solved quickly thanks to open-source intelligence posted on social media that revealed who shot it down and how. But that didn't stop a swirl of rumors that the Rothschilds had the flight shot down to start another world war, or to assassinate Vladimir Putin (who was "supposed to be on the plane"), or to protect Jacob Rothschild's Malaysian business interests, or as part of an Illuminati ritual sacrifice, or to eliminate prominent AIDS researchers linked to the Big Pharma conspiracy theory for some reason. None of it was true, but all of it generated clicks in the frenetic days after the plane was shot down when no theory was too bonkers for someone to believe.[41]

"The Rothschilds own 80 percent of the world's wealth" and/or "are worth 500 trillion dollars": Pinning down the net worth of a family as large and spread out as the Rothschilds has always been difficult, going back to the family struggling to keep accurate balance sheets in the 1800s. But that's never stopped conspiracy cranks from coming up with their own numbers. One in particular has emerged on the internet as the "true" net worth of the family: the astonishing number $500 trillion.

The figure has appeared everywhere from viral Facebook memes about the Rothschilds having "enough money to feed and clothe every man, woman, and child on Earth" to textbooks about the history of capitalism. And like so many others, it's one of those "facts" that people pass on simply because they've heard that the Rothschilds are really rich. But are they *that* rich?

No, because $500 trillion is more than the net worth of the entire planet, including real estate, according to economic data from 2021.[42] While the $500 trillion number is ludicrous, there are other lower—though still outlandish—numbers thrown around on questionable websites, such as $350 billion, $500 billion, $1 trillion, or $5 trillion. But even those are wild overestimations, given that few Rothschilds have ever appeared on vetted lists of the wealthiest people in the world, such as the annual *Forbes World's Billionaires* list. Naturally, conspiracy theorists offer their own explanation for this: the Rothschilds are so powerful that they simply order their names to be removed from said lists so the public will never know how wealthy they really are.

It's impossible to say what the total value of every Rothschild property or company throughout history is, given how many descendants there are. But while the total is unknown, the family's likely net worth is much less than the other wealthy dynasties of the world, such as the Waltons, Kochs, or Mars families, various foreign oligarchs and tycoons, and the British and Saudi royal families.

So where did the "$500 trillion" number come from? It started appearing on message boards around 2010, always with caveats like "it is estimated" or "experts say," so it's easy to dismiss offhand. And it's entirely possible that it was simply made up and had no forethought behind it whatsoever. But these numbers aren't purely internet inventions, even if the meme is.

In 1926's *The Secret World Government*, Count Cherep-Spridovich declared that "Baron Edouard A. Rothschild V is today the 'Uncrowned Ruler of the World.' He controls the 300 men of the Hidden Hand, $300,000,000,000 and 90 percent of the World's press."[43] Fifteen years later, George Washington Armstrong's *Rothschild Money Trust* took that figure, added $100 billion in profit he thought the family made off the Great War, and another $100 billion in profit he assumed they made off the Great Depression to come up with "a very conservative estimate" of "a family fortune [that] is now in the neighborhood of $500,000,000,000."[44] It's possible someone took that number and just turned "billion" into "trillion" because it sounds more sinister, and it became gospel truth online. The truth is that we'll likely never know for sure.

Both the "$500 trillion" and "$500 billion" numbers are absurd. Armstrong's guess of $500 billion, published in 1940, would be the equivalent of more than $10 trillion adjusted for inflation. And while Baron Edouard Rothschild was a wealthy man, much of his property was confiscated by the Nazi-controlled Vichy government, and he fled Paris for New York with "only" about a million dollars' worth of jewels.[45] But the popularity of anti-Rothschild books during the Cold War and Rothschild conspiracy theories online have made these stratospheric guesses at the family's net worth something close to canonized among modern cranks.

"Controlling the world's money supply": There are countless apocryphal quotes assigned to various Rothschilds, including some previously explored in this book, such as Gutle Rothschild's supposed declaration that wars wouldn't exist if her boys didn't want them. But there are two quotes linked to the Rothschilds more than any other, and both are freely employed by cranks and legitimate writers alike.

One is Mayer Amschel's infamous declaration, supposedly from 1790: "Give me control of a nation's money supply, and I care not who makes its laws." The other is the equally outrageous quote supposedly uttered by Nathan Rothschild after Waterloo: "The man who controls the British money supply controls the British Empire, and I control the British money supply." To conspiracy theorists, these quotes sum up the entire ethos of the family—control, domination, manipulation, and blood-soaked greed.

Variations on these two lines existed long before the internet, of course. But while they predate the web, they are *everywhere* in internet-based works that involve the Rothschilds, global government, fiscal tyranny, or Jewish power. Even more disturbingly, the quotes have appeared in legitimate financial history and scholarship about the family. Mayer's supposed quote shows up as an epigraph in the Pulitzer Prize–winning 2009 history of the Great Depression *Lords of Finance*[46] and in frequent Fox News contributor Andrew Napolitano's 2011 book *It Is Dangerous to Be Right When the Government Is Wrong*,[47] among many others. So tackling these quotes here along with other Rothschild internet-era tropes is appropriate.

Most examinations of Mayer's quote start with G. Edward Griffin's 1994 book *The Creature from Jekyll Island*, which claims "it was Mayer Amschel Rothschild who was quoted as saying: 'Let me issue and control a nation's money and I care not who writes the laws.'"

In a footnote to the quote, Griffin writes that the line was

quoted by Senator Robert L. Owen, former Chairman of the Senate Committee on Banking and Currency and one of the sponsors of the Federal Reserve Act, National Economy and the Banking System (Washington, D.C.: U.S. Government Printing Office, 1939, p. 99). This quotation could not be verified in a primary reference work. However, when one considers the life and accomplishments of the elder Rothschild, there can be little doubt that this sentiment was, in fact, his outlook and guiding principle.[48]

Putting aside that "issuing and controlling" the money supply of nations was not, in fact, Mayer's "outlook and guiding principle," at least we now have a source for where Griffin found the quote: Oklahoma senator Robert Owen's 1939 pamphlet. Except Owen's pamphlet doesn't cite the original source of the quote either, merely attributing it to a long speech on early American monetary policy "narrated by Hon. C. G. Binderup in a speech on the floor of the House of Representatives, 76th Cong."[49]

While representative Charles Binderup of Nebraska did rail against "the Rothschild Bank" on the floor of Congress in a May 27, 1938, speech for supposedly causing an economic crisis by refusing to let the Thirteen Colonies print their own money,[50] he never used the quote Owen attributes to him. However, it does appear in the Congressional Record numerous times in the 1930s, owing to the contentious debates about the role of gold and central banking in recovering from the Depression. And it's always in the same context: having been given the ability to "issue and control" the money supply of the US, the Federal Reserve has too much power and risks being an American version of what many antisemites believed Mayer Amschel Rothschild was—a unilateral controller of how much money is printed. Do any of *these* uses have a source with a more accurate attribution?

Most uses of the quote by members of Congress aren't overtly anti-Jewish, but much more in line with the economic antisemitism of pre-WWII America, along with fear of a federal government allowed to print money at will. The first variation on "let me issue and control a nation's money supply" that comes close to the most popular version of the quote in the Congressional Record was by Mississippi Democrat T. Jeff Busby on January 20, 1934—more than four years before Binderup's supposed use. In opposition to the Gold Reserve Act of 1934, Busby brings up the supposed enemies of silver by declaring "the founder of the great Rothschild banking house said 'if you will let me furnish the money of a country, I care not who makes its laws.'" He then rails against the Federal Reserve holding too much money, just one voice in a debate on central banking that would rage for years.[51]

The line would continue to appeal to anti-gold Democrats for years to come as the American economy worsened. As if to prove how slippery the quote is, Indiana Democrat Finly Hutchinson Gray used it in speeches on the House floor four times during the 1930s and gave it a different speaker every time. During the 74th Congress in 1935, he attributes it first to "Anselm Rothschild"[52] and later to "one of the great Rothschild brothers [sic], one of the world's shrewd, crafty financiers."[53] He would use it again, on May 2, 1938, during the 75th Congress, when he attributes it to "the great financier Rothschild,"[54] and one more time a month later, attributed to "Meyer Anselm Rothschild, the world wizard of money and finance."[55] Other users gave it still different attributions, all uttered after Rep. Busby's use—Maryland Democrat Thomas Alan Goldsborough quoted an article from the magazine *Money* in a 1935 speech that claimed it was a saying from "one of the Rothschilds," for example.[56]

And legislators didn't get any better at identifying the "issue and control a nation's money supply" quote in future decades. In just one example, a 1982 House speech by Georgia Democrat Elliott Levitas—that state's first Jewish member of Congress—cites the line simply as "supposed to have been said by Baron Meyer Rothschild."[57]

So clearly Senator Owen was wrong in attributing the quote to Binderup rather than Busby (or Gray, who used it more often), and therefore G. Edward Griffin was wrong in citing Owen's attribution. But if Owen didn't get it from Binderup, where *did* he get it? It's possible that he simply cited the wrong member of Congress and nobody caught the error. Or maybe he got it from an entirely different source. A different version of Mayer's "quote" appears in another Congressional document even further back, this time from 1911—the otherwise anodyne record *Hearings on House Resolution No. 314*, where anti–Federal Reserve author T. Cushing Daniel testifies as a witness that former British prime minister William Pitt "made this statement: 'Let the American people go into their debt-funding schemes and banking systems, and from that hour their boasted independence will be a mere phantom.' He realized the maxim that Rothschilds laid down as fundamental: 'Let us control the money of a country and we care not who makes its laws.'"[58]

It's not known where Daniel got the line or if he wrote it himself, but he might have adapted it from several sources, including an 1890 tract called *Addresses on the Civil Sabbath from a Patriotic and Humanitarian*

Standpoint written by clergyman Wilbur Crafts, who attributed to "the lawless" the phrase "let us appoint the city's police and we care not who makes its laws."[59] And it's likely *that* quote was adapted from an English proverb about music that's attributed to everyone from Scottish author Andrew Fletcher in 1703 to Elizabethan courtier Sir Philip Sidney to Plato: "If a man were permitted to make all the ballads, he need not care who should make the laws of a nation."

Regardless, there's no evidence Mayer said it, or believed anything like it. In 1790 he was still a court Jew bound to the restrictive laws of Frankfurt's *Judengasse* and would have been in no position to "issue and control" any nation's currency.

As for Nathan's "control the British money supply" quote, it appears to originate long after his death. It first appears in an early 1980s' reprint of *Secrets of the Federal Reserve*, in which Eustace Mullins writes that after his Waterloo coup, Nathan "arrogantly exclaimed, during a party in his mansion, 'I care not what puppet is placed upon the throne of England to rule the empire on which the sun never sets. The man that controls Britain's money supply controls the British Empire, and I control the British money supply.'"[60]

Nobody at the time wrote of Nathan saying anything like this, and it runs totally counter to his known business philosophy. But there might be a predecessor quote in *Rothschild Money Trust*, the source of so much other repurposed Rothschild bunk.

In the midst of stomping a barrel of sour grapes over what the Rothschilds "did" to him, George Washington Armstrong declares, "There is a Rothschild Money Trust. It has grown in magnitude and power ever since it was established in 1812. It threatens the destruction of our government and of our civilization. [...] It now controls the British Empire and the American Government. It must be destroyed or we lose our freedom."[61]

Alex Jones and David Icke couldn't have said it better themselves.

WOULDN'T HAVE TO WORK HARD: THE ROTHSCHILDS IN POPULAR CULTURE

Is it even possible to write or talk about the Rothschilds without lapsing into antisemitic conspiracy theories?

As we've seen so far, that question has mostly been answered with hokey biographies and myth-drenched films like *The House of Rothschild*. Because the Rothschilds rarely tell their own stories, it's sadly been left primarily to cranks who, at best, declare "we don't hate Jews, we're just asking questions" before launching into antisemitic diatribes. Overall, the prevailing conspiracy narrative about the family has told the world that the Rothschilds are so evil and have brought so much misery on the world that even other Jews should detest them. At best, they're so wealthy that they are untouched by the cares and concerns of the rest of the rabble, other Jews included.

But we also know that's not how Jews saw the Rothschilds. Other Jews admired their business acumen, their courage in the face of institutionalized antisemitism, and their generosity toward the wider Jewish community. These are many of the same attributes that Gentile writers, particularly in nineteenth and early twentieth century America, extolled as core American virtues. Even now, Americans still revere the self-made individuals who lifted themselves up by their bootstraps and took nothing from the government on the way. What description could more fit Mayer and his boys, who turned a minor patronage into a worldwide empire while surviving waves of oppression and violence?

Go back to Elie Wiesel in 1990 in *The New York Times*, who believed as a child that the Rothschilds were idols who "seem to have been born under a lucky star, the best money can buy: our worst enemies could do them no harm."[1] So where are *these* depictions in the 200-plus-year history of the family? Is the Rothschild myth so pervasive that it's penetrated even into the cinemas and stages and bookstores of people who aren't antisemitic? It turns out that the high esteem other Jews held for the Rothschilds *was* shared by some artists, Jewish and Gentile alike. And it would find its way into works by some of the most acclaimed artists in recent history.

ALL DAY LONG I'D BIDDY-BIDDY-BUM – ROTHSCHILDS IN STORY AND SONG

The Rothschilds were mentioned or caricatured, sometimes cruelly, sometimes admiringly, in the work of Disraeli, Byron, Heine, Balzac, and Thackeray. These portrayals seized on the wealth, the largesse, the millions lent to other nations without a second thought. And while they were (mostly) free of conspiracy theory, they were heavy on mythmaking.

Beyond these literary giants, there was a vast world of Jewishness that saw the very *idea* of the Rothschilds as profound. Their steadfast insistence on retaining their Judaism when so many other banking families had converted was a beacon of aspiration at a time when most Jews still lived at a subsistence level.[2] Where many Gentiles saw scheming puppet masters in the Rothschilds, their fellow Jews saw a fantasy, a pinnacle of achievement, and a name to be almost whispered in revered awe. They were every mother's dream for her boys. After all, Mayer and his sons emerged from the squalor of the ghetto to become wealthy beyond measure—and *they remained Jews*. If they could do it, others could, too.

Just the aura of the name Rothschild was enough to power the imagination of a storyteller. The titular character in Anton Chekhov's 1894 short story *Rothschild's Violin* (also sometimes called *Rothschild's Fiddle*) is a universe away from *those* Rothschilds, merely a "gaunt, red-bearded Jew with a network of red and blue veins on his face, who bore the name of a famous rich man." He plays the flute in his town's Jewish orchestra alongside the miserable elderly Christian coffin maker Yakov, who plays the violin to make a few extra kopeks. Rothschild's playing, even on the merriest of tunes, is so deeply sad that the embittered Yakov "began to conceive a feeling of hatred and contempt for all Jews, and especially for Rothschild." The two fight constantly, to the point where Yakov is thrown out of the orchestra for his disagreeable behavior.

Eventually, Yakov's wife Martha dies, and Yakov himself takes ill, only for Rothschild to come by and declare that the orchestra leader wants Yakov to play. A sick Yakov viciously berates Rothschild and sends him running, chased by dogs and shrieking children. But thrashing about that night, Yakov comes to regret his actions toward the Jew, wondering to himself, "Why, oh why, had he frightened and insulted that Jew just now? Why did people in general always interfere with one another? What losses resulted from this! What terrible losses! If it were not for envy and anger they would get great profit from one another." When Rothschild returns the next day, again seeking to get Yakov to play, the two reconcile, and just before his death, Yakov declares that he wants Rothschild to have his precious violin—which the Jew now plays exclusively.[3]

Chekhov wasn't particularly interested in anti-Jewish sentiment until he took a trip through Siberia to tour a Jewish prison, though he was also moved by the plight of Alfred Dreyfus.[4] Instead, the story is an ironic and deeply sad meditation on the futility of hatred and the baggage that regret saddles us with—quintessentially Chekhovian attributes at the center of much of his work. It's not clear why the author picked that name, but it could be as simple as it being a Jewish name that everyone would know. The power of the Rothschild myth was such that, for better or worse (usually worse), the name itself was inseparable from Judaism.

Rothschild's Violin was a minor footnote in Chekhov's career, and its one adaptation is even less well known—a forty-minute operetta written in 1940 by young Russian musician Veniamin Fleishman, a student of the great composer Dimitri Shostakovich. It was Shostakovich who suggested the idea of adapting Chekhov's story, and after the student was killed fighting for the Soviet Union in September 1941, a heartbroken Shostakovich stepped in to finish the piece. Because it revolved around a Jew, it took until 1968 for the finished operetta to finally be staged even once. Further performances were forbidden by a Communist Party official who believed the "Rothschild" in question was part of the evil Zionist banking family and, as such, an enemy of the state.[5]

But a different musical piece, this one actually based on the mystique of *those* Rothschilds, became one of the most successful musicals in American history. It's probably playing in a high school gymnasium or community theater somewhere in the world at this moment: *Fiddler on the Roof.*

Neither the original English version of the 1964 musical nor its 1971 film adaptation specifically mention the family—part of its creators toning down the "Jewishness" of the source material to give the show more universal appeal. But the Tevye the Dairyman stories that *Fiddler* was adapted from, written by Russian Jewish author Sholom Aleichem, view the Rothschilds much the same as Elie Wiesel did as a child. They were a beacon of hope that one day your hard work would be rewarded with something other than yet more suffering, the people who you hope will someday grace the doorway of your humble home.

In Aleichem's *Tevye the Dairyman* collection, the generic "Rothschild" is the rich Jew our humble hero and those around him mention when needing to reference someone wealthier or luckier than they are, which is almost everyone. But it's in *Tevye's Daughters*, another collection of Tevye stories published after Aleichem's death, that the author truly explores the aspirational model that the Rothschilds represented to the greater Jewish community.

In the short monologue "If I Were a Rothschild," Tevye's vision for what he'd do with unlimited wealth starts small and faintly tragic: he'd buy his and his wife's good Shabbat clothes back from the pawn shop. But his dreams grow like Mayer's fortune—a new roof for the synagogue, a new bathhouse, "a real hospital such as they have in big towns," and various other homes and societies for the poor and unwell. Tevye Rothschild would do what the Rothschilds actually did: help Jews wherever they needed it, while attempting to "do away with war altogether" simply by loaning all the combatants money at a low interest rate, "four or five percent at the most." Of course, being Tevye, he gets carried away to the point where he's imagined himself as so wealthy he's transcended the need for money itself, seeing it as "a delusion, a made-up thing." But you need money to provide the bread and candles for the Sabbath, so poor Tevye is left back where he started, no wealthier or wiser.[6]

The hugely successful musical would keep that sense of aspiration, with *Fiddler* scribes Sheldon Harnick and Jerry Bock tweaking the title "If I Were a Rothschild" to be "If I Were a Rich Man," to make it easier for Western audiences to relate to, and taking some of the song's content from a different story in the same collection. But "If I Were a Rothschild" is still the song's name in the Hebrew translation of the show, and when the first-ever Yiddish adaptation of *Fidler afn Dakh*, as it was called, debuted in New York in 2018, it too stuck to Aleichem's title.[7]

The gesture may seem simple, but it's deeply meaningful for Jews. For generations of Jews across the Diaspora, the great family epitomized what it meant to be safe and secure at a time when the danger of the local authorities or an angry mob always loomed, and backbreaking work was a means to survive the endless array of hardships around you. After all, what were Rothschild pastimes like collecting art, making wine, and raising racehorses if not things you'd do if you "didn't have to work hard"? Who *wouldn't* want to do that?

"WHY WOULD ROTHSCHILDS NEED A JOHN?"

Fiddler was a worldwide smash hit, helping kick off a new interest in Jewish history and culture. But a few years earlier, there was another popular work that combined myth and history to put the Rothschilds on a pedestal—though at times, it was as precarious as that violinist perched on the roof of Tevye's house.

Frederic Morton's 1962 biography, *The Rothschilds: A Family Portrait*, was the first major postwar examination of the Rothschilds, and it was a huge success, becoming a finalist for the National Book Award and hitting #1 on the *New York Times* bestseller list.[8] As the Vienna-born Morton was much more a novelist than a historian, its tone was less of a scholarly exploration of the Rothschilds and more of a gossipy, soap opera–esque look at the glitz and glamour of the family that by now embodied the oft-snarled phrase "old money."

Past chapters of this book have explored Morton's recounting of the Waterloo story, where the author takes an opportunity to serve up new scholarship about this most well-worn Rothschild trope and utterly wastes it perpetuating the myth of Nathan's "scoop." The rest of the book, based on extensive interviews Morton did with Rothschild family members and their business associates, along with past Rothschild biographies like the flawed Egon Caesar Corti books and others, is mostly the same. While Morton writes in the introduction that he's more interested in the "human" side of the family, mostly what he means is what they bought and how much. In just one early example, he gushes over the "white mink and diamond stars" worn by French Rothschild heiress Philippine on the day of her 1961 wedding to a nameless young man singled out by Morton as "very handsome, very talented, [and] very poor."[9]

The wedding is excessively posh—a seven-foot-tall cake, private railroad cars, battalions of gendarmes in silk stockings, paragraphs gushing over the floral arrangements. Morton then moves backward to the beginning of the family's success. And again, it's paragraph after paragraph of satin-lined rooms on their yacht, gold ballrooms in the mansions, massive chandeliers, Alfred de Rothschild's "baton of pure white ivory banded with a circlet of diamonds," which he used to "conduct the symphony orchestra he kept as a private hobby,"[10] "whole galleries of Rembrandts, Watteaus, Ingres, Fragonards, Picassos,"[11] and the like. More is more, and too much is not enough—likely a product of the time Morton spent speaking to family members in their homes and offices.

Contemporary reviews of the book, though positive, single out Morton's lack of detail about the business dealings of the family, while spending most of his time on, as one critic noted, "the visible result of all this victory, [where] the tale grows fascinating."[12] And even though he clearly admires the ability of the Rothschilds to survive whatever is thrown at them, hints of certain tropes can't help but worm their way into Morton's writing.

He starts one early chapter by declaring that "someone once said that the wealth of Rothschilds consists of the bankruptcy of nations"—a quote with no citation that future writers would use against the family.[13] Wars between nations are merely "stepping stones" in their "demonic drive" for wealth. They order around royalty and presidents, and entire nations rise and fall based on their whims. "The history of Rothschild is the history of other people's Waterloos," he concludes at one point, making an uncomfortable point that for a Rothschild to win, someone else has to lose.[14]

Unsurprisingly, some of Morton's hyperbolic claims about the family found their way into more conspiratorial and antisemitic work. Christian conspiracy theorist Des Griffin's 1976 book *Descent Into Slavery?* and Eustace Mullins's *The World Order: Our Secret Rulers* both take quotes from *A Family Portrait* out of context to portray the Rothschilds as piratical bankrupters of nations—and cast Morton as the biographer brave enough to pull back the veil on the Rothschild conspiracy.

The criticism and misinterpretation of Morton's work aside, there is value in his examination of the myth of the Rothschilds. But that value can be found not in the laundry list of artworks the family hung on its walls, but in what he *doesn't* write about: Morton's own relationship with the Rothschilds as figures of aspiration.

Morton, born Fritz Mandelbaum in 1924, narrowly escaped with his family to New York during the Nazi annexation of Austria, with his family changing their name so his father could join an allegedly antisemitic trade union. As such, he writes with great sensitivity about the Rothschilds' difficulties during the early years of the Nazi regime, such as Louis spending months as a hostage of the Gestapo, or Parisian winemaker Philippe's arrest and subsequent escape across the Pyrenees Mountains into Spain and freedom.[15]

The common thread between one Jew fleeing tyranny to another is clear in a piece Morton penned for *The New York Times* in 1970. Remembering his desperate flight from Vienna, he wrote,

> my family and about 600 other Jews were in the Vienna Rothschild palace. We were there to beseech the new tenants, the Jewish Passport Section of the Gestapo, to let us leave the Austria Hitler had taken over. For ten hours we trembled and inched and starved our way up an alabaster staircase. I remember having to go to the bath room and being sure there wasn't any—why would Rothschilds need a john? And when we finally left, precious passports in hand, I remember the SS man coming in at the door. Under the mighty Rothschild portals, he wiped his shoes briefly before he caught himself.[16]

For Morton during those desperate hours, like Elie Wiesel during his poor childhood, the Rothschilds were awe-inspiring legends, with their mere name serving as "a myth which could impose itself on the most hostile mind"—like an SS flunky who shows a modicum of respect for the great house he's using to help decide which Jews can leave and live, or stay and likely die.

The Rothschilds' largesse was victory for all Jews. They were heroes who fought tenaciously for the freedom of other Jews, while never giving in to the temptations of conversion and assimilation. And if they enjoyed vast art collections or bottles of wine that cost more than a house, well, they earned it. At a WNYC author's luncheon around the time of the book's release, Morton gushes over the family's love of fine food and wine. He's particularly impressed with how Mayer would stuff potential business partners or local overlords with rich food to get them drowsy enough to give in to his demands.[17] It was all bigger than life. And a few years after the release of *A Family Portrait*, the theater world at large would see just how dramatic and outsized their already dramatic and outsized story could be.

A MUSICAL PORTRAIT

If history had turned out differently, Tevye wouldn't have sung about what he'd do if he were a rich man, because the Rothschilds could have gotten there first.

Shortly after its publication, the rights to *A Family Portrait* were offered to Sheldon Harnick and Jerry Bock, who turned the book down to continue working on *Fiddler*. But after *Fiddler*, the duo felt like they could musically dramatize the First Family of Judaism to bring out both the opulence of their success and the dangers of their lives as visible Jews. The ensuing years saw the duo write draft after draft of an adaptation of Morton's book, a tortuous process that directly led to the breakup of their lucrative partnership.

But after countless revisions and rewrites, *The Rothschilds* finally hit Broadway in 1970, sporting a massive cast and budget to tell the story of Mayer's rise from the ghetto and Nathan's ascent to "king of the Jews" on the back of the Napoleonic Wars through song and dance.[18] And the show was set up to make the same kind of splash *Fiddler* made. It got solid reviews in the biggest papers in New York and a major promotional push. Its cast members even hit the *Ed Sullivan Show* to sing one of its songs, with Mayer and his cute kids belting out the expositional track "Sons." But Harnick and Bock couldn't make lighting strike twice, and after its initial success, it quickly faded into obscurity.

The initial run of *The Rothschilds* certainly can't be called a failure. It ran for over a year and received numerous Tony Award nominations, including one for Best Musical, and a Best Actor win for Hal Linden for his portrayal of Mayer. It had a stately score and sumptuous sets and costumes, and it took the notable stance of referencing the dark history of Jewish persecution that ultimately resulted in the Holocaust. But it lacked the earworms, the jokes, and the joyous drunk dancing that *Fiddler* boasted. It wasn't universal, and it wasn't aspirational. Listening to it now, it feels stiff and formal, with characters that seem remote and unlikable, singing their way through an overly complicated plot about financial instruments and interest rates—one of the last songs in the show is called "Bonds," and it's literally about selling bonds. Even worse, cultural critics thought it was out of sync with its times, both socially and in terms of musical theater trends, where minimalism, social protest, and equality were replacing big showstoppers and dancing girls.[19]

For a show that debuted when feminism was becoming a mainstream ideology, it almost completely omitted the five Rothschild daughters from the story. Even worse, much of Gutle's character arc and several solo songs were cut from the finished production, and the only other woman of note in the cast is Nathan Rothschild's love interest.[20] Austrian statesman Prince Metternich and various French and English bankers get as much singing time as Gutle or any of the Rothschild women, essentially writing them out of their own story and replacing them with stereotypical portrayals of Jewish men being good at making money.

And attempts by Morton to equate the Rothschilds' struggle in the *Judengasse* to that of the Black American quest to escape the crushing poverty of the inner city came off as hokey and tone-deaf. Morton's 1970 *New York Times* essay "Jewish is Beautiful" was meant as a direct nod to the "Black is beautiful" movement, and despite him speaking openly about his brush with doom in Vienna and how it compared to the danger presented by police to Black Americans, even other Jewish intellectuals didn't buy the comparison.

From a moral standpoint, *The Rothschilds* shows the antisemitism of the time as deeply impacting the family. And it directly addresses at least some of the myths about them. As if written as a response to their cultural depictions as conniving and greedy misers, the musical Rothschilds are honest to a fault, singing in "Sons" about how any boys of Mayer "caught cheating . . . will get a beating." The script even makes a snide reference to "International Conspiracy of the Rothschilds" pamphlets consumed by "ignorant peasants" and produced by the very royalty the family lent money to. But like Gutle's songs, much of the most virulent and hard-hitting anti-Jewish sentiments the Rothschilds faced in their time were cut from the script during its tortuous writing process in the service of a more feel-good story with a happy ending.[21]

Of course, that's the ending that the vast majority of Jews' stories lacked. The Rothschilds chose not to go to the place where Tevye's family in *Fiddler* had no other choice but to go: America. And more than anything, *The Rothschilds* just couldn't escape the shadow of that show, even with their creators differentiating between the two at every turn. Tevye and his cohorts were humble, hardworking, jubilant, steadfast, and relatable—they came from nothing, and had to run away even from that. The Rothschilds, for all the blows they took, were insulated from the vast majority of it.

And while *Fiddler* became a staple of stages around the world, *The Rothschilds* would only return to the stage in a heavily rewritten form at the American Jewish Theatre in 1990, and again in 2015 as a one-act musical retitled *Rothschild and Sons*. Even decades after its debut, the comparison to *Fiddler* was never more than a review away, with Bock himself writing to America Jewish Theatre before it debuted there, "Don't you think, after nineteen years, that it's about time *The Rothschilds* stood on its own two feet?"[22]

It was that 1990 revival that prompted Elie Wiesel to extol the virtues of both *The Rothschilds* and the Rothschilds, not as one rigorously documenting the other, but as a celebration of Jewish perseverance, writing that the fictional family "are not caricatures; they suffer none of the complex neuroses that seem to afflict so many of their counterparts in current novels and plays. No self-hate, no fleeing to 'the other side,' no desire to assimilate."[23] The show portrayed the family as who other Jews needed them to be, not necessarily as how the rest of the world saw them.

THE ROTHSCHILD WOMEN TELL THEIR STORY

More recent works about the Rothschilds have attempted to view the dynasty through a lens other than of men making deals, with a new generation of historical scholarship centered around the women of the family. Yes, it was Mayer's will that decreed that only his sons (and their sons and grandsons) would inherit the Rothschild banks of Europe. But with few business options available, these women and their descendants carved their own path, living lives of distinction that have rarely been explored.

Israeli novelist Sara Aharoni's bestselling 2016 book *The First Mrs. Rothschild* told a fictionalized version of Gutle's nearly century-long life in the *Judengasse*. Of particular interest to Aharoni is why Gutle never moved out of the ghetto, even after her sons' success gave her the ability to live in any number of glittering palaces around the continent. Gutle's ascetic life-style and her seemingly death-defying age fascinated writers of the time, some of whom actually loitered around her small house hoping to learn her secrets—echoes of the magical "Hebrew Talisman" that supposedly made Nathan Rothschild rich. And she was a featured player in some of the many Rothschild jokes of the time, with fellow Jews poking gentle fun at the family's wealth and extravagance as related to Gutle's frugality. But her inner life was sorely neglected in family biographies.

Of course, Gutle was just the first in a long line of remarkable Rothschild women. In her 2021 biography *The Women of Rothschild*, British journalist Natalie Livingstone explores the triumphs, eccentrici-ties, and trailblazing of the Rothschild matriarchs. She separates the story of Nathan's daughter Hannah's marriage to Christian MP Henry FitzRoy from the myth and schmaltz of its portrayal in the 1934 film. Other Rothschild daughters and wives directly advised their husband's political campaigns, fought for Jewish emancipation, made music and outsider art, scandalized male-dominated realms of finance and sport, and made names for themselves in conservation and science. A far cry from the image of priv-ileged heiresses sneering at each other behind fake smiles, the Rothschild women took their good fortune and gave it back to the world in a myriad of ways that no conspiracy crank would ever dare mention.

But there may be no Rothschild woman whose story fired the imagi-nation as much as that of Kathleen Annie Pannonica Rothschild, usually known as "Nica" and often simply called "the Jazz Baroness."

The story of Nica, the great-great-granddaughter of Nathan Mayer Rothschild, was told by her great-niece, the author and filmmaker Hannah Rothschild, in her book *The Baroness*. A young Nica married a French dip-lomat and future war hero, and eventually left him and their children and headed to New York. She fell in with the city's jazz scene, becoming a fi-nancial patron and artistic muse to bebop legends like Thelonious Monk, Bud Powell, Sonny Rollins, Horace Silver, and Charlie Parker—the latter of whom died in one of the hotel rooms Nica lived in and used as impromptu spaces for jam sessions. Nica bought cars and instruments for her beneficia-ries, paid their rent, funded their tours, gave them lifts to gigs in her Bentley, and paid for their funerals when they died destitute, which they often did.

And this wasn't an idle pursuit, like art or wine collecting. Nica's advo-cacy for these artists often put her at risk of police hassle and even got her hit with a three-year prison sentence when she and Monk were busted with marijuana in her car in Delaware in 1958.

Her family begged her to flee the US and avoid prison—but Nica stayed and fought the case, finding kinship as a Jew with Monk and the other Black musicians dealing with racism, unfounded myths, and prejudice.[24] Her determination to stay and keep faith with Monk paid off, as the case was dismissed due to police failing to follow proper procedure. Nica contin-ued as a patron to the jazz world and stayed in New York until her death in 1988. The numerous songs named after her, written and performed by the jazz legends she kept alive and working, will be known long after the works of cranks and hacks fade away.

"SWIMMING IN MONEY"

The Rothschilds are widely represented in a different form of modern storytelling with roots in some of the music that Nica had championed a generation earlier: rap.

Jazz samples, including by artists funded by Nica Rothschild, were a huge part of early rap. Sadly, so was antisemitism, particularly in the music of both Ice Cube and Public Enemy, who were forced to fire their "Minister of Information." Professor Griff for his claims that Jews were responsible for "the majority of the wickedness that goes on across the globe" and helped finance the AIDS virus.[25] Anti-Jewish references had mostly faded from popular hip-hop by the 2000s, though, as rap's biggest stars became household names in white America. The Rothschilds—like the Rockefellers and Gambino crime family kingpin John Gotti—were now a shorthand for "stacking" wealth and accumulating power in hip-hop. Megastar rapper Drake extols Rothschild wine on his 2016 track "You Know, You Know," while rapper the Game is "swimming in money like the Rothschilds" on the same year's "What Your Life Like."

It's definitely not all a mutual admiration society, though. On "Be Right," multiplatinum-selling rapper Nas spits out conspiracy tropes like "Fitted hat high rank officials / World Bank like Rothschilds / Take the wool from over your eyes / Who conspired to deceive you and I," while Run the Jewels's Killer Mike rapped in 2011's "American Dream" that, rightly or wrongly, "In America the crooks get the castles / Never see a Rothschild or Rockefeller shackled." And Kanye West, even before his 2022 turn toward antisemitic conspiracy theories, got in on namechecking the Rothschilds, thanks to a guest verse on his 2021 song "Jesus Lord" by rapper Jay Electronica—who, in turn, mentions Nica and her relationship with Thelonious Monk.

It's Jay Electronica who's made the most headlines when it comes to the Rothschilds, both for his embrace of antisemitic stereotypes and his alleged affair with one: Kate Rothschild, the now ex-wife of British financier Benjamin Goldsmith. Rap magazines were abuzz with news of the affair in 2012, featuring both mentions of the rapper's Jewish jibes and more than one unfortunate reference to the family's wealth. Or as the now-defunct sports and pop culture website Grantland wrote in referencing the conspiracy machine, they were the "famous, shadowy family that has, for the past 250 years or so, secretly governed the world, controlled the economy, commissioned biographies about themselves in order to downplay their power, and generally provided endless sustenance for casual antisemitism everywhere."[26]

Skip ahead a few years, and multiple tracks on Electronica's Grammy-nominated 2020 album *A Written Testimony* reference the deeply antisemitic "Synagogue of Satan" slur, and on one, Electronica specifically raps, "And I bet you a Rothschild I get a bang for my dollar / The synagogue of Satan want me to hang by my collar." Again, though, rap observers couldn't decide if it was truly an antisemitic attack or merely a reference to his affair with Kate Rothschild.[27] Further complicating matters was Electronica including on the song a sample of a speech by Nation of Islam leader Louis Farrakhan, himself renowned for his constant attacks on Jews, including the Rothschilds, who he's claimed "control the entire world" and ran the Atlantic slave trade, among other accusations.[28]

Rappers aren't the only musicians to employ the Rothschilds in their personal conspiracy theories, just the most prolific. Rocker Glenn Danzig, for example, referred to American politics as "a process by people who are handpicked by the Rothschilds and all these other people to do this kind of crap" in a 2017 interview.[29] It was clear that even with a new generation of writers attempting to humanize the Rothschilds and tell their once-neglected stories, the old stereotypes kept creeping in, spouted by people who either didn't know any better or did, and just didn't care.

"ROTHCHILD" VS. ROTHSCHILD

Nica's life story was told in multiple documentaries, including one directed by Hannah Rothschild and another produced by jazz lover Clint Eastwood. She was also given a fictional portrayal in Eastwood's 1988 Charlie Parker biopic *Bird*—released just months before Nica's death. But beyond those, the Rothschilds have been almost entirely absent from both the big and small screens since 1934.

Whether because of the complexity of telling the 200-year story of a multigenerational family, the difficulty many audiences might have in relating to the Rothschilds, or the prevalence of myths and conspiracy theories about them, Rothschild stories have been told mostly in books.

There is one production in development that might break this streak, though—the nascent TV series *Five Arrows*, on the rise of the five sons of Mayer.[30] The new project of *Downton Abbey* and *The Gilded Age* creator Julian Fellowes, *Five Arrows* made a big splash in the trade papers with its announcement in April of 2018—but there's been little news of it since. If it does ever get produced, *Five Arrows* promises to tell a very different story from that of the fictionalized largesse of *Downton*'s Crawley family, instead exploring real Rothschild stories "of fraternal struggles for dominance, of brilliant but disenfranchised women, of generational conflict, of incestuous alliances and of forbidden love with outsiders."[31]

But for all the Rothschild-related projects in various stages, there's one that has nothing to do with the family except, unfortunately for its writer, sharing their name. It inspired a slew of journalists and historians alike to bang their head on the nearest available desk and exclaim, "This can't be real, can it?" It was, though. And its story illustrated everything that makes the Rothschild myth both so alluring and so pernicious.

The project was *Rothchild* [sic], a new script by up-and-coming writer and director John Patton Ford, set to be directed by Jon S. Baird, who had previously made a well-received biopic about legendary comedy duo Laurel and Hardy. It was first announced in May 2019 at the Cannes Film Festival, billed as a "dark satire about New York's super rich" in which "charismatic outcast Becket Rothchild plots his way back into his family's riches, setting himself on a collision course with patriarch Whitelaw Rothchild." Announced as starring in the film, which was set to start shooting later that year, were Shia LaBeouf as Becket, and bizarrely, Mel Gibson as Whitelaw.[32]

Yes, the same Mel Gibson whose father, Catholic fundamentalist Hutton Gibson, claimed that the Holocaust was largely faked by Jewish plutocrats to make money, with Europe actually having *more* Jews after the war than before. It's also the same Gibson who in 1996 reportedly asked Jewish actress Winona Ryder if she was "an oven dodger," then later directed *The Passion of the Christ*, which portrayed the Jews as hook-nosed Christ killers. After attempting to tone down the film's reliance on the deicide trope (because, as he claimed, Jews would be "coming after me at my house. They'd come to kill me"), Gibson attempted to make amends by producing a miniseries on the Holocaust, which was likely never made in part because Gibson was pulled over for drunk driving in July 2006 by a Jewish deputy, only for him to blame the "fucking Jews [who] are responsible for all the wars in the world."[33]

Another round of apologies and amends ensued, with Gibson announcing in 2011 that he was developing a script around Jewish hero Judah Maccabee, who Gibson had supposedly admired since childhood. That project fell apart in a blizzard of accusations from the film's scriptwriter, Joe Eszterhas, who argued that Gibson was an antisemitic Holocaust denier who "hates Jews" and said the Old Testament contained references to sacrificing Christian babies (Eszterhas claimed that these references that Gibson was alluding to were actually from the *Protocols*). Gibson, for his part, denied all of it and said he still wanted to make a film about Judah Maccabee, just not the one Eszterhas wrote.[34]

When *that* Mel Gibson was announced as starring in a film named after the most well-known family in Judaism, it was too much for the internet to bear. Dozens of articles digging up Gibson's past antisemitic remarks came out, and social media was unsparing in attacking both Gibson and whoever thought it was a good idea to cast him in *Rothchild*, essentially likening it to casting a member of the KKK to play Martin Luther King, Jr.[35]

It took about a day for Team Gibson to enter damage control mode, as the actor's publicist sent out an email smugly claiming that "I feel the need to spare you any embarrassment as I'm told this film is about a fictional family (hence the name 'Rothchild') vs the Rothschild family to which you are referring. Completely unrelated to your premise and angle. Hopefully this is helpful to you." In keeping with their general silence on the myths and conspiracy theories, the Rothschild family and their representatives didn't comment about the controversy.[36]

A year later, with Gibson in the midst of yet another career upswing and renewed interest in his antisemitic statements, news very quietly broke that *Rothchild* was "no longer happening."[37] Conspiracy theory accounts on social media continued to push the fiction that Gibson was either starring in or directing the film as an attack on the Rothschilds and the New World Order, but the project was clearly dead, and it was almost certainly dead because it was Mel Gibson starring in a film called *Rothchild*.

But for as annoyingly smug as Gibson's publicist's "I'm sorry if you were offended" statement was, he was correct: the film had nothing to do with the actual Rothschilds. Ford's *Rothchild* script had placed highly on the 2014 Black List, a tally of the most well-regarded unproduced screenplays in Hollywood. Based on that publicly available draft (which likely was rewritten by the time Gibson signed on), Ford's intent truly was to satirize the New York upper crust, and not the Jewish banking elite. The family in the film isn't even Jewish—the name is just one associated with money.

Rothchild is a dark and violent satire on the alluring power of greed. The draft opens with Becket in prison confessing his murderous sins to a Catholic priest just before his execution—something that no Rothschild would ever do. The story then flashes back to Becket's early life with his mother Mary, described by the script as "an heiress to the fourth largest industrial fortune in the world." After Mary is disowned by the patriarch of her family for getting pregnant via a musician, her son Becket is set up to inherit the entire Rothchild fortune of $17 billion, provided all nine other heirs die. Which they do, one by one, by Becket's hand—via shooting, burning, exploding, getting sucked into engines, being hacked to death by a mob of Chinese sweatshop workers with machetes, etc.

Even Mel Gibson's role in the film was overstated, as the grotesquely villainous Whitelaw barely appears until the last twenty-five pages of the script. Eventually, the two collide over the vast fortune, and Becket kills Whitelaw with an arrow through the neck. The rest of the story is about how Becket conspires to get out of jail and get away with the whole thing—incisively satirizing how there's a level of wealth and power that can literally allow one to get away with murder.[38]

Ultimately, the script's complex murder plot is much more an homage to the 1949 revenge comedy *Kind Hearts and Coronets* than any kind of spiritual successor of *The Eternal Jew*. As such, Ford rebounded from the controversy, writing and directing the critically acclaimed drama *Emily the Criminal* in 2022. In turn, the success of that film revived interest in *Rothchild*. Sure enough, nothing in Hollywood ever really dies, and the trade papers announced in early 2023 that Ford would be writing and directing a new iteration of the script, retitled *Huntington*, and presumably without Mel Gibson or references to the world's most well-known Jewish family.[39]

BILLIONAIRE TYRANT

Even if they aren't directly referenced, virtually any fictional family of power or secret society is claimed by someone to be an interpretation of the Rothschilds. In particular, the Rothschilds are often linked to many of the plots and conspiracies found in the sprawling works of novelist Thomas Pynchon, with the users on the r/Pynchon Reddit forum speculating that the reclusive author has included a number of coded references to them in his books *The Crying of Lot 49* and *Gravity's Rainbow*, though it's just idle guessing.

There has also been consistent speculation on the internet that the sneering "billionaire tyrant" character of Springfield Nuclear Power Plant owner C. Montgomery Burns on *The Simpsons* is a fictionalized version of Lord Jacob Rothschild. The octogenarian philanthropist has been unfairly saddled with a similar reputation as a megalomaniacal tyrant—one that Mr. Burns more than deserves on *The Simpsons*, but that Jacob has done nothing to warrant. On the surface, Jacob does bear something of a physical resemblance to the Springfield Nuclear Power Plant owner, and it's not only antisemitic cranks that have noticed: a search for "Jacob Rothschild and Mr. Burns" on the video app TikTok brings up dozens of videos with more than fifty million views, while various internet threads claim the fictional character is based on the real scion's supposed relentless greed and lust for power.

At least one deeply antisemitic meme takes the resemblance even further, contrasting a particularly bad picture of the aged Jacob with a grotesque picture of Mr. Burns and making the usual claims that the Rothschilds are worth 500 trillion dollars, own nearly every central bank in the world, and have financed both sides of every war since Napoleon, and that "you have probably never heard of me."

Most people probably either never *have* heard of Lord Jacob Rothschild or, if they have, saw something about him in a conspiracy video. The real Lord Jacob rarely speaks to the media, starting one amiable chat with the *Financial Times* in 2010 with the understated plea, "I don't, you know, usually give interviews. So if you decide to write anything, I'd rather it wasn't about me." And mostly, the interview is about the usual Rothschild interests—food, wine, and art rather than world domination and space lasers.[40]

Beyond that, the internet is simply wrong. Mr. Burns debuted as a character in 1989 in the very first episode of *The Simpsons*. That same year, the renowned British artist Lucien Freud painted a famous portrait of Lord Jacob, and his 1989 visage looks nothing like the fictional power plant owner. According to *Simpsons* creator Matt Groening and supervising director David Silverman, the personality of Mr. Burns is a mix of John D. Rockefeller and the miserly banker Henry Potter from *It's a Wonderful Life*, while the character's look is based on former Fox Broadcasting head Barry Diller.[41]

One misapplication of the Rothschild myth that *does* include something of a Rothschild connection concerns *Eyes Wide Shut*, the final film of the auteur Stanley Kubrick. No stranger to myths and urban legends about his work, Kubrick's 1999 tale of sexual intrigue and infidelity revolved around a disaffected therapist (played by Tom Cruise) going on a nighttime adventure and finding himself at a masked orgy ritual being held by a mysterious and wealthy secret society.

It's easy enough to assume the orgy is just an artist's interpretation of what an Illuminati ritual might be. But as it turns out, the Paris Rothschilds actually *did* host a masked party full of arcane rituals at which rich people put on costumes to hide their identity—the 1972 Surrealist Ball. It was one of many parties thrown in the legendary Rothschild mansion Château de Ferrières, built in the late 1850s for James de Rothschild and reopened a century later by his heir Guy de Rothschild after its sacking by the Nazis.[42]

And when the photos of the ball were eventually released, they looked *a lot* like the masked ritual at the center of the Kubrick film—women in evening gowns wearing ornate masks (including Guy's wife Marie-Hélène wearing a massive deer head studded with actual diamonds), servants dressed as cats pawing at each other or sleeping in piles, invitations written backward, a number of jarring references to cannibalism in the names of food, and mannequins of naked dead women and babies surrounded by roses on tables.[43]

To the casual viewer, it looks suspiciously like both the impression many people have of the idle rich in general—obsessed with rituals and sex and costumes—and the orgy scene in *Eyes Wide Shut* in particular. And the ultimate "gotcha" for conspiracy theorists seemed to be that one of the English Rothschilds' stately homes, the Buckinghamshire-located Mentmore Towers, was used as a location for the film: it served as the Long Island–set exterior of the mansion where the orgy was held.

So was Kubrick "blowing the lid off" the Rothschilds' occult horror parties like the "Illuminati Ball"? Was the director's fatal heart attack in March 1999, which occurred just a few days after he'd screened the film for Warner Bros., a sign that he'd gotten too close and said too much about a certain family? And, as some have alleged, were changes made to the film after Kubrick's death to absolve certain bad actors of their vile deeds? Conspiracy theories flew that there were secret extended cuts of the orgy scene with direct references to the Rockefellers and Rothschilds that the powers that be demanded be removed, and even that Kubrick was revealing the secret, horrible details of the "Pizzagate" conspiracy theory, alleging that powerful people were trafficking children for occult rituals—nearly twenty years before that term even existed.[44]

Since its release, the film has gotten a reputation as portending the sexual abuses of the elite in the twenty-first century. Rich Cohen, in the *Paris Review*, noted that it "[revealed] a dynamic that had long played out in sectors of elite society but was not glimpsed until our own age, an age of scandal," particularly with disgraced financier Jeffrey Epstein.[45] And it's easy to see glimmers of both conspiracy obsession and classic Jewish tropes in Kubrick's films (the filmmaker was Jewish), including *Eyes Wide Shut*, in which the mysterious patient who introduces Cruise to the underworld orgy cult is a Jewish banker named Victor Ziegler.

But diving into both the Surrealist Ball and the inspirations behind the film, it's clear that they had little, if anything, to do with each other. The Rothschild Ball, for one, was not actually an occult orgy (that we know of, anyway), and many of its attendees weren't masked—including celebrities like Salvador Dali and Audrey Hepburn. Like many of the supposed occult or sexual references in the Pizzagate conspiracy theory decades later, the weird costumes and cat servants featured at the Ball can, at worst, be considered a festival of bad taste and conspicuous consumption.

Logistically, the comparison doesn't work, either. The ball wasn't widely known about until the pictures from it were released in the late 2010s, and there's no evidence Kubrick or his collaborators knew anything about it. The salacious details about Ziegler and his orgies were invented as backstory for the film by its co-writer, Frederic Raphael. The details were so lurid and convincing that immediately after Raphael faxed some pages to Kubrick that purported to be an "FBI dossier" on Ziegler, the director called the writer demanding to know where he'd gotten what he thought was "confidential material," only for Raphael to reassure him, "I'm a writer. I make things up."[46]

Even the "Rothschild mansion" Mentmore Towers has little of the allure that conspiracy researchers attach to it: the house has been used as a location for a number of other decidedly non-Illuminati films, like *Ali G Indahouse*, and was sold off by the family in 1978 to the Maharishi Foundation. Whatever occult or secret connection exists between the Rothschilds and *Eyes Wide Shut*, then, exists in the minds of believers, and nowhere else.

And so it continues; whenever Western pop culture needs a wealthy and secretive family to be running some kind of hidden puppet-master routine, the Rothschilds are available. But it's not just in the West. The Rothschilds have always been a global business, and it's no surprise that they're the subject of conspiracy theories in nations far from their traditional centers of power—even countries with virtually no Jewish population to blame their woes upon.

"MAKING MONEY
THE JEWISH WAY":
ROTHSCHILD
CONSPIRACY
THEORIES AROUND
THE WORLD

Countries like the US, England, France, and Germany have long been traditional centers of Jewish life. And Judaism continues to have a rich tradition
in Eastern Europe, even if it occasionally involves fleeing Eastern Europe.
This combination of heritage and hatred is to be expected in countries
where Jews are highly visible, often persecuted, and seem "overrepresented"
in high-profile fields.

But even countries with virtually no native Jews or Jewish tradi-
tions aren't immune to the contagion of Jew-hatred. After all, religions
might vary by geography, but the need to scapegoat and blame outgroups
is universal. So too are conspiracy theories about who "really" runs the
world—and Jews are entrenched enough in Western culture as "puppet
masters" for the appeal of Jewish control of finance to be universal.

With two millennia of cranks, hate preachers, and political

bomb-throwers blaming Jews for all the woes of their particular country, it's no wonder that antisemitic conspiracy theories can find audiences
in nations without any Jewish culture to speak of. And because the
Rothschilds are still among the best-known Jews, these theories often involve them to an almost absurd degree. Sometimes, it's a familiar form,
like state-sponsored antisemitic attacks based on the *Protocols of the
Elders of Zion* or other seminal anti-Jewish texts using prominent Jews as
stand-ins for centuries of Western colonial imperialism. But just as often,
antisemitism in nations without a Jewish population involves a more be-
nign-seeming kind of exotic fascination—much the same way "Orientals"
were exoticized in Western popular culture of the past. They use the
same "innate Jewish wisdom" tropes that fueled works like *The Hebrew
Talisman* or make paeans to the otherworldly beauty of the "Jewess."

But more often than not, they're just about money. Like the need for
someone to blame, the desire to get rich quickly is also universal—spawning a vast industry of "Jewish business books" in Asia. Most were dodgy
tomes full of amateur advice that, regardless, sold millions of copies to people who have never met a Jewish person in their life but sought to harness
their "power" anyway.

The common thread in all these strands of global thinking about
Judaism, from fairly harmless stereotypes to vicious antisemitism, is that the
Jews are the kings of business and politics, and the Rothschilds are the leaders of the Jews. Despite the linguistic and cultural barriers at work, some
things translate into any language.

"GOLDEN CHAINS": ROTHSCHILD CONSPIRACY THEORIES IN THE MUSLIM WORLD

Antisemitism wasn't always endemic to the Arab world. In the Middle Ages,
Jewish merchants and craftspeople prospered in Muslim lands, freed from
the numerous prohibitions that held them down in Christian empires. And
Jews had no specific monopoly on lending money at interest, dispelling old
notions that the "Jews were the Rothschilds of the Islamic world," as some

previous scholarship has claimed.[1] For hundreds of years, Jews and Muslims enjoyed near-equal rights in much of the Middle East, a coexistence that ended for good with the Mongol destruction of Baghdad in 1258. The aftermath saw centuries of erosion of Jewish rights in the Arab world, ebbing and flowing with the times.

Even as Rothschild myths were emerging in Europe, antisemitism in the Middle East was far from the universal construct that it would later become. Western-style Jew-baiting grew substantially after the Damascus Affair in 1840, with a slew of European antisemitic tracts and ideas finding new minds to poison in the wake of that incident's blood libel accusation and subsequent violence toward local Jewish communities. Jewish leaders were seen as helping perpetrate the ritual killings that Jewish communities were being accused of, and the Rothschilds were deeply involved in helping to tamp the crisis down, making them natural targets for the growth of Middle Eastern Jewish conspiracy theories.

In the decades after Damascus, blood libel accusations spread to Beirut, Jerusalem, Cairo, and numerous other major cities in the Ottoman Empire—almost always beginning in Christian communities, and only later jumping to Arabic-language papers.[2] Starting in 1894, the Dreyfus Affair and the emergence of Zionism and Jewish immigration to British Palestine fueled another spate of attacks and organized violence against Jews in the Middle East.

As usual, they were driven by myths about Jewish money, power, and control. And as usual, the Rothschilds were singled out, particularly over their advocacy for the establishment of a Jewish state and their funding of European colonial adventures (or misadventures). As the Great Depression picked up steam and another world war loomed, the rise in European and American antisemitism ran parallel to another similar spike in the Middle East. Despites differences in language and culture, the two worlds linked up often, with no less than Father Coughlin denouncing the potential founding of a Jewish state in Palestine as a mere front for the Rothschilds tightening their "golden chains" and parasitical toll collection on the Suez Canal—which, of course, he claimed that the Rothschilds had funded.[3]

Around the same time, the printed contagion that is *The Protocols of the Elders of Zion* began to creep into Arabic discourse about Jews. Touted as the leaked Jewish scheme for world domination, the *Protocols* was first translated into Arabic from French by Christian authors in 1926, and by the early '60s there were nearly a dozen different Arabic translations, more than any other language except German.[4] Its lurid descriptions of the grand and terrifying plans the "wise men of Zion" had for the rest of the world meshed with extant ill feelings toward Zionism and the nascent state of Israel, and scapegoated the Rothschilds as the cause of much of it.

During the Second World War, much of the Arab world's enmity toward Jews, and the Rothschilds in particular, was driven by the Nazi propaganda machine. Looking for ways to exploit anti-colonial feelings all over the Middle East, the Nazis spent considerable effort and money broadcasting a constant stream of Arabic-language propaganda over shortwave radio and in printed papers, putting capital into the propaganda scheme up until the final months of the regime. This work didn't revolve around translations of Hitler's speeches or even the *Protocols*, which likely wouldn't have sparked much interest in most Muslims, but in pairing selective readings of the Koran with tales of the wicked imperialism of the US, England, and their masters in worldwide Jewry.[5]

A key vector for the Nazi attempt to win the hearts and minds of the Muslim world was Hajj Amin al-Husseini, the Grand Mufti of Jerusalem under the British Mandate and one of the founders of the Palestinian liberation movement. In 1937, even before the war formally broke out, al-Husseini broadcast a "proclamation" declaring an eternal "battle between Jews and Islam" and demanded that Muslims "not rest until your land is free of the Jews." Al-Husseini would move to Berlin in 1941 and continue spreading antisemitic Nazi propaganda until his arrest by French troops at the end of the war. Much of the Grand Mufti's line of attack focused on the leaders of the Zionist movement going back to the mid-1800s, and there was no shortage of punches thrown at the Rothschilds. Lionel and his son Natty Rothschild in particular were targeted, as Al-Husseini viewed them as colluding with Disraeli and other British officials to be "the driving forces of the destruction of the regime of the Islamic Caliphate," never mind that most of the British Rothschilds of the time, particularly Natty, were opposed to the idea of a Jewish homeland.[6] It would seem that the imaginary feats of Lionel and his family—from dividing the United States to destroying the Middle East—knew no bounds.

With the foundation of the state of Israel in 1948, enmity regarding the Jews, and the Rothschilds' role in the creation of that nation, continued to spread. Linking the Rothschilds to specific anti-Israel sentiment certainly wasn't the domain only of the Arab world, and a number of Christian nationalist writers ran with the idea as well—a 1972 issue of *The Cross and the Flag* decried the existence of a "Talmudic hidden hand" controlled by the Rothschilds, who "financed transplanting 600,000 eastern European Talmudists ('Jews') into Palestine" in order to "have secure and permanent access to their unlimited wealth in the Far East."[7]

But antisemitism in the Middle East had grown considerably by then, to the point where it was almost universal in many Muslim nations. Even in regions where neighboring nations constantly warred with each other over religious doctrine and natural resources, they could unite in their hatred of the Jewish people—Pew Research polling from 2006 showed that o percent of Lebanese and Jordanian respondents had a favorable view of Jews, and Jews had single-digit favorability ratings in majority Muslim nations like Pakistan and Morocco as well. And as always, the Rothschilds were among the most well-known targets for this hatred.[8]

THE ROTHSCHILD *CONSPIRACY*

With countless editions now available in every nation in the Middle East, the *Protocols* would be adapted into multiple successful film and television series. These shows usually were provided large budgets and spooled out over dozens of episodes devoted to the supposed horrors of the Jews and their plan for world conquest. And they didn't air on fringe YouTube channels but were usually broadcast in prime time on state TV around Ramadan, when Islamic TV viewership is traditionally at its highest. These series freely indulged in Jewish money and power conspiracy theories based around the *Protocols*, and one in particular, the lavish 29-part 2003 Syrian miniseries *Al-Shatat* (roughly translated as "The Diaspora"), put the Rothschilds at the very top of a grotesque and ancient conspiracy to rule the world and use the blood of Christian and Muslim children in their rituals.

Al-Shatat opens with its own interpretation of *The House of Rothschild*'s fictional scene of Mayer on his deathbed admonishing his sons to live and trade with dignity. It is, unsurprisingly, not devoted to living and trading with dignity but instead to the patriarch issuing his befuddled sons a set of marching orders to take over the globe.

"All the nations that have accepted non-Jewish faiths should be destroyed and annihilated," this version of Mayer, called Amschel Rothschild, wheezes in a translation by the watchdog think tank the Middle East Media Research Institute. "They should be uprooted. They are wrong and illegitimate. Therefore, take control of them both in secret and openly. You should rule them with might, deceit, and vigilance. Do not allow any nation to share your domination of the world." When one of "Amschel's" dimwitted progeny doesn't understand, the patriarch spells it out as plainly as possible:

"We have been commanded to secretly establish a Jewish government," declares "Amschel" in a long rant. "I am proud to be a member of that government. The mission of this government is to protect the Jewish people, and to rule the entire world. We should use mercenaries and our own people, who have infiltrated various governments and who head them, and thus impose our views and ideas." He then gives each of his five boys meticulous instructions for a different country to take control over, before making them swear on the Torah that they will "carry out my will to annihilate the world."[9]

The series later explicitly depicts the blood libel, with Jewish elders slitting the throats of non-Jewish children and baking their blood into matzo. It features a depiction of Zionist advocate Edmond de Rothschild as a cruel puppet master, makes unhinged claims that the Rothschilds were responsible for the creation of the atomic bomb, and even devotes an entire episode to creating a Jewish conspiracy to deny the veracity of the *Protocols*—while beginning each episode with a disclaimer that *Al-Shatat* was not based on the *Protocols*. *Al-Shatat* wasn't just a hit in Syria; it would air again and again in the Muslim world, including in Iran, dubbed into Farsi and retitled simply *Conspiracy*.[10]

Iranian culture would adopt its own particular version of anti-Rothschild sentiment. Ayatollah Ruhollah Khomeini, the country's first Supreme Leader, regularly attacked the Rothschilds as figureheads of the global cabal dominating the Middle East. And state media pushed bizarre conspiracy theories that the son of the founder of the Baha'i faith had worked with the Rothschilds to help create the state of Israel—fueling the violent persecution of both religions, which continues to this day.[11]

In particular, the country's state-funded antisemitic "Jewish Studies Centre" think tank, one of the biggest purveyors of anti-Jewish conspiracy theories in the Middle East, has published dozens of articles attacking the family for everything from running a secret world government to funding large-scale drug trafficking to encouraging corruption in the fashion industry.[12] Other Iranian papers linked the state of Israel and the Trump administration to the modern Rothschilds through a variety of real and imaginary plots. One especially unhinged piece produced by the Jewish Studies Centre involved accusing retired Israeli general Daniel Rothschild of serving as a "dynasty" member tasked with commanding the legendary Israeli intelligence agency Mossad, despite General Rothschild never heading Mossad and not being related to the banking family.[13]

Other Middle Eastern media outlets spend nearly as much time blasting the Rothschilds for a mind-boggling array of conspiracies, most of which either aren't real or have nothing whatsoever to do with the Rothschilds. A search of the Middle East Media Research Institute archive brings up hundreds of videos of Arabic-language media (much of it state-owned and lavishly produced) claiming the family owns 80 percent of the world's wealth and 99 percent of the media, is the secret source of global drug distribution, created both ISIS and COVID-19, funded the removal of Native Americans during the 1800s, has assassinated every US president who died in office, and controls secret cures for AIDS and cancer. None of this seems any different from the theories peddled by Western conspiracy theory influencers, and that's the point: for as much enmity as the conservative Western press has for the Muslim world, and vice versa, they can unite behind their belief that a powerful German Jewish banking cabal is the real source of all our ills.

CURRENCY WARS

There are only about ten thousand Jews in China, most of whom are expatriates. But while China's Jewish population is essentially the size of a rounding error, Jewish wealth has historically impacted the Chinese economy, particularly in the growth of its cities. The Rothschilds had a number of commercial ventures in China in the nineteenth and twentieth centuries, and the Baghdadi-born Jewish family the Sassoons were often called "the Rothschilds of the East," both for their outsized role in Asian and Middle Eastern banking and for having a similar history—they too had a family-run global business dominating markets in multiple countries, in this case, India, China, and Iraq.[14] Despite most Chinese people never having met a Jew, the nation of over 1.2 billion is just as vulnerable to Jewish stereotypes and hoaxes as any other country with a great wealth divide and a rapidly growing middle class.

Many of these myths revolve around the supposedly preternatural ability of Jews to conjure money out of thin air. As China's economy westernized and upward mobility became reality for millions, it created a massive market for "Jewish business books," with many becoming bestsellers. Reflecting on the generally positive status of Jews in China, they have titles like *The Eight Most Valuable Business Secrets of the Jewish, The Legend of Jewish Wealth, Making Money the Jewish Way*, and *Jewish Entrepreneurial Experience and Business Wisdom*. They make lofty promises to unlock the "ancient secrets" of Jewish financial success and translate them to the peculiarities of doing business in the Chinese market. And they often sell tens of thousands of copies despite murky authorship, numerous inaccuracies, and seemingly little knowledge of Jews or Judaism.[15]

Virtually all of these books reference the Rothschilds, for the simple reason that they're among the most well-known wealthy Jews in the world. Indeed, the Chinese upper class has a particular obsession with Rothschild wines and art, often to the point of delusion. Fake bottles of Château Laffite Rothschild wines have sold for five figures, and a fraudulent member of the family named Oliver Rothschild spent years traveling around China giving speeches and being wined and dined as a philanthropist before he was revealed as having no relation to the actual Rothschilds.[16]

Clearly, the allure of Jewish wealth and wisdom are considerable even in countries where the actual impact of Jews is negligible. But none of the dozens of often slapdash and incoherent "Jewish business books" sold in China made the cultural impact that 2007's bestseller *Currency Wars* did. Because that book is not about how the Rothschilds made their money, but how they control yours.

Upon his return to China in 2007 after living in the United States for over a decade, IT consultant Song Hongbing wrote and published *Currency Wars* (sometimes also called *The Currency War*), first as articles on his blog, then in book form, attempting to understand the 1997 Asian financial crisis and how China could compete with the US.

Like the Great Depression six decades earlier, the 1997 crisis began with a contagion of bank failures and capital flight—this time in Thailand. The slump spread just as quickly as the *Creditanstalt* failure had from Austria to the rest of Europe in the 1930s, infecting countries all over Southeast Asia and imperiling Japan, China, and even the United States before it burned out two years later. And taking inspiration from the family that was scapegoated for the 1931 contagion, Song Hongbing blamed the 1997 crisis on the machinations of the Rothschilds.[17]

Though the book has made little impact in the US or Europe, the basic thrust of *Currency Wars* would be familiar to any reader of *Secrets of the Federal Reserve*, *The Creature from Jekyll Island*, *Descent into Slavery*, the works of Canadian Illuminati conspiracy theorist William Guy Carr—himself a major influence on conspiracy thinkers like David Icke and Gary

Allen—or the antisemitic and anti-interventionist speeches of Charles Lindbergh. Indeed, Song cites these and other conspiracy works dozens of times, basing much of his research around Eustace Mullins in particular.[18]

Song's thesis essentially is that the Rothschilds have a vast and hidden fortune that has gone "unnoticed" by the Western media. They use that money to control the Federal Reserve, while the Federal Reserve controls the dollar, and the dollar controls the global economy. And all of it is connected to the eternal struggle over the supposed return of the gold standard, which the Rothschilds bitterly oppose and take drastic action against—including by starting wars and global depressions.

To extrapolate his "findings," Song digs into the same tropes, conspiracy theories, and myths that generations of past cranks mined for riches. Chinese-centric elements aside, little of what *Currency Wars* presents would look out of place in a posthumous new book by Mullins or Allen: that the Rothschilds control virtually every central bank in the world, have trillions of dollars of hidden wealth, ruthlessly assassinate any world leader that gets in their way, and have manipulated financial markets and global conflicts for their own aims for two centuries, in Asia as well as Europe and the United States.

Song also uses Frederic Morton's *The Rothschilds: A Family Portrait* as a primary source, despite that book's previously noted reliance on myth. In one particularly bizarre passage in the endnotes of *Currency Wars*, Song extrapolates a guess at the Rothschilds' net worth by starting with the figure $6 billion, supposedly given by Morton in his book as the family's combined wealth in 1850. While Morton merely claims that number "has been estimated," Song decides that not only did the family have that much money, but that it would return somewhere between 4 and 7 percent interest each year—capping his estimate of the family's wealth in 2007 at potentially almost one *quadrillion* dollars.[19]

Song relentlessly attacks the Rothschilds, blaming the family for everything from the "suspicious" deaths of Kennedy assassination witnesses to the "free silver" conflicts of the late 1800s to the United States's massive national debt in the 1990s. The book's 2009 sequel, *Currency Wars 2: The*

Power of Gold, is just as brazen in its Infowars-style claims that a "global currency" backed by gold and carbon credits will be introduced by the same elite banking cabal who purposefully crashed the economy in 2008 to hasten their takeover of world finance. The goal of the Rothschild-funded "financial Pearl Harbor," as Song calls it, will be to totally destroy the Chinese economy, remove it as a threat to the West, and undo the massive advancement of China's middle class.[20] Only China hoarding gold—which the country started doing in late 2022—can forestall the Western-driven doom.

Much of *Currency Wars* is devoted to how Jewish power manipulates the United States. But like so many of the Western counterparts he cites, Song claims he personally has nothing against Jews, who are not "singled out" in *Currency Wars*, as he puts it in one interview.[21] Song's protestations aside, antisemitism in China is on the rise in general, fueled by increased nationalism, COVID-19 conspiracy theories, and widespread adoption of social media, where state censors seem to have no problem tolerating anti-Jewish sentiments.[22]

Initially released by the large state-owned publisher CITIC Press, *Currency Wars* was a huge hit in China, with sales fueled by the upheaval of the 2008 subprime meltdown and retroactive claims that Song had "predicted" the crisis. It sold at least two hundred thousand copies in the first two years after its publication after being recommended by high-end lifestyle magazines and celebrities as a way to understand the recent financial calamities. One estimate of the popularity of *Currency Wars* claimed that as many as three million copies were in circulation by 2020, thanks to hundreds of thousands of bootlegged or pirated copies, and it inspired a raft of copycat books that sparked a *"Currency Wars* phenomenon."[23]

Currency Wars and its sequels had a profound impact on how the Chinese elite saw Western power and economic growth. They became extremely popular with government officials and top business leaders as an alternative explanation for Asia's stagnant economy in the 1990s, inspired a slew of other popular books about the need for China to "rise" against the West, and drove a resurgence of pop nationalism based on the fear that the US would do anything to stop China's economic growth—even going to war.[24] Despite pushback by Chinese and Western financial professionals who claim Song has no particular expertise or training in global finance and that he's trading on well-worn antisemitic clichés, Song's conspiracy theory of impending "currency wars" between China and the West have made him one of the wealthiest writers in Asia. And he did it the same way so many others did—taking tropes and clichés about the Rothschilds and updating them to match current events.

Despite the book's enormous success and influence in China, it's had virtually no footprint in the Western world. For years, *Currency Wars* wasn't even available in English, with only small portions translated and posted on Chinese blogs. It was an omission that itself became fodder for conspiracy theories on Chinese social media, theorizing a plot by the Rothschilds to suppress the book and keep its "truth" from Western audiences.

It took until 2021 for *Currency Wars* to be sold in English, offered by a small European house also selling, among other antisemitic tomes, the works of fascist Italian philosopher Julius Evola, translations of extremist bible *The Turner Diaries*, and multiple editions of *Mein Kampf.* Given the popularity of the works Song was inspired by and the extant proliferation of anti-Rothschild theories, it would seem a conspiracy to suppress *Currency Wars* was wholly unnecessary—because its thesis is nothing that can't already be found in a dozen places.

"FORCING THE END": THE ROTHSCHILDS AND AUM SHINRIKYO

Like China, Japan has a tiny community of Jews, numbering less than two thousand and made up almost entirely of expats. But despite the absurdity of scapegoating a population that's not big enough to fill a large church, Japan has a tangled history of how it views Jewish wealth, both extolling it and blaming it for Japan's problems.

Historically, small communities of Jews would often pass through Japan escaping pogroms or expulsions. During the imperial period, when Japan succumbed to the same malignant nationalism that infected its ally Germany and ruthlessly murdered millions of Chinese civilians, the Japanese government refused to expel or exterminate the small number of Jews living either in Japan or occupied Manchuria. Jews were even able to obtain visas to settle in Shanghai, where a small Jewish ghetto was relatively safe from the persecution of both Jews and Chinese, though hundreds of its residents died in its cramped and squalid quarters. Once the war ended, small cadres of Jews remained in the ruins of Tokyo and Kobe, with most of Japan's remaining Jewish community leaving for Israel.

But even if Japan was a safer harbor for Jews than Nazi-occupied Europe, Japan was far from immune to the conspiracy theories that dragged behind Jews wherever they went. *The Protocols of the Elders of Zion* was first translated into Japanese in the late 1920s and became extremely popular during the war years. In the late 1970s, Japan's steadily growing economy exploded, and the country became a world leader in electronics, aviation, and the automotive industry. With this growth came concerted—and often racist—attempts by the West to tamp it down. Seeing themselves as still being oppressed by American occupiers, some Japanese saw Jewish power and wealth as the "real" causes of the economic and cultural tension between the US and Japan. But others were fascinated by the exoticism and wealth of Jews, and found a kind of kinship with what they saw as an oppressed minority who carved out great success in banking, finance, and academia.

Japan in the 1980s was a country seemingly obsessed with Jews and Judaism. Some of it was positive—*Fiddler on the Roof* became one of the most popular musicals in Japanese history, and Anne Frank's *Diary of a Young Girl* sold millions of Japanese-language copies, with her name being appropriated by, among other products, a popular sanitary napkin company. Jews were seen as excelling in business, mathematics, art, and academics—all qualities emphasized by Japanese education. And a 1972 book written by a Jewish expat born and raised in Kobe called *The Japanese and the Jews* sold millions of copies by pointing out the similarities between the two outwardly different cultures. As such, many Japanese saw both themselves and the Jewish people as victims of imperialism and the scapegoating of people scared of their success.[25]

But as always, there was a darker edge to this obsession, and conspiracy theories routinely fell on the European "power brokers" devoted to hampering Japan's "economic miracle." By the late '80s, anti-Jewish book sales started to make up an outsized share of the literature market in Japan, fueled by bestsellers like *The Secret of Jewish Power to Control the World* (written by a member of the Japanese parliament) and the *Protocols*-inspired set of books *If You Understand Judea, You Can Understand the World* and *If You Understand Judea, You Can Understand Japan* by Holocaust-denying fundamentalist preacher Masami Uno. Masami's books sold nearly a million copies in less than a year, making the usual claims of an upcoming Jewish-backed Western takeover of the global economy and adapting them to particularly Japanese fears.[26]

Like it does everywhere else, antisemitism in Japan meshed with the local culture, using fear of foreign power and religion alongside familiar propagandistic images of Jews to push Japanese-centric conspiracy theories. In particular, the authors of the dozens of popular anti-Jewish books in Japan in the '80s and '90s blamed Jewish control for the Western spread of nuclear weapons, US attempts to overvalue Japanese currency, the ever-present fear of Anglo-American takeover, and even earthquakes and nuclear disasters. Many of these books and articles slotted the Rothschilds into their usual roles of globalist puppet masters, hoarders of wealth, and hopelessly inbred Zionist fanatics keen on destroying Japan once and for all and dividing its wealth among themselves.

Besides likely being Japan's most prolific anti-nuclear writer, Tokyo-born Hirose Takashi was a major vector of specifically anti-Rothschild sentiment. In 1991, Hirose published *Red Shield—Mystery of Rothschild*, which took the familiar Rothschild conspiracy and translated it for Japanese audiences, linking Rothschild marriages (and intermarriages) to two centuries of wealth hoarding and control of the West. The book was successful enough to spawn multiple sequels and put Hirose on the map as something of an expert on the Rothschilds. Several years after his Rothschilds book, Hirose published an article in the leftist biweekly paper *Sapio*, with a circulation of nearly a quarter of a million, using graphs and detailed charts to display the Rothschilds' supposed viselike grip on global finance, politics, and media—along with their incestuous connections to each other.[27]

Within a few years, Japanese papers were routinely running advertisements for antisemitic books laundering the *Protocols* for Japanese readers while printing articles and ads alleging global domination plots by the Rothschilds and their Christian puppets. These weren't in fringe rags or extremist newsletters, but in some of the most widely read and respected publications in the country. Splashy ads in popular daily paper *Asahi* and the *Nikkei*, Japan's equivalent of *The Wall Street Journal*, used images of Stars of David and Satan with proclamations of "Jewish cartels surrounding the Rothschilds" attempting to destroy Japan to shill for a three-volume book series called *Get Japan, the Last Enemy: The Jewish Protocols for World Domination*.[28]

Written by a Japanese speaker under the pseudonym "Jacob Morgan," *Get Japan* posited that a vast conspiracy headed by the Rothschilds controlled the Bank of Japan, had put "Jewish symbols" on Japanese money, and was driving the country to ruin through a rigged political system and interest rate cuts. Eventually, Western-backed Jews would "re-conquer" Japan, likely a reference to the US occupation of Imperial Japan after the Second World War. Unchecked by the Japanese media or intellectuals of the time and buoyed by growing xenophobia toward both the West and foreign workers in Japan, Japanese antisemitism grew to the point where Nazi iconography and pro-Holocaust handbills started becoming regular fixtures in Tokyo in the mid-1990s.[29]

It was into this growing acceptance of blatant conspiracy theory–mongering over Jews and Western influence that Shoko Asahara stepped. Born Chizuo Matsumoto in 1955, the legally blind Asahara formed the cult that would become known as Aum Shinrikyo in 1984, mixing elements of Buddhist, Hindu, and Christian tenets with Nostradamus prophecies and End Times eschatology. Seeing himself as the Lamb of God, the "holiest holy man," and the human manifestation of Christ, the increasingly megalomaniacal Asahara believed it was his role to take upon himself the sins of the world and "force the end" of humanity through violent conflict. To hasten things along, he wielded a fanatically devoted cadre of disciples as his weapon.[30]

Despite Asahara basing his apocalyptic ideology at least in part on ancient Jewish concepts of Armageddon, antisemitism played a major role in Aum's rise and its terror campaign of the early 1990s. Like many other prominent Japanese antisemites, the Aum cult was obsessed with nuclear weapons—though positively, seeing them as a vessel to bring about the End Times, as opposed to the extreme negative feelings of figures like Hirose Takashi. Cult followers were also supportive of the Nazis and believed Western governments were agents of oppression. It's not entirely a straight line from the antisemitism and Jewish paranoia of Japan in the 1980s to Aum, given how complex Aum's mythology was. But the two are inextricably linked, finding a common enemy in a highly stereotyped religious group with virtually no footprint in Japan. Asahara declared the cult's enemies to be "Jewish Japanese," a term encompassing everyone from the emperor to major business leaders, all seen as "cosmopolitan" figures controlled by Jewish power.[31]

These "Jewish Japanese" were often singled out for the cult's crude early gas attacks, as Asahara proclaimed that Japan would need to be "karmically cleansed" through nuclear fire as punishment for persecuting him, just as the Jews had suffered such a cleansing for their persecution of Christ.[32] And Aum propaganda material routinely attacked wealthy European and American Jews, including the Rothschilds, using the same vulgar French and German cartoons that pilloried the family a century earlier.

Aum quickly grew to be a worldwide movement with thousands of members in total thrall to their leader. It had its own political party, and as much as a billion dollars in assets. It was also attempting to purchase assault rifles, an attack helicopter, and weapons of mass destruction. In January 1995, the cult's newspaper *Vajrayana Sacca* published a 95-page antisemitic tract called "Manual of Fear: The Jewish Ambition—Total World Conquest." It was a declaration of war against the Jewish people and the "'world shadow government' that murders untold numbers of people and, while hiding behind sonorous phrases and high-sounding principles, plans to brainwash and control the rest." "Japanese, awaken!" extols the hypnotic, photo-laden pamphlet, adding, "the enemy's plot has long since torn our lives into shreds." It then goes into a litany of attacks on Jews for everything from massacres in Cambodia, Rwanda, and Bosnia to exploiting Japan's devastation after the war for their own fiscal advancement.[33]

Two months later, fueled by apocalyptic fantasies of starting its final war against the Jewish-Freemason alliance attempting to enslave the world, Aum carried out a coordinated sarin gas attack on the Tokyo subway, killing thirteen and injuring more than five thousand. It was the group's second major gas attack in less than a year, and in its aftermath, Asahara and most of his leading disciples were arrested. Following the attacks, Aum rebranded under several new names, and even after Asahara's execution it continues to have a small membership that follows variations on the guru's teachings.

Japan's obsession with the exoticism and power of the Jewish people mostly abated after that, but the country still struggles with how to define a people who have almost no footprint there. Some of it continues to be aspirational, such as when the CEO of Japanese investment giants SoftBank told shareholders that he wanted to be seen as a twenty-first century Mayer Amschel Rothschild for the "information revolution."[34] But most of it can charitably be described as ignorant, such as a Tokyo club promoting a Nazi theme night in 2021, or the head of one of Japan's biggest hotel chains giving an interview to a company magazine in which he claimed that "Jewish people control American information, finance, and laws, and they benefit greatly from globalization because they move their massive profits to tax havens so they don't have to pay any taxes."[35]

It might be shocking to read comments like this coming from the Japanese CEO of a modern international company rather than a French pamphlet-pushing crank or a 1930s American radio hate preacher. And they are shocking. But they also represent just one data point in a disturbing twenty-first-century trend: the resurgence of public and unapologetic antisemitism.

From rap stars declaring how much they love Hitler to political candidates dining with open neo-Nazis to pundits sharing nakedly anti-Jewish tropes to audiences of millions, as the acceptability of Islamophobia in the post-9/11 era faded, it was replaced by familiar fears of Jewish power, influence, "overrepresentation," and control. These would be dangerous, fraught years for the world's Jewish population, fueled by what was now nearly two centuries of "legitimate scholarship" on how Jews, and specifically the Rothschilds and their puppets, controlled every aspect of finance and politics.

But what would be different about the 2020s reemergence of antisemitism isn't that it was being spread by powerful people using new technology, but that there was no attempt to couch it in the "not all Jews, just *those* Jews" equivocations of the past. Starting with the embrace of Donald Trump by the far-right, the acceptability of scapegoating wealthy Jews for the ills of the world—from war to COVID-19 to inflation—would reach heights not seen since the days leading up to the Holocaust.

#FLYROTHSFLY: ROTHSCHILD CONSPIRACY THEORIES IN THE AGE OF TRUMP

It was just one angry, incoherent sign in a sea of angry, incoherent signs. Lofted into the sky at a Tea Party rally alongside hand-drawn proclamations about President Barack Obama's "concealed birth certificate" and "Marxist buddies" was one declaring, for all the world to see:

Obama Takes His Orders from the Rothschilds.[1]

Barack Obama, of course, does not take his orders from the Rothschilds. He couldn't even get the support of Lynn Forester de Rothschild, the one member of the family who has played any kind of significant role in American politics. But trivialities like "the truth" don't matter when you're irrationally angry that the United States had the nerve to elect a Black president who was going to put you on a death panel for not buying health insurance.

The Tea Party movement exploded in the US during Obama's first term, fueled by conservative terror over imaginary wealth confiscation and the looming specter of Marxist control and/or martial law. As with many populist movements of the United States's past, such as the Anti-Masonic Party and the Know Nothing Party of the 1800s, its patriotism-tinged allegations of Jewish/New World Order/Communist/Leftist domination were nothing new. And like those movements, it had a tremendous amount of initial success electing outsider candidates who "spoke plainly" on hot-button issues, only to fizzle out in a haze of doctrinal infighting and the realization that most people—even most American conservatives—are just not as extreme as the fringe makes them out to be.

But one American celebrity, mulling over the idea of throwing his considerable cultural and financial weight into politics, was paying attention to what made the Tea Party such a hit in those early days. He noticed the power and appeal of the movement's unhinged conspiracy theories, vague accusations of a global super-government, and "us versus them" rhetoric when they were unleashed by radio talkers and blogs on disaffected Republicans angry about the Black president with a foreign-sounding name.

And Donald Trump wanted in.

THE "KING OF DEBT" MEETS THE "KINGS OF EPOCH"

Donald Trump never claimed to be a politician. He was the opposite of a stuffed-shirt Washington candidate, an outsider beholden to nobody who built a worldwide brand on gut instinct and charisma, doing it his way or the highway. He was a winner, and if he lost, it was only either because some piddly rule got in his way or because he needed to lose now in order to win even bigger later. That was what appealed to so many people about him. That and the conspiracy theories, of course.

His first brush with political aspiration, other than his doomed 2000 Reform Party run for president, was publicly doubting the veracity of Obama's birth certificate and Christianity while spinning wild tales about the death of Hawaii Department of Health director Loretta Fuddy in a plane crash being a targeted hit that "all others survived" after she released Obama's long-form birth certificate in 2011.[2]

The paranoia and conspiracy theories continued as Trump announced his campaign in summer 2015 and began the laborious process of trouncing every other boring, establishment GOP candidate. And where conspiracy theories become coin of the realm, antisemitism always follows. Trump's campaign, and subsequently his presidency, unleashed a deluge of antisemitic tweets, memes, image board posts, podcasts, and cartoons directing unhinged hate at any Jews who were critical of Trump—and even some who supported him, particularly his Jewish son-in-law Jared Kushner, who got no quarter for being married to Trump's daughter Ivanka, who had converted to Judaism.[3]

The "alt-right," as it came to be known, was foundationally powered by antisemitic conspiracy theories about "white genocide," their term for the supposed replacement of whites by imported minorities, transferred through unchecked immigration to "white countries" thanks to Jewish scheming. Many of the most prominent voices in the alt-right and the Trump sphere in general were openly neo-Nazi and lionized fascism. And they railed against "globalism"—the latest term for Jewish control of banking and the media.[4]

The impact on American Jews was immediate, and continues to this day. The ADL reported that 2021 was their worst year on record for tracked incidents of vandalism, harassment, and assault targeted at Jewish people in the US, likely due to conspiracy theories about COVID-19 being a Jewish plot and the rise of extremist movements in general.[5] Antisemitic statements spiked both in polling results and in public, with a wide range of political and cultural figures blurting out unevidenced and hateful things about Jews. It was everyone from rapper Kanye West proclaiming his love of Hitler (while making references to "300 Zionists" who run the world, a clear echo of the "Committee of 300" conspiracy theory) to anonymous trolls leaving antisemitic fliers on car windshields to Trump making the bizarre claim that American Jews needed to "get their act together" and appreciate Israel more "before it's too late."[6]

Again and again, it came back to Trump—who attracted openly antise-mitic influencers and went off on rants full of well-worn Jewish tropes while simultaneously claiming he was "the greatest President for Jews in the his-tory of the world" and was "loved like the King of Israel" in that country.[7] But the antisemitic trolls who worshipped Trump unwittingly also em-braced the Rothschilds. Because the two were tied together going decades back, with Rothschild funds playing a critical role in helping Trump estab-lish his reputation as a bulletproof winner who only loses so he can pull off an even greater triumph down the road.

It was 1990, and Donald Trump was in trouble. His overbuilding in Atlantic City had left him the proud owner of three casinos, the last of which, the Trump Taj Mahal, had been financed through $675 million in junk bonds offered at a 14 percent interest rate. The Taj might have been "the Eighth Wonder of the World," but Atlantic City was losing its luster. By the end of the year, Trump was looking at making huge payments on an underachieving property that he'd massively overspent on. Seeking to re-structure his debt and avoid bankruptcy, he did what European royals and leaders had done for two centuries: he turned to Rothschild.[8]

Or, to be more precise, he turned to Rothschild, Inc.—the newly incor-porated New York–based asset management firm launched by the British and French branches. Rothschild, Inc. had prospered as advisors for the waves of privatization and mergers hitting big business in the 1980s, and one of these areas was bankruptcy restructuring.[9] Rothschild executive Wilbur Ross, who had gone to Yale to become a writer and switched to banking when, he said, he ran out of things to write about, was running the bank-ruptcy division and soon became enjoined in a lucrative partnership with Donald Trump. The first order of business: save the Taj.

Ross took a look at the frenzied celebrity surrounding "the Donald" and came up with a better idea than plain old bankruptcy: Trump would give up half his stake in the casino but get better repayment terms and keep over-all control of the property. Maybe more importantly, his brand wouldn't be tarnished with failure. The deal bailed Trump out, and he bought the stake back in 1996, turning the Taj Mahal into Atlantic City's highest grossing casino for over a decade.[10] With Ross, by then dubbed "the king of bankruptcy," advising the self-proclaimed "king of debt," Trump made similar deals to bail out other struggling Trump properties. And much of it was thanks to Rothschild.

By 2000, Ross had bought Rothschild Inc.'s bankruptcy fund from the firm and went into business himself. Trump would eventually return the favor to Ross by nominating him to be his Secretary of Commerce, and he was one of the few Trump cabinet members to not get fired or resign due to scandal. And the Rothschild/Trump link rarely came up, either on the campaign trail or during his presidential term. Neither supporters nor detractors saw fit to bring it up.

But the Rothschild-masterminded bailout of the Taj Mahal wasn't the only link that Trump and Europe's "kings of epoch" had. There was another relationship between the two—one at the heart of the Russian interference in the 2016 election that likely played at least some role in propelling Trump into office in the first place.

HOLIDAYS IN CORFU

Before the 2016 election, there was little reason for any American who didn't professionally cover Russian business to know who Oleg Deripaska was or how he'd made billions off that country's frequently violent 1990s-era "aluminum wars." But that relative anonymity changed shortly after Trump's inauguration, when journalists discovered that Deripaska had spent much of the previous decade working with Trump's last campaign manager, Paul Manafort, as part of a $10 million per year deal for Manafort to advance American interests in Russia. With speculation about Russia's role in the 2016 election swirling, it seemed like this was an obvious connection between the Trump campaign and Vladimir Putin, given that Putin and Deripaska had a close (though stormy) relationship.[11]

As it would turn out, Deripaska had met Manafort through Manafort's business partner at the time, Rick Davis. And Davis had been introduced to the aluminum titan through one of Deripaska's advisors—Nathaniel

"Nat" Rothschild, the heir to the Rothschild Baronetcy currently held by his father, Lord Jacob Rothschild. According to a redacted filing in the US Senate's investigation of Russian interference in the 2016 election, Rothschild was with Deripaska when Manafort presented him a plan for a "political influence campaign" on behalf of ousted Ukrainian president Viktor Yanukovych in the aftermath of the 2004 Orange Revolution—a plan with at least some ties to organized crime in Russia.[12] While neither the Senate investigation nor US law enforcement accused the Rothschild heir of wrongdoing, it wasn't the first time Nat's relationship to Russian money had made bad headlines for the family.

In 2008, news broke that Nat and Deripaska were among a crowd of uber-rich photographed lounging on a yacht off Corfu with British Conservative politician George Osborne. When Nat claimed that Osborne had tried to solicit a £50,000 donation to his Conservative Party from Deripaska, it was a huge scandal. The ensuing "Yachtgate" farrago raised uncomfortable questions about the role of Russian money in British politics, and whether Osborne, a rising star in the Conservative Party, had potentially violated British law with his solicitation. As usual, everyone involved escaped unscathed, and Osborne later became Chancellor of the Exchequer, one of the highest-ranking offices in the British government.[13]

More scandal ensued a few years later with the news that Nat had brokered a deal between EU Trade Commissioner Peter Mandelson and Deripaska while the group was on a hedonistic weeklong trip through Russia in 2005, several years before "Yachtgate." When the *Daily Mail* wrote about the deal, it used the unfortunate canard "puppet master" to refer to Nat Rothschild's role, prompting Nat to sue the paper for libel. It was one of the few recent times that the Rothschilds actually took action over something written about them in the press, but it also exposed the sheer depths of the megawealth that the Rothschilds have enjoyed for two centuries: a world of impromptu private jet jaunts halfway across the world, a stay in Deripaska's chalet with an in-house traditional Cossack band for entertainment, and "birch-leaf beatings in a communal sauna" in Siberia. Nat would lose the libel case, and he also lost a further appeal, having opened an uncomfortable window into his family's lavish lifestyle that had been closed for a long time.[14]

The Trump base's ill feelings toward the "European bankers" would seem to make the links that Trump, Ross, and Manafort all had to the Rothschilds a serious problem. After all, presidents are ephemeral, but Jewish control of finance is eternal. How could antisemites embrace a man so connected with the Illuminati power brokers who supposedly run everything?

It turns out that they could because there was little Trump could do that they *wouldn't* embrace—even if it meant violating their long-held hatred for Jews. Certainly, there are anti-Rothschild writers and conspiracy theorists who loathed Trump as much as they would any other Jewish-controlled American president. Among the most prominent was David Icke, who claimed Trump was just another Rothschild-funded stooge "chosen by the Hidden Hand" that controlled both parties—a Zionist alliance Icke often refers to as the "Kosher Nostra."[15]

But the majority of Trump acolytes never bring up Trump's links to the Rothschilds, even in their attacks *on* the Rothschilds. In one especially undignified incident, rabidly pro-Trump political cartoonist Ben Garrison was disinvited from Trump's "social media summit" in 2019 after the White House learned of a 2017 cartoon Garrison had drawn invoking classic antisemitic tropes: a decrepit green hand labeled "Rothschilds" serving as the puppet master of George Soros, who in turn was pulling the strings of former Trump National Security Advisor H. R. McMaster and former CIA head David Petraeus—two of the generals often thought to be plotting in secret against Trump.

Rather than blame the White House for rescinding the invitation, Garrison claimed that accusations of him or the cartoon being antisemitic were libelous media creations, and that he was only depicting the Rothschilds as "instrumental in the behind-the-scenes creation of the Federal Reserve," which was "a historical fact."[16] Garrison was so committed to the fiction of the Rothschilds as global controllers that when he sued the ADL the next year alleging that they had defamed him by calling his work antisemitic, he actually included in the suit the "fact" that "ADL knew that the Rothschilds controlled Soros and that Soros controlled McMaster."[17]

If it became absolutely necessary, Trump supporters would deflect from Trump's Rothschild connections by bringing up the family's support of Hillary Clinton or French president Emmanuel Macron's stint from 2008 to 2012 as an investment banker at Paris-based Rothschild & Co. When Macron won a bitter election over far-right candidate Marine Le Pen to become President of France in 2017, a slew of articles brought up Macron's ties to the Rothschilds, claiming he would be subjected to years of conspiracy theories and baseless accusations.

Sure enough, Macron was labeled "Rothschild's choice" to run France, written off as "President Rothschild," and called an "arrogant and idiotic Rothschild employee and gofer President of France" by David Icke.[18] But like the Rothschild connections to Ross and Manafort, most of Trump's biggest fans had little problem with Trump and Macron's public friendship, an alpha male bromance of firm handshakes, obnoxious praise lavished on each other, air kisses, and even the duo planting an oak tree together outside the White House. The friendship between the men eventually soured, and the tree died, but little of the Rothschild/Macron connection stuck to Trump.[19] Just like very little of anything negative sticks to Trump, so too did the Rothschild links fall away. Apparently, when you're Donald Trump, they just let you do it.

"SNOWING OUT OF NOWHERE"

It wasn't all Trump's fault, of course. He came to power at a time when social media was making it easier than ever to spread conspiracy theories, countless earth-shaking world events involving economics and health demanded alternate explanations, and a relentless grift machine stood at the ready to profit off them. It was happening before Trump, and it happened after him.

Despite the Rothschilds being nowhere near the upper reaches of the banking world anymore, they were put at the levers of virtually everything of importance: banking, politics, wars, the very fate of nations. And they went to realms beyond the earth, into the sky and the clouds. Because what could be more terrifying than controlling the very basics of existence: the weather that blesses us with sunshine, or curses us with untimely rain?

The fear that "they" were manipulating the weather through "geoengineering" is much older than the internet. Both US and Soviet scientists were studying the potential of weather modification by the late 1940s, and when then-president Lyndon Johnson was briefed on the looming danger of human-caused climate change in 1965, geoengineering was offered as a potential solution.[20] Like many other conspiracy theories with a toehold in real life, the current iteration of weather control plotting eventually circles back to the Rothschilds. And naturally, the most famous recent resurgence started on Facebook.

"Man, it just started snowing out of nowhere this morning, man," exclaimed Washington, D.C., council member Trayvon White, Sr., on a Facebook Live stream in March 2018 as flakes descended on the nation's capital. "Y'all better pay attention to this climate control, man, this climate manipulation. And D.C. keep talking about, 'We a resilient city [sic].' And that's a model based off the Rothschilds controlling the climate to create natural disasters they can pay for to own the cities, man. Be careful."[21]

Called out for employing antisemitic language, White would quickly apologize for the comment. But in the lexicon of the Rothschilds controlling everything, it sounds totally believable. We've seen countless other writers accuse the Rothschilds of having total control over everything from banking to mining to the media, so why not making it snow? It's just another iteration of the same conspiracy theory—and it wasn't the only one White was referring to. The "resilient city" comment was a reference to a Rockefeller Foundation grant program incentivizing cities to deal with environmental and economic challenges—and it was a program council member White had already wrongly linked to the Rothschilds in past comments.[22]

But more than that, conspiracy theorists had already made hay linking various weather control schemes—imaginary and real—to the Rothschilds.

Initially, the family wasn't accused of *changing* the weather, but of *pretending* the weather was changing—for money, of course. Ex-wrestler, actor, and Minnesota governor Jesse "The Body" Ventura put out a 2009 episode of his show *Conspiracy Theory* purporting to expose the "global warming scam," which he believed had been funded in large part by a conspiracy involving both the United Nations Environment Program and British Rothschild baron Edmund de Rothschild—who had died at the age of ninety-three that year—as a way of profiting off carbon taxes and green energy initiatives.[23]

But that was nothing compared to the storm, if you will, of conspiracy theories in 2011 when E.L. Rothschild, the investment fund set up by Sir Evelyn and Lynn Forester de Rothschild, bought a controlling stake in Weather Central, a company that provided weather forecasting and graphics to TV news programs in North America and Asia. Sir Evelyn claimed the investment was made partially due to climate change, saying, "As weather becomes more extreme around the planet, with greater human and financial ramifications, we believe that Weather Central will play a major role in mitigating damage and improving lives."[24]

Immediately, geoengineering conspiracy theorists started asking why the Rothschilds would take such an interest in weather and decided it was part of a bigger plot. One conspiracy book purporting to blow the lid off the "Full Spectrum Dominance of Planet Earth" took the purchase and connected it both to the Alaska-based atmospheric research array HAARP and to supposed geoengineering patents held by Raytheon, Lockheed Martin, and biotech titan Monsanto. Are weather modelling and forecasting "code for 'scheduling?'" the book rhetorically asked.[25]

Sadly, we never found out, because rival network the Weather Channel bought Weather Central, including the Rothschilds' controlling stake, the next year. Naturally, that got folded into the "weather control" plot as well. Conspiracy theorist James Perloff, whose website has an entire page just of Rothschild family memes and who made a video called *Rothschild's War on Christianity*, wrote on his blog of the connections between the Weather Channel and one of its part owners, the investment firm BlackRock. And who, Perloff reasoned, sat on the board of BlackRock, and was accused of killing off his fellow patent owners in the crash of MH370 to benefit that fund? "Evelyn's powerful cousin Jacob Rothschild," of course. Just two cousins conspiring through "rival" weather forecasters and a network of hedge funds to control the skies.

"Naturally, I don't know how the Rothschilds allocate their market investments," Perloff wrote. "But given their long history of fiscal manipulation, it would seem that weather control, combined with weather forecasting control, would make weather derivatives an irresistible item for any bankster's portfolio."[26]

So when Trayvon White accused the Rothschilds of making it "snow out of nowhere," he was merely following a tradition of conspiracy theorists blaming climate woes not on out-of-control industrial practices or the developed world's addiction to fossil fuels but on the globalist controllers who want you to *think* the climate is changing.

But what's an even more efficient way to exercise control over the sleeping masses than ruling over weather forecasting or making it snow on command? Blowing things up with lasers.

"LASERS OR BLUE BEAMS"

Georgia CrossFit devotee Marjorie Taylor Greene wasn't a political figure in November 2018 when she went on Facebook to offer her opinions on the Camp Fire, one of many wildfires that had recently devastated California. But while she wasn't a conspiracy theorist member of Congress yet, she was definitely a conspiracy theorist. Among other claims Greene would make on social media before entering politics were that the Parkland, Florida, school shooting was a false flag carried out to take away gun rights, that a "so-called plane" had hit the Pentagon on September 11, that Barack Obama was a secret Muslim, and that the unsolved murder of DNC staffer Seth Rich had been carried out by an El Salvadoran street gang on the order of prominent Democrats. None of it was out of the ordinary from what one might hear on the average episode of Infowars or in a thousand other places.[27]

Like with most of her other theories, Greene's 2018 Facebook post about the Camp Fire is an incoherent ramble, and it was deleted from the site for violating terms of service. If she hadn't been elected to Congress just a few years after posting it, it wouldn't have merited any coverage. But reading it reveals everything about where the global conspiracy mindset was, how it used social media to spread its message, and how that message could find interested ears all over the world when delivered in an earnest, "just asking questions" fashion by a skilled troll.

In the post, Greene claimed that Pacific Gas & Electric, one of the major power providers for California, had used a "space based solar generator" developed by the green energy startup Solaren to collect energy from the sun and beam it to earth in something resembling "lasers or blue beams," and that such technology would "replace coal and oil," devastating the American economy. But something went terribly wrong, according to Greene's crack research. In theory, she mused, the beam could "miss a transmitter receiving station" owned by PG&E and instead roast a forest. And wouldn't you know it, there just happened to be a massive fire on remote California woodland that just happened to be earmarked for a $77 billion light rail project that just happened to be run by the husband of California senator Dianne Feinstein. And who sits on the board of PG&E? None other than Roger Kimmel, "vice chairman of Rothschild Inc international investment banking firm [sic]."

"If they are beaming the suns energy back to Earth, I'm sure they wouldn't ever miss a transmitter receiving station right??!! I mean mistakes are never made when anything new is invented. What would that look like anyway? A laser beam or light beam coming down to Earth I guess. Could that cause a fire? Hmmm, I don't know. I hope not! That wouldn't look so good for PG&E, Rothschild Inc, Solaren or [then–California governor] Jerry Brown who sure does seem fond of PG&E," she continued, making up connections and conspiracies as fast as she could type.

It's not clear why a large forest fire in California "wouldn't look good" for an investment bank based in Paris and London. But Greene seemed to have a theory: the entire scheme was perpetrated both to clear land for a green energy boondoggle to keep California politicians happy and to manipulate PG&E's stock prices and make more money—the same motivation that drove everything else the Rothschilds did.[28]

And with that, the "Jewish Space Laser" conspiracy theory was born, with the Rothschilds at the head of a vast plot to reap billions by using secret technology to advance their socialist climate change hoax, killing dozens of people in the process. While it may be beside the point, it's important to note that Greene's post never actually used the phrase "Jewish space laser," or even the word "Jewish." The term likely came from the title of one of the many stories written about the post after it was first rediscovered, with *New York Magazine* columnist Jonathan Chait writing that "Marjorie Taylor Greene Blamed Wildfires on Secret Jewish Space Laser."[29]

That's not to absolve Greene of the obvious connection she was making, though, given that she went out of her way to single out Rothschild, while labeling Kimmel's involvement "very interesting."

It wasn't that interesting. Roger Kimmel was indeed a vice chairman at the investment firm Rothschild Inc. And he was on the board of PG&E at the time of the Camp Fire, though he resigned in early 2019 as the company declared bankruptcy from legal liabilities due to its faulty power line igniting and starting the blaze.[30] In fact, almost the entire leadership suite of PG&E resigned, a move forced by California governor Gavin Newsom as part of its bankruptcy restructuring.[31] But Greene didn't focus on all of those other board members, or the various issues at PG&E that led to the fire, or the climate crisis that likely made the fire considerably worse. She focused only on the one board member who also worked for Rothschild.

News about the post broke just weeks after Greene had been sworn in—and after she'd worn a mask on the floor of the House on January 6, 2021, with TRUMP WON stitched in white letters. Twitter immediately lit up with the hashtag #JewishSpaceLasers, memes sharing pictures from the "Jews in Space" gag from Mel Brooks's 1981 film *History of the World Part I*, and other jokes at Greene's expense. A few commenters saw the story as an opportunity to point out that this was another example of Jews being scapegoated—a trope that often ends in violence. "#JewishSpaceLasers may be funny unless you contemplate how many of these conspiracy theories are rooted in antisemitism and racism and how many elected officials are helping to mainstream them because they frankly don't care if it ends up getting anyone hurt or killed," tweeted CNN's Jake Tapper, trying to throw a little cold water on the fun.[32]

Putting aside the memes, what exactly was she talking about? Conspiracy theories often revolve around magical, unproven technology doing something that "shouldn't happen," and that often didn't actually happen. The "space laser forest fire" was a perfect example, and Solaren quickly released a statement debunking the entire thing as not possible. The company had a contract with PG&E to develop its satellite power transmission technology, but the deal was canceled after Solaren was unable to get funding to further develop the project. No satellites were ever launched, and if they eventually are, they won't use lasers but radio frequencies "to transmit power from Earth Orbit to a Receiving Station on Earth."[33]

Greene wasn't even the only person to blame California's fires on space-based lasers. Fires in 2017, 2018, and 2020 were all blamed by conspiracy theorists on "DEWs"—directed energy weapons. Supposedly, the powers that be are using laser weapons to burn California's forests in order to clear land for various green energy scams, to distract from other false flag incidents, to further the UN's evil Agenda 21 genocide plot, or to control the weather. Or all of those.[34]

The proof of all these different plots, supposedly, is that certain buildings are completely destroyed by the fires, while other buildings and trees are completely untouched. But large fires are complex and can quickly take on a life of their own. They shift with the wind, burn at different levels of intensity based on the materials that fuel them, often spread via windblown embers that can land on one roof and miss another, and don't always burn trees because trees are full of water. None of this has anything to do with lasers or the UN or satellites; it's just the science of how large fires spread, and why they're so hard to put out.[35]

And in just a few specific examples of the Rothschilds being blamed, a 2019 post on prolific anti-5G blog *StopTheCrime* lambasted the "PG&E aka

Rothschild—Burn'em Up and Fix'em Plan" in the wake of the power giant's bankruptcy,[36] while a conspiracy-minded gentleman offering public comment at a City of Chicago Police Board meeting in December 2018 declared that "these fires out in Northern California are obviously directed energy weapon fires. And they're obviously connected to the Rothschilds," after which he was politely told to wrap it up.[37]

After the initial press coverage, the "Jewish space lasers" remark continued to dog Greene, who was well on her way to becoming one of the most media-savvy and TV-friendly members of the Republican Congressional delegation. She tried to explain the comment away, claiming that she "didn't find out until recently that the Rothschilds were Jewish," that the controversy had been ginned up by the liberal media, and, of course, that the people accusing her of antisemitism were themselves the real antisemites.[38]

They were not. The real antisemites were still who they'd always been, and they were busy with their new grand plot: the supposed upcoming purge of the deep state being engineered by a mysterious entity known only as "Q." And Q had big plans for the Rothschilds.

BLACK FOREST BLUES: THE ROTHSCHILDS AND QANON

As the Trump years ground on, it became impossible to talk about worldwide conspiracy theory without talking about QAnon. What began in October 2017 as a few anonymous, prophetic posts about Hillary Clinton getting arrested, posted on the image board 4chan (itself a hive of Rothschild conspiracy theories), bloomed into a full-on conspiracy cult. QAnon even found vocal proponents—most of whom denied knowing anything about it even as they used its catchphrases—at the very top of the Trump pyramid. It was as if someone had finally read *None Dare Call It Conspiracy* and decided to call it a conspiracy. Even though nothing Q ever promised came to pass, and its predictions were met with constant failure, the Q movement was too big and too lucrative to give up on. So believers started to take matters into their own hands, committing a growing list of crimes, including several murders, and numerous Q acolytes invading the US Capitol on January 6, 2021.[39]

Primed by decades of conspiracy theories in popular films and games, Q's story of a secret war between good and evil was deeply alluring to a new generation of fringe believers. Its complex story tips its hat to everything from the blood libel to films like *The Matrix* and *Blade Runner 2049* to currency scams of the 2000s to elements of Bill Cooper's "Silent Weapons for Quiet Wars." And like Cooper would roll up the Rothschilds in that conspiracy, the Q poster (likely a combination of trolls who made different posts without any real plan for their storyline) would reference the Rothschilds when there was a need for a rich Jewish villain to blame for things not happening on schedule.

The mysterious Q "drops" pegged the Rothschilds as having a fortune of $2 trillion,[40] hinted that they helped develop AIDS,[41] claimed they kept the population enslaved through opioids, cleaning products, and tobacco,[42] and accused family members of being intwined with the NXIVM sex cult.[43] Q even helpfully used four posts to provide a list of "ROTHSCHILD OWNED & CONTROLLED BANKS"—in reality just a rundown of central banks around the world that was cribbed from a 2013 post on a blog called "Humans Are Free."

But Q didn't just see the Rothschilds as a powerful banking interest, but as depraved and deranged, using their victims in bizarre occult rituals that smacked of the lurid hysteria of John Todd's tapes. In early 2018, just a few months after it launched, Q responded to tweets from California congress member Adam Schiff, a longtime thorn in Trump's side, with this bizarre allegation:

Would POTUS make a serious accusation if the TRUTH wasn't about to come to LIGHT?

Black Forest.

Austria.

Rothschild.

FIRE sale days after post?

What went on there?

Dopey.

You have more than you know.

Q

A few hours later, Q mentioned "Rothschild estate sale [Black Forest]" as part of a longer ramble covering a range of conspiracy theories encompassing Soros, the Clintons, and others. Q "researchers" took these crumbs and "baked" them into a shocking conspiracy theory: the Rothschilds had used one of their secluded properties in the Black Forest as a hunting ground for human beings, tracking and killing people in bizarre and horrifying rituals, and doing God only knows what with their bodies. When caught by the Trump team, they had no other option to cover up their depravity but to sell the property and make a run for it.[44]

There are, of course, a number of problems with this theory. The biggest is that Q is not especially good at geography: the Black Forest is in Germany, not Austria. Nor have the Rothschilds owned any land in the Black Forest. But the Rothschilds did own a vast Austrian woodland parcel called Langau—the same parcel confiscated from Louis de Rothschild by the Nazis. The family had gotten most of it back from the Soviets in 1952 but found the palaces in disrepair and unlivable. Much of the forest was donated to the Austrian government, with Louis's heirs building lodges on the land that remained.

By 2018, when Q's deranged conspiracy landed, one of the parcels was owned by Albert von Rothschild's great-grandchildren Geoffrey Hoguet and Nancy Clarice Tilghman, the latter of whom had written lovingly of the hunting lodge's history and quirks in an article for *Architectural Digest*.[45] The other was owned by another great-granddaughter, arts patron Bettina Burr. Tilghman and Hoguet sold their parcel in February 2018, with Burr selling a year later.[46]

While the deals netted the heirs north of $200 million, there's no indication that this was a "family fire sale" necessitated by authorities being on the verge of busting their "human hunting ring." It's likely that Q got the idea from yet another past blog post with fake information, this one about a "Ninth Circle Satanic Child Sacrifice Cult" full of European royalty who hunted children at their lodges.[47]

Numerous other Q influencers used the Rothschilds as props in their own media, linking them to plots and conspiracies of all types, most of which had little to do with reality. And what was probably the most influential of all the different pro-QAnon videos, Dutch director Jan Ossebaard's ten-part series *Fall of the Cabal*, was full of typical references to the family, including claiming that "all central banks are in the hands of the Rothschilds," who funded Hitler and the Nazi war machine, and that they will assassinate any leader who gets in their way.[48] Despite being made up of reheated leftovers, *Fall of the Cabal* was a hugely popular series that social media companies freely allowed to spread and "red pill" new converts to QAnon, up until they cracked down on Q content after the 2020 election. By then it was much too late to stop the spread of QAnon—it had become a hugely important part of the plot to get Donald Trump a second term he didn't win.

STOP THE STEAL

The far-right Rothschild obsession grew to the point that a speaker at the 2020 Republican National Convention, Women for Trump member Mary Ann Mendoza, had to be pulled due to her history of sharing antisemitic conspiracy theories, including one by a QAnon influencer that extolled the *Protocols* and claimed the Rothschilds and other "malevolent Jewish forces in the banking industry are out to enslave non-Jews and promote world wars."[49]

When Biden did the "unthinkable" and won the election, it was the same conspiracy theorists who concocted a vast Democratic Party plot to steal the contest using rigged voting machines, cloned ballots, and rolls full of dead voters, all funded by globalist money. And only the patriots of Trump's movement, with God and some armed extremists on their side, could stop them. As Alex Jones hoarsely screamed at a crowd at the "Stop the Steal" rally in Washington, D.C., the day before the insurrection, it was God who was in control, "not Bill Gates, not Warren Buffett, not Lord Rothschild, not the globalists!"[50]

Unfortunately for Jones and his compatriots, God did not intervene in the election, and Biden was inaugurated two weeks after the Capitol riot. Even then, Rothschild-centric conspiracy theories about the contest continued unabated. The family were the puppet masters who picked Biden to help take the fall for the worsening global economy, as one hugely popular thread on Reddit forum r/conspiracy put it.[51] Alex Jones continued pushing nonsense about the family, while 2022 midterm election candidates included them in their increasingly reality-deprived conspiracy theories and hoaxes. A mention of the family could even be found in Trump's second impeachment filing, entered into evidence in a news article where a January 6 rioter tells a reporter the day before that the Democratic establishment "have destroyed our country and sold [it] to the Rothschilds and Rockefellers."[52]

The incidents are so bizarre they defy belief, while also being completely on par with past Rothschild inanities. A "prophet" working on the campaign of Pennsylvania GOP gubernatorial candidate Doug Mastriano claimed that "the truth" about the Rothschilds and "their power over their wicked and fraudulent government" was coming,[53] while Arizona Senate hopeful Blake Masters was reported to have posted in 2006 on a libertarian site of a conspiracy by the "Houses of Morgan and Rothschild" to get the United States into the First World War by arranging the sinking of the *Lusitania*. Masters had adapted his conspiracy from *Creature From Jekyll Island* author G. Edward Griffin and ended his post with what he described as a "representative and poignant quotation" from *Reichsmarschall* Hermann Goering at the Nuremberg trials, a figure not usually renowned for his heart-tugging quotes.[54] Both Mastriano and Masters lost, part of an extremely poor showing for election deniers and conspiracy theorists overall. And the Rothschilds were among the many bad actors implicated in the "Great Reset" conspiracy theory claiming the World Economic Forum had embarked on a COVID-19-fueled push to transform humanity into a bug-eating, perpetually locked-down slave race under the control of European financiers.[55] There was even a supposed Rothschild connection in WEF president and "Great Reset" villain Klaus Schwab—a viral rumor that he was "part of the family" because a woman who happened to have the last name Rothschild had married a man with the last name Schwab. Neither had anything to do with either the family, the WEF, or Klaus Schwab, but it didn't matter. The mere linking of the names was all it took. And sometimes it didn't even take that—such as the bizarre hoax that young Swedish climate change activist Greta Thunberg is secretly the great-granddaughter of British banker and prominent Zionist Lionel Walter Rothschild. The claim that "Walter," as he was usually known, had an illegitimate son named "Joachim Rothschild" who is Thunberg's grandfather is entirely untrue: there was no "Joachim" among Walter's descendants, and Thunberg has no relation to the family. But it spawned videos that got millions of views and shares on social media from conspiracy theorists looking to tie the Rothschilds to Thunberg, who, like the Rothschilds, occupies a place of almost fanatical hatred among many fringe dwellers.[56]

NEW DISEASE, SAME OLD TROPES

When the COVID-19 pandemic hit, the volume of invective aimed at China, Asian Americans, and Asian people everywhere was disturbing and consequential. But the Jewish people weren't spared, being assigned their familiar roles of "rootless" disease vectors, moving from place to place sucking up resources and leaving only sickness behind. Even the makers of *The Eternal Jew*, a film that went out of its way to call Jews human plague rats, would have marveled at the instant spread of disinformation and bigotry that accompanied the pandemic.

The entire world went into lockdown, becoming socially isolated with too much time on its hands thanks to a little-understood new disease. It was a perfect environment for conspiracy theories to grow, and the search for a scapegoat quickly led to the Rothschilds.[57] The family was relentlessly accused of using COVID-19 alongside longtime targets Bill Gates and George Soros to finally unleash their long-planned genocide of "useless eaters" and Gentiles, the horror that so many anti–one world government writers had prophesied.

A rumor started spreading on social media that usual villain Jacob Rothschild "owned" the copyright on the terrifying new disease, which was bioengineered through a front group he also owned (with Bill and Melinda Gates, of course) called the Pirbright Institute. The theory took off in QAnon circles, with conspiracy gurus digging up old patents and grant applications as "proof" COVID was a Rothschild-created bioweapon. And in keeping with conspiracy theorists easily adapting to new technology, the rumor also found viral fame on TikTok, becoming just one of a slew of COVID hoaxes and anti-vaccine videos that went viral during the lockdown and beyond.[58] In reality, Jacob Rothschild had no link to the Pirbright Institute, which is a real infectious disease research center in England that had gotten a few grants from the Gates Foundation. Pirbright researchers had actually patented several strains of coronavirus, but they were attenuated versions of chicken viruses that could be used as a potential vaccine for bird flu, not COVID-19.[59]

Once that hoax fizzled out, it was replaced with the claim that one Sir Richard Rothschild, banking dynasty member and bioweapons researcher, had patented a "System and Method for Testing for COVID-19." And that he'd done it in 2015—a clear, unmistakable sign that the New World Order had spent years planning to unleash COVID, only to leave a tiny clue behind for conspiracy researchers to find and blow open the entire horrifying scheme.

Like so many times before, it was all either misinterpreted or bogus. While Richard A. Rothschild is a real researcher with multiple patents to his name, there's no evidence that he's related to the banking dynasty, nor is he a knight. Even if he had been related, it wouldn't be more than an unfortunate coincidence, because the 2015 application was merely for a "System and Method for Using, Processing, and Displaying Biometric Data." The portions about COVID-19 were part of a supplemental application filed in 2020 to apply the same design for COVID testing, which was still in its early stages. The dates on the application clearly show that the 2015 patent came first, with most of the viral memes being doctored versions of the supplemental application. Also, it's not likely that if the cabal had invented COVID-19 years before the outbreak of the pandemic they'd leave such an obvious clue lying around to be found by conspiracy researchers later.[60]

Isolated people everywhere were desperate for answers as to what was really going on and who was responsible. Major conspiracy influencers saw an open door and shoved a dump truck full of books and paranoia through it. David Icke in particular took the lead on spreading rumors of a "super-conspiracy" created by the Rothschilds and Rockefellers, who were devoted to using COVID to create a "global Orwellian state" based on depopulation and total surveillance of the few survivors. Icke's videos on the Rothschild "super-conspiracy" were hugely popular, with one early video that accused the family of helping plan the outbreak getting nearly six million views in just a few days.[61]

And once there were vaccines for COVID-19, the conspiracy theory industry didn't give up; it merely shifted focus to claiming they were untested, dangerous, and rewrote the DNA of their recipients, causing them to drop dead without warning.

One particularly loathsome idea to conspiracy believers was that of "vaccine passports," electronic documents you could show proving you'd been vaccinated or had recently taken a negative COVID test. Despite vaccine identification being a common and easily implemented way to submit proof of inoculation, the idea launched a hotbed of fears that the New World Order would use these documents to track who had complied with supposed mandated injections, and who had strayed and needed to be punished.

In June 2021, Rothschild & Co. managing director Arielle Malard de Rothschild met with officials from the Republic of Georgia to discuss potential investment opportunities. Months later, in a completely unrelated development, the country announced it would be instituting a passport system that would allow fully vaccinated, COVID-free Georgians to enjoy indoor activities and events. Because two things can't happen in the same country without being a conspiracy, Christina Pushaw, the spokeswoman for Florida governor Ron DeSantis, himself a vocal opponent of mandated COVID mitigation measures, including vaccine requirements, tweeted to her large following:

"Georgia decided to enact a 'Green Pass' system (biomedical security state). Immediately after that, the Rothschilds show up to discuss the attractive investment environment in Georgia (lol). No weird conspiracy theory stuff here!"[62]

Subsequent posts saw Pushaw claim she was "just making observations"—which, of course, were wrong. The Rothschild & Co. meeting took place months before Georgia instituted its Green Pass system, it had nothing to do with vaccines or vaccine mandates, and "the Rothschilds" had no sway over other countries instituting vaccine passports. Like Marjorie Taylor Greene with her Rothschild Inc. laser beam before, Pushaw tried to weasel her way out of the comment by adding context that "the Georgian government is intentionally fueling antisemitic Rothschild conspiracy theories in order to smear anyone who opposes vaccine passports as a 'conspiracy theorist.'"[63] She also claimed, before she deleted the tweet, that it was "an attempt at sarcasm," and that she opposes both antisemitism *and* the Georgian government.[64]

Of course, this was a variation on the same line used by everyone from John Reeves in the 1880s to Gary Allen in the 1970s to David Icke in the 2000s to right-wing trolls in the 2020s—that not all Jews are evil, but some Jews definitely are, and it's not anti-Jewish to point out the bad ones or ask questions. In fact, it's pro-Jewish, because the good Jews should hate the bad ones. After all, nobody is above criticism, right?

One very prominent Jew would be forced to answer these pedantic questions over and over: George Soros. And where conspiracy theorists once focused their ire on the Rothschilds, increasingly they found a more inviting and relevant target in Soros, a Jewish billionaire who openly supported progressive politics and causes, and seemed to have his claws into everything. Many of the same cranks who made millions off the Rothschilds effortlessly pivoted to using the same tropes on Soros, with devastating effects on both politics and culture. It would seem that Rothschild conspiracy theories were so prevalent that they didn't even need the Rothschilds anymore.

IT'S NOT EASY BEING GOD: HOW GEORGE SOROS BECAME THE ROTHSCHILDS OF THE TWENTY-FIRST CENTURY

As antisemitism surged in the Trump years, scholars and experts saw the looming danger and went on the offensive. Some of the most prolific chroniclers of the history of attacks on Jews spoke at length, in the US and elsewhere, about the perilous moment facing Jews and how it was rooted in past surges in antisemitism.

The Rothschilds were part of that conversation, naturally. But by then, Hungarian billionaire George Soros had surpassed the family as the primary focus of anti-Jewish plots, conspiracy theories, and hoaxes. In speaking at a World Jewish Congress event in France in fall 2022, author and United States Special Envoy for Monitoring and Combating Anti-Semitism Deborah Lipstadt bridged the gap between the Powerful Jewish Puppet Masters of the Old World and those of the New World by referring to Soros as "the Rothschilds of the twenty-first century."

"The stereotype remains the same," Lipstadt explained. "[It's] used somewhat differently on the extreme left, used somewhat different on the extreme right, but the stereotype is the same."[1]

Every bizarre accusation, trope, and conspiracy theory pushed out about the Rothschilds would be repurposed and updated for Soros. The secret links to the Nazis, the total control of global politics, the leadership of a cabal of shadowy string pullers, the obscene hoarding of wealth, the meddling in worldwide affairs, the funding of secular forces bent on race mixing and equality—all of them were recycled into a new narrative that wasn't actually new, but merely about a new target.

Soros was perfect for scapegoating in the social media era. He was Jewish and incredibly rich, of course. But there are plenty of rich Jews out there. Soros seems to have plenty of other tempting attributes for conspiracy theorists to latch on to. He was old, and easy to portray as a kind of decrepit power broker, like a Jewish Emperor Palpatine from Star Wars. He spoke in a thick foreign accent and often used oddly phrased sentences that lent themselves to being taken out of context. He unabashedly supported liberal causes and opposed authoritarianism. And he openly threw his weight into the American electoral process, something the Rothschilds had refused to do for nearly two centuries.

But the biggest difference between the Rothschild myth and the Soros myth isn't the particulars of the smears, it's in how fast they grew. Cranks and antisemites took just a few years to do with Soros what took over a century with the Rothschilds, rapidly creating an industry dedicated to willfully misinterpreting the basic facts of his existence in the service of antisemitism.

THE BOY FROM BUDAPEST

Soros and the Rothschilds share unimaginable wealth, European roots, an outsized public profile, and their Jewishness. But for everything they have in common, there's much more that they don't.

The Rothschilds have been passing their fortune down since Mayer's death, but Soros made his himself, going from being an almost destitute young man to one of the richest men in the world in middle age. Georgy Schwartz, as he was named at birth in 1930, was the son of middle-class Hungarian Jews Erzsébet and Tividar Schwartz. The Schwartz family was comfortable compared to many other Jewish families in Budapest and engaged in upper-middle-class pursuits like the study of the auxiliary language Esperanto and magazine writing. But they certainly weren't wealthy, and Soros's parents had little to their name when they eventually joined their son in the US.

Even their religion was more of a difference than a commonality. The Rothschilds were deeply devoted to their practice and to worldwide Judaism, but the Schwartz family was almost incidentally Jewish. Not that it mattered in the context of the times, as Jewish Hungarians of the 1930s faced an onslaught of antisemitic laws and scrutiny, no matter their level of belief. The family didn't convert, but in 1936, as a safety measure, Tividar changed their last name to Soros, meaning both "the next in line" in Hungarian and "to soar" in Esperanto.[2]

Hungary joined the Axis Powers in 1940, and German troops later marched through the country on their way to invade the Kingdom of Yugoslavia. As the war went on, the country became a German client state, with the Hungarian Army all but wiped out at Stalingrad in 1943. By early 1944, German tanks and troops would return, this time as occupiers: Nazi Germany formally took control of Hungary and installed a pro-Nazi government. For the Soros family and Budapest's other Jews, what had been a few years of repression without the threat of deportation turned into the same nightmare inflicted on the other nations of Europe suffering under the Nazi bootheel. Among these indignities were mass deportation and removal from society. Jewish children like thirteen-year-old George were forbidden from attending school and instead sent to the newly established Jewish Council to hand out deportation notices—which George claims his father refused to let him do.[3]

Seeing the peril his family was in, Tividar purchased false papers for George and his brother Paul and sent them to live in the countryside with

Gentile families. It almost certainly saved their lives—in just two months, from May to July in 1944, 440,000 Hungarian Jews would be shipped to the camps, most to Auschwitz and immediate gassing. George spent the rest of the war hiding, first with a Hungarian civil servant who took the boy on a trip to survey the confiscated estate of a wealthy Jewish family who had fled to the West. It was an act that not only would be used against the adult George, but that forced the young George into another hiding spot after he was recognized.[4] Months of moving around and hiding ensued, sometimes with Tividar and Paul, other times alone, before the Red Army expelled the Germans following the brutal Siege of Budapest, which left the city in ruins and over fifteen thousand Jews dead in a spate of executions by pro-Nazi militias.

With Hungary coming under Soviet control after the war, George emigrated to London. He took odd jobs and enrolled in the London School of Economics, having little to his name when he got his first job in finance in 1954. At that point, he was still struggling, and stymied by refining the manuscript of a book he'd never publish. So Soros set out for New York to get his share of the United States's postwar economic dominance. One biography claims the future billionaire left with just $5,000 to his name and was soon joined by his parents, who started a coffee stand on Coney Island that immediately failed.[5]

But what Soros lacked in immediate financial resources he made up for in knowledge of how American firms could get a piece of Western Europe's rapid recovery. With his experience in the European market, Soros started rising and landed at the New York investment bank Arnhold and S. Bleichroeder, founded in 1803 by Samuel Bleichröder, the father of the Rothschild family's agent in Berlin during the Bismarck era. By 1973, Soros was successful enough to launch his own hedge fund, the Soros Fund, with $13 million in assets. Countless purchases, investments, stock sales, and dividends would follow, with what was later renamed the Quantum Fund growing to a portfolio of more than $6 billion a quarter century later— making both Soros and the shareholders in his fund wealthy.[6]

Like the Rothschilds' myriad financial transactions, the intricacies of every deal and investment Soros made are far beyond the scope of this book.

But one victory in particular would start his journey toward being on the lips of every crank and antisemite in the world. It was 1992, and the then 62-year-old George Soros made billions off shorting the British pound sterling, betting it would crater in value relative to the rest of Europe's currencies.

When Soros shorted the pound, it was one of countless gambles he'd made on worldwide financial upheavals. Some were unsuccessful, such as when the Quantum Fund lost $800 million incorrectly betting that Japan's stock market would crash alongside the rest of the world in 1987.[7] But in 1992, inflation and interest rates were on the rise all over Europe, and the United Kingdom was mired in a recession. With his deep knowledge of the European bond market, Soros believed that Britain would be forced to withdraw the pound from the European Exchange Rate Mechanism when its value against the deutschmark fell below a certain threshold. And that's exactly what happened.

On September 16, 1992, the pound sharply dropped and Britain, in turn, withdrew from the ERM. Soros and the Quantum Fund had sunk $10 billion into the bet, and came up a billion dollars richer—while ordinary Britons lost substantial amounts of value in their paychecks and mortgages due to the pound's plunge.[8] Much like Morton had salaciously written of the Rothschilds' "score" from Waterloo as a defeat for everyone else, media profiles of Soros touting his profit off what became known as "Black Wednesday" put this once fairly unknown figure right into the faces of people around the world. And many saw a smiling Jew gladly profiting off what they saw as the misery of others, and teed up the usual scapegoating allegations.

It wasn't true, of course, and even Soros acknowledged that while Britain had lost and he'd gained, it wasn't a catastrophe. Soros was far from the only trader to short the pound, the crash would have happened even if Soros hadn't made his bet, and, ultimately, the event was seen as a seminal step toward Britain's recovery from its yearslong recession.[9]

But for Soros, the media scrutiny and profiles after Black Wednesday— some fawning, others scabrous—would be a preview of the conspiracy theory industry that would evolve around him, his philanthropy, and his very existence.

EMERGENCE

Like the Rothschilds even now, Soros once shunned interviews or press coverage. Despite his growing profile as a financial savant capable of gambling vast sums of money on a hunch, he was rarely written about beyond a few mid-'70s articles about the success of his hedge fund.[10] The typical Soros profile of the period, such as one from *Time* magazine in May 1987, extolled his "uncanny knack for switching successfully between stock, bond and money markets" with the seeds of the Quantum Fund provided by "members of the Rothschild family and other rich Europeans."[11] That article, incidentally, pointed out that Soros "argues that financial disaster of some kind is quite likely in the future"—and the Dow plummeted by more than 22 percent on a Monday just five months later.

Soros didn't profit off "Black Monday" in 1987. But he did off Black Wednesday in 1992. And afterward, it became impossible for him to ignore the throngs of reporters camped out around his London home. So he started giving interviews and talking more about both his background and his methodology. The *Financial Times* ran a front-page interview with the hyperbolic title "The Man Who Broke the Bank of England" and extolled the risky bet Soros had made on the pound's failure. The nickname stuck, and most of the profiles around that time focused on the gambles he took through the Quantum Fund rather than his prolific philanthropy toward anti-authoritarian causes—in 1982 Soros had started his first foundation, called the Open Society Fund (later called the Open Society Foundations) after a book written by his mentor, the philosopher Karl Popper.[12]

Soros was an emerging example of Jewish wealth in the '90s, but in the firmament of "globalist controllers," he was still far below the Rothschilds and other stalwarts like the Rockefellers, Council on Foreign Relations Bilderberg Group, and, of course, the Clintons. But that would finally start to change for good in December 1998, with an interview on the US magazine show *60 Minutes* that delved deeply into his past, and contorted events of his childhood into a story that didn't reflect what actually happened.

The stories Soros has told about living under Nazi rule tend to contradict each other and are often taken out of context—and none more so than here. In a bizarre sequence that would be used against Soros for the next two decades, journalist Steve Kroft asked Soros if he felt survivor's guilt over making it through the Holocaust—survival aided in part by posing as the godson of a Christian Hungarian civil servant. "[A]s hundreds of thousands of Jews were being shipped off to the Nazi death camps," Kroft intoned, "a thirteen-year-old George Soros accompanied his phony godfather on his rounds, confiscating property from the Jews."[13]

This was clearly a misinterpretation of what happened when Soros was in hiding, compounded by Kroft then telling Soros, "My understanding is that you went out with this protector of yours [. . .] and helped in the confiscation of property from the Jews." But Soros, who seemed befuddled at being asked about the "complicity" of a Jewish child in the Nazi horror, was only able to say that he had no role in taking anything away from anyone and had "no sense of guilt" over something he didn't do. Combined with other comments from Soros that hiding with his father was "the happiest" time of his life—because he got to see his father, who he deeply admired, acting bravely in the face of overwhelming danger—the impression that many of Soros's opponents got was of a collaborator who felt no guilt over participating in the slaughter of his coreligionists to enrich himself.[14] It was essentially the same "fake Jew" accusation as the ones leveled at the Rothschilds time and time again. But this time, it seemed to be confirmed by the man himself—even if those statements had to be twisted free from their context to make sense.

Despite the reputation he'd later get among American conservatives as a malevolent puppet master, Soros was once routinely praised by anti-communist Republicans, and was an admirer of Ronald Reagan.[15] After all, he'd fled both fascism and communism, making his own fortune and lifting himself up by his proverbial bootstraps. But after the fall of the Soviet Union, Soros directed his philanthropy toward opening up once-authoritarian cultures to liberal ideas of freedom and democracy—and it would make him enemies on both the American and European right.

He funded dissidents, liberals, scientists, students, and the free press in Russia, Hungary, Poland, what was then Czechoslovakia, and others.

And he was regularly attacked by right-wing Eastern European leaders and thinkers trying to impose their own versions of control on the chaotic region. Increasingly, he was seen as the primary funding source for coups, uprisings, revolutions, and economic crashes. These attacks predictably devolved into swipes at his Judaism, even though he wasn't particularly outspoken or observant.

There was a time when the Rothschilds would likely have been singled out for these types of bizarre accusations, as their name is often synonymous with Jewish wealth in Eastern Europe. But far-right leaders and the oligarchs they enriched instead found it easier and more impactful to attack Soros, whose Open Society Foundations made him "a puppet of Jerusalem," as one Hungarian far-right pundit put it in 1992.[16]

As if to prove how interchangeable Soros and Rothschild conspiracy theories would become, while Song Hongbing became a celebrity in China by blaming the Rothschilds for the 1997 Asian crash, Malaysian prime minister Mahathir bin Mohamad wasted little time blaming the contagion on Soros instead.

Referencing rumors that Soros had caused the crash by massively shorting Thai currency, Mahathir told an organization of Muslim leaders that "we may suspect that [Jews] have an agenda, but we do not want to accuse them," before promptly accusing them of "ruling this world by proxy. They get others to fight and die for them" and later calling Soros a "moron."[17] Soros responded with public jabs of his own, and the feud went on for several years. It was one of a number of public spats Soros would have with far-right leaders around the world—including one who'd previously been the recipient of funds from the Open Society Foundations.

By the late 1990s, Soros was giving substantial sums to progressive organizations and causes in the US, with an emphasis on marijuana legalization, voting rights, economic opportunities for marginalized communities, and criminal justice reform. Even then, Soros was still far from Public Enemy #1 for conspiracy theorists, and still continued to identify as a Republican. That changed for good in 2004, when Soros started throwing his financial weight around in American politics by donating over $27 million to the failed Democratic effort against George W. Bush, who he excoriated for rushing into war with Iraq.[18]

But while that was the moment when mainstream conservative media and politicians zeroed in on Soros, the onslaught of myths had been going on for years in fringe publications and conspiracy sites. And it began with the writings of a group that had once been renowned for its conspiracy theories about the Rothschilds, making a seamless transition from one all-powerful Jewish scapegoat to another.

If someone has to be blamed for the genesis of the Soros conspiracy, blame it on Lyndon LaRouche.

THE CLUB OF THE ISLES

The myths about George Soros would eventually become inseparable from reality, but for his first few decades in the public eye, most of this was confined to things he'd actually done. It wasn't until a November 1996 article in the LaRouche publication *Executive Intelligence Review* that the far-right made the jump to pure conspiracy mongering.

An infamous agitator and conspiracy theorist, LaRouche spent nearly half a century as a perennial political candidate, running on a third-party slate in every US presidential election from 1976 to 2004. A prolific publisher and activist with a knack for getting attention, he started his career as a voice for labor and the far left before flipping to the far right in the 1970s, creating a mass movement that was considered a neofascist cult and reviled on both sides of the aisle.[19] The "LaRouche Movement" was a gumbo of advocacy for utopian science and engineering, opposition to the modern monetary system, and hardcore conspiracy theories. But like almost all conspiracy theories, it eventually boiled down to a European cabal running things. In LaRouche's case, it was the Soviet Union, the British Royal Family, the Illuminati, various opium lords, and other Jewish elites who were all conspiring to enslave humanity through drugs and debt. Naturally, the movement accused the Rothschilds of all manner of ritual, conspiracy, collusion, and horrific crime in countless books and articles like *The*

Rothschild Roots of the KKK and *The Rothschilds: From Pitt to Rockefeller.*

Executive Intelligence Review (*EIR*), founded by LaRouche in 1974 and continuing after his 2019 death, is a grab bag of conspiracy theories and accusations about various enemies of the LaRouche movement, Jews in particular. The 1996 "EIR Investigation," written by economic researcher and "peak oil" conspiracy theorist F. William Engdahl, is called "The Secret Financial Network Behind 'Wizard' George Soros," and it shouldn't be a surprise who the leaders of that "secret network" were. All of the now-expected tropes are here, including the baseless accusations that they aren't "real Jews," the mangling of historical fact, and the charter membership in a secret society that isn't real.

Echoing shadowy, nonexistent cabals like Cecil Rhodes's "Society of the Elect" or the "Hidden Hand," Engdahl accused Soros of being a puppet of another such group called the "Club of the Isles," which he claims was "built upon the wreckage of the British Empire after World War II." Relegating Soros to the status of being a mere twentieth century court Jew, Engdahl goes on to create a spurious link between him and the Rothschilds, calling them "the most important of such 'Jews who are not Jews,'" and falsely accusing them of having "launched Soros's career."

"They are members of the Club of the Isles and retainers of the British royal family," Engdahl continues, providing no evidence for his claims about the family. "This has been true since Amschel Rothschild [sic] sold the British Hessian troops to fight against George Washington during the American Revolution."[20]

It should be noted that there's scant evidence that the "Club of the Isles" exists, and the only mentions one can find in print or online of it are in other conspiracy theorist works, particularly other LaRouche publications. But as always, those details don't matter. There is one detail that's different, though: Engdahl's attacks aren't *on* the Rothschilds, but on one of their supposed protégés. Engdahl accuses Soros of seeding his Quantum Fund with Rothschild associates and claiming he "owes" his success to their stewardship, particularly his role at Arnhold and S. Bleichroeder in the late 1960s. While the obsessively private Rothschilds might use "golems" like

Soros as their public proxies, Soros had also created his own brand of financial manipulation and "ruling of nations," according to Engdahl.[21]

Essentially, he was once just a pupil learning the art of global control—but now he was on his way to becoming the master. The article quickly spread on the nascent conspiracy internet, with one portentous alt.conspiracy post from 1997 even claiming that "N.M. Rothschild of London [. . .] has been linked to the more unsavory elements of international organized crime."[22]

The *EIR* article about Soros might have been the first, but it would quickly have company. Because while the internet was a boon to Rothschild theories, it was pure rocket fuel for the same theories about Soros.

INTERNET DRUG GROUPS

While LaRouche publications continued attacking Soros, it was hard for more mainstream conservatives to get past the stink of crankery in *Executive Intelligence Review* articles like the one accusing Soros of being a "drug pusher" for Queen Elizabeth II and a cog in the Nazi persecution machine.[23] Other attacks on Soros came in similar conspiracy publications, such as the reliably antisemitic rag *Instauration*, which freely lumped Soros, the Rothschilds, and the Rockefellers among other "international financier[s] and meddler[s]" throwing their backing behind "One World causes for the Great Unwashed."[24]

The real "passing of the torch" from the fringe to the mainstream came in 2004, as Soros began to get involved in US presidential politics. A naturalized American citizen, Soros was still a Republican, even if his philanthropy was directed at traditionally leftist causes. But he saw US involvement in Iraq as indicative of both a party and a country heading off the rails, passing laws, including the USA Patriot Act, that unacceptably abrogated the openness Soros held so dearly. "I decided the most important thing I could do to foster global open societies was to get Bush out of the White House," Soros told Jane Mayer of *The New Yorker* a few weeks before the election.[25] So Soros gave generously to liberal groups, taking advantage of new laws that allowed endless amounts of money to pour into "PACs" or political action committees. Fully united behind George W. Bush and still drunk on post-9/11 "with us or with the terrorists" patriotism, the far-right media machine pounced.

Mainstream attacks on Soros started with articles on the far-right site Newsmax, funded and produced by many of the same people who had created the Clinton conspiracy industrial complex a decade earlier. They were full of accusations that Soros had spent the last three decades "recruiting, training, indoctrinating, and installing a network of loyal operatives in fifty countries" dedicated to regime change in the US, and that Soros was "a lone wolf, answering to no particular master and loyal to no one"—a clear, purposeful echo of the "rootless cosmopolitan" slur thrown at Jewish business leaders in century after century.[26]

From there, the hysteria made its way up the ladder to Fox News stalwart Bill O'Reilly, who relentlessly attacked Soros and his political activism, comparing him to both Fidel Castro and Don Corleone and calling him "the most powerful Democrat in America." Other prominent Republicans subsequently went on Fox News before the election to call him a "robber baron" who "hates America," a "sleazoid" who wanted to purchase John Kerry's victory, and a Nazi collaborator who was somehow personally responsible for the mass murder of Jews—with some even accusing Soros of being *in* the SS, thanks to a popular fake picture. The attacks ramped up to the point where Soros had to hire substantial armed security.[27]

And it wasn't just pundits and cranks, but actual members of Congress who apparently felt it was in their constituents' best interests to attack a Hungarian hedge fund investor. Republican Speaker of the House Dennis Hastert made attacking Soros all but a second job, routinely going on Fox News to echo incoherent LaRouche conspiracy theories about Soros being funded by unspecified "drug groups" through small payments on the internet.

"George Soros has been for legalizing drugs in this country. So, I mean, he's got a lot of ancillary interests out there," Hastert bellowed to a befuddled Chris Wallace. "The fact is, we don't know where this money comes from. Before transparency—and what we're talking about in transparency in election reform is you know where the money comes from. You get a $25 check or a $2,500 check or $25,000 check, put it up on the internet. You know where it comes from, and there it is."[28]

As the election neared, Speaker Hastert continued attacking Soros for "nobody knowing where his money came from," while simultaneously attacking Soros for getting vast amounts of his money from drug cartels. Ultimately, none of these accusations were substantiated, which can't be said for Hastert, who went to prison for over a year after pleading guilty to illegally structuring cash withdrawals to pay off boys he'd molested as a teacher before entering politics.[29]

However much Soros gave to the Kerry campaign, or was rumored to have given, it wasn't enough, as Kerry lost the 2004 election to Bush. But the itch to blame Soros for all of the evils of the world wouldn't be scratched, particularly as the supposed far-left socialist Kenyan Muslim usurper Barack Obama brought his "orders from the Rothschilds" to the White House four years later.

The conspiracy theory industry around Obama was a perfect fit with the conspiracy theory industry around Soros. And together, they took Tea Party paranoia and antisemitism to new heights, fueled by pundits and influencers who truly thought they'd found the head of the snake that was Western leftism and deputized themselves to chop it off.

THE PUPPET MASTER

Like the Rothschilds before him, Soros became almost comically easy to blame for whatever conspiracy theorists believed had gone wrong—whether it was world events, like the various anti-authoritarian "Color Revolutions" Soros was accused of funding in Europe, or self-inflicted personal problems, like former House Majority Leader Tom DeLay's indictment for campaign finance violations in 2005, which he blamed on Soros funding (DeLay was convicted, though the verdict was overturned on appeal).[30]

Like Mayer Amschel's supposed quote about "controlling the world's money supply," Soros hysteria even found its way into the Congressional record. In just one example from 2006, Indiana Republican Mark Souder used his platform not to improve the lives of the people who voted for him, but to rail against what he called "The Guilt-Free Record of George Soros," taking clips from the infamous *60 Minutes* interview out of context and merging them with accusations that Soros was funding prostitution, had compared George W. Bush to Hitler, and had even "funded a pro-marijuana children's book."[31]

All of it would be deeply familiar to anyone versed in the slew of accusations against the Rothschilds. But with the Rothschilds, the most prevalent conspiracy theories took decades to percolate—it was thirty years after Waterloo that the "Nathan made millions by lying about the outcome" trope first appeared in the scabrous pamphlet by "Satan." In the case of Soros, new accusations and attacks appeared on a daily basis, spread quickly on social media and on far-right blogs, and were given outsized airtime by the most popular cable news outlet in the United States.

It can't be overstated how much Fox News relied on Soros conspiracy theories during its rise to national prominence. O'Reilly would routinely monologue about the horrors of the one world government Soros sought to force upon America. On almost daily segments and then later a two-night special event in 2010, Glenn Beck used blackboards and charts to track the conspirators and plots revolving around "puppet master" Soros—sometimes even using actual puppets. Even after Beck and O'Reilly were taken off the network, Tucker Carlson and Lou Dobbs continued attacking Soros as funding all manner of anti-democratic plots and schemes.[32] Other major conservative figures like Rush Limbaugh, Andrew Breitbart, Sean Hannity, Mark Levin, and countless others relentlessly accused Soros of pulling strings, controlling governments, and funding godlessness. And for as often as Alex Jones attacked the Rothschilds, he did it even more with Soros starting in 2009, casually linking him to everything from the COVID-19 outbreak to his own personal legal problems.

As Obama's presidency gave way to the tumultuous 2016 election, Soros helped fund Democratic candidate Hillary Clinton to the tune of more than $9 million. But while other billionaires, including one of the cofounders of Facebook, gave much more than Soros, it was Soros who was primarily singled out for conspiracy theories about his secret "shadow network" of "'60s radicals" looking to take over the government. When trolls and hackers linked to Russian intelligence needed the name of a wealthy progressive to link to "corrupt" Hillary Clinton, they used Soros—creating a slew of fake social media profiles to spread rumors about him and dumping hacked emails from Soros and the Open Society Foundations on Russian-created blogs like DCLeaks.[33]

After Trump's victory, Soros was accused of paying for virtually every dirty deed under the sun, some of which were warped versions of causes he actually had funded, and others that were simply fake. Soros was falsely linked to the supposed funding of the George Floyd protests in 2020 and accused of paying for women to accuse Trump of sexual misconduct, of paying NFL quarterback Colin Kaepernick to kneel during the National Anthem in 2018, of funding both the protests and counterprotests around the "Unite the Right" rally in Charlottesville in 2017, and of paying Hillary Clinton to wear purple during her 2016 Democratic National Convention speech as a sign of support for "Purple Revolutions"—which were also supposedly funded by Soros.[34]

Any act of rebellion or anti-Trump protest anywhere could be blamed on unspecific but omnipresent "Soros funding," from the Black Lives Matter movement to the nebulous groups of activists lumped by conservatives under the label "antifa." In almost every case, the "paid protestors" weren't being paid by Soros (or anyone else), but some were found to be employees of groups or foundations that had, at one point or another, taken donations linked to Soros or the Open Society Foundations. Some of these donations were in the thousands of dollars, and had been given years or even decades before the "paid protesting" took place. It was a paper-thin connection, but it was enough for anti-Soros pundits and content creators to dine on.[35]

Much of this supposed "paid protesting" coincided with the world's plunge into lockdown. When COVID-19 hit, conspiracy theorists suddenly had nothing but time on their hands and imaginary demons to fight. And while some blamed the Rothschilds, more of them wasted no time blaming Soros and his various allies for creating and spreading the pandemic. First on Facebook groups, then at in-person anti-lockdown rallies, Soros was accused of funding the disease, personally contracting Dr. Anthony Fauci to coordinate its spread, and paying to use the vaccine as a vector for either global genocide or implanting tracking microchips in people. The methods were different, but the goals were the same: one world government, total control of behavior, massive wealth confiscation, and a society where patriots are mere slaves to the whims of the insiders.[36]

During four consecutive US elections, a growing number of Trump supporters accused Soros of owning the companies that built voting machines, controlling the methodology of vote counting, or of simply paying vast sums to criminal "mules" to dump fake ballots into drop boxes. The majority of these theories were either based on the actual owners of these companies having once been connected to the Open Society Foundations in some negligible way or just made up.[37] Even Trump targeted Soros directly, claiming on Twitter that protestors against the Supreme Court nomination of Brett Kavanaugh were "paid for by Soros and others" while sharing other tweets accusing Soros of sending "billions" to the Biden campaign.[38]

Soros also continued to be a target for right-wing leaders around the world. Hungarian prime minister Victor Orbán had once gratefully accepted money from the Open Society Foundations as a student, but after taking office he made Soros a target of relentless antisemitic conspiracy theories, "anti-Soros" laws, inflammatory billboards, and accusations about putting Europe under his control through mass migration. Soros, for his part, fought back by claiming Orbán was turning his homeland into a "mafia state" and running "an elaborate kleptocratic system to rob the country blind."[39] Some of the attacks against him even came from other Jews—such as the two Jewish American political consultants who essentially created the anti-Soros conspiracy industry in Eastern Europe while helping facilitate Orbán's rise to power.[40]

And Soros was a central figure in the QAnon conspiracy theory, which mixed classic antisemitic canards with its riddles and predictions. The mysterious Q claimed Soros ran massive slush funds for the Democrats, funded "domestic terrorism" through antifa and intentionally set forest fires, was "targeted" for arrest alongside the Clintons and others, bought the video game company Blizzard to use it as a front to exchange secret messages, took "orders" from a mysterious entity known as "P," and was the perpetrator in countless other bizarre accusations. Believers rarely, if ever, asked for evidence of these claims—all that was needed was for one to become "awake" and see what was "really happening."

Liberals often mocked the far-right's tendency to blame Soros for literally anything, while Soros himself either ignored them or pushed back forcefully. But the sheer tonnage of Soros conspiracy theories mixed with the general ramping up of extremism and antisemitism in the West during the time of Trump and Brexit would have serious consequences. They inspired acts of violence and murder, carried out by deranged conspiracy believers utterly convinced that a Hungarian nonagenarian and his antifa horde were to blame for all of the woes of the world—and that something had to be done about it.

"THE DESTRUCTION OF OUR WHITE CULTURE"

It's difficult to link recent individual acts of violence to specific myths about the Rothschilds. Essentially, historical Rothschild myths are so integral to the fabric of modern conspiracy theories that they can start to feel like background noise, indistinguishable from simply blaming "Jewish money" or "European bankers" or "the Illuminati."

But Soros has specifically been invoked by name in a slew of crimes, killings, and acts of terrorism directed toward both the Jewish community and prominent left-leaning people in general. The Rothschilds may have been the physical target of a few cranks and brick-throwing revolutionaries in their day, but Soros has repeatedly had people try to kill him because they think he rules the world. And if they couldn't get to him, any other Jew would suffice.

The last week of October 2018 saw a wave of antisemitic rhetoric and violence that wouldn't have been out of place at a pogrom or Nuremberg rally. Much of it was driven by the impending midterm election, as conspiracy theories about what various Jewish controllers—mainly Soros—were doing to ensure Democrats would win dominated right-wing media. And it was long past the domain of fringe figures. Donald Trump Jr. tweeted that Soros was a Nazi, former New York City mayor turned Trump lawyer Rudy Giuliani claimed on social media that Soros was the "Antichrist" and should have his assets seized by the government, and so on.[41]

In particular, conservative hysteria focused on what they saw as a massive horde of migrants approaching the US–Mexico border. Mainstream and fringe outlets ran an endless loop of fearmongering and cleverly edited B-roll showing menacing-looking Latinos piling into vans and slowly making their way to Texas, seemingly intent on doing who-knows-what to American women and jobs. And it was all funded by giant wads of cash handed out in the open by Soros flunkies. The message was clear: Soros was paying for these invaders, and if Democrats took over the government, they would be the beachhead in nothing less than a full-scale invasion meant to destroy America for good.

In reality, the caravan was much smaller than most estimates claimed, and was made up mostly of women and children fleeing violence and crushing poverty. At the time, it was nowhere near the US–Mexico border, and would arrive well after the election. Many caravan travelers weren't even intending to enter the US, instead hoping to gain political asylum in Mexico.[42]

But there was a midterm to win, and fear to be mongered. As the leader of the Republican Party, President Trump tweeted relentlessly about the caravan and told reporters at the end of October that he "wouldn't be surprised" if Soros was funding the migrant groups, because "a lot of people" said he was.[43]

And in that sense, Trump was right. A lot of people were saying it. Multiple Congressional Republicans, a slew of Fox News personalities, and professional conspiracy theorists all claimed without evidence that Soros was definitely funding the caravan, it was definitely being coordinated with the Democrats, and it was definitely a clear and present danger to white Americans. Fox News host Lou Dobbs in particular helped connect Soros to a worldwide Jewish conspiracy, with a guest on his show claiming that "a lot of these folks have affiliates that are getting money from the Soros-occupied State Department"—a clear reference to the "Zionist Occupation Government" trope of Jews controlling US politics that's a staple of white nationalist and antisemitic content.[44]

Not only were a lot of people saying it, a lot of people were listening. On October 23, deep in the middle of caravan hysteria, a caretaker at Soros's house in the affluent New York City suburb of Bedford found a pipe bomb in the mailbox. Half a foot long and full of explosive powder, the device was in an envelope dressed up to make it look like an ordinary package (with "Florida" misspelled on the return address), and was later detonated by the bomb squad. Soros wasn't at the house, but the device easily could have maimed whoever found it—and it was just one of a wave of pipe bombs sent to other frequent conspiracy theorist targets like Barack Obama, Joe Biden, Hillary Clinton, and the offices of CNN.[45]

Without a suspect, it was a tricky line for conspiracy theorists to walk, since they'd spoken freely of their desire for terrible things to happen to Soros and cultivated the deranged hoaxes that led to the attempted bombing but also didn't want to seem happy that someone was committing mass terrorism. Some Soros haters—Rush Limbaugh, Lou Dobbs, various neo-Nazis—simply wrote it off as a false flag perpetrated to make Trump supporters look bad.[46] Others took a darker tone—on the day after the bomb was found in Soros's mailbox, Alex Jones went on a bizarre rant about how maybe some of these people deserved what was happening, and screamed "I am death" over and over about "bullying evil jerks" like "George Soros and Hillary Clinton and Lord Rothschild."[47]

Ultimately, Florida resident Cesar Sayoc, who lived in a van covered in anti-Democratic, pro-Trump stickers and memes, was arrested for the bombings. Sayoc seemed to have an especially sharp axe to grind against Soros, to the point where the day the bomb was discovered in Bedford, Sayoc posted a meme on Facebook claiming, "the world is waking up to the horrors of George Soros." He routinely told acquaintances that Soros was "buying the whole Democratic Party" and to blame for whatever was wrong in the United States at the moment.[48]

Sayoc, who blamed his attacks on steroid addiction and mental illness, pleaded guilty to domestic terrorism and was sentenced to twenty years in prison. And none of the crude explosive devices he sent actually went off. But the victims of another Soros-obsessed terrorist weren't so lucky.

"HIAS likes to bring invaders in that kill our people," wrote 46-year-old Robert Bowers on the far-right message board Gab, referencing a Jewish American nonprofit focused on humanitarian issues and often attacked by antisemitic conspiracy theorists as a Soros front. He added, "I can't stand by and watch my people get slaughtered. Screw your optics. I'm going in."[49]

And then he went in.

Bowers entered the Tree of Life Synagogue in Pittsburgh, allegedly screamed "All Jews must die," and opened fire with an AR-15. He killed eleven worshipers and wounded six others before being shot by police and arrested. The shooter's social media footprint was full of references to both Soros by name and conspiracy theories linked to Soros, including that he was funding the same Honduran migrant caravan that Trump and Fox News had been obsessing about. Trump, for his part, offered his condolences, then went right back to spreading conspiracy theories about Soros—his statement that he "wouldn't be surprised" if Soros was paying for the migrant caravan took place days *after* Bowers used the same conspiracy theory as fodder for his murderous delusions.[50]

Soros and his evil empire were constantly evoked at Trump rallies, MAGA gatherings, anti-vaccine protests, QAnon and Christian nationalist conventions, and even in the rhetoric around the January 6 insurrection, where nebulous "Soros-funded antifa" members were blamed for supposedly fake violent acts meant to make the "peaceful protestors" who had violently breached the Capitol look bad.

Even with the constant invoking of antisemitic tropes, most of the people going to these events and spreading these theories had no intention of committing a violent act—and certainly not mass murder. But the nature of trolling and online hate is that it's virtually impossible to separate out the majority of people who are just talking about taking up arms from the small number that will actually take up arms.

One of the latter was Payton Gendron, who shot and killed ten people at a supermarket in a majority-Black neighborhood in Buffalo, New York. Gendron's manifesto justifying the murders, something of a standard issue rant posted by spree-killers in the digital age, swiped huge blocks of text from another manifesto, that of Christchurch, New Zealand, mass killer Brenton Tarrant. But while both documents were rambling diatribes full of cut-and-pasted trolling and self-serving paeans to misguided notions of whites "being replaced" by minorities, Gendron's included a long original section of antisemitic rhetoric. He specifically singled out Soros, who not only was "attacking the west," but was explicitly the enemy of the common man through "shorting currencies" and funding "the destruction of our white culture."[31]

The sheer hatred and conspiratorial nature of the document was shocking to the mainstream media outlets, who breathlessly reported on the shootings and manifestos, often unwittingly spreading their toxic ideas without context or redaction. It should not have been even slightly surprising.

THE NEW OLD EXTREMISTS

None of these shooters or terrorists specifically mentioned the Rothschilds. But they didn't have to. If George Soros is the Rothschild family of the twenty-first century, and the Rothschilds "gave Soros his start," then invoking him is invoking them. And, in turn, invoking two hundred years of hate, conspiracy theories, unhinged plots, and paranoia—dark forces that sometimes lead to repression, and occasionally to genocide.

Rothschild conspiracy theories have proven to be remarkably durable. They build on each other, with each new one based on the old ones, perpetuating and spreading the myths with new details. It hasn't always been as bad as it was in the immediate post-Trump era, but it's never entirely gone.

Antisemitism cycles up when there aren't other enemies or outgroups for cranks and the disaffected to focus on. And new generations of extremists now emerge constantly, pumping out hateful hoaxes and propaganda that constantly work their way upward from the dank pits of the internet to the biggest social media companies and media giants on the planet.

These professional conspiracy mongers spread their message with a speed and ease that Dairnvaell or Drumont or Pound couldn't comprehend when they got started smearing the "insiders" of "the Hidden Hand." Some are clean-cut young fascists in suits doing podcasts, others are celebrities too divorced from reality to know antisemitism is wrong, and some are the same cadre of discontented and forgotten "common folk." And now they all have platforms. They've always been among us, but now they're *among us*. They say what they want in the guise of "free speech" and are platformed by outlets hungry for clout. Some are miserable and alone, screaming to nobody. Others make money hand over fist. And the tools that social media companies and regulators have to stop them are woefully inadequate.

Together, the new extremists are espousing the same hateful tropes that were once relegated to being fodder for fringe pamphlets and whispered accusations. But now they aren't fringe, and they aren't whispering. Fueled by the same ancient conspiracy theories and hate, the new extremists make no pretense of leveling their accusations only against "those Jews"—meaning the Rothschilds, and later Soros—but against all Jews everywhere.

They are a danger to everyone. And they'll never stop—because they never have.

THE ROTHSCHILDS OF NORDSTETTEN

Marx Rothschild wasn't born with that famous last name. For one, it wasn't famous when he came into the world sometime in 1735. He likely had no last name at all, as Jews in the southwest of what's now Germany weren't allowed to take them, usually going by a combination of their Hebrew name and their father's first name.

At some point, Marx settled in the tiny hamlet of Nordstetten, a satellite community of the small town Horb am Neckar nestled into the northern edge of the Black Forest. He and his wife had one known child there, Emanuel Marx, born in 1755. Emanuel Rothschild, as he was called after a while, was a successful merchant who build his own house in Nordstetten in 1808. He and his wife Judith had seven children, including six sons. Two of those sons—Samuel Emanuel Rothschild and Moses Emanuel Rothschild—set out for the promised land of America. Samuel emigrated to New York City, while Moses Emanuel and his children settled in Davenport, Iowa, on the west bank of the Mississippi River across from

Moline, Illinois. Their children would eventually spread out to the rest of the Midwest, including Kansas City and Chicago.[1]

The Nordstetten Rothschilds prospered, like so many German Jews forced out of their homeland by antisemitism and poverty. They founded stores and banks, they built residential and commercial buildings that still stand in Chicago and Kansas City. They became doctors and lawyers, authors and artists, merchants and financiers, professors and judges, religious and community leaders. Melville Nelson Rothschild, the grandson of Moses Emanuel and a prosperous businessman in Chicago, even had a motto that he passed down to his children: "the Rothschilds have always worked and the Rothschilds will always work."[2] And they are the reason I exist—Moses Emanuel's son Isaac's grandson Arthur was my grandfather. He was no "financial ruler of nations," but a good man who served his country and his community.

So despite their vast differences in wealth, power, fame, and status, the Rothschilds of Nordstetten and the Rothschilds of Frankfurt were not all that different from each other. My family line certainly didn't smuggle gold across the English Channel to fund Wellington, help England purchase a stake in the Suez Canal, or establish the railways of Europe. Their stories weren't told in musicals or Hollywood films. But they made their mark and found success and community wherever they went, like so many other Jews of the Diaspora. And other Rothschilds, from other villages in Germany and other nations, also carry the name without having any known relation to the children of Mayer Amschel.

One famous example is the author and satirist Dorothy Parker, born Dorothy Rothschild and the granddaughter of Prussian Jews from Bavaria. And in one particularly odd irony, Parker's uncle Martin Rothschild was one of the many souls who went down on the *Titanic*, a disaster that various conspiracy theories have pinned on the Rothschilds of Frankfurt as part of their evil plot to found the Federal Reserve and take control of the US money supply.[3]

Still, the question of *those* Rothschilds nagged at various Nordstetten Rothschild descendants enough to fund a book of family genealogy, which was partially inspired by the desire to see if there was a connection to the famous family. There was no evidence the two families were related, nor any particular reason to think they would be. But the book tracing the line of Nordstetten Rothschilds freely acknowledges the idea of a connection—and the power of the Rothschild myth.

"The name Rothschild has an exciting and magical sound to it," the family history writes. "Because of its association with the famed European banking family which originated in Frankfurt, the name is synonymous with wealth, glamor, success, philanthropy, and dedication to the Jewish people." And while they aren't connected, the Nordstetten Rothschilds "exhibit some of the same characteristics of the more famous Rothschilds."[4]

From the wealthy Rothschilds of Frankfurt to the fake Anna de Rothschild of Mar-a-Lago to the countless other unrelated Rothschilds who share only a last name, *the name Rothschild* indeed carries enormous weight. It could, in the past, almost literally move mountains and shift the destinies of nations. Even now, it opens doors for people who only pretend to carry it. It embodies wealth and success, yes. But also hoaxes and hate, conspiracy theories and deranged notions of power and control spawned by two centuries of such allegations making their creators wealthy and famous. Even beyond the conspiracy theories and accusations, there are the simple suggestions—how many other family names spark innocuous questions of "Are you related to *those* Rothschilds?"—and assumptions that the holder of the name is wealthy.

And that power will persist, driven far more by myth, legend, distorted history, and wishful thinking than anything resembling modern reality. Rothschild assets have splintered and diluted, or have been sold off or subsumed by other companies. The investment bank and financial services firm now known as Rothschild & Co., created by the merger of the British and French branches in 2003, has nowhere near the assets of any of the top hundred financial institutions in the world. It does not control the world's central banks or trillions of dollars or an arsenal of orbital death rays. The only Rothschild on the 2022 *Forbes* list of billionaires, encompassing more than 2,500 of the richest humans on earth, is Facebook founding engineer

Jeff Rothschild—who isn't related to the Frankfurt Rothschilds.[5] And the family is nowhere near "above the law," as so many cranks allege—family-connected banks have recently both been fined by the IRS for helping clients evade tax laws[6] and sanctioned for not doing due diligence in the 1MDB-money laundering scandal.[7]

While the myth will endure, its focal point will change, by necessity. Conspiracy theories excel at recontextualizing themselves and keeping their believers hooked on the main thrust of a story even when the details change extensively. "Rothschild of the twenty-first century" George Soros is in his early nineties. Even with all his billions, he will not live forever. Once he's gone, another wealthy Jew will have to become the principal target of the conspiracy theories and hoaxes that both Soros and the Rothschilds before him were attacked with.

A few Rothschilds could potentially take over for Soros, though Evelyn de Rothschild died in 2022 and Lord Jacob Rothschild, the current chief punching bag of the family, is in his late eighties. And few of the younger crop of Rothschilds have the public profile or financial background to quite work as a conspiracy figurehead. Many don't even work in finance.

Two of Soros's financier sons, Alexander and Jonathan, might draw the ire of the far-right conspiracy machine for their political activism and advocacy for progressive causes. Alexander Soros in particular is already a frequent target of online conspiracy theorists for his ties to Barack Obama, Emmanuel Macron, and other "globalist" figures; he is also the heir apparent to take over the Open Society Foundations.[8] It would at least save the conspiracy theorists time by letting them use the same memes. Or it might be some other wealthy, progressive Jewish figure who becomes Public Enemy #1 for the crank set. Maybe they won't be involved in banking or finance. They don't even need to actually be Jewish—it's not like facts matter to the crowd that will crown them as the new "king of Jews."

Klaus Schwab, the German chair of the World Economic Forum since 1971, has become a lightning rod for conspiracy theorists since he wrote the 2020 book *COVID-19: The Great Reset*, and has been accused of planning to shut down the global power grid, force humans to eat bugs and give up their property, and plunge the world into a slave state.[9] But Schwab is nearly as old as Soros, and also Catholic. So the "puppet master" mantle might go straight to Schwab's protégé and advisor, the Israeli writer and historian Yuval Noah Harari. The bestselling *Sapiens* author and Hebrew University of Jerusalem professor has quickly become a top-tier target for conspiracy theorists. In particular, Harari is often linked to Schwab's "great reset" idea, and accused by anti-vaccine and pro-Trump pundits of being the driving force behind an upcoming "mass extinction event" involving biotechnology and the COVID-19 vaccine that will kill billions of people and leave the rest as slaves.[10]

Humans are simply too hard-wired to ever leave behind the demand for someone to blame their problems on. And the need for that target to be Jewish and wealthy is almost hard-wired in modern discourse, as proven by decades of Soros conspiracy theories, which crawled out of the slime of centuries of Rothschild conspiracy theories, begat by millennia of antisemitism and prejudice in Europe.

And it doesn't matter that the seminal texts of antisemitism have been debunked time after time. We know the *Protocols* were a Russian forgery, that there is no all-powerful Illuminati, and that the Rothschilds do not and never have had the wealth and power that their tormentors claim they have. Those who believe they're real want them to be real, and that's enough for them. The antisemitic canard is flexible enough to provide an explanation for almost anything—from bad weather to global fascism. It will always center on an outgroup that has "too much power" and needs to be taken down a peg. It spreads efficiently through the use of new technology, unbothered by facts and unmoored from reality. And it will always be easier to blame rich Jews for the problems of society than it will be to do the hard work of actually fixing them.

But the Rothschilds have also been a beacon to follow in the dark times created by relentless scapegoating and antisemitism. Many Jews, from those emigrating from the real Nordstetten to those fleeing Tevye the Dairyman's fictional Anatevka, have followed that beacon. If they are nothing else, they are a model of aspiration. Beyond all of the outlandish plots and schemes, the accusations and false history, the "space lasers" and secret cabals, the Rothschilds of Frankfurt show what unity, tenacity, courage, and generosity can accomplish—from the squalor of the *Judengasse* to the opulence of their own palaces and the tables of kings and prime ministers in just a few short generations.

It is a remarkable achievement. And no conspiracy theory will ever change that.

ACKNOWLEDGMENTS

My eternal thanks to everyone who provided research material, avenues of investigation, corrections, or primary sources for *Jewish Space Lasers*— Seth Cotlar, Seth Daire, JJ Macnab, Arieh Kovler, Sarah Hightower, Jun Amamiya, and numerous anonymous researchers. The Alex Jones quotes come from the hard work of Dan Friesen and Jordan Holmes of the Knowledge Fight podcast, who listen to more Infowars than any human being should. And thanks to my fellow disinformation researchers and writers for keeping me sane on this very strange journey.

Special thanks to Melanie Aspey at the Rothschild Archive and Professor Rainer Liedtke at the University of Regensburg for early inspiration and answering my very pedantic questions.

Because of the obscurity and unavailability of many of the primary sources, and my desire to not buy the antisemitic material of cranks, this book would not have been possible without the vast digital library of the Internet Archive, archive.org. My special thanks to Jason Scott of textfiles. com, who walked me through ways to find deeply buried newsletters and extremist materials in the Archive. And a brief note on terminology: in keeping with what has become the prevailing spelling of the term among researchers and experts, I refer to anti-Jewish feelings as "antisemitism" without a hyphen. Other variations on the term used in past works have been kept as they were written.

I'm fortunate to now have published two books through Melville House, and have come to rely on their tenacity, passion, and enthusiasm to take chances and move fast. Editing on this project started with Athena Bryan, and was picked up by Carl Bromley. Carl expertly guided me through my many misuses of English versus British, regaled me with knowledge on the Holy Roman Empire and David Ricardo, and never changed anything just for the sake of making changes. I'm grateful to both of you. My thanks to the publicity, social media, and design teams at Melville House as well.

Thanks to my agent, Kristen Moeller at Waterside Productions, who made simple yet epochal suggestions when refining my pitch, like, "Let's make sure we can actually get access to the Rothschilds." And special thanks to my manager and friend Seth Nagel at 5X Media for immediately calling me after the publication of my last book and saying, "Time to come up with another book."

And thanks most of all to my family for their enthusiasm and love, and above all, my wife and our boys. Maybe one day you won't be so bored by your dad rambling on about what he does.

ENDNOTES

INTRODUCTION

1 Michael Sallah, et al, "Inventing Anna: the Tale of a Fake Heiress, Mar-a-Lago, and an FBI Investigation," *Pittsburgh Post-Gazette*, August 26, 2022, https://newsinteractive. post-gazette.com/anna-de-rothschild-trump-mar-a-lago-security-fbi-investigation/.

2 Ibid.

3 Michael Sallah, et al, "Fake 'Rothschild' Was Chased by Russian Organized Crime When She Took Pictures With Trump at Mar-a-Lago," *Organized Crime and Corruption Reporting Project*, December 2, 2022, https://www.occrp.org/en/investigations/ fake-rothschild-was-chased-by-russian-organized-crime-when-she-took-pictures-with-trump-at-mar-a-lago.

4 Sallah, "Inventing Anna."

5 Liam Stack, "Antisemitic Attacks in New York Are at Highest Level in Decades," *The New York Times*, April 26, 2022, https://www.nytimes.com/2022/04/26/nyregion/an-tisemitic-attacks-new-york.html.

6 Adam Enders, et al. "Are Republicans and Conservatives More Likely to Believe Conspiracy Theories?" *Political Behavior* (2022), https://doi.org/10.1007/s11109-022-09812-3

7 Elie Wiesel, "STAGE VIEW; Treasured Family Is the Secret Wealth Of 'The Rothschilds,'" *The New York Times*, September 23, 1990.

CHAPTER I

1 Benjamin Ivry, "The Secret Jewish History of Napoleon Bonaparte," *The Forward*, August 19, 2019, https://forward.com/culture/319002/the-secret-jewish-history-of-napo-leon-bonaparte/.

2 Sara Toth Stub, "Remembering Hadrian, Destroyer of the Jews," *The Tower Magazine*, March 2016, http://www.thetower.org/article/remembering-hadrian-destroy-er-of-the-jews/.

3 Eric Hananoki, "Fox Nation host Lara Logan shares conspiracy theories about 'Putin's purge of the Rothschild money changers,' Jewish people masterminding U.S. Civil War," *Media Matters*, March 22, 2022, https://www.mediamatters.org/lara-logan/fox-nation-host-lara-logan-shares-conspiracy-theories-about-putins-purge-rothschild.

4 Caleb Ecarma, "Lara Logan's Latest Anti-Semitic Comments Are 'More Suited to a White Supremacist Chat Room,'" *Vanity Fair*, March 29, 2022, https://www.vanityfair. com/news/2022/03/lara-logan-anti-semitic-comments.

5 David A. Hollinger, "Rich, Powerful, and Smart: Jewish Overrepresentation Should Be Explained Instead of Avoided or Mystified," *The Jewish Quarterly Review* 94, no. 4

[University of Pennsylvania Press, Center for Advanced Judaic Studies, University of Pennsylvania] (2004): 595–602, http://www.jstor.org/stable/1455593.

6   See Amazon.com, https://www.amazon.com/Investing-Code-Ancient-Jewish-Investor/dp/1535144696. Accessed 7 Apr. 2022.

7   Alux.com, "15 Reasons Why JEWISH People Are RICHER," Video, *YouTube*, https://www.youtube.com/watch?v=GeSrp-7TYGY. Accessed 7 Apr. 2022.

8   Abraham Foxman, *Jews and Money: The Story of a Stereotype* (New York: Palgrave Macmillan, 2010), 59.

9   Aaron Kirschenbaum, "Jewish and Christian Theories of Usury in the Middle Ages," *The Jewish Quarterly Review* 75, no. 3 [University of Pennsylvania Press, Center for Advanced Judaic Studies, University of Pennsylvania] (1985): 270–89, https://doi.org/10.2307/1454076.

10   Marvin Perry and Frederick R. Schweitzer, *Anti-Semitism: Myth and Hate from Antiquity to the Present* (New York: Palgrave Macmillan, 2005) 122–124.

11   "The Chosen Few: A New Explanation of Jewish Success," PBS NewsHour, April 18, 2013, https://www.pbs.org/newshour/economy/the-chosen-few-a-new-explanation-of-jewish-success.

12   Perry and Schweitzer, *Anti-Semitism*, 124.

13   Perry and Schweitzer, *Anti-Semitism*, 126–127.

14   Kirschenbaum, "Jewish and Christian Theories of Usury in the Middle Ages."

15   Adam Smith, *The Wealth of Nations*, Volume 1 (New York: The Modern Library, 1937), 401.

16   Perry and Schweitzer, *Anti-Semitism*, 133.

17   Osama bin Laden, "Letter to America," Reprinted in *The Guardian*, November 20, 2022, https://www.theguardian.com/world/2002/nov/24/theobserver.

18   Perry and Schweitzer, *Anti-Semitism*, 128.

19   Philologos, "Why Judas Still Conjures Up Images of the Jew as Christ-Killer," *The Forward*, June 30, 2013, https://forward.com/culture/179389/why-judas-still-conjures-up-images-of-the-jew-as-c/.

20   Jerusalem Post Staff, "Van Morrison's 'They Own the Media' faced with antisemitism claims," *The Jerusalem Post*, May 20, 2021, https://www.jpost.com/diaspora/antisemitism/van-morrisons-they-own-the-media-faced-with-antisemitism-claims-667607.

21   Van Morrison, "For the avoidance of doubt, the "They" in They Own The Media refers to Boris Johnson's (UK) government," *Twitter*, May 20, 2021, https://twitter.com/vanmorrison/status/1395363232185991172.

22   Giorgio Spagnol, "Banksters and Warmongers," *Institut Européen des Relations Internationales*, June 7, 2019, https://www.ieri.be/en/publications/wp/2019/juillet/banksters-and-warmongers.

23   Menasseh ben Israel, *How Profitable the Nation of the Jews Are*, quoted in *The Jew in the Modern World*, edited by Paul Mendes-Flohr and Jehuda Reinharz (London, Oxford University Press, 1995), 10.

24   Holland Cotter, "From the Court Jews' Uneasy Heyday," *The New York Times*, September 13, 1996, https://www.nytimes.com/1996/09/13/arts/from-the-court-jews-uneasy-heyday.html.

25 Natalie Zemon Davis, "The Life of a Court Jew," *Tablet Magazine*, March 23, 2020, https:// www.tabletmag.com/sections/arts-letters/articles/natalie-zemon-davis-court-jews.

26 Samuel G. Freedman, *Jew vs. Jew: The Struggle for The Soul Of American Jewry* (New York: Simon & Schuster, 2000), 276.

27 Hannah Arendt, *Jewish Social Studies* 14, no. 2 (1952): 176–78, http://www.jstor.org/ stable/4465066. Accessed 6 Apr. 2022.

28 Johnathan Myers, "Aaron of Lincoln shows us the uncertain legacy of success," *The Jewish Chronicle*, March 12, 2021, https://www.thejc.com/news/all/aaron-of-lincoln-shows-us-the-uncertain-legacy-of-success-1.513079.

29 Shlomo Eidelberg, "A Note on Joseph Süss Oppenheimer's Death Sentence," *Jewish Social Studies* 30, no. 4 (1968): 272–74, http://www.jstor.org/stable/4466430. Accessed 7 Apr. 2022.

30 Yair Mintzker, *The Many Deaths of Jew Suss* (Princeton, NJ: Princeton University Press, 2017), 5–8.

31 Lauren Weber, *In Cheap We Trust* (New York: Little Brown, 2009), 45.

32 Weber, *In Cheap We Trust*, 46.

33 Foxman, *Jews and Money*, 139.

34 Ron Kampeas, "2 Kentucky lawmakers apologize for saying 'Jew them down,'" *The Times of Israel*, February 24, 2022, https://www.timesofisrael.com/2-kentucky-lawmakers-apologize-for-saying-jew-them-down/.

35 Jessica Langer, "Ohio State Assistant Professor Uses Anti-Semitic Slur in Class," *The Lantern*, December 22, 2021, https://www.thelantern.com/2021/12/ohio-state-assistant-professor-uses-antisemitic-slur-in-class-incident-under-investigation-by-university/.

36 Dan Amira, "Oklahoma Lawmaker Uses the Term 'Jew Me Down' and Everybody Laughs, Because Oklahoma," *New York Magazine*, April 18, 2013, https://nymag.com/ intelligencer/2013/04/oklahoma-jew-me-down-dennis-johnson-video.html.

37 Angelo Bruscas, "'Jew Down the Price': Grays Harbor Commissioner Apologizes for Comment," *The Daily World*, March 23, 2017, https://www.chronline.com/stories/jew-down-the-price-grays-harbor-commissioner-apologizes-for-comment, 33047.

38 David Wildstein, "Trenton councilwoman calls "Jew down" a verb, says it referred to 'negotiating and not hate,'" *New Jersey Globe*, September 15, 2019, https://newjerseyglobe.com/local/ trenton-councilwoman-calls-jew-down-a-verb-says-it-referred-to-negotiating-and-not-hate/.

39 Foxman, *Jews and Money*, 94.

CHAPTER 2

1 Amos Elon, *Founder: A Portrait of the First Rothschild and His Time* (New York: Viking, 1996) 19–21.

2 Peter H. Wilson, *The Holy Roman Empire: A Thousand Years of Europe's History* (London: Penguin Random House UK, 2016), 102–103.

3 Elon, *Founder*, 27.

4 The Rothschild Archive, "House of the Green Shield, The Judengasse, Frankfurt, Germany," https://family.rothschildarchive.org/estates/68-house-of-the-green-shield.

5 Elon, *Founder*, 43.

6 Elon, *Founder*, 44–45.

7   Derek Wilson, *Rothschild: A Story of Wealth and Power* (London: Andre Deutsch, 1988), 6–7.

8   Niall Ferguson, *The House of Rothschild, Volume 1: Money's Prophets* (New York: Viking, 1998), 71.

9   Ferguson, *The House of Rothschild, Volume 1*, 43.

10 Elon, *Founder*, 71–74.

11 Wilson, *Rothschild*, 20.

12 Wilson, *Rothschild*, 17–19.

13 Elon, *Founder*, 106–107.

14 S. D. Chapman, "The Establishment of the Rothschilds as Bankers," *Jewish Historical Studies* 29 (1982): 177–93, http://www.jstor.org/stable/29779815. Accessed 12 Apr. 2022.

15 Ferguson, *The House of Rothschild, Volume 1*, 67.

16 Elon, *Founder*, 147–153

17 Gavin Daly, "Napoleon and the 'City of Smugglers,' 1810–1814," *The Historical Journal* 50, no. 2 (2007): 333–52. JSTOR, http://www.jstor.org/stable/4140133. Accessed 25 Jul. 2022.

18 Elon, *Founder*, 157.

19 Wilson, *Rothschild*, 45.

20 Niall Ferguson, "Investors Are Often the First Casualties of War, Bloomberg News, February 20, 2022, https://www.bloomberg.com/opinion/articles/2022-02-20/niall-ferguson-investors-may-be-the-first-casualty-of-a-ukraine-war.

21 Ferguson, *The House of Rothschild, Volume 1*, 238.

22 The Rothschild Archives, "Rothschild and Gold," https://www.rothschildarchive.org/collections/rothschild_faqs/rothschild_and_gold.

23 Brenda Maddox, "All in the Rothschild Family," *The Washington Post*, April 29, 2003, https://www.washingtonpost.com/archive/lifestyle/2003/04/29/all-in-the-rothschild-family/3e196527-ed93-427b-9cd9-b1960228f42f/.

24 Ibid.

25 Ferguson, *The House of Rothschild, Volume 1*, 328–335.

26 Reiner Liedtke, "Agents for the Rothschilds: A Nineteenth Century Information Network," excerpted from Rainer Liedtke, *N M Rothschild & Sons. Kommunikationswege im europäischen Bankenwesen im 19. Jahrhundert* (Cologne 2006), https://www.degruyter.com/document/doi/10.1515/9783110415162-003/pdf.

27 Ferguson, *The House of Rothschild, Volume 1*, 296.

28 Ferguson, *The House of Rothschild, Volume 1*, 299.

29 Ferguson, *The House of Rothschild, Volume 1*, 304.

30 Liedtke, "Agents for the Rothschilds," 7.

31 Jewish Virtual Library, "The Damascus Blood Libel," https://www.jewishvirtuallibrary.org/the-damascus-blood-libel.

32 Glenn R. Sharfman, "Jewish Emancipation," *Encyclopedia of Revolutions of 1848*, October 26, 2000, https://www.ohio.edu/chastain/ip/jewemanc.htm.

33 Salo W. Baron, "The Impact of the Revolution of 1848 on Jewish Emancipation," *Jewish*

Social Studies 11, no. 3 (1949): 195–248, http://www.jstor.org/stable/4464829. Accessed 22 Apr. 2022.

34 Ferguson, *The House of Rothschild, Volume 1*, 458–460.

35 The Rothschild Archive, "Exhibition, Rothschilds in Caricature," https://www.roth-schildarchive.org/exhibitions/rothschild_in_caricature/frankfurt_revolt_1848.

36 Ferguson, *The House of Rothschild, Volume 1*, 462–467.

37 See Ian Sansom, "Great Dynasties of the World: The Rothschilds," *The Guardian*, September 16, 2011, https://www.theguardian.com/lifeandstyle/2011/sep/17/roth-schild-great-dynasties-ian-sansom, with the "French journalist" possibly being the anti-Rothschild socialist Alexandre Weill. Other sources attribute it to early twentieth century German economist Werner Sombart.

38 Ferguson, *The House of Rothschild, Volume 1*, 233–234.

39 Giles Constable and Malcolm J. Rohrbough, "The Rothschilds and the Gold Rush: Benjamin Davidson and Heinrich Schliemann in California, 1851–52," *Transactions of the American Philosophical Society* 105, no. 4 (2015): i–115. JSTOR, http://www.jstor.org/stable/44650947. Accessed 22 Jul. 2022.

40 Niall Ferguson, *The House of Rothschild, Vol. 2: The World's Banker* (New York: Penguin Books, 2000), 5–8.

41 Ferguson, *The World's Banker*, 20–23.

42 Virginia Cowles, *The Rothschilds: A Family of Fortune* (New York: Futura Publications, 1973), 122.

43 Ferguson, *Money's Prophets*, 127.

44 Ferguson, *The World's Banker*, 180.

45 The Rothschild Archive, "Brief History of the Naples House," https://www.rothschildarchive.org/business/c_m_de_rothschild_and_figli_naples/.

46 Ferguson, *The World's Banker*, 150–156.

CHAPTER 3

1 The Rothschild Archive, "Exhibition: the Rothschilds in Caricature," https://www.rothschildarchive.org/exhibitions/rothschild_in_caricature/a_view_from_the_royal_exchange.

2 The British Museum, "Nathan Meyer Rothschild," https://www.britishmuseum.org/collection/term/BIOG161439.

3 Ferguson, *Money's Prophets*, 257–258.

4 Cowles, The Rothschilds: A Family of Fortune, 69.

5 Alfred Rubens, "The Rothschilds in Caricature," *Transactions & Miscellanies* (Jewish Historical Society of England) 22 (1968): 76–87. JSTOR, http://www.jstor.org/stable/29778770. Accessed 14 Jul. 2022.

6 Gordon A. Craig, "Prophets," *The New York Review of Books*, January 9, 1997, https://www.nybooks.com/articles/1997/01/09/prophets/.

7 Frederick Busi, "The Balzacian Imagination and the Dreyfus Affair," *Nineteenth-Century French Studies* 6, no. 3/4 (1978): 174–88, http://www.jstor.org/stable/23536011. Accessed 15 Apr. 2022.

8   Brian Cathcart, *The News from Waterloo* (London: Faber &Faber, 2015), 294–295.

9   The Rothschild Archive, "October 2018: "The land that never was": correspondence between Gregor MacGregor and N M Rothschild, 1821," https://www.rothschildarchive. org/collections/treasure_of_the_month/october_2018_the_land_that_never_was_correspondence_between_gregor_macgregor_and_n_m_rothschild_1821.

10 Ferguson, *Money's Prophets*, 28.

11 Ferguson, *Money's Prophets*, 56.

12 Ibid.

13 Ferguson, *Money's Prophets*, 65.

14 W. T. Stead, "The Money Kings of the Modern World," *The Windsor Review* 18 (1903): 170–182.

15 "The Empire of Rothschild," The American Monthly Review of Reviews, Volume 31 (1905).

16 Cathcart, *The News from Waterloo*, 169.

17 Egon Caesar Corti, *The Rise of the House of Rothschild* (New York: Cosmopolitan Books, 1928), 158–159.

18 Ferguson, *Money's Prophets*, 98–100.

19 John Reeves, *The Rothschilds, the Financial Rulers of Nations* (Chicago: A. C. McClurg and Co., 1889), 17–19.

20 Reeves, *The Rothschilds*, the Financial Rulers, 86.

21 Ibid.

22 Reeves, *The Rothschilds*, the Financial Rulers, 170–175.

23 56 Cong. Rec 33, 514.

24 David Starr Jordan, "The Waste of War," reprinted in *The Maryland Peace Society Quarterly*, 1910.

25 Ignatius Balla, *The Romance of the Rothschilds* (London: Eveleigh Nash, 1913), 88–92.

26 Anti-Defamation League, "A Hoax of Hate: The Protocols of the Learned Elders of Zion," January 5, 2013, https://www.adl.org/resources/backgrounders/hoax-hate-protocols-learned-elders-zion.

27 *The International Jew, Vol 1: The World's Foremost Problem* (Detroit: The Dearborn Press, 1920), 188–189.

28 Fredric Morton, *The Rothschilds: A Family Portrait* (New York: Atheneum, 1962), 49–50.

29 Staff, "Anti-Semitic theory in Bitcoin firm email," *The Jewish Chronicle*, July 6, 2021, https://www.thejc.com/news/uk/antisemitic-theory-in-bitcoin-firm-advert-1.518376.

30 Samantha Sharf, "Carrier Pigeon Commerce: How Knowing First Helped The Rothschilds Build A Banking Empire," *Forbes*, June 18, 2014, https://www.forbes.com/sites/samanthasharf/2014/06/18/carrier-pigeon-commerce-how-knowing-first-helped-the-rothschilds-build-a-banking-empire/?sh=6c8349cb2b08.

31 *Endgame*, Dir. Alex Jones (2007).

32 Cowles, The Rothschilds: A Family of Fortune, 46–49.

33 Ferguson, *Money's Prophets*, 96.

34 Ferguson, "Investors Are Often the First Casualties of War."

35 Ferguson, *Money's Prophets*, 100.

36 Cowles, *The Rothschilds: A Family of Fortune*, 49.

37 The Rothschild Archives, "Nathan Mayer Rothschild and Waterloo," https://www.rothschildarchive.org/business/n_m_rothschild_and_sons_london/nathan_mayer_rothschild_and_waterloo.

38 Chapman, "The Establishment of the Rothschilds as Bankers," 187.

39 Cathcart, *The News from Waterloo*, xi–xii.

40 Cathcart, *The News from Waterloo*, 211.

41 Cathcart, *The News from Waterloo*, 212.

42 Cathcart, *The News from Waterloo*, 211.

43 Quoted in Wilfried Parys, "Samuelsonian Legends About Ricardo's Finances Lack Historical Evidence," European Society for the History of Economic Thought, May 10, 2019.

44 The Rothschild Archive, "Review of the Year April 2013–March 2014," https://www.rothschildarchive.org/materials/annual_review_2013_2014_complete_pdf_copy_4.pdf.

45 Gavin Daly, "Napoleon and the 'City of Smugglers,' 1810–1814," *The Historical Journal* 50, no. 2 (2007): 333–52. JSTOR, http://www.jstor.org/stable/4140133. Accessed 25 Jul. 2022.

46 Cathcart, *The News from Waterloo*, 294–295.

47 For more about Ricardo and the intricacies of the British consol market in the days of Waterloo, see Parys, "Samuelsonian Legends."

CHAPTER 4

1 Peter W. Sinnema, "Representing the Railway: Train Accidents and Trauma in the 'Illustrated London News,'" *Victorian Periodicals Review* 31, no. 2 (1998): 142–68, http://www.jstor.org/stable/20083063. Accessed 10 May 2022.

2 The Rothschild Archives, "Rothschild Timeline," https://www.rothschildarchive.org/exhibitions/timeline/.

3 Julie Kalman, "Rothschildian Greed: This New Kind of Despotism," https://h-france.net/rude/wp-content/uploads/2017/08/vol1_Kalman2.pdf.

4 Victor Hugo, *Les Misérables* (New York: Penguin Classics Deluxe Edition, 2005), 1412.

5 Melanie Aspey, "Making Tracks: Promoting The Rothschild Archive as a Source for Railway History," http://www.docutren.com/HistoriaFerroviaria/Semmering2004/pdf/01.pdf.

6 Jay R. Berkovitz, "The French Revolution and the Jews: Assessing the Cultural Impact," *AJS Review* 20, no. 1 (1995): 25–86, http://www.jstor.org/stable/1486474.

7 Ibid.

8 Julie Kalman, "Sensuality, Depravity, and Ritual Murder: The Damascus Blood Libel and Jews in France," *Jewish Social Studies* 13, no. 3 (2007): 35–58, http://www.jstor.org/stable/4467774. Accessed 16 May 2022.

9 Quoted in Victor M. Glasberg, "Intent and Consequences: The 'Jewish Question' in the French Socialist Movement of the Late Nineteenth Century," *Jewish Social Studies* 36, no. 1 (1974): 61–71, http://www.jstor.org/stable/4466802. Accessed 9 May 2022.

10 Quoted in Ferguson, *Money's Prophets*, 232.

11 See Dan Desmarques, *The Secret Empire: The Hidden Truth Behind the Power Elite and the Knights of the New World Order* (22 Lions Publishing, 2020), Chapter 25, for one example of Gutle's apocryphal quote in antisemitic literature.

12 Julie Kalman, "Rothschildian Greed: This New Kind of Despotism."

13 Pierre-Joseph Proudhon, "On the Jews," 1847, reprinted on Marxists.org, https://www.marxists.org/reference/subject/economics/proudhon/1847/jews.htm.

14 Edmund Silberner, "Pierre Leroux's Ideas on the Jewish People," *Jewish Social Studies* 12, no. 4 (1950): 367–84, http://www.jstor.org/stable/4464914.

15 Glasberg, "Intent and Consequences."

16 Edmund Silberner," Friedreich Engels and the Jews," *Jewish Social Studies* 11, No. 4 (1949): 323–342, https://www.jstor.org/stable/4464841.

17 Kalman, "Rothschildian Greed: This New Kind of Despotism."

18 Zosa Szajkowski, *Jews and the French Revolutions of 1789, 1830 and 1848* (New York: Ktav Publishing House, 1970), 1112.

19 Georges Dairnvaell, *Histoire édifiante et curieuse de Rothschild Ier, Roi des Juifs* (Paris, 1846).

20 Ibid.

21 Ibid.

22 Ibid.

23 William I. Brustein, Louisa Roberts, *The Socialism of Fools?: Leftist Origins of Modern Anti-Semitism* (New York: Cambridge University Press, 2015), 37.

24 Dairnvaell, *Histoire édifiante et curieuse.*

25 Ibid.

26 Ibid.

27 Ibid.

28 Ibid.

29 Kalman, "Rothschildian Greed: This New Kind of Despotism."

30 Anon, "The Hebrew Talisman" (1836).

31 The Rothschild Archive, "Principal acquisitions, 1 April 2005–31 March 2006," https://www.rothschildarchive.org/materials/ar2006acquisitions.pdf.

32 Quoted in Kalman, "Rothschildian Greed: This New Kind of Despotism."

33 Ferguson, *Money's Prophets*, 585.

34 Ferguson, *Money's Prophets*, 432.

35 Kalman, "Rothschildian Greed: This New Kind of Despotism."

36 Quoted in Anka Muhlstein, *Baron James: The Rise of the French Rothschilds* (New York: The Vendome Press, 1982), 147.

37 Ferguson, *Money's Prophets*, 432.

38 Corti, *Reign of the House of Rothschild*, 247.

39 Quoted in Herbert R. Lottman, *The French Rothschilds* (New York: Random House, 1995), 32.

40 Quoted in Kalman, "Rothschildian Greed: This New Kind of Despotism."

41 Emile Barrault, *Letter to M. Rothschild* (Paris: Lettres 31 Contemporarines, 1848).

42 Corti, *Reign of the House of Rothschild*, 247.

43 Corti, *Reign of the House of Rothschild*, 248–250.

44 Ferguson, *Money's Prophets*, 433.

45 Morton, *The Rothschilds: A Family Portrait*, 117.

46 Corti, *Reign of the House of Rothschild*, 247–248.

47 Cathcart, *The News from Waterloo*, 164–168.

48 "Book on Rothschilds Arouses a Defender," *The New York Times*, January 19, 1913.

49 Cowles, *The Rothschilds: A Family of Fortune*, 49.

50 Muhlstein, *Baron James*, 148.

CHAPTER 5

1 Ferguson, *The World's Banker*, 156.

2 The Rothschild Archive, "The Siege of Paris: Sundry Papers," https://guide-to-the-archive.rothschildarchive.org/the-paris-banking-house/depts/de-rothschild-freres-sundry-papers/the-siege-of-paris-sundry-papers.

3 Ferguson, *The World's Banker*, 205.

4 Ferguson, *The World's Banker*, 244.

5 Ferguson, *The World's Banker*, 294.

6 The Rothschild Archive, "Suez Canal Loan Receipts," https://www.rothschildarchive.org/collections/treasure_of_the_month/march_2015_suez_canal_loan_receipts_1876.

7 Ferguson, *The World's Banker*, 299.

8 Ron Chernow, "A Canal Runs Through It," *The New York Times Magazine*, December 1999, https://archive.nytimes.com/www.nytimes.com/library/magazine/millennium/m1/chernow.html.

9 Ferguson, *The World's Banker*, 353–355.

10 Bernard M. Magubane, The Making of a Racist State: British Imperialism and the Union of South Africa, 1875–1910 (Trenton, NJ: Africa World Press, 1995), 225,

11 Ferguson, *The World's Banker*, 360–361.

12 Derek Wilson, *Rothschild: A Story of Wealth and Power*, 304–305.

13 Ferguson, *The World's Banker*, 461.

14 Miles F. Shore, "Cecil Rhodes and the Ego Ideal," *The Journal of Interdisciplinary History* 10, no. 2 (1979): 249–65. JSTOR, https://doi.org/10.2307/203336. Accessed 24 Jan. 2023.

15 Robert Hortle, "Rhodes scholars: can you justify taking the money of the 'godfather of apartheid'?" *The Guardian*, February 1, 2016, https://www.theguardian.com/commentisfree/2016/feb/02/rhodes-scholars-can-you-justify-taking-the-money-of-the-godfather-of-apartheid.

16 Eustace Mullins, *The Secrets of the Federal Reserve: The London Connection* (Staunton, Virg.: Bankers Research Institute, 1952), 143.

17 Ron Linker, "Who's behind the world banking cartel? The Rothschild family!," *The Athens News*, June 26, 2013, https://www.athensnews.com/opinion/letters/who-s-behind-

the-world-banking-cartel-the-rothschild-family/article_7c477d34-866b-5a5b-bd2b-5b9995743b73.html.

18 *The Spanish Fork*, March 21, 1907, https://chroniclingamerica.loc.gov/lccn/sn85058245/1907-03-21/ed-1/seq-5/.

19 Nancy L. Green, "The Dreyfus Affair and Ruling Class Cohesion," *Science & Society* 43, no. 1 (1979): 29–50. JSTOR, http://www.jstor.org/stable/40402147. Accessed 25 May 2022.

20 John Ganz, "The Socialism of Fools?" *Unpopular Front*, November 7, 2022, https://johnganz.substack.com/p/the-socialism-of-fools.

21 Edouard Drumont, *La France juive* (Paris, 1886).

22 R. F. Byrnes. "Edouard Drumont and La France Juive." *Jewish Social Studies* 10, no. 2 (1948): 165–84. JSTOR, http://www.jstor.org/stable/4615301. Accessed 26 May 2022.

23 Ibid.

24 Ferguson, *The World's Banker*, 269.

25 Quoted in *Business Insider*, "The Rothschild Gang: Shadow Conspiracy Or Rumor?," June 1, 2011, https://www.businessinsider.com/the-rothschild-gang-shadow-conspiracy-or-rumor-2011-6.

26 Scott D. Seligman, "He was the father of anti-Semitic publishing in America," *The Forward*, February 5, 2020, https://forward.com/culture/439401/he-was-the-father-of-anti-semitic-publishing-in-america/.

27 Quoted in Ferguson, *The World's Banker*, 269.

28 The Rothschild Archive, "Leopold de Rothschild," https://guide-to-the-archive.rothschildarchive.org/rothschild-family-collection/depts/english-family-papers/leopold-de-rothschild-1845-1917.

29 William I. Brustein and Ryan D. King, "Anti-Semitism in Europe Before the Holocaust," *International Political Science Review* 25, no. 1 (2004): 35–53.

30 Theodore Herzl, *The Jewish State* (Dover Publications, New York: 1988), 40.

31 Ferguson, *The World's Banker*, 279–293.

32 "Rothschild Frankfort House to Close," *The New York Times*, August 11, 1901.

33 Ferguson, *The World's Banker*, 457.

34 Ferguson, *The World's Banker*, 240–241.

35 The Rothschilds Archives, "Rothschilds on Active Service," https://www.rothschildarchive.org/exhibitions/rothschilds_and_the_first_world_war/rothschilds_on_active_service.

36 *Endgame: Blueprint for Global Enslavement*, Dir. Alex Jones (2007).

37 Martin Horn, "A Private Bank at War: J.P. Morgan & Co. and France, 1914–1918," *The Business History Review* 74, no. 1 (2000): 85–112. JSTOR, https://doi.org/10.2307/3116353. Accessed 27 May 2022.

38 Cowles, *A Family of Fortune*, 195.

39 Ferguson, *The World's Banker*, 459.

40 N. Forbes, "Family banking in an era of crisis: N.M. Rothschild & Sons and business in central and eastern Europe between the World Wars," *Business History* 55, no. 6 (2013): 963–980. http://dx.doi.org/10.1080/00076791.2012.744586.

41 Liaquat Ahamed, *Lords of Finance: The Bankers Who Broke the World* (Penguin, New York: 2009), 404.

42 Ferguson, *The World's Banker*, 465.

43 The Rothschild Archives, "*Creditanstalt* crisis: a chronology," https://guide-to-the-archive.rothschildarchive.org/the-vienna-banking-house/depts/the-creditanstalt/creditanstalt-crisis-a-chronology.

44 Ahamed, *Lords of Finance*, 409.

45 Ahamed, *Lords of Finance*, 412.

46 Ahamed, *Lords of Finance*, 416.

47 Ahamed, *Lords of Finance*, 422–424.

48 Sebastian Doerr, et al, "How failing banks paved Hitler's path to power: Financial crisis and right-wing extremism in Germany, 1931-33," Vox.EU, March 15, 2019, https://voxeu.org/article/financial-crisis-and-right-wing-extremism-germany-1931-33.

49 Ahamed, *Lords of Finance*, 420.

50 Hannah Stamler, "Art and Exile in the Third Republic," *The Nation*, August 16, 2021, https://www.thenation.com/article/culture/house-fragile-things-france-review/.

CHAPTER 6

1 Rothschild Archive, "Letter from August Belmont, 1837," https://www.rothschildarchive.org/collections/treasure_of_the_month/may_2016_letter_from_august_belmont_1837.

2 Ferguson, *Money's Prophets*, 61.

3 Xaviant Haze, *The Suppressed History of American Banking* (New York: Bear & Company, 2016), 16.

4 David Icke, *The Robots' Rebellion* (Bath: Gateway Books, 1994), 157.

5 David Allen Rivera, *Final Warning: A History of the New World Order* (Oakland, CA: Conspiracy Books, 1998), 46.

6 Rothschild Archive, "Letter from August Belmont, 1837," https://www.rothschildarchive.org/collections/treasure_of_the_month/may_2016_letter_from_august_belmont_1837.

7 Ferguson, *Money's Prophets*, 369.

8 Haze, *The Suppressed History*, 90.

9 Lucas Kawa, "The Story Behind The Most Insidious Rothschild Dynasty Conspiracy Theory", *Business Insider*, January 8, 2013, https://www.businessinsider.com/rothschild-family-war-of-1812-conspiracy-2013-1.

10 Mullins, *The Secrets of the Federal Reserve*, 88–92.

11 Rudolf Glanz, "The Rothschild Legend in America," *Jewish Social Studies* 19, no. 1/2 (1957): 3–28. JSTOR, http://www.jstor.org/stable/4465515. Accessed 10 Jun. 2022.

12 Ibid.

13 Ibid.

14 Richard Hofstadter, *The Age of Reform: From Bryan to FDR* (New York: Alfred A. Knopf, 1955), 78–79.

15 Haze, *The Suppressed History*, 165.

16 Mary E. Hobart, *The Secret of the Rothschilds* (Chicago: Charles H. Kerr and Co., 1898), 48.

17 Jon E. Lewis, *The Mammoth Book of Conspiracies* (Robinson: London, 2012), 39.

18 Anti-Defamation League, "A Hoax of Hate: The Protocols of the Learned Elders of Zion," January 5, 2013, https://www.adl.org/resources/backgrounders/hoax-hate-protocols-learned-elders-zion.

19 Ibid.

20 Victor E. Marsden, *The Protocols of the Learned Elders of Zion*, reprinted by Liberty Bell Publications, 7.

21 Arthur Cherep-Spiridovich, *The Secret World Government, or "The Hidden Hand"* (New York: 1926) 44.

22 Cherep-Spiridovich, *The Secret World Government*, 174.

23 Naval History and Heritage Command, "The Russian Navy Visits the United States," United States Navy, https://www.history.navy.mil/research/library/online-reading-room/title-list-alphabetically/r/the-russian-navy-visits-theunited-states.html.

24 "Count Spiridovich, Rabid Anti-Semite Under Czar Dies in N.Y. a Suicide at 75," *The Wisconsin Jewish Chronicle*, October 29, 1926, https://www.newspapers.com/clip/14295048/the-wisconsin-jewish-chronicle/.

25 Rev. Charles E. Coughlin, *Driving Out the Money Changers* (Radio League of the Little Flower, 1933).

26 Matthew Sweet, "Could you spot a conspiracy theorist?," UnHerd.com, April 23, 2021, https://unherd.com/2021/04/could-you-spot-a-conspiracy-theorist/.

27 *New Jersey Jewish News,* MetroWest Edition, "Grant Backs Anti-Semitic Article," (July 31, 1959), 4

28 John L. Coleman, *The Rothschild Dynasty* (World Intelligence Review, 2006), 54.

29 Andrew Leonard, "Was Abe Lincoln a Jewish pawn of the Rothschilds?" Salon.com, June 2, 2011, https://www.salon.com/2011/06/02/was_abe_lincoln_a_jewish_pawn_of_the_rothschilds/.

30 Elaine Penn, "Interfered with by the state of the times," The Rothschild Archive, 2003, https://www.rothschildarchive.org/materials/ar2003_state_of_the_times.pdf.

31 Vincent P. Carosso, "A Financial Elite: New York's German-Jewish Investment Bankers," *American Jewish Historical Quarterly* 66, no. 1 (1976): 67–88. JSTOR, http://www.jstor.org/stable/23880424. Accessed 6 Jul. 2022.

32 Niall Ferguson, *The Ascent of Money* (Penguin: New York, 2008), 93.

33 Wilson, *Rothschild: A Story of Wealth and Power*, 184–185.

34 Penn, "Interfered with by the state of the times."

35 Ferguson, *The Ascent of Money*, 97.

36 August Belmont to Abraham Lincoln, May 9, 1862, Library of Congress.

37 Quoted in Ferguson, *The World's Banker*, 115.

38 *Chicago Tribune*, November 6, 1864.

39 Jay Sexton, "The Funded Loan and the 'Alabama' Claims," *Diplomatic History*, 27, no. 4 (2003): 449–78. *JSTOR*, http://www.jstor.org/stable/24914292. Accessed 27 Jul. 2022.

40 55 Cong. Rec 32, 2503.

41 Ferguson, *The World's Banker*, 117.

42 "Washington Officials Approve the Fraud," *The Advocate and Topeka Tribune*, December 7, 1892.

43 "Traitors Triumph," *Kansas Agitator*, November 2, 1893.

44 "Emperor Rothschild's Soliloquy," *Kansas Agitator*, April 28, 1892.

45 Hofstadter, *The Age of Reform*, 78.

46 "Furor Over Mary Leese," *The New York Times*, August 11, 1896.

47 James Ledbetter, "Has the Famous Populist 'Cross of Gold' Speech Been Unfairly Tarred by Anti-Semitism?" Daily JStor, July 6, 2016, https://daily.jstor.org/william-jennings-bryan-cross-of-gold/.

48 Ronald R. Stockton, "McGuffey and the Jews: An Assessment of the Baldwin Thesis," Social Science Colloquium Series, University of Michigan-Dearborn, October 8, 2008, https://deepblue.lib.umich.edu/bitstream/handle/2027.42/168233/McGuffeyConferencePaper.doc?sequence=1.

49 Ferguson, *The World's Banker*, 399.

50 Roger Lowenstein, *America's Bank: The Epic Struggle to Create the Federal Reserve* (New York: Penguin, 2015), 67.

51 "Great Bank Group Takes the New Bonds," *The New York Times*, April 23, 1908.

52 Lowenstein, *America's Bank*, 107–108.

53 Anti-Defamation League, "Jewish 'Control' of the Federal Reserve: A Classic Antisemitic Myth," January 30, 2017, https://www.adl.org/resources/backgrounders/jewish-control-federal-reserve-classic-antisemitic-myth.

CHAPTER 7

1 Dietrich Eckhart, "To All Working People!," reprinted in *Nazi Ideology Before 1933: A Documentation*, edited by Barbara Miller Lane and Leila J. Rupp (University of Texas, Austin: 1978), 31.

2 Ferguson, *Money's Prophets*, 23.

3 Alfred Rosenberg, *The Myth of the 20th Century* (Berlin, 1930).

4 Glen W. Gadberry, editor, *Theatre in the Third Reich, the Prewar Years: Essays on Theatre in Nazi Germany* (Westport, CT: Greenwood Press, 1995), 66–68.

5 "Rothschild Linked to Marx by Nazis," *The New York Times*, July 8, 1937.

6 Ferguson, *Money's Prophets*, 23.

7 John E. Dolibois, *Pattern of Circles* (Kent, OH: Kent State University Press, 1989), 117.

8 Nesta Webster, *World Revolution: The Plot Against Civilization* (Boston, Small Maynard & Company: 1921), 241.

9 Webster, *World Revolution*, 297–308.

10 Excerpted in *The Fear of Conspiracy*, ed. David Brion Davis (Ithaca, NY: Ithaca Press, 1971), 239–240.

11 American Jewish Congress, "American Jewish Yearbook: Review of the Year 5697," 254–255.

12 Sarah Kate Kramer, "When Nazis Took Manhattan," *NPR Code Switch*, February 20, 2019, https://www.npr.org/sections/codeswitch/2019/02/20/695941323/when-nazis-took-manhattan.

13 Seva Gunitsky, "These are the three reasons fascism spread in 1930s America—and might spread again today," *The Washington Post*, August 12, 2017, https://www.washingtonpost.com/news/monkey-cage/wp/2017/08/12/these-are-the-three-reasons-that-fascism-spread-in-1930s-america-and-might-spread-again-today/.

14 "New Anti-Jewish Booklet Circulated on Coast," *The Anti-Jewish Propaganda Front*, American Jewish Committee, no. 1 (1937).

15 "How Do They Do It," *American Bulletin*, July 7, 1936.

16 "New Lights on the Italian-Ethiopian Question," *American Bulletin*, September 18, 1935.

17 Elizabeth Dilling, *The Octopus* (self-published, 1940; reprinted by the Sons of Liberty, 1985).

18 Leon B. Blair, "George Washington Armstrong, 1866–1954," Texas State Historical Association, https://www.tshaonline.org/handbook/entries/armstrong-george-washington.

19 Kenneth E. Hendrickson, Jr., "The Last Populist: George Washington Armstrong and the Texas Gubernatorial Election of 1932, and the 'Zionist' Threat to Liberty and Constitutional Government," *East Texas Historical Journal* 40, no. 1, article 6 (2002), https://scholarworks.sfasu.edu/ethj/vol40/iss1/6.

20 George Washington Armstrong, *Rothschild Money Trust* (self-published, 1940), 21.

21 Armstrong, *Rothschild Money Trust*, 36.

22 John T. Flynn, *Men of Wealth: The Story of Twelve Significant Fortunes from the Renaissance to the Present Day* (New York: Simon & Schuster, 1941), 86.

23 Flynn, *Men of Wealth*, 124–125.

24 "John T. Flynn, 81, Rightist, Is Dead," *The New York Times*, April 14, 1964.

25 Arnold Leese, *Gentile Folly: The Rothschilds* (self-published, 1940), preface.

26 Leese, *Gentile Folly*, 42.

27 Anthony David Moody, *Ezra Pound: Poet. A Portrait of the Man and His Work. II: The Epic Years 1921–1939* (Oxford: Oxford University Press, 2014), 239.

28 John Tytell, *Ezra Pound: The Solitary Volcano* (New York: Doubleday, 1987), 257–259.

29 James Dowthwaite, "'CRIME Ov Two CENturies:' Anti-Semitic Conspiracy Theory as a Narrative Arc in Ezra Pound's 'Cantos,'" *Amerikastudien / American Studies* 62, no. 3 (2017): 413–36. JSTOR, http://www.jstor.org/stable/44982343. Accessed 15 Jul. 2022.

30 The Cantos Project, *Canto LII*, http://ezrapoundcantos.org/index.php/canto-lii?start=1.

31 "Rothschild Play in London," *The New York Times*, May 8, 1912.

32 Colin Crisp, *Genre, Myth and Convention in the French Cinema, 1929–1939* (Bloomington, IN: Indiana University Press, 2002), 12.

33 Ben Urwand, *The Collaboration: Hollywood's Pact with Hitler* (Cambridge, Massachusetts: The Belknap Press of Harvard University Press, 2013), 72–76.

34 Urwand, *The Collaboration*, 71.

35 Urwand, *The Collaboration*, 82.

36 *The House of Rothschild*, Dir. Alfred Werker (Twentieth Century Pictures, 1934).

37 Ibid.

38 Ibid.

39 Urwand, *The Collaboration*, 84.

40 "*The House of Rothschild* Review," *The Hollywood Reporter*, February 23, 1934, https://www.hollywoodreporter.com/news/general-news/house-rothschild-review-movie-1934-1276275/.

41 Urwand, *The Collaboration*, 94.

42 Scott Beekman, *William Dudley Pelley: A Life in Right-wing Extremism and the Occult* (Syracuse, NY: Syracuse University Press, 2005), 133.

43 Ibid.

44 William Dudley Pelley, "Poor Old George Arliss Becomes a Jewish Propagandist," *Liberation* 5, no. 23 (January 27, 1934).

45 Urwand, *The Collaboration*, 90.

46 Ute Stargardt, "'Rassenpolitik' in National Socialist Cinema," *Shofar* 16, no. 3 (1998): 1–27, *JSTOR*, http://www.jstor.org/stable/42943943. Accessed 20 Jul. 2022.

47 Kate Connolly, "Jud Süss: the Nazis' inglorious blockbuster," *The Guardian*, February 25, 2010, https://www.theguardian.com/film/2010/feb/25/jud-suss-film-without-conscience.

48 *The Rothschilds' Shares in Waterloo*, Dir. Erich Waschneck (UFA Film, 1934).

49 Ibid.

50 Stargardt, "'Rassenpolitik' in National Socialist Cinema."

51 Dr. Stig Hornshoj-Moller, "The Eternal Jew: A Blueprint for Genocide in the Nazi Archives," Yale Center for International and Area Studies, October 1998.

52 *The Eternal Jew*, Dir. Fritz Hippler (1940).

53 Ibid.

54 Ibid.

55 Ibid.

56 Urwand, *The Collaboration*, 204.

57 Hornshoj-Moller, "The Eternal Jew: A Blueprint for Genocide in the Nazi Archives."

58 Ferguson, *The World's Banker*, 470–472.

59 Ferguson, *The World's Banker*, 474–477.

60 Ferguson, *The World's Banker*, 471.

61 "21 More Jews Commit Suicide in Austria; Arrests Mount; Border Control Tightened," *Jewish Telegraphic Agency*, March 21, 1938, https://www.jta.org/archive/21-more-jews-commit-suicide-in-austria-arrests-mount-border-control-tightend.

62 "Baron Louis De Rothschild Dead: Paid $21,000,000 Ransom to Nazis," *Jewish Telegraphic Agency*, January 17, 1955, https://www.jta.org/archive/baron-louis-de-rothschild-dead-paid-21000000-ransom-to-nazis.

63 Jenni Frazer, "The women in WWII Paris who 'did what they had to' for survival," *The*

Times of Israel, September 2, 2016, https://www.timesofisrael.com/the-women-in-wwii-paris-who-did-what-they-had-to-for-survival/.

64 Hannah Rothschild, *The Baroness: The Search For Nica, the Rebellious Rothschild* (New York: Alfred A. Knopf, 2013), 119.

CHAPTER 8

1 Robert S. Wistrich, "Anti-Semitism in Europe Since the Holocaust," *The American Jewish Year Book* 93 (1993): 3–23. *JSTOR*, http://www.jstor.org/stable/23605811. Accessed 10 Aug. 2022.

2 Ibid.

3 In one example, Father Coughlin had his massive audience stripped to virtually nothing when the National Association of Broadcasters took him off the air for violating the morals clause it wrote into its bylaws specifically in response to his pro-Nazi ranting. See Thomas Doherty, "The Deplatforming of Father Coughlin," *Slate*, January 21, 2021, https://slate.com/technology/2021/01/father-coughlin-deplatforming-radio-social-media.html.

4 Elliot Cohen, "Mr. Zanuck's 'Gentleman's Agreement': Reflections on Hollywood's Second Film About Anti-Semitism," *Commentary*, January 1948, https://www.commentary.org/articles/elliotecohen/mr-zanucks-gentlemans-agreementreflections-on-hollywoods-second-film-about-anti-semitism/.

5 Ferguson, *The World's Banker*, 480–483.

6 Anti-Defamation League, "Eustace Mullins, Anti-Semitic Conspiracy Theorist, Dies at Age 86," February 4, 2010, https://www.adl.org/resources/news/eustace-mullins-anti-semitic-conspiracy-theorist-dies-age-86.

7 Tytell, *Ezra Pound*, 304.

8 Mullins, *Secrets of the Federal Reserve*, 6.

9 Ibid.

10 Mullins, *Secrets of the Federal Reserve*, 9.

11 Mullins, *Secrets of the Federal Reserve*, 108.

12 Eustace Mullins, "Adolf Hitler: An Appreciation," *National Renaissance Bulletin*, October 1952.

13 Margaret Edds and David M. Poole, "VA Militias Defend Their Rage and Fears," *The Roanoke Times*, April 30, 1995.

14 Alex Jones, Infowars, September 28, 2005, https://archive.org/details/AlexJonesInterviewsEustaceMullins.

15 Graeme Wood, "Into the Psyche of Eustace Mullins, *The Atlantic*, September 23, 2010, https://www.theatlantic.com/entertainment/archive/2010/09/into-the-psyche-of-eustace-mullins/63457/.

16 Anti-Defamation League, "Eustace Mullins, Anti-Semitic Conspiracy Theorist, Dies at Age 86."

17 Oliver Willis, "Beck promoted the work of an anti-Semitic 9-11 truther," Media Matters, September 22, 2010, https://www.mediamatters.org/glenn-beck/beck-promoted-work-anti-semitic-9-11-truther.

18 Eustace Mullins, *Murder by Injection; The Story Of The Medical Conspiracy Against America* (Staunton, VA: National Council for Medical Research, 1988), 113.

19 Lynn Darling, "Spotlight on Conspiracy with the Liberty Lobby," *The Washington Post*, May 25, 1979.

20 Max Blumenthal, *Republican Gomorrah* (New York: Nation Books, 2009), 18–19.

21 Group Research Inc., *Periodicals on the Right* (September 20, 1966), 23.

22 "Rothschild Bank Syndrome," *Common Sense*, no. 562 (June 1970).

23 "Andrew Johnson Reconsidered," *Instauration* 23, No. 4 (March 1998).

24 Ned Touchstone, "Rothschild Agent Lehman," Louisiana Citizens' Council, "The Councilor," March 1963.

25 Jill Lepore, "Reigns of Terror in America," *The New Yorker*, November 12, 2018, https://www.newyorker.com/magazine/2018/11/12/reigns-of-terror-in-america.

26 Group Research Inc., *Periodicals on the Right*.

27 Sean Wilentz, "Confounding Fathers," *The New Yorker*, October 11, 2010, https://www.newyorker.com/magazine/2010/10/18/confounding-fathers.

28 Carroll Quigley, *Tragedy and Hope* (New York: Macmillan, 1966), 280.

29 W. Cleon Skousen, *The Naked Capitalist* (self-published, 1970), 50.

30 Skousen, *The Naked Capitalist*, 8.

31 "Round Table Review: *The Naked Capitalist*," *Dialogue Journal*, 1970, https://www.dialoguejournal.com/articles/roundtable-review-the-naked-capitalist/.

32 Wilentz, "Confounding Fathers."

33 Alexander Zaitchik, "Meet the Man Who Changed Glenn Beck's Life," *Salon*, September 16, 2009, https://www.salon.com/2009/09/16/beck_skousen/.

34 William Gayley Simpson, *Which Way Western Man* (Hillsboro, WV: National Vanguard Books, 1978), 827.

35 Simpson, *Which Way Western Man*, 913.

36 Robert Tracinski, "Which Way, Western Man?," *Discourse Magazine*, April 14, 2022, https://www.discoursemagazine.com/politics/2022/04/14/which-way-western-man/.

37 Simpson, *Which Way Western Man*, 268.

38 Gary Allen and Larry Abraham, *None Dare Call It Conspiracy* (Seal Beach, CA: Concord Press, 1972), 22–23.

39 Ibid.

40 Hua Hsu, "A Global Government Is Waiting in the Wings," *New York Magazine*, November 15, 2013, https://nymag.com/news/features/conspiracy-theories/new-world-order/.

41 Owen Gleiberman, "'Alex's War' Review: A Gripping and Disturbing Look at Alex Jones and the Politics of Unreality," *Variety*, July 30, 2022, https://variety.com/2022/film/reviews/alexs-war-review-alex-jones-1235329491/.

42 Alexander Zaitchik, "Meet Alex Jones," *Rolling Stone*, March 2, 2011, https://www.rollingstone.com/culture/culture-news/meet-alex-jones-175845/.

43 Michael Shermer, "Conspiracy, Inc.," July 29, 2022, https://michaelshermer.substack.com/p/conspiracy-inc.

44 George Kellman, "Anti-Jewish Agitation," *The American Jewish Year Book* 56 (1955):

221–29, *JSTOR*, http://www.jstor.org/stable/23604877. Accessed 23 Aug. 2022.

45 Glen Jeansonne, *Gerald L. K. Smith, Minister of Hate* (New Haven, CT: Yale University Press, 1988), 23–30.

46 Jeansonne, *Gerald L. K. Smith*, 89.

47 Jeansonne, *Gerald L. K. Smith*, 140.

48 "Christian Nationalism's Racist Past Precludes Revival Except Among GOP's Trumpiest," MSNBC, July 25, 2022, https://www.youtube.com/watch?v=oKrjhaPI95Y.

49 *The Cross and the Flag* 26, no. 5 (August 1967).

50 *The Cross and the Flag* 30, no. 3 (June 1971).

51 Henry Makow, "Illuminati Defector: Rothschilds Rule with Druid Witches," Rense.com, October 31, 2007, reposted at https://www.bibliotecapleyades.net/sociopolitica/esp_sociopol_illuminati_27.htm.

52 Jesse Walker, *The United States of Paranoia* (New York: HarperCollins, 2013), 186–188.

53 Walker, *The United States of Paranoia*, 190.

54 Makow, "Illuminati Defector."

55 Pat Robertson, *The New World Order* (Dallas: Word Publishing, 1991), 96.

56 Robertson, *The New World Order*, 123.

57 Robertson, *The New World Order*, 181.

58 Jacob Heilbrunn, "His Anti-Semitic Sources," *New York Review of Books*, April 20, 1995, https://www.nybooks.com/articles/1995/04/20/his-anti-semitic-sources/.

59 Letters to the Editor, "Is Pat Robertson an Anti-Semite?" *Commentary*, January 1996, https://www.commentary.org/articles/reader-letters/is-pat-robertson-an-anti-semite/.

60 Umberto Eco, "Ur-Fascism," *The New York Review of Books*, June 22, 1995, https://www.nybooks.com/articles/1995/06/22/ur-fascism/.

61 Milton William Cooper, *Behold a Pale Horse* (Flagstaff, AZ: Light Technology Publications, 1990), 76.

62 Cooper, *Behold a Pale Horse*, 36.

63 Cooper, *Behold a Pale Horse*, 41.

64 Cooper, *Behold a Pale Horse*, 42.

65 Hartford Van Dyke, Letter to the editor, *Paranoia Magazine*, December 17, 2003, http://www.thelivingmoon.com/45jack_files/02archives/Letters_from_the_Author_of_Silent_Weapons_for_Quiet_Wars.html.

66 Cooper, *Behold a Pale Horse*, 267.

67 Amazon rankings as of 2/14/23.

68 Lewis Beale, "Conspiracy Monger William Cooper Was the Titan of Tin Hats," *The Daily Beast*, August 31, 2018, https://www.thedailybeast.com/conspiracy-monger-william-cooper-was-the-titan-of-tin-hats.

69 "BEST SELLERS: November 17, 1991," *The New York Times*, November 17, 1991.

70 Asawin Suebsaeng, "The Story Behind 'The Creature From Jekyll Island,' the Anti-Fed Conspiracy Theory Bible," *The Daily Beast*, November 26, 2015, https://www.thedailybeast.com/the-story-behind-the-creature-from-jekyll-island-the-anti-fed-conspiracy-theory-bible.

71 William T. Still, *New World Order: The Ancient Plan of Secret Societies* (Lafyette, LA: Huntington House Publishers, 1990), 136

72 Office of the Director of National Intelligence, "Bin Laden's Bookshelf," https://www.dni.gov/index.php/features/bin-laden-s-bookshelf?start=5.

CHAPTER 9

1 Emma Grey Ellis, "The Internet Protocols of the Elders of Zion," *Wired Magazine*, March 12, 2017, https://www.wired.com/2017/03/internet-protocols-elders-zion/.

2 Mark Fenster, *Conspiracy Theories: Secrecy and Power in American Culture* (Minneapolis, MN: University of Minnesota Press, 1999), 185.

3 "Rothschild: The Head of the Beast," alt.sport.horse-racing, October 24, 1994, archived at Usenet Archives, https://www.usenetarchives.com/view.php?id=alt.sport.horse-racing&mid=PDE5OTQxMDI0MTYyMS5MQUEwMTI0NUBHZW5zeXMuY29tPg.

4 "Revelations of Awareness," *Cosmic Awareness Communications* 94, no. 14, http://cdn.preterhuman.net/texts/conspiracy/Cosmic.Awareness/Issue%2094-14.

5 "The Rothschild Formula," alt.conspiracy, September 7, 1996, archived at Usenet Archives, https://www.usenetarchives.com/view.php?id=alt.conspiracy&mid=RHR6V2x6TzVndFU.

6 "The Rothschild-Rockefeller Luciferian Conspiracy!" alt.politics.usa.misc, April 2, 1997, archived at Usenet Archives, https://www.usenetarchives.com/view.php?id=alt.politics.usa isc&mid=PDVkNm1uaSQ5anFAYWxleGFuZGVyLklOUy5DV1JVLkVkdT4.

7 A partial list of early conspiracy-themed websites, almost all of which are dead links, can be found at http://www.padrak.com/alt/WEBSITES.html#CN.

8 *Conspiracy Nation* 1, no. 1 (1994), archived at http://www.textfiles.com/conspiracy/CN/cn1-01.txt.

9 *Rothschild's Choice*, RiverCrest Publishing, DVD, 2009, http://www.rivercrestpublishing.com/dvd_rothschilds_choice.htm.

10 *Conspiracy Nation* 12, no. 44, archived at: http://www.textfiles.com/conspiracy/CN/cn12-44.txt.

11 *Conspiracy Nation* 12, no. 46, archived at: http://www.textfiles.com/conspiracy/CN/cn12-46.txt.

12 Sherman H. Skolnick, *Overthrow of the American Republic* (Chicago: Dandelion Books, 2007), 68–69.

13 Philip Weiss, "Off the Grid," *New York Times Magazine*, January 8, 1995, https://www.nytimes.com/1995/01/08/magazine/off-the-grid.html.

14 "Americans are Rothschild Proxies in Iraq," HenryMakow.com, March 14, 2004, https://henrymakow.com/000357.html?_ga=2.210117333.1908058131.1661799890-1165896808.1661799890.

15 Andrew Carrington Hitchcock, *The Synagogue of Satan* (Austin, TX: RiverCrest Publishing, 2007), 251.

16 Dan Friesen and Jordan Holmes, hosts. "David Rothschild [sic] Interview," *Knowledge Fight*, episode #129, February 14, 2018, https://knowledgefight.libsyn.com/knowledge-fight-david-rothschild-interview.

17 Allen and Abraham, *None Dare Call It Conspiracy*, 56.

18 See Dan Friesen and Jordan Holmes, hosts, "July 21–23, 2003," *Knowledge Fight*, episode #659, March 14, 2022, and Dan Friesen and Jordan Holmes, hosts, "July 31—August 1, 2003," *Knowledge Fight*, episode #680, May 13, 2022.

19 Quoted in "The House of Rothschild / The World's Banker," *The Peace Revolution Podcast*, episode #35, July 17, 2011.

20 Dan Friesen and Jordan Holmes, hosts, "April 27, 2009," *Knowledge Fight*, episode #636, January 14, 2022.

21 Chris Rovzar, "Insanely Wealthy, Titled Aristocrat Thinks Barack Obama Is 'Elitist,'" *New York Magazine*, September 17, 2008, https://nymag.com/intelligencer/2008/09/insanely_wealthy_titled_aristo.html.

22 "Rothschilds & Rockefellers: Trillionaires Of The World," Infowars.com, January 17, 2010, archived at https://web.archive.org/web/20100120040323/https://www.infowars.com/rothschilds-rockefellers-trillionaires-of-the-world/.

23 For more of the back and forth by Wikipedia editors over Alex Jones's true belief about Jews, see "Talk: Alex Jones/Archive 1," Wikipedia.org, https://en.wikipedia.org/wiki/Talk:Alex_Jones/Archive_1#Anti_Semitism.

24 Information on Rothschild mentions on Infowars scraped from http://fight.fudgie.org/

25 Will Offley, "David Icke and The Politics Of Madness," Political Research Associates, February 29, 2000, http://www.publiceye.org/Icke/IckeBackgrounder.htm.

26 David Icke, *And the Truth Shall Set You Free* (self-published, 1995), 88.

27 Icke, *And the Truth Shall Set You Free*, 92.

28 David Icke, *The Biggest Secret: The Book that Will Change the World* (Ryde, UK: Bridge of Love Publication, 1999), 31–32.

29 Icke, *The Biggest Secret*, 80.

30 David Icke, *The Trigger: The Lie That Changed the World* (Ryde, UK David Icke Books Ltd., 2019), 677.

31 David Icke, *Human Race Get Off Your Knees: The Lion Sleeps No More* (Ryde, UK: David Icke Books Ltd., 2010), 78–79.

32 Quoted in David Icke, "Was Adolf Hitler a Rothschild?," DavidIcke.com, August 17, 2003, archived at https://cdn.preterhuman.net/texts/conspiracy/David%20Icke%20-%20Was%20Hitler%20A%20Rothschild.pdf.

33 Ian Kershaw, *Hubris: Hitler 1889–1936* (New York: Norton, 1999), 7–9.

34 Ibid.

35 Kershaw, *Hubris*, 604.

36 Simon Sebag Montefiore, *Young Stalin* (Toronto: McArthur & Company, 2007), 76–80.

37 Kerry Capell, "The Stunning Collapse of Iceland," *NBC News*, October 9, 2008, https://www.nbcnews.com/id/wbna27104617.

38 Daryl Bradford Smith, "The History of the House of Rothschild," December 2005, https://web.archive.org/web/20051217133551/http://www.iamthewitness.com/DarylBradfordSmith_Rothschild.htm.

39 Stephen Shankland, "Freescale's Internet-of-things controller chip cut down to size," *CNET*, February 25, 2014, https://www.cnet.com/tech/mobile/freescales-internet-of-things-controller-chip-cut-down-to-size/.

40 David Mikkelson, "Malaysia Air 370 Patent Conspiracy," Snopes, March 13, 2014, https://www.snopes.com/fact-check/mh370-patent-disappearance/.

41 Matthew Blake, "From CIA assassination cock-up to nefarious Illuminati involvement: The MH17 conspiracy theories doing the internet rounds." *The Daily Mail*, July 18, 2014, https://www.dailymail.co.uk/news/article-2697293/From-CIA-assassination-cock-nefarious-Illuminati-involvement-The-MH17-conspiracy-theories-doing-internet-rounds.html.

42 Ollie Williams, "World's Wealth Hits Half A Quadrillion Dollars," *Forbes*, June 10, 2021, https://www.forbes.com/sites/oliverwilliams1/2021/06/10/worlds-wealth-hits-half-a-quadrillion-dollars/?sh=7e54028d309d.

43 Cherep-Spridovich, *The Secret World Government*, 48.

44 Armstrong, *Rothschild Money Trust*, 36.

45 "France to Seize Fortunes of Rothschild, Louis-Dreyfus and Other Noted Exiles," *The New York Times*, April 1, 1940.

46 Ahamed, *Lords of Finance*, 179.

47 Andrew Napolitano, *It Is Dangerous to Be Right When the Government Is Wrong* (New York: Thomas P. Nelson, 2011), 205.

48 Griffin, *Descent into Slavery*, 218.

49 Robert L. Owen, *National Economy and the Banking System* (Washington, D.C.: U.S. Government Printing Office, 1939), 99.

50 75 Cong. Rec 83, 7676.

51 72 Cong. Rec 38, 993.

52 73 Cong. Rec 78, 11693.

53 73 Cong. Rec 79, 6817.

54 75 Cong. Rec 83, 6050.

55 75 Cong. Rec 83, 8157.

56 74 Cong. Rec 80, 9800.

57 97 Cong. Rec 128, 7761.

58 Hearings on House Resolution No. 314., December 15, 1911, 40.

59 Wilbur Fisk Crafts, *Addresses on the Civil Sabbath from a Patriotic and Humanitarian Standpoint* (New York, 1890), 5.

60 Mullins, *Murder by Injection*, 104.

61 Armstrong, *Rothschild Money Trust*, 221.

CHAPTER IO

1 Elie Wiesel, "STAGE VIEW; Treasured Family Is the Secret Wealth Of 'The Rothschilds,'" *The New York Times*, September 23, 1990.

2 Ferguson, *Money's Prophet*, 170.

3 Anton Chekhov, *Rothschild's Violin*, 1896.

4 Donald Rayfield, "What Did Jews Mean to Chekhov?" *European Judaism: A Journal for the New Europe* 8, no. 1 (1973): 30–36, JSTOR, http://www.jstor.org/stable/41442422. Accessed 12 Oct. 2022.

5 Peter Laki, "Veniamin Fleishman, Rothschild's Violin," American Symphony, https://

americansymphony.org/concert-notes/veniamin-fleishman-rothschilds-violin/.

6   Sholem Aleichem, "If I Were a Rothschild," *Tevye's Daughters* (New York: Crown Publishing, 1949).

7   Joseph Berger, "How Do You Say 'Tradition' in Yiddish?," *The New York Times*, July 11, 2018, https://www.nytimes.com/2018/07/11/theater/fiddler-on-the-roof-yiddish-folksbiene.html.

8   Christopher Lehmann-Haupt, "Alfred A. Knopf Jr., Influential Publisher, Dies at 90," *The New York Times*, February 16, 2009.

9   Morton, *The Rothschilds: A Family Portrait*, 13.

10 Morton, *The Rothschilds: A Family Portrait*, 152.

11 Morton, *The Rothschilds: A Family Portrait*, 237.

12 William Harlan Hale, "Only the Family Knows the Secret," *The New York Times*, February 18, 1962.

13 Morton, *The Rothschilds: A Family Portrait*, 36.

14 Morton, *The Rothschilds: A Family Portrait*, 72.

15 Morton, *The Rothschilds: A Family Portrait*, 216–219.

16 Frederic Morton, "Jewish is Beautiful," *The New York Times*, October 18, 1970.

17 WNYC Book and Author Luncheon, March 18, 1962, https://www.wnyc.org/story/frederic-morton-jane-jacobs-and-patrick-dennis-and-cris-alexander/.

18 Alisa Solomon, "Family Fortune," *Tablet Magazine*, December 27, 2006, https://www.tabletmag.com/sections/arts-letters/articles/family-fortune.

19 Ibid.

20 Jessica Hillman, *Echoes of the Holocaust on the American Musical Stage* (Jefferson, North Carolina: McFarland & Company, 2012), 138.

21 Hillman, *Echoes of the Holocaust*, 132–135.

22 Hillman, *Echoes of the Holocaust*, 128.

23 Wiesel, "Treasured Family Is the Secret Wealth Of 'The Rothschilds.'"

24 Rothschild, *The Baroness*, 231–232.

25 See Robert Christgau, "The Shit Storm," for more on Public Enemy's early embrace of antisemitic tropes, http://www.robertchristgau.com/xg/music/pe-law.php.

26 Hua Hsu, "Jay Electronica and the Rothschild Affair," *Grantland*, June 13, 2012, https://grantland.com/features/jay-electronica-kate-rothschild-hip-hop-illuminati-obsession/.

27 Gabe Friedman, "Rapper Jay Electronica sparks anti-Semitism controversy with Rothschild and 'synagogue of Satan' lyrics," *Jewish Telegraph Agency*, March 17, 2020, https://www.jta.org/2020/03/17/culture/rapper-jay-electronica-sparks-anti-semitism-controversy-with-rothschild-and-synagogue-of-satan-lyrics.

28 Anti-Defamation League, "Farrakhan: In His Own Words," January 12, 2013, https://www.adl.org/education/resources/reports/nation-of-islam-farrakhan-in-his-own-words.

29 Kory Grow, "Glenn Danzig on Dark New LP, Misfits Plans, Why He Hates Recent Presidents," *Rolling Stone*, May 26, 2017, https://www.rollingstone.com/music/music-features/glenn-danzig-on-dark-new-lp-misfits-plans-why-he-hates-recent-presidents-120225/.

30 Peter White, "'Downton Abbey' Creator Julian Fellowes Developing Rothschild Dy-

nasty Drama With Jemima Khan At Sky Atlantic," *Deadline Hollywood*, April 16, 2018, https://deadline.com/2018/04/downton-abbey-creator-julian-fellowes-developing-rothschild-dynasty-drama-with-jemima-khan-sky-atlantic-1202365145/.

31 Instinct Productions, "The Rothschilds," https://instinctproductions.com/the-rothschilds/.

32 Andreas Wiseman, "Shia LaBeouf & Mel Gibson Set For Satire 'Rothchild' From 'Stan & Ollie' Director Jon S. Baird; HanWay Launches Sales—Cannes," *Deadline Hollywood*, May 13, 2019, https://deadline.com/2019/05/shia-labeouf-mel-gibson-rothchild-jon-sbaird-hanway-cannes-1202613457/.

33 PJ Grisar, "Absolutely every anti-Semitic thing Mel Gibson has ever said," *The Forward*, June 24, 2020, https://forward.com/culture/449521/mel-gibson-anti-semitism-timeline-winona-ryder/.

34 Sharon Waxman and Brent Lang, "Warner Bros. Shelves Mel Gibson Maccabee Movie (Exclusive)," *The Wrap*, April 11, 2012, https://www.thewrap.com/warner-brothers-pulls-plug-mel-gibson-maccabee-movie-exclusive-36952/.

35 Briana R. Ellison, "Trending: Whoever green-lit this casting needs to retire. Just a thought," *The Washington Post*, May 14, 2019, https://www.washingtonpost.com/express/2019/05/15/trending-whoever-green-lit-this-casting-needs-retire-just-thought/.

36 Tarpley Hitt, "Mel Gibson's Rep. Claims Controversial 'Rothchild' Movie Is 'Completely Unrelated' to the Rothschild Family," *The Daily Beast*, May 14, 2019, https://www.thedailybeast.com/mel-gibson-rep-claims-controversial-rothchild-movie-is-completely-unrelated-to-the-rothschild-family.

37 Alex Ritman, "Mel Gibson Has Busy Film Slate Despite Renewed Anti-Semitism Claims," *The Hollywood Reporter*, June 30, 2020, https://www.hollywoodreporter.com/news/general-news/mel-gibson-has-busy-film-slate-renewed-anti-semitism-claim-1300903/.

38 John Patton Ford, *Rothchild* script, 2013 draft.

39 Matt Grobar, "'Emily The Criminal's John Patton Ford Prepping Comedic Thriller 'Huntington'", *Deadline*, March 8, 2023, https://deadline.com/2023/03/john-patton-ford-huntington-studiocanal-next-feature-1235282656/.

40 Jackie Wullschlager, "Lunch with the FT: Jacob Rothschild," *Financial Times*, April 16, 2010, https://www.ft.com/content/03ccc110-48da-11df-8af4-00144feab49a.

41 Shawn Tully, "Who is the Real Montgomery Burns?," *Fortune Magazine*, March 7, 2015, https://fortune.com/2015/03/07/who-is-the-real-montgomery-burns/.

42 Ferguson, *The World's Banker*, 488.

43 Ed Cripps, "Party Animals: The Rothschild Surrealist Ball," *The Rake*, October 2022 issue, https://therake.com/stories/icons/party-animals-the-rothschild-surrealist-ball/.

44 Robert Phillip Kolker and Nathan Abrams, *Eyes Wide Shut: Stanley Kubrick and the Making of His Final Film* (New York: Oxford University Press, 2019), 142–144.

45 Rich Cohen, "Behind the Mask of Corruption," *The Paris Review*, April 6, 2020, https://www.theparisreview.org/blog/2020/04/06/behind-the-mask-of-corruption/.

46 Quoted in Nathan Abrams, "Kubrick and the Paranoid Style: Antisemitism, Conspiracy Theories, and *The Shining*," *Senses of Cinema*, no. 95 (July 2020), https://www.sensesofcinema.com/2020/the-shining-at-40/kubrick-paranoid-style-antisemitism-conspiracy-theories/.

CHAPTER II

1   Marvin Perry and Frederick M. Schweitzer, *Anti-Semitism: Myth and Hate from Antiquity to the Present* (New York: Palgrave Macmillan, 2005), 265.

2   Bernard Lewis, *The Jews of Islam* (Princeton, NJ: Princeton University Press, 1984), 158–159.

3   Robert Wistrich, ed., *Anti-Judaism, Antisemitism, and Delegitimizing Israel* (University of Nebraska Press, 2016), 127.

4   Bernard Lewis, Semites and Anti-Semites: An Inquiry into Conflict and Prejudice (New York: Norton, 1986), 199–208.

5   See Jeffrey Herf, *Nazi Propaganda for The Arab World* (New Haven: Yale University Press, 1999) for an in-depth examination of how the Nazis adapted and reflected the key works of Islam back for propaganda purposes.

6   Herf, *Nazi Propaganda*, 186.

7   *The Cross and the Flag* 30, no. 11 (February 1972).

8   Richard Wike and Juliana Menasce Horowitz, "Lebanon's Muslims: Relatively Secular and Pro-Christian," Pew Research, July 26, 2006, https://www.pewresearch.org/global/2006/07/26/lebanons-muslims-relatively-secular-and-pro-christian/.

9   Translated by the Middle East Media Research Institute, August 30, 2009, https://www.memri.org/tv/rothschild-legacy-controlling-world-syrian-produced-antisemitic-tv-series-al-shatat-aired-iranian.

10 Menahem Milson, "A European Plot on the Arab Stage: The Protocols of the Elders of Zion in the Arab Media," Middle East Media Research Institute, May 20, 2011, https://www.memri.org/reports/european-plot-arab-stage-protocols-elders-zion-arab-media.

11 Paul Salmons, "Debunking the Rothschild conspiracy," February 12, 2021, https://paulsalmons.associates/blog/conspiracy-theories.

12 Behnam Gholipour, "Special Report: The Bone-Chilling Insanity of Iran's 'Jewish Studies Center,'" IranWire, April 26, 2022, https://iranwire.com/en/society/103407-special-report-the-bone-chilling-insanity-of-irans-jewish-studies-center/.

13 Salmons, "Debunking the Rothschild conspiracy."

14 Jordyn Haime, "The Dramatic Decline of the 'Rothschilds of the East,'" *Tablet Magazine*, November 2, 2022, https://www.tabletmag.com/sections/community/articles/decline-sassoon-family.

15 Ariana Eunjung Cha, "Sold on a Stereotype," *The Washington Post*, February 7, 2007, https://www.washingtonpost.com/archive/business/2007/02/07/sold-on-a-stereotype-span-classbankheadin-china-a-genre-of-self-help-books-purports-to-tell-the-secrets-of-making-money-the-jewish-wayspan/da06370a-5c28-4220-8d4c-cdb03edbc449/.

16 Nicholas Moore, "China's fascination with the Rothschild family," *CGTV*, February 28, 2018, https://news.cgtn.com/news/7951544e35677a6333566d54/share_p.html.

17 Richard McGregor, "Chinese buy into currency war plot," *The Australian*, September 27, 2007, http://www.theaustralian.news.com.au/story/022487560-3637500.html.

18 While the bulk of *Currency Wars* is in Chinese, many of the endnotes and citations are in English.

19 See Morton, *The Rothschilds: A Family Portrait*, 56, for the initial estimate that Song Hongbing uses.

20 Chris Buckley, "China bestseller sees plots and profit in financial crisis," *Reuters*, September 20, 2009, https://www.reuters.com/article/us-china-economy-book/china-best-seller-sees-plots-and-profit-in-financial-crisis-idUSTRE58K0RR20090921.

21 Ibid.

22 Tuvia Gering, "Antisemitism with Chinese Characteristics," *Tablet Magazine*, February 15, 2022, https://www.tabletmag.com/sections/news/articles/antisemitism-with-chinese-characteristics.

23 Sunny Han Han, "'Hypothetical West' and 'Rise of China': On Pop-nationalism in China Today—Centering on Currency War's Spread and Acceptance in China," *Cambridge Journal of China Studies* 15, no. 2, https://www.repository.cam.ac.uk/bitstream/handle/1810/317358/202002-3-article4.pdf?sequence=1.

24 Ibid.

25 David G. Goodman and Masanori Miyazawa, *Jews in the Japanese Mind* (New York: The Free Press, 1995), 5–6.

26 Clyde Haberman, "Japanese Writers Critical of Jews," *The New York Times*, March 12, 1987.

27 Goodman and Miyazawa, *Jews in the Japanese Mind*, 138.

28 Perry and Schweitzer, *Anti-Semitism*, 117.

29 Goodman and Miyazawa, *Jews in the Japanese Mind*, 254–255.

30 Robert Lifton, *Destroying the World to Save It* (New York: Harry Holt and Company, 1999), 166–167.

31 Lifton, *Destroying the World to Save It*, 180.

32 Lifton, *Destroying the World to Save It*, 197.

33 Christopher L. Schilling, "Buddhist Anti-Semitism," *Jewish Political Studies Review* 31, no. 3/4 (2021): 18–28, JSTOR, https://www.jstor.org/stable/27083953. Accessed 2 Dec. 2022.

34 Sam Shead, "SoftBank CEO says he wants to be a 21st century Rothschild," *CNBC*, June 23, 2021, https://www.cnbc.com/2021/06/23/softbank-ceo-masayoshi-son-says-he-wants-to-be-21st-century-rothschild.html.

35 Kevin Lui, "The Head of One of Japan's Biggest Hotel Groups 'Made Anti-Semitic Remarks in a Company Magazine,'" *Time Magazine*, February 16, 2017, https://time.com/4672913/japan-apa-hotels-antisemitic-toshio-motoya/.

CHAPTER 12

1 Arthur Goldwag, *The New Hate: A History of Fear and Loathing on the Populist Right* (New York: Pantheon Books, 2012), 40.

2 In reality, Fuddy died of a heart attack after the light plane carrying her and several others went down off the coast of Hawaii, with the other passengers all unharmed. See Philip Bump, "Birthers Seize on Death of Hawaii Official as Fuel for Birtherism," *The Atlantic*, December 12, 2013, https://www.theatlantic.com/politics/archive/2013/12/birther-conspiracy-theorists-seize-death-hawaii-official-fuel-birther-conspiracy-theory/356080/.

3 Jonathan Mahler, "Anti-Semitic Posts, Many From Trump Supporters, Surge on Twit-

ter," *The New York Times*, October 19, 2016, https://www.nytimes.com/2016/10/19/us/politics/anti-semitism-trump-supporters-twitter.html.

4 For one example of how the alt-right used antisemitic tropes as a rallying cry in support of conspiracy theories, see the testimony of author Deborah Lipstadt in the lawsuit against Unite the Right founder Jason Kessler, July 20, 2020, https://files.integrityfirstforamerica.org/14228/1611248500-832-1-expert-report-of-d-lipstadt.pdf.

5 Michelle Goldberg, "Antisemitism Increased Under Trump. Then It Got Even Worse," *The New York Times*, April 29, 2022, https://www.nytimes.com/2022/04/29/opinion/antisemitism-post-trump.html.

6 Rachel Treisman, "How antisemitic rhetoric is impacting Jewish communities, and what to do about it," *National Public Radio*, November, 6, 2022, https://www.npr.org/2022/11/06/1133608843/antisemitic-rhetoric-kanye-jewish-communities-reaction.

7 Jonathan Chait, "Trump Says Jews Should Love Him Because He's Almost Literally Jesus," *New York Magazine*, August 21, 2019, https://nymag.com/intelligencer/2019/08/trump-jews-jesus-wayne-allyn-root.html.

8 Chase Peterson-Withorn, "Getting Donald Out Of Debt: The 25-Year-Old Ties That Bind Trump and Wilbur Ross," *Forbes*, December 8, 2016, https://www.forbes.com/sites/chasewithorn/2016/12/08/trump-and-his-commerce-secretary-wilbur-ross-a-look-at-25-years-of-connections/?sh=62dcf919f820.

9 Ferguson, *The World's Banker*, 494–495.

10 Peterson-Withorn, "Getting Donald Out Of Debt."

11 Jeff Horowitz and Chad Day, "Before Trump job, Manafort worked to aid Putin," *Associated Press*, March 22, 2017, https://apnews.com/article/122ae0b5848345faa88108a-03de40c5a.

12 United States Senate Select Committee on Intelligence, *Russian Active Measures Campaigns and Interference in the 2016 Election, Volume 5*, 48–50, https://www.intelligence.senate.gov/sites/default/files/documents/report_volume5.pdf.

13 Matthew d'Ancona, "Doesn't 'Yachtgate' give you that sinking feeling?," *The Daily Telegraph*, October 26, 2008, https://www.telegraph.co.uk/comment/columnists/matthewd_ancona/3563042/Doesnt-Yachtgate-give-you-that-sinking-feeling.html.

14 Peter Walker, "Nat Rothschild loses libel case against Daily Mail over Mandelson trip," *The Guardian*, February 10, 2012, https://www.theguardian.com/politics/2012/feb/10/nat-rothschild-loses-libel-daily-mail.

15 Icke, *The Trigger*, 31.

16 Susan Ingram, "Cartoonist Disinvited from White House Defends Image Labeled Anti-Semitic," *Jewish Times*, July 10, 2019, https://www.jewishtimes.com/cartoonist-disinvited-from-white-house-defends-image-labeled-anti-semitic/.

17 See Garrison v. Anti-Defamation League, Western District of Virginia, July 10, 2020, Page 6, https://www.courtlistener.com/docket/17344321/1/garrison-v-anti-defamation-league/. – the case was dismissed in early 2021.

18 Icke, *The Trigger*, 488.

19 Kim Willsher, "Trump and Macron's symbolic friendship tree dies," *The Guardian*, June 10, 2019, https://www.theguardian.com/us-news/2019/jun/10/tree-planted-to-mark-trump-macron-friendship-dies

20 Victor, David G., et al. "The Geoengineering Option: A Last Resort Against Global Warming?" *Foreign Affairs* 88, no. 2 (2009): 64–76, JSTOR, http://www.jstor.org/stable/20699494. Accessed 3 Oct. 2022.

21 Jesse Bernstein, "D.C. Lawmaker Pins Recent Snowfall On The Rothschilds," *Tablet Magazine*, March 19, 2018, https://www.tabletmag.com/sections/news/articles/d-c-lawmaker-pins-recent-snowfall-on-the-rothschilds.

22 Ibid.

23 Kate Sheppard, "Jesse Ventura Body-Slams the Climate Change 'Conspiracy,'" *Mother Jones*, December 23, 2009, https://www.motherjones.com/politics/2009/12/jesse-ventura-body-slams-climate-change/.

24 Andrew Edgecliffe-Johnson, "EL Rothschild Buys Stake in Weather Central," *Financial Times*, January 31, 2011, https://www.ft.com/content/67ee5828-2d8d-11e0-8f53-00144feab49a.

25 Elana Freeland, *Chemtrails, HAARP, and the Full Spectrum Dominance of Planet Earth* (Port Townsend, WA: Feral House, 2014), 187.

26 James Perloff, "Are the Rothschild Elite Banking on the Weather?," July 19, 2016, https://jamesperloff.net/rothschild-banking-weather/.

27 Eric Hananoki, "Marjorie Taylor Greene penned conspiracy theory that a laser beam from space started deadly 2018 California wildfire," MediaMatters.org, January 28, 2021, https://www.mediamatters.org/facebook/marjorie-taylor-greene-penned-conspiracy-theory-laser-beam-space-started-deadly-2018.

28 Ibid.

29 Jonathan Chait, "Marjorie Taylor Greene Blamed Wildfires on Secret Jewish Space Laser," *New York Magazine*, January 28, 2021, https://nymag.com/intelligencer/article/marjorie-taylor-greene-qanon-wildfires-space-laser-rothschild-execute.html.

30 Reuters Staff, "Rothschild vice chairman resigns from PG&E board," *Reuters*, January 15, 2019, https://www.reuters.com/article/us-pg-e-director/rothschild-vice-chairman-resigns-from-pge-board-idUSKCN1P919X.

31 Ivan Penn, "PG&E Appoints a New Board as It Eyes Its Bankruptcy Exit," *The New York Times*, June 10, 2020, https://www.nytimes.com/2020/06/10/business/energy-environment/pge-new-board-gavin-newsom.html.

32 Rachel Steinberg, "Rothschilds linked to California wildfires," *The Jewish Chronicle*, January 29, 2021, https://www.thejc.com/news/us/congresswoman-s-comments-linking-rothschilds-to-california-wildfires-prompt-mockery-and-outrage-1.511357.

33 Solaren, Inc, "Facebook Post Referencing Solaren Space Solar—Setting the Record Straight," January 20, 2021, https://www.solarenspace.com/2021/01/29/facebook-post-referencing-solaren-space-solar-setting-the-record-straight/.

34 Anna Merlan, "California's Wildfires Have Spawned a Truly Weird New Conspiracy Theory," Gizmodo, November 16, 2018, https, https://gizmodo.com/californias-wildfires-have-spawned-a-truly-wild-new-con-1830418656.

35 Jim Robbins, "Fierce and Unpredictable: How Wildfires Became Infernos," *The New York Times*, August 13, 2018, https://www.nytimes.com/2018/08/13/science/wildfires-physics.html.

36 Stop the Crime, "PG&E aka Rothschild—Burn'em Up and Fix'em Plan," October 22,

2019, https://stopthecrime.net/wp/2019/10/22/pge-aka-rothschild-burnem-up-and-fixem-plan/.

37 "City of Chicago Police Board Public Meeting," December 13, 2018, https://www.chicago.gov/content/dam/city/depts/cpb/PubMtgMinutes/PubMtgTranscript12132018.pdf.

38 Jacob Kornbluh, "Marjorie Taylor Greene has a new spin on the Jewish space lasers remark," *The Forward*, March 18, 2021, https://forward.com/fast-forward/466090/marjorie-taylor-greene-has-a-new-spin-on-the-jewish-space-lasers-remark/.

39 As previously stated, for much more detail on the rise and spread of QAnon, see *The Storm is Upon Us: How QAnon Became a Movement, Cult, and Conspiracy Theory of Everything* (New York: Melville House, 2021).

40 https://qposts.online/post/133.

41 https://qposts.online/post/252.

42 https://qposts.online/post/1010.

43 https://qposts.online/post/341.

44 Mike Rothschild, "The Rothschild Human Hunting Lodge," June 13, 2019, https://themikerothschild.com/2019/06/13/rothschild-human-hunting-lodge/.

45 Nancy Hoguet, "Writer Nancy Hoguet Takes AD Inside Her Family's Hunting Lodge in the Austrian Alps," *Architectural Digest*, June 11, 2017, https://www.architecturaldigest.com/story/rothschild-hunting-lodge-austria.

46 Mattias Wabl, "Rothschilds Sell Last Piece of Austrian Empire After 200 Years," *Bloomberg*, January 24, 2019, https://www.bloomberg.com/news/articles/2019-01-25/rothschilds-sell-last-piece-of-austrian-empire-after-200-years.

47 Rothschild, "The Rothschild Human Hunting Lodge."

48 Pepjin van Erp, "Debunking *Fall of the Cabal*, Part 2," April 25, 2020, https://www.pepijnvanerp.nl/2020/04/debunking-fall-cabal-by-janet-ossebaard-part-2/.

49 Meredith Deliso and Will Steakin, "Mary Ann Mendoza pulled from RNC lineup after retweeting anti-Semitic QAnon conspiracy," *ABC News*, August 25, 2020, https://abcnews.go.com/Politics/mary-ann-mendoza-pulled-rnc-lineup-retweeting-anti/story?id=72607904.

50 Brandon Gage, "Alex Jones Declared Holy War Against Joe Biden on Eve of Capitol Insurrection," HillReporter.com, February 7, 2021, https://hillreporter.com/alex-jones-declared-holy-war-against-joe-biden-on-eve-of-capitol-insurrection-92413.

51 https://reddit.com/r/conspiracy/comments/ufam66/theory_joe_biden_was_chosen_for_the_sole_purpose/.

52 117 Cong. *Impeachment of Donald John Trump, Evidentiary Record Volume II*, February 2, 2021, Pg. 1275, https://www.govinfo.gov/app/details/CDOC-117hdoc9/CDOC-117hdoc9-vol2/context.

53 Eric Hananoki, @ehananoki, Twitter post, September 1, 2022, "During a video today, Doug Mastriano campaign 'prophet' Julie Green claimed (via prophecy): 'The truth about the Rothschilds is coming. A whistleblower has the truth, and all they need to destroy their narrative and their power over their wicked and fraudulent government.'" https://twitter.com/ehananoki/status/1565378544078913539.

54 Jonathan Weisman, "The Strident Writings of a Young Blake Masters Dog His Senate Run," *The New York Times*, July 6, 2022, https://www.nytimes.com/2022/07/06/us/politics/blake-masters.html.

55 "'The Great Reset' Conspiracy Flourishes Amid Continued Pandemic," December 29, 2020, ADL.org, https://www.adl.org/blog/the-great-reset-conspiracy-flourishes-amid-continued-pandemic.

56 Christian Haag, "Greta Thunberg is related to the Rothschild family and Klaus Schwab," *Logically AI,* February 9, 2023, https://www.logically.ai/factchecks/library/717655d5.

57 Rainer Zitelmann, "The Corona Crisis: The Rothschilds? Bill Gates? The Search For A Scapegoat Has Begun," *Forbes Magazine*, March 23, 2020, https://www.forbes.com/sites/rainerzitelmann/2020/03/23/the-corona-crisis-the-rothschilds-bill-gates-the-search-for-a-scapegoat-has-begun/?sh=6a0c68282283.

58 Yasmine Summan, "How viral coronavirus hoax videos are blowing up on TikTok," *Dazed Digital*, February 3, 2020, https://www.dazeddigital.com/science-tech/article/47763/1/how-viral-coronavirus-hoax-videos-are-blowing-up-on-tiktok.

59 Matthew Brown, "Fact check: Neither Pirbright Institute nor Bill Gates owns novel coronavirus patent," *USA Today*, March 27, 2020, https://www.usatoday.com/story/news/factcheck/2020/03/27/covid-19-fact-check-bill-melinda-gates-foundation-did-not-patent-coronavirus/2919503001/.

60 Reuters Staff, "Fact check: Rothschild did not patent a test for COVID-19 in 2015 and 2017," October 27, 2020, https://www.reuters.com/article/uk-factcheck-patent/fact-check-rothschild-did-not-patent-a-test-for-covid-19-in-2015-and-2017-idUSKBN-27C34O.

61 Center for Countering Digital Hate, "#DeplatformIcke: How Big Tech powers and profits from David Icke's lies and hate, and why it must stop," May 2022, https://counterhate.com/wp-content/uploads/2022/05/DeplatformIcke.pdf.

62 Jonathan Chait, "DeSantis Spokesperson Blames Vaccine Passport on the Rothschilds," *New York Magazine*, November 17, 2021, https://nymag.com/intelligencer/2021/11/desantis-spokesperson-georgia-vaccine-passport-rothschilds-anti-semitism-conspiracy-theories.html.

63 Christina Pushaw, @christinapushaw, Twitter post, November 17, 2021, "The Daily Beast is preparing a hit piece on me because I suggested the Georgian government is intentionally fueling antisemitic Rothschild conspiracy theories in order to smear anyone who opposes vaccine passports as a 'conspiracy theorist.' Twitter is not for nuance." https://twitter.com/christinapushaw/status/1460996118343565322.

64 Chait, "DeSantis Spokesperson."

CHAPTER 13

1 Marc Rod, "French antisemitic violence is 'not unique anymore,' Lipstadt warns," *JewishInsider.com*, Oct 25, 2022, https://jewishinsider.com/2022/10/ambassador-deborah-lipstadt-antisemitism-envoy-france-world-jewish-congress/.

2 Emily Tamkin, *The Influence of Soros: Politics, Power, and the Struggle for an Open Society* (New York: HarperCollins, 2020), 8–11.

3 Michael Lewis, "The Speculator," *The New Republic*, January 9, 1994, https://newrepublic.com/article/74330/the-speculator.

4 Tamkin, *The Influence of Soros*, 14.

5 Robert Slater, *Soros: The Life, Times & Trading Secrets of the World's Greatest Investor* (New York: McGraw Hill, 1996), 39.

6   Michael T. Kaufman, *Soros: The Life and Times of a Messianic Billionaire* (New York: Knopf, 2002), 134–135.

7   Lewis, "The Speculator."

8   Kaufman, *Soros*, 235.

9   Slater, *Soros*, 186.

10 Kaufman, *Soros*, 157.

11 Frederick Ungeheuer, "George Soros: World's Champion Bull Rider," *Time Magazine*, May 4, 1987, https://content.time.com/time/subscriber/article/0,33009,964280,00.html.

12 Kaufman, *Soros*, 73.

13 Emily Tamkin, "Five Myths About George Soros," *The Washington Post*, August 6, 2020, https://www.washingtonpost.com/outlook/five-myths/five-myths-about-george-soros/2020/08/06/ad195582-d1e9-11ea-8d32-1ebf4e9d8e0d_story.html.

14 Kaufman, *Soros*, 5.

15 Kenneth Vogel, et al., "How Vilification of George Soros Moved From the Fringes to the Mainstream," *The New York Times*, October 31, 2018, https://www.nytimes.com/2018/10/31/us/politics/george-soros-bombs-trump.html.

16 Peter Maass, "U.S. Interests Try to Counter Hungarian Rightist," *The Washington Post*, October 20, 1992, https://www.washingtonpost.com/archive/politics/1992/10/20/us-interests-try-to-counter-hungarian-rightist/ed26f474-a87f-4770-b27b-eff89aadba72/?utm_term=.5e4cb56ed2ef.

17 Thomas Fuller, "Mahathir: a master of progress and offense," *The New York Times*, October 20, 2003, https://www.nytimes.com/2003/10/20/news/mahathir-a-master-of-progress-and-offense.html.

18 Vogel, et al., "How Vilification of George Soros."

19 John Mintz, "Ideological Odyssey: From Old Left to Far Right," *The Washington Post*, January 14, 1985, https://www.washingtonpost.com/wp-srv/national/longterm/cult/larouche/main.htm.

20 F. William Engdahl, "The Secret Network Behind 'Wizard' George Soros," *Executive Intelligence Review* 23, no. 44 (November, 1, 1996), https://larouchepub.com/eiw/public/1996/eirv23n44-19961101/eirv23n44-19961101_054-the_secret_financial_network_beh.pdf.

21 Ibid.

22 "Soros = Rothschild = CFR = Currency Collapes? [sic]", alt.conspiracy, February 2, 1997, archived at Usenet Archives, https://www.usenetarchives.com/view.php?id=alt.conspiracy&mid=PDM0ODNlMTczLjQ4MDg3MzhAbmV3cy5sbS5jb20%2B.

23 Michael Wolraich, *Blowing Smoke* (Cambridge, MA: Da Capo, 2010), 153–154.

24 *Instauration* 22, no. 12 (November 1, 1997).

25 Jane Mayer, "The Money Man," *The New Yorker*, October 18, 2004, https://www.newyorker.com/magazine/2004/10/18/the-money-man.

26 Quoted in Wolraich, *Blowing Smoke*, 156–157.

27 Mayer, "The Money Man;" Eric Alterman, "The Soros Slander Campaign Continues," *The Nation*, July 5, 2004, https://www.thenation.com/article/archive/soros-slander-campaign-continues/.

28 Jack Shafer, "Dennis Hastert on Dope," *Slate*, September 1, 2004, https://slate.com/news-and-politics/2004/09/dennis-hastert-on-dope.html.

29 Dylan Matthews, "A man two heartbeats away from the presidency was a serial child molester," *Vox*, April 28, 2016, https://www.vox.com/2016/4/28/11520156/dennis-hastert-child-molestation-explained.

30 Anne E. Kornblut, "The War Against Tom DeLay," *The New York Times*, October 2, 2005, https://www.nytimes.com/2005/10/02/weekinreview/the-war-against-tom-delay.html.

31 109 Cong. Rec E1917.

32 Robert Mackey, "The Plot Against George Soros Didn't Start in Hungary. It Started on Fox News," *The Intercept*, January 23, 2019, https://theintercept.com/2019/01/23/plot-george-soros-didnt-start-hungary-started-fox-news/.

33 Scott Shane, "The Fake Americans Russia Created to Influence the Election," *The New York Times*, September 7, 2017, https://www.nytimes.com/2017/09/07/us/politics/russia-facebook-twitter-election.html.

34 Marcus Baram, "A Timeline of George Soros Conspiracy Theories," *Fast Company*, October 5, 2018, https://www.fastcompany.com/90247335/a-timeline-of-george-soros-conspiracy-theories.

35 Tamkin, "Five Myths About George Soros."

36 Luke Mogelson, *The Storm is Here: An American Crucible* (New York: Penguin Press, 2022), 31.

37 For an extremely tenuous link between the owner of Smartmatic, a voting machine company, and the Open Society Foundations, see Lori Janjigian, "George Soros is the subject of one of the more misguided conspiracy theories of the election," *Business Insider*, October 25, 2016, https://www.businessinsider.com/george-soros-connection-to-voting-machines-2016-10.

38 Vogel, et al. "How Vilification of George Soros."

39 Shaun Walker, "George Soros: Orbán turns to familiar scapegoat as Hungary rows with EU," *The Guardian*, December 5, 2020, https://www.theguardian.com/world/2020/dec/05/george-soros-orban-turns-to-familiar-scapegoat-as-hungary-rows-with-eu.

40 Hannes Grassegger, "The Unbelievable Story of The Plot Against George Soros," *Buzzfeed News*, January 20, 2019, https://www.buzzfeednews.com/article/hnsgrassegger/george-soros-conspiracy-finkelstein-birnbaum-orban-netanyahu.

41 Vogel, et al. "How Vilification of George Soros."

42 Dara Lind, "The Migrant Caravan, Explained," *Vox Media*, October 25, 2018, https://www.vox.com/2018/10/24/18010340/caravan-trump-border-honduras-mexico.

43 Brett Samuels, "Trump: 'I wouldn't be surprised' if Soros were paying for migrant caravan," *The Hill*, October 31, 2018, https://thehill.com/homenews/administration/414171-trump-i-wouldnt-be-surprised-if-soros-were-paying-for-migrant-caravan/.

44 Daniel Politi, "Why Did Synagogue Suspect Believe Migrant Caravan Is Jewish Conspiracy? Maybe He Watched Fox News," *Slate*, October 27, 2018, https://slate.com/news-and-politics/2018/10/robert-bowers-suspected-synagogue-shooter-believes-migrant-caravan-is-jewish-conspiracy.html.

45 William K. Rashbaum, "At George Soros's Home, Pipe Bomb Was Likely Hand-Delivered, Officials Say," *The New York Times*, October 23, 2018, https://www.nytimes.com/2018/10/23/nyregion/soros-caravan-explosive-bomb-home.html.

46 David Neiwert, "Mail-bomber 'false flag' theories overwhelm discourse on terrorism," *Hatewatch*, October 27, 2018, https://www.splcenter.org/hatewatch/2018/10/26/mail-bomber-false-flag-theories-overwhelm-discourse-terrorism.

47 Dan Friesen and Jordan Holmes, hosts, "October 23, 2018," *Knowledge Fight*, episode #220, October 24, 2018, https://knowledgefight.libsyn.com/knowledge-fight-october-23-2018.

48 "Why is billionaire George Soros a bogeyman for the hard right?," *BBC News*, September 7, 2019, https://www.bbc.com/news/stories-49584157.

49 Tara Isabel Burton, "The centuries-old history of Jewish 'puppet master' conspiracy theories," *Vox Media*, November 2, 2018, https://www.vox.com/2018/11/2/15946556/antisemitism-enlightenment-george-soros-conspiracy-theory-globalist.

50 *BBC News*, "Why is billionaire George Soros a bogeyman for the hard right?"

51 ADL Center on Extremism, "Striking Similarities Between Gendron and Tarrant Manifestos," May 24, 2022, https://www.adl.org/resources/blog/striking-similarities-between-gendron-and-tarrant-manifestos.

EPILOGUE

1 My paternal family genealogy is taken from Charles B. Bernstein, *The Rothschilds of Nordstetten* (Private Press: Chicago, 1989).

2 Bernstein, 8.

3 Kevin Fitzpatrick, "Sad Demise of Dorothy Parker's Uncle on the Titanic," *DorothyParker.com*, April 11, 2012, https://dorothyparker.com/2012/04/sad-demise-of-dorothy-parkers-uncle-on-the-titanic.html.

4 Bernstein, vii.

5 Ryan Mac, "Meet New Billionaire Jeff Rothschild, The Engineer Who Saved Facebook From Crashing," *Forbes*, February 28, 2014, https://www.forbes.com/sites/ryanmac/2014/02/28/meet-jeff-rothschild-the-hidden-facebook-billionaire-old-enough-to-be-zuckerbergs-dad/?sh=1c1192a555ed.

6 Robert W. Wood, Rothschild Bank Enters Deferred Prosecution Agreement, Triggering More IRS Disclosures," *Forbes*, June 4, 2015, https://www.forbes.com/sites/robertwood/2015/06/04/rothschild-bank-enters-deferred-prosecution-agreement-triggering-more-irs-disclosures/?sh=2cb55453af5a.

7 Reuters Staff, "Private bank Rothschild fined in 1MDB case: source," *Reuters*, June 22, 2017, https://www.reuters.com/article/us-malaysia-scandal-rotschild/private-bank-rothschild-fined-in-1mdb-case-source-idUSKBN19D149.

8 Nicholas Kulish, "George Soros Is Making Changes at His Foundation While He Still Can," *The New York Times*, September 12, 2021, https://www.nytimes.com/2021/09/12/business/george-soros-philanthropy-open-society-foundation.html.

9 Mark Hay, "COVID Truthers Have Found a New 'Pandemic' to Freak Out About," The Daily Beast, April 30, 2022, https://www.thedailybeast.com/conspiracy-theorists-are-already-freaking-out-about-the-next-pandemic-as-part-of-the-so-called-great-reset.

10 Logically AI, "Yuval Noah Harari has a plan to control people with 'organism hacking,'" May 17, 2022, https://www.logically.ai/factchecks/library/879553bb.